BOSTON
HANDBOOK

BOSTON HANDBOOK

FIRST EDITION

JEFF PERK

MOON
TRAVEL
HANDBOOKS

BOSTON HANDBOOK
FIRST EDITION

Published by
  Moon Publications, Inc.
  P.O. Box 3040
  Chico, California 95927-3040, USA

Printed by
  Colorcraft Ltd.

Printing History
1st edition—January 1999

ISBN: 1-56691-136-2
ISSN: 1098-6732

Editor: Pauli Galin
Map Editor: Gina Wilson Birtcil
Copy Editors: Deana Corbitt Shields, Emily Kendrick
Production & Design: David Hurst
Cartography: Chris Folks and Mike Morgenfeld
Index: Asha Johnson

Front cover photo: Back Bay Brownstone on Commonwealth Avenue. © Walter Bibikow; courtesy of the
                     Picture Cube

All photos by Jeff Perk unless otherwise noted.

Distributed in the United States and Canada by Publishers Group West

Printed in China

To Dad,
with love

CONTENTS

ABBREVIATIONS

a/c—air-conditioning
AT—Appalachian Trail
B&B—bed and breakfast
CCC—Civilian Conservation Corps
d—double
HI—Hostelling International
MBTA—Massachusetts Bay Transit
   Authority
pp—per person

Rt.—Route
SPNEA—Society for the Preservation of
   New England Antiquities
s—single
T—commonly used nickname for the
   subway, from MBTA
tel.—telephone
TTOR—The Trustees of Reservations

ACCOMMODATION PRICING KEY

Rankings represent the average price charged for a double. Call specific accommodations for single, seasonal, and special rates.

Budget: $35 and under

Inexpensive: $35-60

Moderate: $60-85

Expensive: $85-110

Premium: $110-150

Luxury: $150 and up

ACKNOWLEDGMENTS

Although writing is not unlike sailing solo through unfamiliar waters, even the most intrepid single-handers know in their heart of hearts that their feat would be next to impossible without the aid of the folks back on shore, lending support, sharing tips, or simply checking in with the cheery "Bon voyage!" It's my great good fortune to have Professor J.L. "Luo Lili" Romeo and Steve *New Hampshire Handbook* Lantos there on the dock, both of whom conveniently ignored their past experience with this loose-ruddered rustbucket of a writing vessel, and willingly lent their support again. Thanks to you both.

Edward Hasbrouck, another Moon author (of *The Practical Nomad*), also weighed in with some thoughtful suggestions and feedback. I can't get enough of that sort of stuff, Edward, it's always appreciated. Martha Sullivan and Linda McConchie were standouts among the PR and tourism professionals who brightened my job of gathering information, making the nuts-and-bolts assembly of this guide a lot less of a chore than it could be otherwise. Thanks, all.

A special bow of appreciation goes to Ken Dumas, of the Central Transportation Planning Staff, for invaluable GIS assistance. I'm also grateful to Cindy Cohen for permission to use excerpts from her work, and to Norman Leventhal for permission to draw upon his map collection.

Thanks to Pauli Galin, Gina Birtcil, Bill Newlin, Bob Race, and many invisible others at Moon, my journey is actually as well-charted and shoal-free as a trip through a duck pond. Thanks, you guys, for helping chalk up another successful trip.

As always, I owe a great big hug to my family for their resolute support of my wayward career choice. Dad, David, Henia, and Joel, thanks for lending your hearts—and ears—to my onward journey.

Finally, *cestas de besos* to Jackie *mi corazón,* whose companionship and understanding brought fair weather and smooth sailing from start to finish.

WE WELCOME YOUR COMMENTS

It's a little-known law of geographical dynamics that the rate of change in any given place is directly proportional to the number of travel guides written about it. For Boston, that's a darn high figure, so the rate of change here has been accelerating quite a bit lately. The best any of us writers can do is capture a snapshot of the city in motion, and then apply a warning like this one, stating the obvious: things change. Naturally, no effort has been spared in making the picture in these pages as faithful to reality as humanly possible, up to cultivating insomnia so as not to miss one blessed hour of city life. But since two heads are inevitably better than none, holding such high standards is only possible in part with contributions from readers like you. So if you find in your travels details that differ from what's in these pages—or any inconsistencies, ambiguities, or misleading statements—jot them down on the back of a postcard, or make notes in the margins of this handbook and then transcribe them into an e-mail when you get home.

Don't feel you have to limit correspondence to complaints, either. It's always a pleasure to read a good word from people who've been won over by Boston's charms, or who want to share a discovery with readers of the next edition. So keep in touch—and thanks in advance.

Boston Handbook
Moon Travel Handbooks
P.O. Box 3040
Chico, CA 95927-3040

THERE IS NO FRIGATE LIKE A BOOK

TO TAKE US LANDS AWAY

~ Emily Dickinson

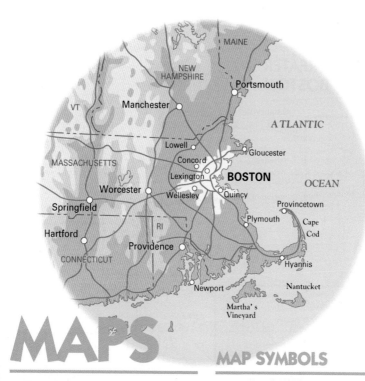

MAPS

MAP SYMBOLS

★ Point of Interest   ⊤ MBTA Terminal

● Accommodation   🛡 Interstate

▼ Restaurant/Bar   ⬭ US Highway

■ Other Location   ○ State Route

Λ Campground

Toll   Toll

Divided Highways

Primary Roads

Secondary Roads

Railroad

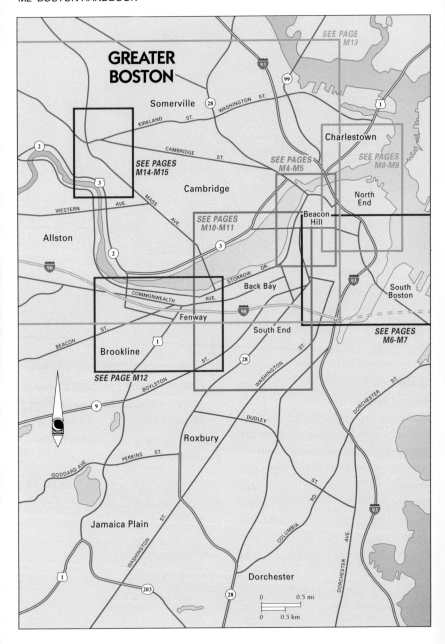

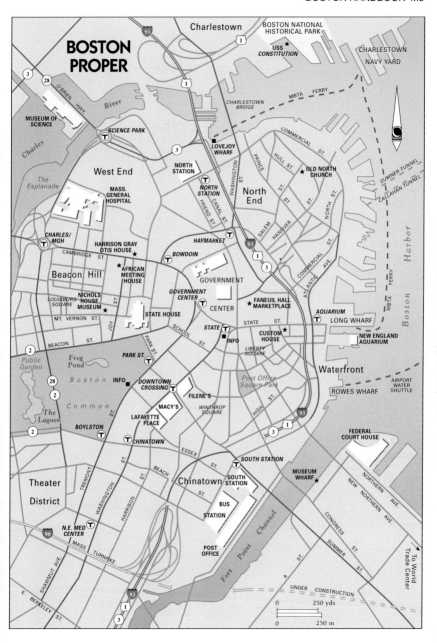

BOSTON PROPER

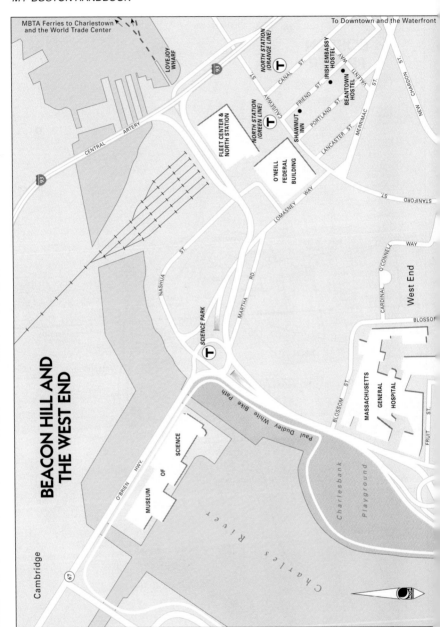

BEACON HILL AND
THE WEST END

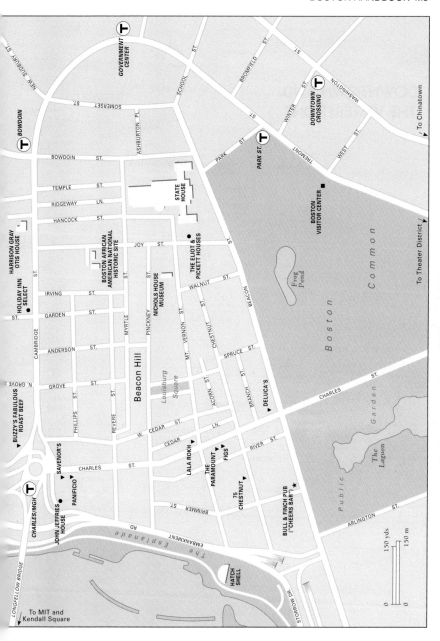

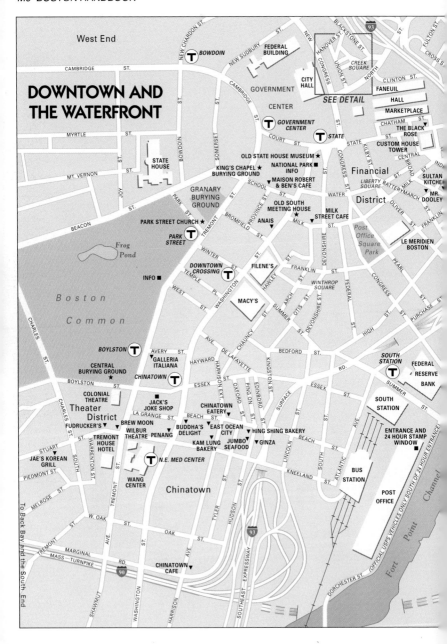

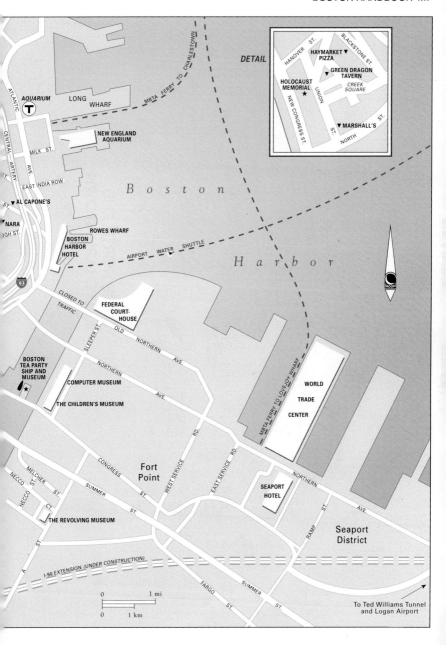

DETAIL

HANOVER ST.
BLACKSTONE ST
HAYMARKET ▼
PIZZA
GREEN DRAGON
▼ TAVERN
CREEK
SQUARE
HOLOCAUST
MEMORIAL
★
UNION
ST.
NEW CONGRESS ST.
▼ MARSHALL'S
NORTH
ST.

AQUARIUM
ⓣ
LONG WHARF

MBTA FERRY TO CHARLESTOWN

ATLANTIC

CENTRAL ARTERY

MILK ST.
AVE.
EAST INDIA ROW.

ST.

NEW ENGLAND
AQUARIUM

B o s t o n

▼ AL CAPONE'S

NARA

IGH ST.

ROWES WHARF

BOSTON
HARBOR
HOTEL

AIRPORT WATER SHUTTLE

H a r b o r

Moor

93

CLOSED TO

TRAFFIC

SLEEPER ST.

OLD

FEDERAL
COURT-
HOUSE

NORTHERN

AVE.

MBTA FERRY TO LOVEJOY WHARF

WORLD

TRADE

CENTER

BOSTON
TEA PARTY
SHIP AND
MUSEUM
★

COMPUTER MUSEUM

NORTHERN

AVE.

THE CHILDREN'S MUSEUM

WEST SERVICE RD.

EAST SERVICE RD.

NECCO
MELCHER ST.
NECCO
CT.
ST.

CONGRESS

SUMMER

ST.

ST.

Fort
Point

NORTHERN

SEAPORT
HOTEL

AVE.

THE REVOLVING MUSEUM

A

ST.

RAMP
ST.

Seaport
District

I-90 EXTENSION (UNDER CONSTRUCTION)

FARGO

ST.

SUMMER

ST.

To Ted Williams Tunnel
and Logan Airport

0   1 mi

0   1 km

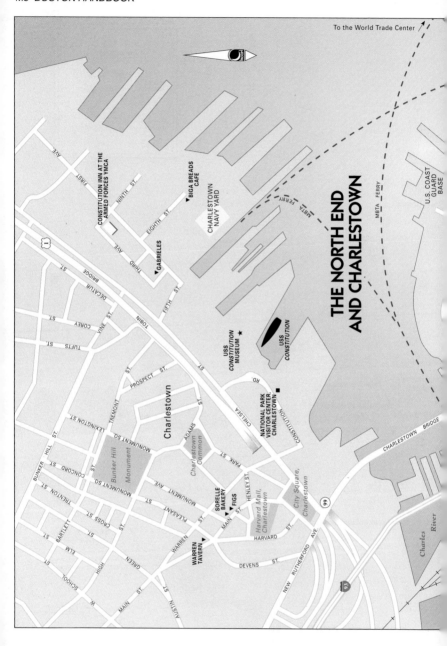

THE NORTH END AND CHARLESTOWN

To the World Trade Center

U.S. COAST GUARD BASE

MBTA FERRY

Charles River

CHARLESTOWN BRIDGE

FIRST AVE

CONSTITUTION INN AT THE ARMED FORCES YMCA

NINTH ST.

BIGA BREADS CAFE

CHARLESTOWN NAVY YARD

EIGHTH ST.

GABRIELES

THIRD AVE

FIFTH ST.

TOBIN

DECATUR

BRIDGE

COREY ST.

VINE ST.

TUFTS ST.

PROSPECT ST.

TREMONT ST.

LEXINGTON ST.

Charlestown

ADAMS ST.

Monument Sq.

Charlestown Common

Bunker Hill Monument

MONUMENT SQ.

BUNKER HILL ST.

CONCORD ST.

TRENTON ST.

MONUMENT AVE.

PARK ST.

PLEASANT ST.

CROSS ST.

BARTLETT ST.

ELM ST.

HIGH ST.

SCHOOL ST.

GREEN ST.

AUSTIN ST.

MAIN ST.

W. SCHOOL ST.

WARREN ST.

SORELLE BAKERY

FIGS

HENLEY ST.

Harvard Mall, Charlestown

WARREN TAVERN

HARVARD ST.

DEVENS ST.

NEW RUTHERFORD AVE.

City Square, Charlestown

99

USS CONSTITUTION MUSEUM ★

USS CONSTITUTION

CHELSEA ST.

RD.

NATIONAL PARK VISITOR CENTER, CHARLESTOWN

CONSTITUTION RD.

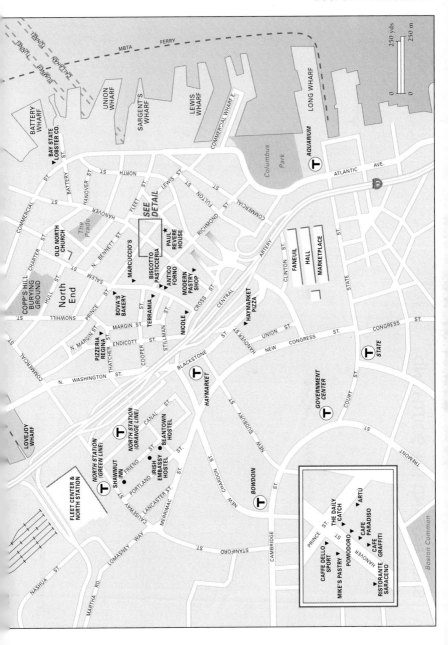

250 yds
250 m

MBTA ---- FERRY

SULLIVAN TUNNEL
CALLAHAN TUNNEL

BATTERY WHARF

BAY STATE LOBSTER CO.

UNION WHARF

SARGENT'S WHARF

LEWIS WHARF

COMMERCIAL WHARF E.

Columbus Park

AQUARIUM

LONG WHARF

ATLANTIC AVE.

I-93

COMMERCIAL ST.
HANOVER ST.
BATTERY ST.
NORTH ST.
FLEET ST.
LEWIS ST.
FULTON ST.
RICHMOND ST.

SEE DETAIL

OLD NORTH CHURCH

The Prado

HANOVER ST.

CHARTER ST.

COPP'S HILL BURYING GROUND

North End

HULL ST.

SALEM ST.

N. BENNETT ST.

MARCUCCIO'S ▶

BISCOTTO PASTICCERIA ▶
ANTICO FORNO ▶

PAUL REVERE HOUSE ★

MODERN PASTRY SHOP ▶

PRINCE ST.

BOVA'S BAKERY ▶

TERRAMIA ▶

NICOLE ▶

CROSS ST.

CENTRAL ST.

FANEUIL HALL MARKETPLACE

CLINTON ST.

STATE ST.

MARGIN ST.

STILLMAN ST.

N. MARGIN ST.

ENDICOTT ST.

COOPER ST.

HAYMARKET PIZZA ▼

PIZZERIA REGINA ▶

THATCHER ST.

BLACKSTONE ST.

UNION ST.

HANOVER ST.

NEW CONGRESS ST.

CONGRESS ST.

COMMERCIAL ST.

N. WASHINGTON ST.

HAYMARKET T

GOVERNMENT CENTER T

COURT ST.

STATE T

LOVEJOY WHARF

NORTH STATION (GREEN LINE) T

NORTH STATION (ORANGE LINE)

CANAL ST.

BEANTOWN HOSTEL ●

SHAWMUT INN ●

FRIEND ST.

IRISH EMBASSY HOSTEL ●

PORTLAND ST.

NEW SUDBURY ST.

NEW CHARDON ST.

BOWDOIN T

FLEET CENTER & NORTH STATION

CAUSEWAY ST.

LANCASTER ST.

MERRIMAC ST.

NASHUA ST.

MARTHA RD.

LOMASNEY WAY

STANIFORD ST.

CAMBRIDGE ST.

TREMONT ST.

Boston Common

PRINCE ST.

ST.

THE DAILY CATCH

ARTÙ

CAFFÈ DELLO SPORT ▶

POMODORO

CAFE PARADISO

HANOVER ST.

CAFE GRAFFITI

MIKE'S PASTRY ▶

RISTORANTE SARACENO ▶

BACK BAY AND THE SOUTH END

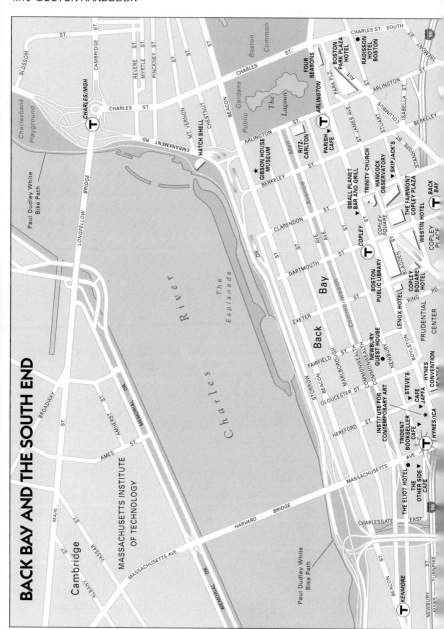

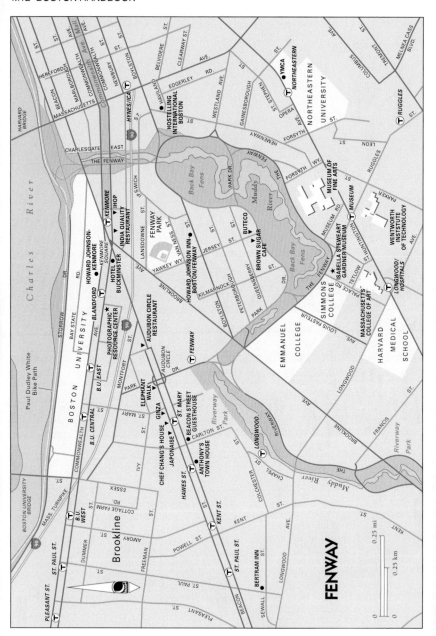

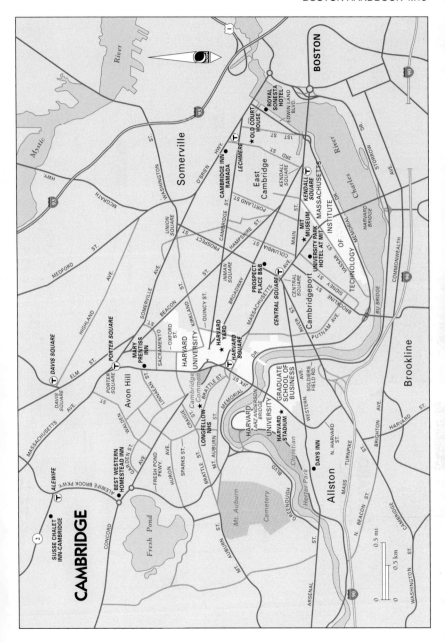

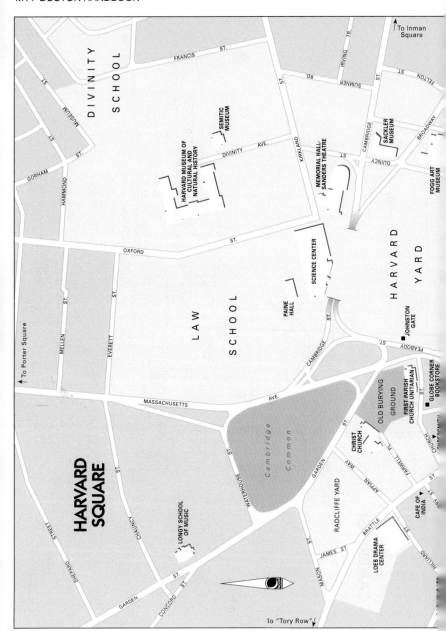

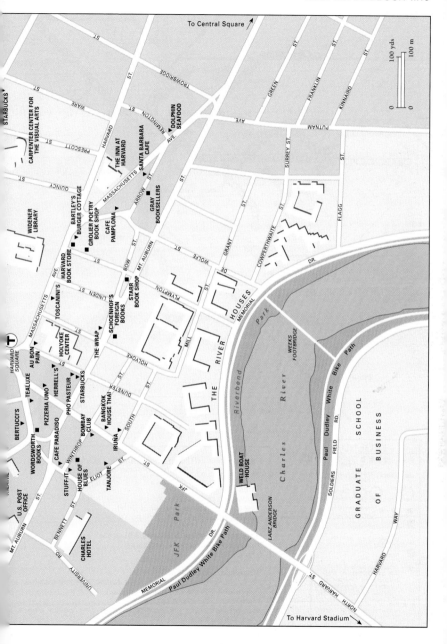

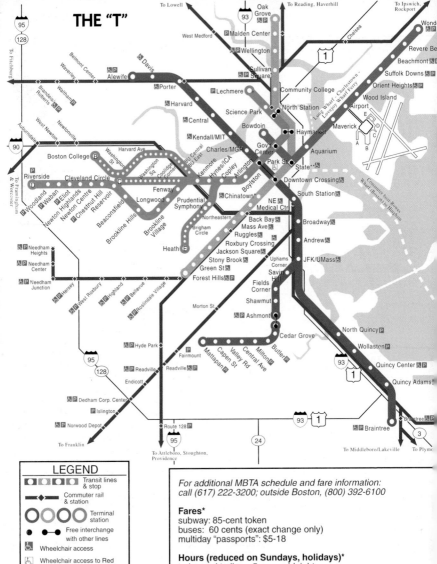

THE "T"

LEGEND

- Transit lines & stop
- Commuter rail & station
- Terminal station
- Free interchange with other lines
- Wheelchair access
- Wheelchair access to Red Line only
- P Parking
- * Wheelchair access Oak Grove side only. Southbound riders exit train at NE Medical Center transfer to Oak Grove train. Exit Chinatown on Oak Grove side.
- ** Blue Line wheelchair access outbound only. Inbound riders transfer to outbound train at Government Center. Exit at State outbound.

For additional MBTA schedule and fare information: call (617) 222-3200; outside Boston, (800) 392-6100

Fares*
subway: 85-cent token
buses: 60 cents (exact change only)
multiday "passports": $5-18

Hours (reduced on Sundays, holidays)*
trains and trolleys: 5 a.m.-midnight
buses: 5 a.m.-1 a.m.

Wheelchair access*
Red, Orange, and Blue Lines, via elevators at some stations
Call (800) LIFT-BUS for bus information.

*certain restrictions and exceptions apply. See "Boston Basics" for complete information

© 1997 MBTA
Internet address:
www.mbta.com

INTRODUCTION

Tomorrow night I appear before a Boston audience—4,000 critics.

—Mark Twain,
in a letter to his sister, 1869

Boston has been the setting for so much American history that every block seems layered with people and events straight out of the textbooks: wharves where angry colonists dumped British tea into the harbor, pulpits from which abolitionists lambasted slavery, a plaque denoting Alexander Graham Bell's workshop, the bar that inspired television's most famous watering hole. Steeped in such a heady brew, Boston understandably lapses every so often into tipsy braggadocio. Whether the "Autocrat at the Breakfast Table," Oliver Wendell Holmes, had his tongue in his cheek when he called Boston's State House "the Hub of the solar system," the city promptly adopted the nickname for itself and has worn it without irony ever since. The Hub it is, and shall remain—especially if there's a New Yorker or, worse, Yankees fan within earshot.

The rough side of history's mantle is a mulish aversion to change. This is perhaps a legacy of the founding Puritans, who cherished status quo with as much ferocity and litigation as any modern NIMBY activist (although the Puritans pilloried their opponents in irons instead of print). Boston's parochialism has been satirized at least since Edgar Allan Poe nicknamed the city "Frogpondium," but unless you try producing experimental theater or applying for a late-night entertainment license, you probably won't even notice.

Far more obvious to casual visitors are the city's students—more than 200,000 of them, attending 60 colleges, universities, and seminaries in the metro area, supposedly a higher concentration than anyplace else on the planet. Collectively, they justify another of Boston's sobriquets—"Athens of America." They also lend a great varsity youthfulness to city shopping, nightlife, and personal ads.

For anyone who doesn't have homework due or a thesis to write, Boston also offers world-class museums, top-notch performing arts, and three major-league sports franchises.

Block after block of neoclassical architecture and the intimacy of historic buildings preserved amid imposing modern office towers give Boston a distinctly European flavor, but the city's notoriously close-knit neighborhoods are becoming increasingly polyglot (a fact manifest in multilingual signs, brochures, and ATMs). You can literally sample the results of this melting pot all over town: from Vietnamese spring rolls to Sicilian calamari, Brazilian *feijoada* to glatt kosher quiche, there's no shortage of ethnic alternatives to cod and baked beans. (It's through association with this last dish that Boston has been dubbed "Beantown," but rest assured that Bostonians themselves *never* use the term.)

Because of the city's small size (Houston, Texas, almost has more open water within its limits than Boston has dry land), all these charms are best appreciated at a pedestrian's pace—especially since touring by car is about as convenient as walking around inside your house with a wheelbarrow. So ditch the gas-guzzler and bring comfortable walking shoes. And welcome to the Hub.

CLIMATE

There is a sumptuous variety about the New England weather that compels the stranger's admiration—and regret.

—Mark Twain

When the first European explorers wrote of their impressions of Massachusetts, they almost invariably heaped as much praise on its wonderful climate as on its abundance of fruits and fishes. When the first colonists compelled by such tantalizing descriptions ventured to establish permanent residence, they discovered that the explorers had omitted a few things from their reports. Like winter. This actually isn't so surprising: even today, the warmer months of the year somehow so intoxicate most Bostonians that the return of cold weather is greeted with a measure of genuine surprise—Isn't there a finite supply of this stuff? And didn't we use it up last year? Massachusetts weather is famously (and understandably) fickle. It is influenced by both the ocean and a number of high and low pressure systems interacting with some half dozen different air masses over the region. Recent years have produced record-breaking cool summers and snowy winters—and also unusually *mild* winters, dry summers, late springs, and early frosts. In short, prediction is difficult in this state and must always be regarded with a skeptical eye. That said, it is possible to make a few generalizations.

Temperatures in Boston's coastal basin are moderated by the proximity of the ocean, whose vast capacity for gradual heat absorption (and discharge) ensures that the mercury on the waterfront doesn't climb as high in summer—or drop as low in winter—as it does in inland areas. However, remember that wind chill can make temperature irrelevant, and that the wind is *always* cooler coming off the ocean. This means that if you go whalewatching on a broiling, 90° F August afternoon, you'll probably regret it if you don't dress for 68° F. In winter, when the prevailing wind shifts around to the northeast, a simple waterfront walk can become downright painful. Unless the Bermuda high pressure system stalls weather over the coast, though, summer's prevailing southwesterly winds blow air masses through the region quickly. This heightens variability, but it also means that bad weather tends not to stick around very long.

There is no dry season in Massachusetts. Precipitation occurs throughout the year—on average, once every three or four days. In spring, consistently warm weather doesn't arrive until well into May, although temperatures may spike up into the short-sleeve zone for a day or three as early as March. Similarly, fall's resurrection of long-sleeve weather and overnight frosts in late September is broken in October by "Indian summer," a modest but unforgettable series of georgeous warm days that rival summer itself. Once fall sets in, the days grow short and the temperatures chilly. Winter's first snows hit the suburbs before the city—the influence of the ocean again—but residents often have occasion to put snow shovels and ice scrapers to some use by the end of December. January and February are the city's coldest months. Despite thaws in March and April, snowstorms are not at all unheard of right through the end of March.

HISTORY

The fact that much of Boston predates the advent of professional archaeology hasn't made the city's prehistoric record very easy to read, but subway and building excavations have at least unearthed proof that the local fondness for seafood dates back some 4,000 years. While ancient Egyptians stacked big blocks and perfected the art of embalming, their Late Archaic contemporaries in Boston supped on fish caught in the vicinity of Copley Square and clams gathered near present-day Quincy Market. A wooden fish weir (preserved in estuarine mud), shell middens, stone tools, and ashes of the cremated aren't the oldest artifacts of human habitation in the area, but higher sea levels have made traces of the earliest residents—Paleoindians from 8,000 to 9,000 years ago—even scarcer.

When 16th-century European fishermen started coming over to catch some dinner of their own, southern New England's indigenous Native Americans are estimated to have numbered in the thousands, representing bands of some half dozen tribes: the Massachusett, Wampanoag, Nipmuck, Pawtucket, Pocumtuck, and Mahican. Each tribe comprised many bands, some more loosely allied than others. All shared the language of the Eastern Algonquian, the linguistic group encompassing most of the tribes on the East Coast between the Carolinas and the Iroquois Confederation. Although effectively a dead language (the last native speaker died in the early 1900s and, in 1995, a Wampanoag Indian who had spent some 21 years working to revive it passed away, too), several Algonquian nouns have made their way into English, including "skunk," "chipmunk," and "powwow."

The Europeans brought with them, among other things, several diseases against which the natives had no resistance. These afflictions, particularly smallpox, proved disastrous for New England's Indians. An epidemic in the years just prior to the arrival of the Pilgrims at Plymouth virtually depopulated the entire Boston basin (Squanto, famous for serving as both a friend to and interpreter for the Pilgrims, was kidnapped from his village on Plymouth Bay in 1614, and by the time he returned from his adventures in Spain and England, the Patuxet band to which he belonged had been utterly wiped out by disease). A second major epidemic swept the New England tribes again after the Puritan migration in the 1630s, and smaller scourges took place periodically well into the 1700s. But despite the depredations of disease, loss of tribal identity through acculturation, and two devastating wars with the English, the Native Americans did not entirely vanish. Indeed, they're still here: several bands of the Wampanoag and Nipmuck tribes reside in Massachusetts alone, and two have even obtained federal recognition.

England Plants the Flag

The English claim to North America is based on John Cabot's 1497-98 voyage along the Atlantic coast. It's uncertain whether Cabot ever actually laid eyes on New England, but rivalry with other colonial powers—including the Dutch and the French—inspired Queen Elizabeth to use his voyage as grounds for bestowing the first royal sanction upon a New England colony in 1578. Sir Humphrey Gilbert was the lucky fellow who obtained her permission to try housekeeping on the Maine coast. Unfortunately, Gilbert's ship sank on its first voyage to Gilbert's prize.

In the first decade of the 17th century, Elizabeth's successor,

John Cabot

King James I, made new grants and patents—royal permissions—to various wealthy financiers and aristocrats, who invested in settlements from the Kennebec River in present-day Maine to the James River in Virginia. The results were decidedly mixed; most of the settlements fell far short of their founders' aspirations. Ships laden with cod, sassafras, and beaver pelts motivated the deep-pocketed speculators, but domestic problems in England made colonization as important as profit-making. Exploding population, crop failures, and the societal shift from self-sufficient villages to a market society created a large migrant pool of tenant farmers and landless artisans willing to emigrate to wherever they might be able to eke out a living. Thousands had already gone to Europe in the decade before the *Mayflower* set sail. Any risks in the New World—violent clashes with Indians, for a start—were conveniently dismissed by colonial promoters.

Captain John Smith, the founder of Virginia's successful Jamestown, was one author of glowing reports on New England's bountiful resources. Among the audience for his public relations campaign was a group of disaffected Protestants, who had fled to Holland after "Bloody Mary" forcefully reimposed Catholicism on England. These "Saints," as they called themselves, declined Smith's offer to guide them to the new colony, frugally preferring to simply buy his book and sea chart and try their luck on their own. Backed by venture capitalists in London and half-believing that they would be united with the Lost Tribe of Israel when they reached their new home, these emigrants were joined by a cadre of middle-class allies known as the Merchant Adventurers (graciously dubbed "Strangers" by their saintly shipmates). Aboard the tiny *Mayflower,* the 102 passengers and an unknown number of crew succeeded in crossing the stormy Atlantic in 1620, where the emigrants established their "plantation" on Cape Cod Bay.

Half of these settlers died their first winter in the new land. But eventually, with infusions of new blood from home and life-saving agricultural lessons from their new Native American neighbors, these Pilgrims (as they came to be called only after 1840) did well enough to both completely repay their investors and attract a slew of new homesteaders to burgeoning outposts from Boston Harbor to Cape Cod.

The *Arbella* Brings Company

Eight years after the arrival of the Pilgrims, a small group of "lord brethren," keen on "purifying" the Anglican Church (instead of rejecting it outright, as the Pilgrims had done), arrived in present-day Salem and laid hold of an English fishing community, a remnant of a failed settlement farther up the coast. Within two years, these zealous brethren's simple land grant was converted into a royally chartered trading organization called the Massachusetts Bay Company, setting the stage for John Winthrop, an influential autocrat, to come a-calling in the *Arbella* and a fleet of nine other ships. This huge flock of "Puritans," dissatisfied with their first landfall and seeking something better, moved south along the coast.

Back home, dissent against the Anglican bishops and economic stagnation from farm shortages proved so widespread that within a generation, 20,000 English—predominantly from East Anglia—joined the Great Migration to the Bay Colony.

City on a Hill

We must Consider that we shall be as a City upon a Hill, the eyes of all people are upon us.

—John Winthrop, 1628

At the time of first contact with 16th-century Europeans, Boston's future home was a hilly, treeless, 750-acre peninsula. The area's indigenous Massachusett Indians, one of two tribes living in the surrounding coastal basin, called the bulbous neck of land *mushauwomuk* ("tide fishing area"), a typically utilitarian Algonquian name shortened to "Shawmut" by Anglo-Saxon tongues. Smaller than New York City's Central Park—and virtually an island at high tide—the peninsula was apparently unoccupied by the disease-ravaged tribe when the young Reverend William Blaxton arrived, in the 17th century.

A refugee from a failed 1623 fishing colony on the nearby South Shore, Blaxton was one of a handful of Englishmen who took up residence around the Charles River estuary and harbor islands in the 1620s. The happy hermit lived alone with his orchard and library until the summer of 1630, when some 800 of the newly arrived Salem Puritans showed up in search of well-watered land. Admiring the strategic heights, abundant springs, and easily defended umbilical to the mainland, John Winthrop and his flock accepted Blaxton's invitation to join him, and by fall their new settlement was officially christened "Boston," after the Lincolnshire hometown of some of the Puritan leaders.

John Winthrop

But Blaxton soon decided that he hadn't escaped England's lord bishops only to wind up in the laps of Salem's lord brethren. With his cattle and his books, he rode beyond the frontier to the banks of the river that now bears his name, the Blackstone, near the present-day Rhode Island border.

Puritans Pull a Fast One

Like the Pilgrims, the Puritans eluded direct English control by design. Winthrop, a well-trained lawyer, recognized an omission in the text of his company's charter: while stockholder meetings to direct the company had to be held where the charter was kept, nothing required the charter to be kept in England. This loophole made it possible to simply pocket the document and bring it along to America—putting the whole wide Atlantic between the colony and oversight by Parliament and the Crown.

Unlike the hereditary or proprietary (i.e., feudal) royal charters given to Maryland's plantation owners or the Duke of York, the Massachusetts Bay political framework of "freemen" (stockholders) assembling in a General Court established the basis for representative government by a company of equals. This may sound democratic, but only shareholders could vote, and out of 1,000 emigrants, exactly four were first enfranchised in the Great & General Court. Only mutinous threats forced revision of the court's composition, creating a bicameral chamber— one part elected by all freemen, the other appointed by Bay Company officers—and expanding voter eligibility to other men of property.

Healthy, Wealthy, and Wise

Spared the "three great annoyances of Woolves, Rattle-snakes and Musketoes" (as William Wood reported in his 1634 chronicle, *New England's Prospect*), Boston quickly became the head and heart of the Puritan Massachusetts Bay colony. As seat of the colonial government and center of seaborne trade, Boston quickly overtook nearby Newtown (now Cambridge), home of the Puritans' first ministerial college (now Harvard University), and other coastal communities engaged in the lucrative import-export business. Until superseded by Philadelphia well into the 18th century, Boston's size and wealth made it the British capital of North America.

Although dried cod was Boston's top export for over a century, the city profited mightily from seafaring "triangular trades"—shipping fish, timber, rice, indigo, and other local supplies to Caribbean sugar plantations or Southern Europe, for example; exchanging them there for tropical commodities; and trading these in England for manufactured goods. The most nefarious triangle consisted of trading New England rum in Africa for slaves, who were sold in the French West Indies for molasses, which was brought back to Boston to be distilled into more rum. (The West Indies were barred from making their own liquor because French cognac producers had successfully lobbied their king to prevent the competition.) Duty-evading commerce with non-English ports flagrantly violated England's Trade and Navigation Acts, but colonial smugglers made too much money to care about legality.

Puritanism alone couldn't protect the new riches of Boston's merchant class, so it embraced politics and trade associations on the one hand and Unitarianism—a religion with a more liberal attitude toward their secular activities—on the other.

Revolutionary Acts

As capital of a veritable empire built on smuggling, Boston soon found its economic interests clashing with Mother England's. In principle, colonial leaders recognized the Crown's right to regulate commerce, but laughably weak enforcement of, for example, the 1733 Molasses Act, designed to discourage the molasses trade with the French, made paper scruples easy to afford. With customs officers bribed to avert their eyes and a Royal Navy far too small to interdict every smuggler, business went on as usual.

Facing enormous debts from the 1756-63 Seven Years War—a conflict known on this side of the Atlantic as the French and Indian War—Parliament tried to close tax loopholes and capture what it perceived to be lost revenue. The colonies, reasoned Parliament, had to share the cost of their defense. But colonial assemblies from Massachusetts to Georgia felt they had already paid a disproportionately large price, in lives, devastated frontier settlements, and outfitting of their many local militias. They also resented the peace treaty that ended the war, in which England agreed to restrict colonists from settling in Indian territory west of the Appalachians.

Boston merchants were among the vanguard of those who resisted Parliament measure for measure. Imported English goods subject to tax were boycotted. Lobbying efforts brought solidarity from neighboring colonies, and sympathy from the opposition Whig party in Parliament. But England's new king, George III, was rigidly unyielding, and his Loyalist majority in the House of Commons grew increasingly vindictive toward American petitioners seeking to curb Parliament's right to tax the colonies. Exemplary of the Crown's dimwittedness was the 1767 Stamp Act, which required a two-penny royal revenue

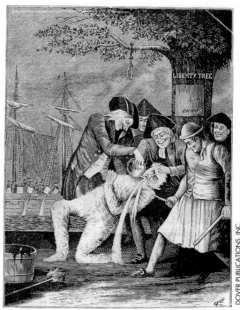

A British cartoon of 1774 captures the colonists' disregard for royal authority—here they force British tea down the tarred and feathered tax collector's throat.

stamp be purchased in order to consummate almost any transaction whatsoever—notarizing a contract, probating an estate, obtaining a marriage license, landing a cargo, registering a birth, even selling newspapers. Since the stamps were to be available only in each colony's major port town, such as Boston, the response from citizens was swift and unambiguous: supplies of the stamps were seized and destroyed by mobs, royal customs agents were threatened and harassed, and district courts either shut down in protest or ignored the law altogether.

Though short-lived, the Stamp Act and its successors steadily frayed the bonds of kinship and loyalty between the colonies and England. As each restrictive measure backfired, King George III and his ministers grew vengeful, particularly toward Massachusetts, which was perceived to be the most seditious. Coerce the Bay Colony into submission, the Loyalists believed, and its neighbors would fall meekly into line. The Whig party prophesied that the colonists loved English liberties too much to willingly bow to the yoke of political slavery, but the "little minds" ruling the Britannic empire were deaf to all objections. (Whig parliamentarians such as John Wilkes, Isaac Barré, and William Pitt were castigated by the king for siding with the colonies during various critical debates, but grateful Americans eventually repaid them with civic pride: thus the existence of such towns as Wilkes-Barre, Pennsylvania, and Pittsfield, Massachusetts.)

Boston's kettle had indeed been steaming for years, even before the March 1770 Massacre or December 1773's Tea Party. But it came to a full boil with the closing of Boston's port in 1774—one of Parliament's much-despised Coercive Acts. Far from isolating Massachusetts, these punitive measures evoked even more radicalism from neighboring colonies than before, although the English remained in denial about the depth of this solidarity for another 10 years.

Revolution finally sprang up in Lexington and Concord in April 1775, when the Redcoats and their fellow German soldiers (hired by the short-handed English from their Prussian allies) fired on local militia while attempting to seize a stash of munitions. It advanced to Boston's threshold with the bloody Battle of Bunker Hill two months later. After enduring an eight-month seige by newly commissioned General Washington and his fledgling Continental Army, Boston's British occupiers finally evacuated under the threat of their own cannon, which had been captured from Fort Ticonderoga and dragged to Dorchester Heights by the indefatigable Henry Knox. Boston remained free for the duration of the war.

Pacific Traders

After the Revolution, Americans were understandably denied access to English markets and credit. Initially, this proved a severe hardship for Boston merchants and mariners, many of whom had profited as privateers during the war. But shipbuilding and exports rebounded to record heights by the start of the 19th century, thanks to trade with the Pacific Northwest and China. Although pioneered by Salem and New York, the sea otter fur trade between "the Coast" and Canton was so dominated by ships of Boston registry and crew that Native Americans in Oregon initially called all U.S. sailors "Boston men."

En route to the Far East, Boston's vessels inaugurated contact with the Marquesas Islands in the South Pacific and the Spanish missionaries on the California coast. Following Captain Cook to Hawaii, they initiated the sandalwood trade to Asia. The Boston ship *Columbia,* later the namesake of the Northwest's mightiest river, in 1790 brought the first of many colorfully feathered "Owyhee" emissaries back to meet Massachusetts's governor; in return, Boston sent to Hawaii horses, bricks (called *pohaku winihepa,* or "Winship stones," after the family that introduced them), infectious diseases, and Calvinist missionaries. One of those missionaries was Sanford Ballard Dole, who became Hawaii's provisional president after the 1893 overthrow of Queen Liliuokalani. (Appropriately, the warship that delivered Marines for the coup was the USS *Boston.*) A slightly more salutary contribution to the Oregon Territory was made by Boston's Colonel Wilder: the first cultivars of d'Anjou pears, planted in 1842. And during the California Gold Rush, Boston's famous clipper ships sped passengers, provisions, and supplies to the Golden Gate—establishing sailing records that would stand unbroken for over 130 years. (The tons of Telegraph Hill stone brought back as

Another cartoon shows America (in the Indian headdress) being forced to take British tea.

DOVER PUBLICATIONS, INC.

ballast gave rise to the modern lament that some of San Francisco's best real estate lies at the bottom of Boston Harbor.)

The Landscapers

Boston is truly a manmade city—not merely the buildings but even the ground beneath them. Making usable land out of tidal mudflats abutting the original peninsula began early in the colonial era, but the most extensive quarrying of the city's drumlins (oval hills of glacially deposited soil and stone) began in the Federal era, following U.S. independence. In various stages throughout the early 19th century, property developers cut down Beacon Hill—once as tall as the State House is now—and its neigboring eminences, and carted their crowns into the adjacent flats to create commercial and residential lots (present-day Charles Street and much of the North End), sometimes amid lawsuits from owners of homes undermined by removal of so much earth. Most of the peninsula's original hills are now preserved only in the layout and naming of downtown streets, many of which still conform to the long-vanished topography. (Stray cows, despite what some people still believe, are *not* to blame for Boston's crooked thoroughfares.)

Even more ambitious than the project of flattening the peninsula was the late-19th-century filling in of the Back Bay, which nearly doubled the city's size. Once part of the lower Charles River's enormous tidal basin, this 580-acre mudflat between Boston and Brookline had become a noxious cesspool by the 1840s, literally bubbling with fermenting raw sewage trapped behind a failed mill dam and a skein of railroad levees. While Thoreau enjoyed his Walden woods, Boston was stewing in its own effluent; after much debate, the state seized the land by eminent domain and implemented a plan to develop the Back Bay as a high-class residential area —in one stroke burying the health hazard, relieving city overcrowding, and raising money through the sale of the new property. Trainloads of Needham sand and gravel started arriving at the foot of present-day Commonwealth Avenue shortly before the Civil War and continued to arrive every 45 minutes, day and night, for the next 35 years.

The Great Fire

Despite the modern additions to Boston's skyline, much of the streetscape is old enough to suggest that it has always been this way. Not so. Very few buildings actually predate the Civil War, thanks in large part to the city's many early fires—the most devastating of which hit Boston right on the heels of Chicago's encounter with Mrs. O'Leary's cow. On November 9, 1872, sparks in a department store at Summer and Kingston Streets raced through the store's hoop skirts and other combustible wares until the building was a fireball; within 24 hours, over 700 of its downtown neighbors had been engulfed. Most of the densely packed structures had flammable wooden roofs two stories higher than the reach of any available fire equipment. Blazing-hot walls of supposedly fireproof granite became explosive stone grenades when doused with water. Aging mineral-clogged water mains, an equine flu epidemic among fire-department horses, gas lines buried too near the surface, and crowds of rubberneckers and looters made a bad situation even worse. Numerous regional fire companies responded to the general alarm—some by train, others running 10 miles or more—but suburban hoses didn't fit city hydrants, and fights broke out over the lack of coordination and fuel for steam-powered pumpers. Not that there weren't heroes: firemen from Portsmouth, New Hampshire, used sea water pumped from the harbor to halt the flames at the very doors of the landmark Old South Meeting House. And the postmaster not only rescued the city's mail, but even kept up deliveries.

By the time the conflagration spent itself, some 65 acres of real estate and $75 million worth of commercial stock had become a smoldering ruin. Compassionate citizens from across the country quickly responded with aid, including major contributions from a sympathetic (and resurrected) Chicago. Although reforms were instituted over such matters as building heights and materials, private interests with a stake in the burned blocks opposed any proposed comprehensive change in urban design. Aside from a few street alterations and the creation of Post Office Square, much of the affected area was rebuilt nearly exactly as before. (Harvard, whose operating budget depended upon rental income from its property in the area, actually *expanded* its holdings.) As for the generosity of the nation, with characteristic Bostonian propriety, surplus money not disbursed by relief agencies after one year was returned—with interest.

Fleeing Yankees

And this is good old Boston
The home of the bean and the cod,
Where the Lowells talk to the Cabots,
And the Cabots talk only to God.

—Dr. John Collins Bossidy, 1910

The insularity of the Lowells, Cabots, and their upper-crust Boston Brahmin peers has become a topic of benign humor, best exemplified by Cleveland Amory's unsurpassed anecdotal study of the breed, *The Proper Bostonians.* Teasing stories about their ossified social conventions and limited repertoire of first names aside, the clubbiness of these powerful 19th-century mercantile dynasties shaped the city's design as significantly as landfill and fire. Their wealth supported Boston's banks, backed its real estate, invested in its capital bonds, and endowed many of its institutions, from hospitals and schools to the Athenæm and the symphony. Allied by marriages, education, and church affiliations against Boston's swelling foreign-born population, Boston's Harvard-educated Unitarian and Episcopalian Yankee oligarchy held disproportionate sway over civic affairs through much of the 1800s. Even a bank founded in 1816 at the behest of a Catholic archbishop and patronized predominantly thereafter by Irish immigrants wasn't immune: no Irish Catholic was named to its board of directors until the end of WW II.

But as these merchant princes improved the downtown streetscape with stately townhouses and museums, they may also unintentionally have changed the appearance of Boston's turn-of-the-century neighborhoods—results of a backlash to their long political dominance.

In 1910, John "Honey Fitz" Fitzgerald, in one of the great political upsets in American history, won the mayoral election. His victory gave Yankees reason to rue the decades of their bigotry and discrimination. Honey Fitz had been mayor before, but reformers confident of a Yankee victory had since altered the city charter to give the office unprecedented executive powers and double the length of the term in which to exercise them. The richest of Beacon Hill's bluebloods could always count on their fortunes and private social clubs to insulate them from the populist rabble, but middle-class Yankees around the city were given a taste of comeuppance. A generation of mostly Irish Democratic pols used municipal payrolls and city services to build a dedicated constituency among Irish, Italians, Eastern Europeans, and other ethnic groups previously excluded from the city's feedbag. Boston's densely populated poor and working-class wards acquired new roads, schools, playgrounds, and bathhouses, while more affluent Yankee enclaves were all but neglected. As the end of WW I brought a flood of tenement dwellers to the city, districts that only a decade earlier seemed destined to be developed as streetcar neighborhoods of single-family homes for Yankee professionals were instead forested with multi-family three-deckers. Affordable to city workers and their families, anathema to conservative Anglo property owners, three-deckers fueled the Yankee exodus to greener suburban pastures. These days, this indigenous housing style has become as emblematic of Boston as Bulfinch's Federal mansions on Beacon Hill, and remains an important symbol of a constituency essential to any mayor's election.

"The People's Choice"

Where I found a muddy lane, I left a
broad highway; where I found a barren
waste, I left a hospital; where I found a
disease-breeding row of tenement houses,
I left a health center; where I found a
vacant lot, I left a magnificent temple of
learning; where I found a weed-grown
field, I left a playground: throughout life,
wherever I have found a thistle, I
endeavored to replace it with a rose.

—James Michael Curley

The most successful Irish politician to come after Honey Fitz was, without a doubt, James Michael Curley. A true populist, perhaps a demagogue,

Mayor James Michael Curley throws out the first pitch.

Curley was a flagrant but beloved scoundrel whose skill at machine politics, from wielding patronage to controlling blocks of votes, earned him numerous electoral victories to every local, state, and national office between alderman and Congress. Famous for his sharp wit and rich baritone oratory, Curley could charm the skin off a tiger. The famous couplet, "Vote early and often/For Mayor Curley of Boston" can't begin to capture the genuine affection he inspired in every Bostonian born without a silver spoon in his mouth.

Before President Franklin Roosevelt's New Dealers gave public works a shred of respectability, Curley incensed Bay State conservatives with his willingness to treat government as one big job opportunity for the down-and-out masses. Though he dispensed gifts and pocketed graft as well as any boss of the late 19th- and early 20th-century era of the big-city machines, many of whom had already been discredited before his own rise to power, Curley was unrepentant about his record. To accusations of being ossified and out of touch during a 1938 run for governor, Curley replied, "No, this leopard has no desire to change his spots. If to keep faith with the people and lead the fight for liberal legislation, to give jobs to the jobless, food to the hungry, and to rescue children and mothers from malnutrition and exploitation and bring comfort and security to the aged constitutes leopard spots, than I submit that I am covered with them." He was also covered with other spots: the criminal record that grew over the years, eventually including stints behind bars for two felony convictions, and one civil penalty for taking a payoff while mayor. Though scandal dogged Curley's career from start to finish, it never disqualified him in the minds of his constituents. The first state representative in Massachusetts history to face criminal conviction (he defrauded the government by taking a civil service exam on behalf of a supporter), Curley proceeded to run for and win election to Boston's Board of Aldermen while in jail, in 1904. And even as their fourth-term mayor was shipped off to a Federal penitentiary in 1947 at age 73 (for mail fraud while serving in Congress, related to kickbacks on government contracts), 62% of Bostonians polled by the *Boston Globe* still approved of his performance in office.

Finally rejected by corruption-weary voters during his fifth run for mayor, Curley was literally chased out of office on his last day by a sheriff trying to serve a restraining order on his blatant lame-duck favors for cronies. Family tragedy and more failed attempts at elected office kept the man in the public eye well into his 80s, but the real jump into immortality came with the help of *The Last Hurrah,* Edwin O'Connor's best-selling 1956 novel about a well-intentioned but bare-knuckled Irish politician, last of a dying breed, at the end of his career. Hollywood went one better with a sentimental film version by John Ford, starring Spencer Tracy as the enobled Mayor Skeffington. Although Curley himself virtually adopted them as official biographies, both book and movie are romanticized views of a life that was in fact *not* his own; nonetheless, myth has prevailed, making Curley a fondly remembered Boston icon. Readers wanting a more factual recounting of both fact and legend—with generous helpings of the frequently hilarious anecdotes that characterize Curley's career—should pick up a copy of Jack Beatty's *The Rascal King,* published in 1992.

"A GOOD SHOEMAKER AND A POOR FISH PEDDLER"

During the first half hour of August 23, 1927, as thousands of protesters from around the globe held a vigil outside, three so-calledradical conspirators were sent to the electric chair for the murder of two shoe-factory employees during a 1920 payroll robbery south of Boston. Convicted almost entirely on the basis of their "suspicious behavior" (i.e., their anarchist beliefs), the immigrants arrested for the crime—shoemaker Nicola Sacco, fishmonger Bartolomeo Vanzetti, and the often-forgotten Celestino Madeiros —might have been executed in obscurity but for a diligent letter-writing campaign that awakened the world to miscarried justice.

Despite State House picketing, reams of newspaper editorials, entreaties from foreign leaders, and a bombing of the American ambassador's house in Paris, Massachusetts's civil authorities stubbornly opposed the mounting international outcry for a retrial. Distinguished law professor and future Supreme Court justice Felix Frankfurter's exposé in the *Atlantic Monthly* of the original trial's flaws was roundly rebutted by the Boston *Evening Transcript,* the newspaper of the city's elite. All-powerful Cardinal William O'Connell (who would later salute Generalissimo Francisco Franco as a fighter for Christian civilization) flatly refused to intercede for clemency. The Dedham trial judge swatted down one appeal after another while boasting to friends what he was doing to those "anarchist bastards."

After several years, a governor-appointed blue-ribbon panel—including the presidents of both Harvard and MIT—reviewed the case to determine whether a retrial was warranted but wound up rubber-stamping the original findings. Public consciences thus salved, the tyranny of xenophobia finally proceeded with the electrocution. At the end, Vanzetti wrote, "Never in our full life could we hope to do such work for tolerance, for justice, for man's understanding of man as now we do by accident." Two hundred thousand people turned out for the funeral procession to a Jamaica Plain crematorium.

Papers and artifacts from the Sacco-Vanzetti Defense Committee are now kept by the Boston Public Library (artifacts include a model by Gutzon Borglum, sculptor of Mt. Rushmore, for a memorial sculpture, which was rejected by both the city and the state). The two men's ashes are there, as well. A shelf of books has been written about the case; among the more interesting are Katherine Ann Porter's *Never-Ending Wrong,* Francis Russell's *Tragedy in Dedham,* and Upton Sinclair's *Boston,* which was banned locally upon its release.

I had a relative, a poet who lived in New York City and in Maine, who came up for the protests about Sacco and Vanzetti. And I can remember, and this was in 1927, when the two men were executed. And there was an enormous outturning of literary people (Katherine Ann Porter and Edna St. Vincent Millay) and lots of people from the arts as well as from politics.

And I remember that night well, although I must say my family didn't think much of Edna Vincent's political and social and other activities.

And I remember going to the vigil outside the prison. And I think I remember, I think I remember . . .

There were always people who believed, and maybe it was a fact, but that when people were executed . . . (It was in Charlestown, just across the river from where the Science Museum is now) . . . that when people were electrocuted, they always said it took so much power (this may have been just a street myth) that the lights blinked. But I think I could say that I remember the lights dimming when they were executed.

—Recollected by Pauline Swift,
from *From Hearing My Mother Talk:
Stories of Cambridge Women,*
collected and edited by Cynthia E. Cohen

The Athens of America Atrophies

As the populism of Irish mayors scared away private Yankee capital and low-wage Southern labor siphoned away any manufacturing still intact after the Depression, Boston entered an economic and cultural tailspin, becoming something of a provincial backwater neighbor to New York. The population leveled off during the Roosevelt and Truman years and then declined, a process arrested only briefly by WW II's boosted payrolls. (The city is ending the 20th century with nearly the same number of residents it had at the beginning—a full 25% below its peak of 800,000.)

But outfitting the military didn't improve the city skyline any more than Depression had, and entertaining the military made some districts even seedier. The blue-blooded Watch and Ward Society, de facto public censors for the city since 1878, had become so active before the war that "Banned in Boston" became a national joke. Civic culture guardians were no more open-minded afterwards: in 1948, Boston's Institute of Modern Art changed the "modern" in its name to "contemporary" in order to disassociate itself from such avant-garde work as Abstract Expressionism (branded by an Institute spokesman as "a cult of bewilderment").

The growth of service industries brought new economic life to the city in the early 1960s—around the same time that urban renewal and the interstate highway system transformed the city's face. Neglected old neighborhoods like Beacon Hill and the South End also got new life from bumper crops of middle-class university graduates, who settled down after obtaining their degrees. While these young constituents of the "new" Boston and the blue-collar workers who grew up here often shared allegiance to the Democratic Party, their views about the city's future diverged widely. The clash between social conservatives and liberals who would remake Boston as a multicultural society finally culminated in the painful and violent battle over school desegregation, an eruption so long and loud that it splashed into headlines across the nation. Repercussions and aftershocks are still felt in the city today.

Hackers, Bankers, Brokers, Students

Despite rents in the the city's social fabric over issues of class and race in the 1960s and '70s, mushrooming skyscrapers attest to Boston's having shed at least *some* of its old strictures. All that's new is no longer anathema. Even Robert Mapplethorpe doesn't threaten Boston's foundations as Isadora Duncan or D. H. Lawrence once did. Business—insurance, money management, high technology—and academia have wrought significant, visible changes over the past two decades. Why, half Boston's current population has been here only since 1980. The core of the city is lively and liveable, and promises to become even more so as the multi-billion-dollar Central Artery/Tunnel project buries the aging elevated interstate dividing downtown from its waterfront and the residential North End. Perhaps the city's millenial energy will even bring baseball's Boston Red Sox the World Series victory they have sought for so long.

COURTESY OF THE BOSTON PUBLIC LIBRARY, PRINT DEPARTMENT

SIGHTS

Most of Boston's major historical attractions lay within the confines of the city's old seagirt boundaries, which effectively means they're all within a short, walkable radius from Boston Common. Being of more modern vintage, most of the city's cultural institutions are widely scattered about, but don't let that be an excuse to reach for the car keys—any blitz of the typical tourist Top 10 would require a good bankroll for parking fees and a saint's patience for navigating the city's streets. Better to rely on public transportation or the unlimited boarding privileges offered by sightseeing trolleys that loop around the major attractions on both sides of the Charles River. Some of the attractions described below are best reached by public bus; in such instances, the route number and destination will be identified just as they're displayed over the bus windshield. For nitty-gritty details about navigating the city via the subways, trolleys, buses, and ferries of the **Massachusetts Bay Transportation Authority** (the MBTA, or "T," for short), see **Transportation** in the Boston Basics chapter.

BOSTON SIGHTS

BEACON HILL AND THE WEST END

Beacon Hill is Boston's cornerstone. New, modern sections of the city are generic enough for Toronto to be used as its movie double, but these slopes—on which the city was founded over 350 years ago, decked out with Federal-style mansions and crowned by the gold dome of the State House—are unequivocally and irreplaceably Old Boston. Beacon and its lower adjoining hills, Pemberton and Mt. Vernon (known collectively to early colonists as "Trimountain," or, more colloquially, "Tremont"), remained undeveloped boondocks for Boston's first century. Isolated behind a town with its feet in the harbor, the settlement that finally grew up on the backside of the hills in the early 1700s included a red light district so steeped in a "torrent of vice" that Mt. Vernon was all but renamed "Mt. Whoredom" in colonial annals and maps. When government outgrew the Old State House in the late 1700s, real estate speculators who were aware that the new building was planned for Beacon Hill acquired most of Trimountain's summit acreage, cropped the top of Beacon Hill, altogether erased Mt. Vernon, and developed the area, during the first decades of the 19th century, into a fashionable mansion district. By the Civil War, changing notions of acceptable urban density replaced trees and gardens with townhouses, making even the chic "sunny" side resemble the rowhouse-dominated servants' neighborhood on the shadier north slope. But the resemblance was only superficial: socially and ethnically, the south side of Beacon Hill remained a bastion of Brahmin WASPs until Boston's 20th-century malaise further subdivided many a fine home into small apartments and faded the finery of the rest. Since the 1970s, Beacon Hill has both recovered its appeal as one of the city's most desirable addresses and received recognition (and protection) as a National Historic Landmark.

Strolling the undulating brick sidewalks of the Hill's labyrinthine streets and alleyways is an end in itself. Notice the bootscrapers embedded in granite front steps, the occasional hitching posts, and the abundance of lacy wrought-iron fencing. Among the facades of Beacon Street facing the Common, look for rare purple window panes; these are chemically flawed panels of clear glass turned amethyst by early 19th-century sunlight. Discover William Ralph Emerson's "House of Odd Windows," at 24 Pinckney St., whose design might be called postmodern if Ralph Waldo Emerson's architect nephew had conceived it in 1984 instead of 1884. Hunt for the cul-de-sacs off Revere and Phillips Streets, or for Boston's most photogenic block of cobblestones—Acorn Street. And don't miss Louisburg Square, the epitome of the Hill's classical elegance and proportion, centered upon a tiny private park jointly owned by adjacent residents. Among past holders of a key to the park gate are Louisa May Alcott (who was living at No. 10 when she died) and *Atlantic Monthly* editor William Dean Howells (who introduced Mark Twain to local literary circles); Massachusetts Senator John Kerry is among those who have one now.

Charms of a more commercial nature are found at the foot of Beacon Hill along Charles Street, whose gas lamps and red brick frame cute little boutiques and a thicket of antique shops. Can't afford deacquisitioned museum pieces, $10,000 Asian furniture, Scandinavian long clocks, or turn-of-the-century china dinnerware? Perhaps the always-interesting Beacon

BULFINCH~THE BUILDER OF BOSTON

The individual arguably most influential in shaping the look and feel of Boston during the decades following American independence was Charles Bulfinch. Born in 1763 to a Boston doctor, Bulfinch was sufficiently privileged in upbringing and education initially to pursue "no business but giving gratuitous advice in architecture." But a bankrupted residential scheme drove Bulfinch into becoming America's first professional architect.

In practice, his adaptations of English design pioneered what is known as the Federal style of architecture. In Boston, he designed mansions, churches, a theater, entire blocks of townhouses, the grid plan for the whole South End, offices, hospitals, banks, markets (including the expanded Faneuil Hall), schools, halls for Harvard (his alma mater), a courthouse, state and local jails, and the State House—one of three New England capitols in which he had a hand. It's no wonder that he felt that architects had so little left to do that it would be useless to encourage his children to join the profession. Many of his buildings are long gone, or—like the curve of Franklin St. from his failed Tontine Crescent development—remain in nothing more than the merest outline.

But as an architect, a developer, a town planner, the de facto mayor (Chairman of the Board of Selectmen), and even the police superintendent, Bulfinch built a 30-year career in Boston that has accurately been described as having transformed a small town of wood into a city of brick and granite (much of which *does* remain).

However, while Boston prospered, Bulfinch did not. Perennially poor, in 1818 he accepted a presidential appointment to rebuild Washington's war-ravaged U.S. Capitol. After 12 well-paid years (his happiest), he finally returned to Boston. There, he rested on his laurels until his death, at 81.

Hill Thrift Shop, at No. 15, has something more in your range; the antiques in front are generally priced under four figures. Sustain your buying and strolling with a big muffin from the bakery case of **DeLuca's,** 11 Charles, tel. (617) 523-4343, near Beacon (a vastly better value than the dainty morsels from Starbucks next door), or give your soles a rest over an inexpensive lunch (great focaccia, lousy croissants) and coffee from attractively casual **Panificio,** 144 Charles, tel. (617) 227-4340, open till 10 p.m. On the landfilled flats of Beacon Hill, beneath the stout brick facade of the Hampshire House, on Beacon Street opposite the Public Garden, is one of the city's most popular tourist attractions, the Bull & Finch Pub. Better known as the *Cheers* **bar,** it's a far cry from the quiet neighborhood spot that once caught the television producers' fancy (nor does it bear great similarity to the TV series' set), but don't let that stop you from hoisting a few at the bar with the million other pilgrims who've come to pay their respects.

House and Garden Tours

One of the few Beacon Hill houses open to the public is the 1804 **Nichols House Museum,** 55 Mt. Vernon St., tel. (617) 227-6993. Per the bequest of its last owner, Rose Standish Nichols, the place is a window into heirloom-filled Beacon Hill gentility; tours (noon-4:15 p.m. Monday, Wednesday, and Saturday; $5) highlight Miss Rose's idiosyncrasies as well as her possessions. The house itself was built by wealthy Jonathan Mason, one of the original Mt. Vernon Proprietors—the group whose ringleader, Harrison Gray Otis, used his knowledge of impending State House construction to acquire the adjacent 18-acre farm of expatriate painter John Singleton Copley. A Tory sympathizer who moved to London before the Revolution, Copley made several hundred percent profit on the sale of his hillside pastures. To his everlasting regret, however, even that sum was a pittance compared to the killing Otis, Mason, and their cronies made on the property.

The son of a Declaration of Independence signer and sometimes elected officeholder himself, Harry Otis made his mint developing Boston land while most of his wealthy contemporaries fattened their bank accounts with maritime trade or shipbuilding. The fruits of Otis's Midas touch

are preserved on and around Beacon Hill in part through his three private mansions, all built by his friend Charles Bulfinch (whose own ill-timed property developments were often profitably acquired by the deeper-pocketed Otis). The first of the three homes, the 1796 **Harrison Gray Otis House,** 141 Cambridge St., is the only one open to the public. Compensating for the plain facade, lost gardens, and much-altered neighborhood is the opulence of the interior, restored to the busy patterns, bright colors, and expensive materials with which Otis and his wife surrounded themselves. Tours of the property—now headquarters for SPNEA, the Society for the Preservation of New England Antiquities—are given on the hour, noon-4 p.m. Tues.-Fri. and 10 a.m.-4 p.m. Saturday ($4; tel. 617-227-3956).

SPNEA also offers guided walks of Beacon Hill starting at 10 a.m. every Saturday, June-Oct. ($10; reservations recommended), commencing with a slide show here at Harry's old digs. For anyone more interested in horticulture than history, the Beacon Hill Garden Club offers a famous **Hidden Garden Tour** ($20; tel. 617-227-4392). Rain or shine, this annual self-guided rite of spring takes place the third Thursday of May; tickets and maps are sold from booths set up on Charles Street for the occasion. The first weekend of June offers another peek behind closed doors and gates—this one free—during the annual **Beacon Hill ArtsWalk,** when local artists hold a grand yard sale of their works in courtyards, backyards, and indoor studios all over the funkier north slope.

Beacon Hill's Other Half

Beacon Hill's shady side was a center for the city's African American community from colonial times through the Great Depression, initially because it was affordable (it was a buffer between town propriety and riverside brothels), then because it was convenient for residents employed in mansions on the other side of Pinckney Street. But it wasn't all laborers' rooming houses and servants' quarters; after Massachusetts abolished slavery, in 1783, Boston's free black community grew to include tradesmen and professionals, from barbers and printers to doctors and lawyers (including the first black lawyer to argue a case in front of the U.S. Supreme Court—*before* the end of the Civil War or ratification of the 13th Amendment, abolishing slavery). The support these residents gave to the abolitionist movement also made Beacon Hill's north slope a major stop on the Underground Railroad, helping fugitive slaves escape to freedom in the northeast, England, and Canada.

The **Boston African American National Historic Site** pays tribute to this underappreciated community, partly with exhibits at the **Abiel Smith School**—46 Joy St. (currently under restoration until early 1999), tel. (617) 739-1200—and partly through excellent ranger-led neighborhood walks (thrice daily late May through early September, or Mon.-Fri. with advanced reservations the rest of the year, even during construction). Behind the Smith School—established by the city in the 1830s to avoid desegregating existing public schools—is the **African Meeting House**, 8 Smith Court, the nation's oldest remaining black church and home to the contemporary gallery of the **Museum of Afro American History,** tel. (617) 742-1854, open daily late May through early Sept., otherwise Mon.-Fri. only; free, but $5 donation suggested. Built for black Baptists who faced discrimination in other local churches, the 1806 structure is most famous as the site of the 1832 founding of the New England Anti-Slavery Society by the unequivocal abolitionist William Lloyd Garrison, and for being the Civil War recruiting center for the Massachusetts 54th Colored Infantry Regiment. As the religious, educational, and civic cornerstone in the African American community for decades, it was also a forum for 19th-century campaigns for integrated schools, women's suffrage, and other nearly forgotten chapters from Boston's history. Take a tour, mentally block out the anachronistic plastic seating (a product of the hall's continued use for public lectures, concerts, and even weddings), and even today you can almost hear echoes of those old debates. Though you won't find it equal in depth or scope to the ranger-led tours, do-it-yourselfers can pick up a free, self-guided **Black Heritage Trail** brochure at either the Meeting House or Smith School, describing 14 well-preserved sights around Beacon Hill's north slope.

The State House

Whatever you do, *don't* call it the Capitol: Charles Bulfinch's 1797 gold-domed masterpiece is properly referred to as the State House, and the elected representatives and senators who gather inside to make the Commonwealth's laws are collectively known as the Great and General Court. From the pine cone ornament (symbolizing the state's abundant timber—most of which was then in what eventually became the state of

---

"I HAD A TEACHER": BEING BLACK IN BOSTON

I had a teacher at Cambridge High and Latin who I think helped me a great deal. She was head of the department of Office Practice, and she sent me on a job.

One of the papers in Boston wanted some girls to do some typing, and I was a good typist, and she sent me with three or four other girls, and it just so happened that I was the only black one, and I was the only one that wasn't taken, and I couldn't understand. I knew I was a faster typist than any of the others. And she took me in her room, and talked to me.

Her name was Miss Dennis; I'll never forget her. She called them and asked them why they didn't take me and they said, "We only needed so many."

And she said, "But I sent my best." I can hear her now, I was sitting right there. But she took me in her room, and she said, "Henrietta, you are going to see this over and over and over. But remember, I told them and I know, I sent my best." And she said, "You just remember that when you go to do something, if you don't get it, if you're rejected for any other reason than performance, don't let it get to you. Just remember that you are capable."

She gave me such a feeling of worth. I think she had even more influence than my mother, because much of what my mother did was from love, you know, but this woman had no reason to build up my ego other than her belief that I was worth something. And she went out of her way to make opportunities.

I'll always remember that afternoon. I was bitterly disappointed.

—Henrietta Jackson,
from *From Hearing My Mother Talk: Stories of Cambridge Women,*
collected and edited by Cynthia E. Cohen

JEFF PERK

*the Massachusetts
State House*

Maine) on top of the (originally wood-shingled) dome to the commemorative Dog and Horse tablet in the east wing, there are many stories to this place. Some of them are related on the Mon.-Fri. tours that begin amid the tall Doric columns inside the front entrance. Not all the young guides have their facts straight, unfortunately; some don't correctly explain, for example, that the Sacred Cod hanging over the second-floor House of Representatives chamber was a 1783 gift from a merchant who wished to remind the legislators where the state earned its bread and butter—kind of an 18th-century "it's the fisheries, stupid."

Across the street from the State House is the **Robert Gould Shaw Memorial,** honoring the Civil War commander of the Massachusetts 54th Regiment, who was slain with scores of his men in a suicidal attack on Fort Wagner, South Carolina. Sculptor Augustus Saint-Gaudens, known for his Adams Memorial in Washington, D.C., spent over a decade working on this bas-relief, which the abolitionist Shaw family intended to honor black enlisted men as much as their son. The young colonel is also memorialized at Cambridge's Mount Auburn Cemetery, with a plaque on the family monument.

Around the corner from the State House, the **Appalachian Mountain Club,** 5 Joy St., tel. (617) 523-0636, dispenses books, maps, field guides, and other planning aids for hikers, campers, and paddlers contemplating outdoor excursions anywhere in New England. If you hadn't yet considered taking to the hills, dales, and streams of the region, check out the bookshelves here at headquarters. The AMC is also an excellent resource for Appalachian Trail hikers; besides buying topos and incredibly detailed trail guides to the famous 2,100-mile Georgia-to-Maine footpath, you can find out how to make reservations for the AMC's network of alpine huts and mountain lodges in New Hampshire and western Massachusetts.

The Museum of Science

Behind Beacon Hill and across busy Cambridge Street lies the old West End, birthplace of Leonard Nimoy and one of the nation's first casualties of federally funded urban renewal. Where once were tenement-crowded streets, street-corner social clubs, and laundry on lines now stand massive institutional office complexes and apartment towers. Although the project was initially hailed for eradicating a blighted part of the city, hindsight has brought rueful awareness that outsize modern buildings often subtract more than they add to a city's quality of life.

Atop the Charles River Dam, off the banks of the West End, sits Science Park and its Museum of Science, tel. (617) 723-2500, best approached via a walk along the river (cross Storrow Drive via the footbridge at the end of Charles St.) or by riding the T. Almost always abuzz with crowds of school groups, families, and faithful members returning to explore yet another of its innumerable exhibit halls, this is one museum that doesn't make you keep your hands to yourself or your voice down. Catch a demo of the world's largest Van de Graaff generator, whose whip-cracking bolts of indoor lightning are showcased in the Theater of Electricity. Let interactive exhibits teach you to think like a scientist. Play virtual reality volleyball. Or take an elevator deep under Boston Harbor to learn more about the Big Dig construction project causing so many of downtown's traffic woes. Planetarium shows take you through the solar system and beyond—especially at one of the trippy laser presentations set to music from the Grateful Dead, Jimi Hendrix, or Smashing Pumpkins. There's a giant OmniMax film theater, too. Open daily year-round ($8 adults, $6 kids and seniors, planetarium and Omni shows additional, combination and family discounts available).

DOWNTOWN AND THE WATERFRONT

Ever since the first State House and Market Square sat at the head of the town wharves, Boston's civil, financial, and commercial functions have been close neighbors. Although that original waterfront lies buried beneath hotels and multistory glass boxes, "downtown" retains its multiple identity in Government Center's bureaucracy, the Financial District's money managers, and Washington Street's department stores. City planners may lump it with Midtown, but Boston Common, too, is "downtown" to most locals (as are Chinatown and the Leather District around South Station—unless you live there).

THE FREEDOM TRAIL

You may have noticed a red stripe threading all around the downtown area, connecting various high-profile historic attractions that date back to the colonial era. This 2.5-mile stripe and its 16 accompanying historic sites comprise the Freedom Trail.

While first and foremost a walk among actual places associated with events leading up to the American Revolution, the Trail encompasses or connects to sites relevant to other elements of Boston's political, religious, and cultural history. Taking in much more than just dead patriots and battle monuments, the Trail touches on the contributions of colonial women to the cause of liberty, 19th-century artifacts of African Americans' and immigrants' struggle to share in the Revolution's freedoms, the very visible architectural legacy of the city, and the downtown neighborhoods whose changing ethnicity mirrors the city's evolving identity.

If you walk the trail on your own, of course, you can start where you like. But most Trail brochures and guidebooks begin at the Common. Allow most of a day to cover the whole route—or you can divide it into smaller segments: downtown, the North End, and Charlestown. You can also cut some of the walking mileage by taking the $1 MBTA water shuttle between the downtown waterfront (Long Wharf, next to the Aquarium) and the Charlestown Navy Yard, where the USS *Constitution* is berthed. Day-trippers coming into the city will find both Commuter Rail stations to be within blocks of the Trail, but at the Navy Yard you will find abundant parking—at more attractive rates than downtown—including some lots offering four hours free.

Between Patriots Day, in mid-April, and Thanksgiving weekend, in late November, National Park Service rangers offer free abbreviated Trail tours starting in front of the **Boston National Historical Park Visitor Center,** at 15 State St., tel. (617) 242-5689, opposite the

It will take most of a day to walk the entire trail.

JEFF PERK

This is the city's economic heart, nearly 200,000 workers strong. With several thousand apartment dwellers and a mix of luxury and working class residential neighborhoods on nearly all sides, downtown Boston isn't the kind of inner city that rolls up its sidewalks after 5 p.m., either. With the vast majority of the city's 17th- and 18th-century remnants—burying grounds, certain streets, and a handful of buildings—downtown would seem to exemplify Boston's commitment to preservation of the past. But with every megasized skyline addition, it affirms a stronger desire to face the future. Here the city's urban history is as condensed as a college survey course, from its first page—the purchase of the Common—through pages yet unwritten, awaiting the day the dust clears from burying

the now-elevated Central Artery. Maybe those pages, when filled, will explain the paradox of the Big Dig, whose high-capacity subterranean interstate promises to deliver a lot more vehicles to the one part of Boston most ill-suited to accommodate them.

For those visitors who wisely skip driving, one of the pleasures of strolling downtown is discovering alleys like Spring Lane, off lower Washington Street, or Winthrop Lane between Arch and Otis Streets, whose landmark- and history-inspired "City Bricks" beguile the downward-cast eye. Observant strollers will also find numerous plaques affixed to buildings or embedded in pavement, each one designating a pinch of city history. When the weather's nice, do what the locals do: find a sunny spot in a small urban

Old State House entrance to the Orange Line's State Street station. These walks cover most of the sites in downtown and the North End but (like most paid tours, too) stop short of crossing into Charlestown. Besides ranger programs, the visitor center also has free Trail brochures, scores of great local-interest books for sale (including a good self-guiding booklet to the 46 sites of Boston's scantily recognized Women's Heritage Trail), and, perhaps most important, public bathrooms.

It's worth noting that while the Boston NHP and the Freedom Trail overlap, they are *not* synonymous. (One of the National Historic Park's eight components is far off the Trail, in Dorchester—and nine of the Trail stops have nothing to do with the NHP.) Also note that there are no consistent rules about admission fees—most components of both the Trail and the NHP are free, but not all. Fortunately, those that do charge admission are among the most inexpensive attractions in Boston.

To coordinate your visit with any of the special events scheduled along the Trail, contact the Freedom Trail Foundation, tel. (617) 227-8800, for your free copy of their annually updated map and guide.

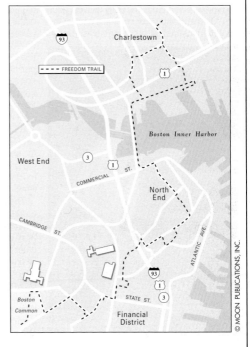

© MOON PUBLICATIONS, INC.

oasis like Winthrop Square, Liberty Square, Post Office Square, or adjacent Angell Memorial Park. A brief respite in any of these art-filled spaces is a great antidote to the weariness that otherwise attends walking on hard pavement all day.

The Common

Misleadingly billed as the nation's oldest public park, Boston Common was originally set aside in 1634 as a military training field and public pasture for grazing cattle. Although greatly altered botanically and topographically—the 17th-century Common had several more hills and ponds, but only one or two trees—the size and boundaries are about the same as when it was first purchased from Rev. William Blaxton. Besides feeding the town's early dairy herd and accommodating centuries of soldiers, the Common was home to the Great Elm, from whose stout branches were hanged many petty thieves, adulterers, Quakers, and other criminals back in the days when capital punishment was proper

JEFF PERK

Peter Banner's 1810 Park Street Church at the entrance to Boston Common

Boston sport. (Executions were often cause for a holiday and could attract boisterous mobs; one triple hanging on the Common in 1789 attracted an estimated 20,000 spectators.) Gallows gave way in the 19th century to healthier recreations: the Oneida Football Club, credited as the first American football team, which played on the Common during the Civil War. A detailed map of nearly all the Common's statuary and monuments, including the plaque to the undefeated Oneidas, is available free at the visitor center along the Tremont Street side. The one statue omitted is the troop of gaunt horseback riders on Charles Street near the corner of Beacon; called *The Partisans,* the modern metal casting by Polish-born Andrzei Pitynski wasn't supposed to be permanent, but 20 years later the city is still waiting for the artist to pick it up.

Besides nice public art, pushcarts selling tourist claptrap, and the Frog Pond—where toy boats sail in summer and skaters congregate in winter ($3 skate rental; for winter conditions, call 617-635-2197), one oft-overlooked feature is the 1756 **Central Burying Ground.** Initially this plot was for marginal figures, such as Boston's first Catholics (note the Celtic crosses), Freemasons, paupers (painter Gilbert Stuart among them), and foreigners, such as the British soldiers who occupied Boston during the Revolution, and Chow Manderien, a teenage Chinese sailor who fell from a ship's mast in 1798. Located on the short, Boylston Street side, this historic burying ground is across from the concentration of musical instrument showrooms known as Piano Row.

The Boston Park Rangers conduct one-hour tours around the Common every Saturday in July and August, and at least once a month April-Oct.; for a precise schedule of these and other Common events, call the Boston Parks & Recreation **Events Line,** tel. (617) 635-3445.

Downtown Crossing

The intersection of Washington, Summer, and Winter Streets and several adjacent blocks form a brick-paved pedestrian shopping mall, anchored by Macy's and Filene's department stores. Major chains like Borders, HMV, the Gap, and General Nutrition Center are well represented, along with a handful of new and used camera shops on Bromfield Street, but the major retail trend in the area is toward off-price clothing stores. Shoppers in search of something unique should hunt out the **Society of Arts and Crafts'** downtown gallery, in the shopping concourse of 34 Summer/101 Arch St., behind Filene's. Also in a class by itself is **The Brattle Book Shop,** on short little West St. a block south of Macy's, whose quarter million used and rare books are a magnet for both serious antiquarians and general used book lovers. The outdoor racks of thousands of $1 books have been an all-season West St. fixture for decades. The book shop's original incarnation opened in 1825, on long-vanished Brattle St., one of a warren of streets erased by Government Center. Run for many years by Elizabeth Palmer Peabody (whose sister Sophia married Nathaniel Hawthorne in the back), the shop was for a time like a 19th-century Algonquin Club, with Margaret Fuller, editor of that notable Transcendentalist publication *The Dial,* hosting a regular series of literary evenings for Boston women.

Though now an entirely separate company from its aboveground namesake, **Filene's Basement,** tel. (617) 542-2011, remains the city's semi-sacred bargain-hunters' mecca, located in what used to be, prior to the 1872 Great Fire, Trinity Church's catacombs. Don't settle for the suburban or out-of-state satellites—they're pale imitations of Washington Street's 1912 original, connected directly to the Downtown Crossing T station. From coats to lingerie, famous labels to generic store brands, there's no shortage of wearables to choose from. There's no shortage, either, of eagle-eyed Basement veterans who brook no interference with their Holy Grail-quest-like search for that bargain of a lifetime. Some one-day blowout sales on high-end items like furs and wedding dresses unleash such human tsunamis through the aisles that accidental visitors may feel as if they've been swept into a re-union of punk-rock moshers and their elbow-swinging mothers.

Although there is a food court at The Corner, opposite Filene's, and various purveyors of sweets and sandwiches are installed all around the skirts of that venerable department store, peckish walkers should keep eyes aloft to spot **Anais,** a convenience store-cum-Armenian luncheonette on the second floor of the **Jewelry Exchange Building,** at 333 Washington St.,

across from Marshall's. Fresh, delicious falafel, hummus, lahmajun, grape leaves, and great honeyed treats baked by owner Arto's wife are complemented by an unsurpassed bird's-eye view of Downtown Crossing's crowds. Anyone in the market for a diamond tiara or gold wedding band will want to shop the building's dozen other tenants, whose combined window displays create a sparkling labyrinth of precious metals and stones.

Pews and Graves

Lower Tremont Street, between the Common and Government Center, is lined with two of Boston's historic graveyards and several equally historic houses of worship. Among the latter is the 1810 **Park Street Church,** opposite the Park Street T station, whose 21-story steeple is as

---

CEMETERIES AND BURYING GROUNDS

A cemetery (from the Greek word for "a sleeping place") was conceived in the mid-19th century as landscaped gardens in which the dead reposed peacefully. The first (and perhaps still this country's most outstanding) was Mount Auburn Cemetery, across the river in Cambridge.

By contrast, burying grounds were unkempt plots of land to which the dead were rudely consigned to molder in their graves until Judgment Day. The idea that decent burial and the maintenance of the grave of the dearly departed might make one whit of difference to the disposition of his or her soul was foreign to the Puritans, who set aside and named Boston's burying grounds. The Puritans believed in predestination: if you were of the Elect, you'd make it to Heaven, and if you, like most people, shared in the sins of Adam and Eve, you didn't. In either case, there was no point in wasting effort prettying up your grave.

The fact that the city's 17th- and 18th-century burying grounds today bear a strong, manicured resemblance to 19th-century cemeteries is the result of modern-day tidying up. What you see on the surface is wholly unlike the true state of affairs underground—where the residents are actually strewn about haphazardly, often unmarked; piled in on top of previous burials; or evicted by later interments.

exemplary of New England's Congregational architecture as they come. Gunpowder stored in the basement during the War of 1812 is said to have prompted the name Brimstone Corner, although Unitarians also used the nickname to mock the church's Bible-thumping Trinitarian preachers. The corner's previous occupant, a storage house, lent its name to the next-door **Granary Burying Ground,** founded in 1660 (wheelchair-accessible entrance is at the end of Tremont Place off Beacon Street). Among the illustrious Bostonians interred here are Crispus Attucks and the other victims of the Boston Massacre; patriots James Otis and Paul Revere; signers of the Declaration of Independence Samuel Adams, John Hancock, and Robert Treat Paine; Ben Franklin's parents (whose memorial obelisk bears an epitaph from their famous son); Boston's first mayor; and John Hull, whose 1652 Pine Tree Shilling was the first coin of the English colonies. Elizabeth Foster Goose is believed to be buried in an unmarked grave somewhere near the marked plot of her son-in-law Thomas Fleet, who collected and published the verses "Mother" Goose recited to her kids. (The stone for Mary Goose, despite what some may say, does *not* mark the famous nursery rhymer. For that matter, Elizabeth isn't the first, either: that honor belongs to the unnamed and possibly fictitious Mother Goose, *mère l'oye,* whose stories were published in 17th-century France by Charles Perrault 22 years before Fleet's alleged collection, no copy of which has ever been found by modern scholars.) Occasionally in summer and around Halloween you'll encounter some of these historical figures wandering around in costume giving autobiographical speeches; their resurrection is courtesy of the Boston Parks & Recreation Department. As in all Boston's historic burying grounds and cemeteries, grave rubbings are absolutely *verboten,* since the stones can't stand the abuse.

The city's oldest graveyard is just down the block: the 1630 **King's Chapel Burying Ground,** near the corner of School Street. Compare the bare-toothed skulls on the Puritans' slate markers with the plump-cheeked cherubs of a later age to get a rough idea of what the Bay Colony's earliest settlers felt about death and dying. Among the most prominent residents awaiting their maker here are Puritan leaders and colonial governors John Endicott and John Winthrop, who took turns as top office holder for 28 of the Bay Colony's first 36 years. Other notables include *Mayflower* passenger Mary Chilton, Paul Revere's fellow alarm rider William Dawes, and Elizabeth Pain, who may have been the inspiration for Nathaniel Hawthorne's *The Scarlet Letter.* Despite common usage, the burying ground actually predates its neighboring namesake by more than half a century. Prior to becoming the first Unitarian church in the U.S. after the Revolution, King's Chapel was headquarters for the Church of England. Its location is a deliberate insult: epitomizing the Anglican contempt for those who tried to escape its high bishops, the original structure was unceremoniously built atop the Puritans' graves. If the current squat stone building, erected in the 1750s, looks like it's missing something, it is: a planned tower was never built for lack of funds.

Just minutes' walk away at the other end of short School Street is **Old South Meeting House,** 310 Washington St., tel. (617) 482-6439. Like the slightly older Old North Church, this landmark 1729 building is remembered primarily for the events of a single night during the prelude to the Revolution. On December 16, 1773, an overflowing crowd of 5,000 Bostonians hotly aired their resentments over a tea tax the English Parliament had refused to rescind. The debate—which had been running for days—was prompted by a recently arrived shipment of tea waiting to pass through customs. (To learn more about the outcome of the evening's alcohol-stoked gathering, head down to the waterfront and visit the Boston Tea Party Ship & Museum.) Old South's ecclesiastic history ended in 1872, but its role as a traditional New England meeting-house—a forum for public address and debate—has never ceased. Highlighting three centuries of upholding freedom of expression, exhibits chronicle the controversies surrounding speakers from those now enshrined as heroic patriots and noble abolitionists to others, like Ku Klux Klan leader David Duke, who challenge the notion of unconditional rights. Some cases have contemporary resonance: the eventual success of birth-control advocate and Planned Parenthood founder Margaret Sanger's campaign to give women unfettered access to contraception may be taken for granted by millions of adult Americans today, but if Sanger's ghost could return to Boston and call for distributing condoms in schools, she'd still cause a fuss. Gift shop and exhibits are open daily; "Middays at the Meeting House" public lectures and concerts are held Thursdays at noon, year-round (admission charged).

Ben Franklin's baptism at Old South and the years he spent at the nation's first public school —Boston Latin—are among the thin threads by which Boston tries to lay an honest claim to the great Philadelphian's legacy. Tenuous or not, they won Franklin a statue in front of the Old City Hall, midway up School Street (you passed it coming from King's Chapel), and a place on the Freedom Trail. Far more obscure is his memorial on the Milk Street side of Old South, in the middle of the facade at No. 17 across the way— you have to look up or you'll miss it.

If it's time to strap on the feed bag, step over to the **Milk Street Cafe,** 50 Milk St., near Devonshire, tel. (617) 542-2433 (you can call for the daily menu; open 7 a.m.-3 p.m.), whose quiches, salads, soups, pizzas, fish, and other strictly kosher goodies draw such a big following from surrounding office workers that it discounts lunches before noon and after 2 p.m. to try to thin out the midday crush. In warm weather, its second cafe, up the street in Post Office Square, is an ideal place to enjoy Boston's best pocket-sized urban park.

Old State House

Opposite the Boston National Historical Park Visitor Center and atop the subway entrance is the 1712 Old State House, one of Boston's few 18th-century buildings. The gilded lion and unicorn roof decorations, once despised symbols of the English crown rule, are an easily identified landmark over one of downtown's busier intersections, but for some inexplicable reason many of the passing pedestrian throng have never visited the **Old State House Museum,** tel. (617) 720-3290, within (open daily; $3). They don't seem to realize they're missing one of the most interesting (and inexpensive) historical museums the city has to offer. Permanent and changing exhibits complement the legacy of a structure that witnessed the Boston Massacre on its doorstep and the reading of the Declaration of Independence from its balcony. Annual reenact-

ments of these two events (every March 5 evening and July 4 afternoon, respectively) are only the most visible of the museum's programs; as steward of Boston history, the museum also hosts lectures, teacher workshops, and walking tours (nominal fees apply and reservations are recommended; tel. 617-720-3292), as well as regular gallery talks on a diverse set of topics (free with museum admission).

Faneuil Hall Marketplace

Since its rebirth in the mid-1970s, this renovated set of 19th-century market buildings, built over the original Town Cove docks, has become emblematic of the New Boston. As a high-quality tourist trap its singlehanded success in revitalizing what was then just another dilapidated downtown was so spectacular that nearly every major American city decided it had to have a copy of its own. Many have been developed by the same firm—the Rouse Company—and most follow a now-familiar theme: take a big run-down artifact whose original purpose has become obsolete, fill it with specialty food vendors and gift-oriented retailers, liberally decorate with pushcarts and colorful banners, and anchor where necessary with a museum, aquarium, or hotel. Derelict wharves, factories, and golden-age-of-steam railroad stations become an instant magnet for yuppies, suburbanites, tourists, and anyone who appreciates urban renewal à la Disney. But why knock it: hot food, cold drink, and clean bathrooms are in ready supply, and from the Disney Store off in the wings to Waterstone's Booksellers above the food court, you can scratch that shopping itch till your credit card cries uncle. The people-watching possibilities are superb, too, and street performers take to the cobblestone courtyards in summer (for a schedule of events and performers, call 617-446-8364).

Technically, the big shopping spread is Quincy (rhymes with "flimsy") Market, as the gold lettering over the mighty Greek Revival facade attests. Although locals apply its name to the whole modern complex, Faneuil (rhymes with "spaniel") Hall, tel. (617) 635-3105, is really just the small rectangular building with the golden grasshopper on top. This structure is the third, designed by Charles Bulfinch in 1805; both name and weathervane were keepsakes from the first, which was donated to the city by wealthy merchant

Peter Faneuil (whose tomb records his last name as "Funnel") and eventually destroyed by fire.

The anti-royalist gatherings that inspired the Cradle of Liberty nickname belong to Faneuil Hall's second incarnation. Such colonial rabblerousing is revived each summer during mock town meetings staged by the National Park Service, whose costumed interpreters debate political self-determination yards from the tumult of the marketplace just as people did in Sam Adams' day. Besides providing the stage for these ranger programs, the present portrait-filled and column-lined second-floor meeting hall (the centerpiece of the Bulfinch make-over) has hosted everything from declarations of presidential candidacies and primary debates to school graduations, concerts, and book signings (open daily unless pre-empted by special events; free). Not all the paintings are originals: the famous Gilbert Stuart portrait of America's first president—purposely posed next to his horse's posterior by the underpaid artist—is actually a copy by his daughter.

Occupying the attic is the **Armory of the Ancient and Honorable Artillery Company,** tel. (617) 227-1638, displaying old documents, uniforms, weapons and other mementos of the nation's oldest existing military unit (Mon.-Fri.; free). Commissioned as a Puritan defense force in 1638, its subsequent ceremonial role (and blue-blooded membership) inspired James Michael Curley's irresistible quip: "Invincible in peace. Invisible in war."

Faneuil Hall still serves a commercial function, too, as it has since it was first built. Among its modern retailers is the basement **Boston City Store,** tel. (617) 635-2911, open Mon.-Sat. and selling real Beantown souvenirs—old porcelain enamel street signs, parking meters, traffic lights, and other cast-off pieces of City property. This shop will never stand accused of dealing in stylish contemporary design—city budgeteers paid for utility more than beauty—but you never know what quirky object may strike your fancy.

T riders should note that the nearest stations to Faneuil Hall and Quincy Market are Government Center and State Street; the three Quincy stations on the Red Line are outside Boston entirely, in the South Shore suburb of Quincy.

Haymarket
While Boston's early waterfront was erased by the great market built under mayor Josiah Quincy (whose identically named son and great-grandson also served as mayors), its character is partially preserved in the adjacent Haymarket. In the center of the so-called Blackstone Block, behind the luxury hotel whose stripped awnings face Faneuil Hall Marketplace from across North St., is a neglected remnant of the city's original shoreline. Enter from the wide alley next to the hotel's glass elevator to find informative historical displays hidden in diminutive **Creek Square.** But for the metal restaurant dumpsters and parked cars, the tight little lanes are as authentic a part of Olde Boston as you'll find anywhere in the city—smells and all. The 200-year time warp is reinforced a few yards west at Marshall Street, where the 1767 Ebenezer Hancock House and a pair of taverns from the early 1800s face each other across the old cobblestones.

The inscribed Boston Stone by the gift shop door has a story behind it, now often mangled in the retelling. It was originally part of a paint mill's mixing trough, later made a cornerstone of a private house built on the mill grounds. Since the mill was such a popular local landmark, the old trough was made into a Boston facsimile of the London Stone, and occasionally used as a surveyor's reference for measurement of distances from Boston—a function now served by the State House dome. In 1835, when the current building was erected, the trough was broken up into four pieces, with only the inscribed portion retained here in the foundation, reunited by mortar with its "mullen," the round stone that ground and mixed the trough's contents.

Imagine what other stories these stones could tell: Ben Franklin and his siblings scampering around here as sprats (their father's ship chandlery sat on the corner, about where the Bell in Hand Tavern now stands); patriots wetting their whistles at the Green Dragon, originally around the corner on Union Street. Isaiah Thomas, publisher of the outspokenly pro-independence *Massachusetts Spy,* probably trod these lanes as he went about his business opposing compromise with George III on the second floor of today's Union Oyster House. Ironically, in 1797 the same digs were rented by the Duc de Chartres, the future King Louis Philippe, in flight from the sharp tongue of Madame Guillotine; although Bostonians initially rallied in support of the French Revolution, by the time the Duke arrived Franco-American diplomatic relations were near breaking point.

Facing the Central Artery on the Blackstone St. side of the block is the Haymarket itself, the raucous, colorful, and almost insufferably crowded Friday and Saturday descendant of the meat and produce mart that once spilled out of Faneuil Hall and Quincy Market. Wooden stalls with pyramids of fruit, bushels of greens, and tables of iced seafood constantly threaten to overflow from either end of the street, particularly on Saturday, the most hectic and picturesque of the two market days. Unlike the farmers' markets that sprout up around the city in summer, these gruff whaddaya-want and don't-touch guys are retailers, not growers; their prices are kept low mostly by selling straight off the back of the truck. Deals that are too good to be true generally are: whatever it is, half will be spoiled rotten. A worthy reward for anyone wading into the shopping horde is a fast, cheap, tasty slice or two from **Haymarket Pizza,** midway along the block; weekdays, when the open-air stalls are stacked away, it's even easier to sniff out.

In sober counterpoint to such a festive contemporary and colonial brew stand the glass towers of the **Holocaust Memorial,** in Carmen Park on Union Street. Each column represents one of the principal Nazi death camps: Majdanek, Chelmno, Sobibor, Treblinka, Belzec, and Auschwitz-Birkenau. Etched on the glass are numbers recalling the victims' identification tattoos, numbers no bigger than your signature covering every inch of every pane on every side, rising by the million up each five-story tower—six million numbers, one for every man, woman, and child murdered by the Third Reich simply for being Jewish. Their memory reaches out through inscriptions by survivors; annotations

also remind us that Nazi persecution touched Gypsies, Jehovah's Witnesses, gays, Communists, and Catholic priests. At the dedication of the towers, Elie Wiesel said they bid us to remember that "no one should ever speak again about racial superiority."

Waterfront

In any reasonable weather, one of the best ways to spend an aimless hour or two is taking a prowl along the city's **Harborwalk.** For the full self-guided tour of Boston's waterfront, pick up a brochure from the Boston National Historical Park Visitor Center on State Street. Alternatively, just find your way down to the wharves and start moseying. Eventually encompassing some 40 miles of intermittently connected promenades, piers, and beaches, Harborwalk is still very much a work in progress; presently its most accessible sections are between the North End's Christopher Columbus Park (next to the Long Wharf Marriott) and the huge brick and glass Federal courthouse on Old Northern Avenue's Fan Pier. Fetch some great Turkish takeout from **Sultan's Kitchen** or a giant slice of pizza (cut in two just to make it manageable) from **Al Capone's,** both on Broad Street landward of the Central Artery. Then persevere through the Big Dig's massive construction zone to the harbor's edge, and sate your hunger while soaking up the rays and listening to halyards smack against masts of gently rocking yachts. Here and there, stone walls, benches, or bollards provide a front-row seat on the marine minuet of small sloops and big motor cruisers, while everywhere greedy seagulls eye unattended snacks, or brazenly excavate discarded pizza crusts from trash receptacles. The truly eagle-eyed may be so lucky as to spot an endangered peregrine falcon—one of only a handful in the entire state—coasting high overhead, perhaps returning to its nest in the cliff-like crevices of the tall granite Custom House clocktower on State Street. Across the harbor, jetliners wing in and out of Logan Airport, whose flat meadows provide the hunting grounds for those peregrines, while giant container cargo carriers inch through the dredged shipping channel between the open seas and the Chelsea docks. Although their collective tonnage barely puts Boston among the nation's top 40 ports, these leviathans are the local lifeline for oil, road salt, beer, shoes, raspberry concentrate, porcelain sinks, and olive oil, among other things.

For a look at life below the waterline, head over to the **New England Aquarium**, on Central Wharf, tel. (617) 973-5200 (daily; $11 weekdays and $12.50 weekends for adults, $10-11.50 seniors, $5.50-6.50 kids). The free outdoor exhibit of harbor seals and sea otters alone can bring a smile to the grumpiest kid or adult; the three-story saltwater tank and its surrounding aquaria —filled with creatures large and small, from sharks to nudibranches, sea turtles to sea anemones—will have you speaking like Jacques Cousteau. Penguins, sea lions, rainforest exhibits, and interactive displays on Boston's own harbor ecology add to the infotainment. The Aquarium's highly recommended whalewatching tours, departing from their doorstep, run weekends in April and late October, daily May through early October; reservations are strongly advised and may be held with a credit card, but payment must be made in cash or traveler's checks ($24 adults, $16.50-19 kids and seniors; tel. 617-973-5281). Throughout July and August you can also join daily "Science at Sea" excursions ($9 adults, $6.50-7 kids and seniors), taking part in various basic experiments designed to gather data about water quality and the overall health of Boston Harbor's ecosystem. And yes, tickets to either the whale watch or science cruises may be used to obtain a discount on Aquarium admission.

The Aquarium is flanked by downtown's two major ferry terminals, Long Wharf and Rowes Wharf. The former is for year-round MBTA water shuttles to Charlestown Navy Yard and Lovejoy Wharf at North Station; the latter is for the Logan Airport Water Shuttle and commuter boats to the South Shore. Various harbor and whale watch cruises and Harbor Island ferries also depart from these wharves; see the **Fun in the Hub** chapter, below, for details.

The rich history of Long Wharf and associated remnants of Boston's golden maritime age, in-

cluding State Street's landmark Custom House, is the subject of walking tours offered throughout the tourist high season (late April to mid-October) by National Park Service rangers affiliated with the Harbor Islands. Inquire at their small white kiosk amid the tee-shirt vendors and boat gangways at the base of Long Wharf for the latest timetable of these urban rambles.

South Station

Like grand old rail terminals throughout the country, the distinctive curved headhouse of South Station, a magisterial Beaux Arts beauty of a building on the corner of Atlantic Avenue and Summer Street, is a reminder of the former glory of American passenger rail. When it opened in 1899 as the city's second consolidated terminal (North Station, now a mere shadow of its former self, was Boston's other "union" station), it had a facade over 2,000 feet long, filling the entire block. With 28 tracks and over 700 daily departures, it was the nation's largest and busiest railroad station, an honor retained well into the early 1900s. Though shorn of most of its original granite bulk after WW II, when America defected to the automobile, South Station still captures a smidgen of that pre-war bustle thanks to the steady flow of Amtrak and Commuter Rail passengers hurrying through its oversized portals. Besides train schedules, newsstands, and—at last!—public restrooms, the big skylit concourse within also holds a food court, offering everything from pizza and salads to croissants and yogurt. Dessert mavens and devotees of Judy Rosenberg's *All-Butter Fresh Cream Sugar-Packed No Holds Barred Baking Book* will be thrilled to know there's an outpost of the author's famed **Rosie's Bakery** here, too. Of course, if you're like Julia Child you may prefer to stick with the french fries from McDonald's.

The skyscraper opposite South Station, whose aluminum skin is reminiscent of the St. Louis Gateway Arch, is Alan Greenspan's house. Okay, not quite: it's actually just one of the nation's dozen Federal Reserve Banks, that outfit that merely regulates the American money supply, tweaks interest rates, and performs other hocus-pocus that enables you to, among other things, get cash for little signed slips of paper made out in your name. Those rate-setting decisions are made behind closed doors, but free public tours of the check- and cash-processing operations are available year-round on the first and third Friday of each month, starting at 10:30 a.m. Due to security considerations and limits on group size, don't even *think* of walking in on a whim: reservations must be made at least one week in advance by calling (617) 973-3464.

Fort Point

Narrow Fort Point Channel divides the South Station area from South Boston, a mostly residential neighborhood whose commercial and industrial edge along the Channel is distinguished by block upon block of 19th-century warehouses. Threescore or more of these large brick buildings, decorated with faded old advertisements and wearing metal medallions stamped with their construction date and the logo of their owner, the Boston Wharf Company, sit squarely across the Channel from downtown's shiny modern towers. Shunned for years by commercial renters, the huge warehouses, with their magnificent light and unfinished beam-and-brick interiors, became home to scads of artists; then, during the real estate boom of the 1980s, office-hungry professionals suddenly looked across the Channel, liked what they saw, and jump-started Fort Point's transformation into prime commercial space, crowding out the artists. The economic lull of the early 1990s gave the arts community the opportunity to buy or take long-term leases on a couple of buildings, thus preserving *some* permanent studio space for working artists, but plans for a mammoth convention center at the mouth of the nearby Ted Williams tunnel to Logan Airport plus projected off-the-chart demand for new office space are causing the professionals to start licking their chops again over these lovely old industrial buildings. The sad paradox is that the artists whose presence and vitality make derelict industrial neighborhoods trendy and desirable then become victims of their own success. The city's movers and shakers have been slow to recognize the value of protecting artists' habitat; for now, Fort Point is still funky and art-savvy, but it seems inevitable that the cubicles and Dilberts and Starbucks will come. Until then, though, several nifty shops and galleries on the 300 blocks of both Summer and Congress Streets are worth a visit, especially if you enjoy vintage

1950s accessories and furnishings, theatrical masks and costumes, or fancy natural cosmetics. Don't miss the Fort Point Arts Community's autumn Open Studios Weekend, tel. (617) 423-4299, either, if you're around the weekend after Columbus Day. Who knows? If you help ring the cash registers loudly enough, it may even wake up City Hall.

Permanently anchored in the middle of the Fort Point Channel next to the Congress Street bascule bridge is the *Beaver II,* a reproduction of one of the three brigs boarded that December night in 1773 by groups of colonials who dumped the ships' cargo—nearly 45 tons of Ceylon tea—into Boston Harbor. If it sounds like an event that shouldn't have been missed, step aboard the **Boston Tea Party Ship & Museum,** tel. (617) 338-1773, and take part in a reenactment, complete with bales of "tea" that you may heave into the drink (daily March-Nov.; $7 adult, $3.50-5.50 kids and seniors). Sailors aboard the vessel acquaint you with life on an 18th-century merchant ship; dockside exhibits explain what motivated the colonials' actions. The nominal tax imposed by the English Parliament's April 1773 Tea Act is the most frequently cited spark, but equally offensive to many of Boston's most influential patriots was the monopoly that legislation gave to the financially troubled East India Company, at the expense of local importers. Winter visitors in town on the Sunday closest to December 16 can catch the Tea Party's anniversary, a spectator event celebrated with the aid of the costumed Middlesex County Volunteers, who swarm the ship and apply their axes to tea chests in a rousing demonstration of patriotic fervor.

On the South Boston side of the Channel a stone's throw from the *Beaver II* stands the three-story Milk Bottle, a home-grown example of "googie," that Southern California idiom of oversized fast-food architecture. One of a handful built around the state in the 1930s to advertise and sell milk products for locally based J. P. Hood Dairy, this particular bottle was destined to be scrapped but was revived as a summertime dairy bar and snack shop. It's also become the emblem for **Museum Wharf,** whose giant brick warehouse holds two outstanding places to while away an afternoon or two. One is **The Computer Museum,** tel. (617) 423-6758, the world's only museum wholly devoted to computational machinery, from a relic-filled history of computer evolution to a walk-through PC (the mouse is half as big as a Honda Civic). Even R2-D2 is here. If you've never read Steven Levy's *Hackers,* or Tracy Kidder's *Soul of a New Machine,* than Boston may seem to be an incongruous host for such a place (compared to, say, Silicon Valley), until one notices how many computer milestones came out of Massachusetts research labs, particularly at MIT. Fascinating as the history may be, the extensive interactive exhibits are, of course, where visitors spend most of their time, discovering the computer's power to teach and amuse (and often do both at once). Open daily mid-June through early September, Tues.-Sun. and Monday holidays the rest of the year ($7, half price Sunday 3-5 p.m.).

Sharing the warehouse with the high-tech stuff is **The Children's Museum,** tel. (617) 426-8855, one of the leading museums for kids in the country, with hours of activities and plenty of encouraging staff. Here, too, emphasis is on interaction: karaoke in a soundproof booth, an ingenious climbing cage, giant Legos. Mock-ups of such places as grandma's house (frozen in 1959, from toys to TV commercials), a Japanese home, and a Latino supermarket are full of things to play with. Exhibits such as Teen Tokyo engage older children, too. A popular place for kids' birthday parties, adult office parties, and even weddings, the museum is open daily June-Sept., Tues.-Sun. and Monday holidays the rest of the year ($7 adults, $6 kids 2-15, $2 for one-year olds, infants free; Friday after 5 p.m. all admissions are $1).

Sharing another nearby building with over 50 artists' studios is **The Revolving Museum,** 288-300 A St., tel. (617) 439-8617. After 14 years of pioneering arts education programs for urban kids (including the I Scream Art Truck, an ice cream wagon-turned-public art catalyst), in early 1998 the museum expanded into the realm of traditional gallery exhibitions on the sprawling ground floor of its formerly industrial home, augmented by performance art and music in its Lab and Coal Room. While the venue may share some physical similarities to other museums, the content decidedly does not: a visit here will disabuse any notion that Boston is wholly mired in dead art by dead artists. Open Wed.-Sun.

noon-6; enter around the back of the building, off Necco Court. Admission charged for selected parties and performances only. For info on special events, opening receptions, and off-site public installations sponsored by the museum, call (617) 439-8617.

Chinatown

Though geographically quite tiny, Chinatown's outsized appeal is based on its food and unruly urban atmosphere. It's also the natural destination for shoppers seeking the chunky porcelain table settings or industrial aluminum cookware found in your average Chinese restaurant. For a traditional Chinese remedy to restore balance to your *ch'i,* consult the friendly and helpful herbalists in the dispensaries on Harrison or Washington Street; just look for the aromatic storefronts whose walls are covered with wooden apothecary cabinets. Or, for some simple attitude adjustment, check out **Jack's Joke Shop,** 38 Boylston, near Tremont, a unique assemblage of silly, sophomoric, and playful gifts, gags, and disguises.

Beneath the gift shops and culinary attractions, Chinatown has a rich and variegated history as deep as any section of Boston. The yards-wide Roxbury Neck that joined the peninsular town to the mainland lay under present-day Washington Street (which by a commemorative legislative fiat runs all the way to the Rhode Island line). In the early 1800s, the rural isthmus was widened with landfill for new middle-class housing; a generation later, these tradesmen's houses were subdivided into tenements for the new influx Chinese, Irish, Europeans, and Syrians. Like every other Chinatown on the East Coast, Boston's carries a legacy of labor disputes and the 1869 completion of the transcontinental railroad, which made low-wage workers from California viable strike-breaking alternatives to those from Europe. Boston's community can be traced specifically to North Adams, in western Massachusetts: after strike-breaking Chinese shoemakers imported from San Francisco had served their purpose, many were drawn to the state's capital port. Some stayed, employed by local garment manufacturers. Tyler Street's restaurants are one result; the oldest has been serving Chinese cuisine since 1879.

Since the arrival of the railroad at South Station in the late 1800s, the neighborhood has been continually eroded at the edges: first by the industry that lent its name to the Leather District next to South Station, then by highways and street widenings on two sides, and finally by burgeoning growth in the hospitals and medical schools at its southwestern corner. For 20 years, it was also hemmed in by the Combat Zone, a city-sanctioned strip of porn shops and triple-X cinemas that once inhabited three blocks of Washington Street. Made nationally famous by Arkansas congressman Wilbur Mills and his swimming partner Fanne Fox (the "Argentine Firecracker" whose companionship sank Mills' career in the mid-1970s), the Zone has all but vanished under asphalt parking lots and new office construction. But lack of residential character doesn't mean lack of residents; since the post-WW II adoption of its modern sweatshop-free identity, the replacement of tenement rowhouses with huge apartment blocks has made the neighborhood far and away the city's most crowded.

The human throng and overlapping layers of multilingual signage give the area an exciting high-octane, gotta-hurry feel well into the late-night hours, but if you slow down you might notice minor details, such as the ancient Liberty Tree embellishment on the brick facade of one renovated Washington Street building, or the soot-blackened bust of Shakespeare next to a Beach Street doorway. For some historical guidance, purchase a Women's Heritage Trail booklet from the Boston National Historical Park Visitor Center on State Street—Chinatown is one of its four discrete tours.

The Theater District

Although Boston's Puritan taboos on public music, art, and even Christmas lingered well into the 19th century, by the end of the Civil War the city had begun sharing in widely popular entertainments such as burlesque and vaudeville. (It was a pair of Hub business partners, B.F. Keith and Edward Albee, who first packaged formerly risqué vaudeville as wholesome family fare in 1885; their "Sunday school circuit" of tightly orchestrated variety shows in lavishly decorated theaters launched the careers of many fa-

mous American hoofers and comedians, and shaped popular entertainment for almost a century.) So many Broadway-bound productions were whipped into shape here that Boston was typecast as Times Square's testing ground, but by the 1920s celluloid was eclipsing all but the bawdiest live acts. During the Depression, many of the city's 55 theaters became cinemas, but time, TV, and the lure of the suburbs have wiped out numerous once-proud landmarks. Along with the demolition of legitimate theaters, urban renewal and fewer Navy Yard battleship visits forced the retirement of less virtuous Boston icons like Zorita the Snake Girl, whose act at Scollay Square's Old Howard was the talk of swabbies around the world.

After a long dry spell, a series of multimillion-dollar renovations has brought some of the original luster back to a smaller, less cohesive Theater District around the intersection of Tremont and Stuart Streets, between the Orange and Green lines. None of the theaters currently offers public tours, but you can usually peek inside with a simple box office visit. From the outside, **The Wang Center for the Performing Arts** looks like it could be an old department store in downtown Chicago or Philadelphia, but the interior is possibly the district's most breathtaking, with its bedazzling multistory marble and gold-leaf lobby modeled after Versailles, and a cavernous auditorium copied from the Paris Opera. Originally built as a movie palace in 1925 —then as now one of the world's largest stages —the Wang is one of three opulent Theater District confections by Clarence Blackall, Boston's preeminent theater architect. The more staid 1914 **Wilbur Theatre,** next door; the beautiful fin de siècle **Colonial Theatre,** on Boylston St.; and two others a few blocks away (no longer used as theaters) are the last remaining of the 14 he designed.

The T is heir to the nation's oldest subway system, and if you take the Green Line to the Theater District you'll get a taste of its early days when you get off at Boylston Street. From the granite entrance kiosks to the heavy rivets on the underground support beams, the Boylston station is essentially unaltered since it opened in 1897.

THE NORTH END

The North End is Boston's Italian neighborhood. It hasn't always been; a century ago, it was still a strong Irish and Jewish quarter, along with the neighboring West End. As both groups moved up socially and migrated toward more spacious neighborhoods—Jews to Roxbury, Irish to South Boston and Jamaica Plain—the new Italian and Sicilian immigrants took their places. The old-world feel remains stronger here than in many parts of the city despite the conversion of waterfront apartment buildings and warehouses into high-priced yuppie condos. History's currents are as strong as the espresso, and Paul Revere is as ubiquitous as Elvis in Memphis.

Overlooking the picturesque granite cobblestones of handkerchief-sized North Square—where Sun Court meets Moon Street—is the home of America's most famous messenger and silversmith, and Boston's only 17th-century building open to the public. The **Paul Revere House** was modified in both the century before Revere lived in it and in the centuries since, but it remains a fine example of what much of early Boston looked like. Besides interpreting Revere's life and times, this and the associated 1711 Pierce-Hichborn House, next door (Nathaniel Hichborn was one of Paul's cousins), are a museum of Boston's pre- and post-Revolutionary history (daily except winter Mondays; $2.50; tel. 617-523-2338).

The fame and attention accorded the **Old North Church** (Christ Church), tel. (617) 523-6676, on Salem St. derives almost entirely from its role on April 18, 1775. That night, two men hung lanterns in its steeple as part of Paul Revere's contingency plan to convey a message he himself might be detained from delivering—namely, that British troops were on the march to Lexington and Concord, and someone in Charlestown needed to raise the alarm. As it turned out, Revere succeeded in evading the cordon of British security thrown up around the city and was able to carry the message in person. At the same time, the anonymous express rider who *did* set off to raise the alarm after seeing the signal lights was apparently intercepted by a British patrol. An 18th-century meetinghouse across from Paul Revere's home had a nickname so similar—"Old North Meeting"—that it raised modern questions about which structure actually deserved the credit for being the scene of all this nocturnal intrigue. The people involved (Christ Church's sexton and vestryman lit the lanterns), the less suitable nature of North Meeting's lower steeple (nowhere near as visible from Charlestown), and unconvincing suggestions that Revere confused an Anglican church with a Puritan meetinghouse in his subsequent testimony on the affair all argue against the meetinghouse, which was dismantled by the British in 1776.

As for the remaining Old North, it's a beauty, built in 1723 after the inspiring designs of London church architect Sir Christopher Wren (open daily; free; special events scheduled the Sunday and Monday closest to April 19). The present 175-foot steeple is the third—and less than 50 years old; its predecessors both fell victim to strong winds. Housed in the tower are the nation's oldest church bells, cast in 1744. (Paul Revere served as one of the ringers as a teenager.) In the rear of the next-door gift shop are an assortment of curios, from a misprinted Bible to tea leaves from the Boston Tea Party. Behind the church, a narrow walkway between apartment gardens descends into the **Paul Revere Mall** ("the Prado" to neighborhood residents), a popular tree-lined plaza adorned with bronze tablets commemorating local people and events. The former 1802 New North Church (now St. Stephen's), across from the Hanover Street end, is the only remaining of five Boston churches by noted Federal-style architect Charles Bulfinch.

Up Hull Street from the front of Old North is 17th-century **Copp's Hill Burying Ground.** Fine views and interesting stories attend the stones here, atop what was originally known as Windmill Hill, where the Puritan ministerial Mather dynasty shares the dust with a state governor, Revolutionary War patriots, sexton Robert Newman of Old North, and some thousand mostly unidentified colonial African-Americans. From here, British cannon shelled Charlestown during the Battle of Bunker Hill; during their occupation of Boston, the Redcoats also took potshots at Copp's Hill grave markers, as you can still see.

What today is the playground on Commercial Street below Copp's Hill was the epicenter of Boston's most improbable disaster: the **Molasses**

Flood. On January 15, 1919, a ruptured metal storage tank unleashed a tidal wave of 2.5 million gallons of molasses onto North End streets. The 14,000-ton surge swept dozens of buildings off their foundations, bent the iron stanchions of the elevated street railway like paper clips, injured 150 people and gruesomely drowned or asphyxiated over a score more in the viscous brown syrup. The cleanup took weeks, and the smell lingered for years.

Boston may yet be the home of the bean and the cod, but a modern rhymer might be moved to add lobster to that list. If you want some of these crustaceans of your own—live, cooked, prepared as a salad or packed to ship anywhere in the U.S.—stop by **Bay State Lobster Company,** 395 Commercial St., the region's largest wholesale and retail seafood market, open daily except Christmas, tel. (617) 523-7960.

CHARLESTOWN

Like Boston, Charlestown was once a bulbous, hilly peninsula whose original outline has been obscured by extensive landfill. Unlike Boston, Charlestown had a resident population of Native Americans when the first English settler, Thomas Walford, arrived, in 1628. Inhabitants of one of several Pawtucket villages on the north side of the Charles River, Walford's hosts endured a humiliating encounter with Plymouth soldiers in 1621 (who insisted on buying the Native American women's clothing until they were stripped naked), the 1629 arrival of John Winthrop and his Salem crowd, and a 1633 smallpox epidemic before finally being forced to move off the peninsula by its steadily expanding Puritan settlement.

Founded a year before Boston, Charlestown was a separate community until 1874, when it was annexed by the growing metropolis next door. Traces of the colonial past were all but erased when the town was destroyed by British incendiary shells during the Battle of Bunker Hill; one exception is the 1630 **Phipps Street Burying Ground**, a block south of Main, noted for especially fine carvings and its monument to university namesake John Harvard. After the Revolution, the town was rapidly rebuilt, producing the maze of narrow streets that confuse and frustrate all

but resident "Townies." The late-18th- and early-19th-century architecture abounding between City Square and the Bunker Hill Monument is by itself excellent reason to make the decidedly unattractive hike across the bridge from the North End, but if you need further inspiration, simply take a deep breath inside the **Sorelle Bakery Cafe,** 1 Monument Ave., or **Figs,** a wood-fired brick-oven pizzeria around the corner at 67 Main St. Or continue up Main another block to sample one of the best renditions of a New England chowder—properly rich and clam-filled without a hint of cheap thickeners—from the historic 18th century **Warren Tavern,** at the corner of Main and Pleasant (open daily).

Charlestown Navy Yard
Until it was given to the Boston National Historical Park, after the Vietnam War, this 17-acre chunk of the Charlestown waterfront was one of the nation's half-dozen naval shipyards. Numerous reminders of its 174-year history of building

"Old Ironsides"

and repairing warships remain: drydocks (still in use), a quarter-mile-long ropewalk (a long shed in which rope was once made—this one the work of the same architect who designed Quincy Market), the WW II destroyer USS *Cassin Young*, and the crown jewel, the **USS *Constitution***, "Old Ironsides" (tour schedule tel. 617-242-5601). Nicknamed for its resistance to British cannonballs in the War of 1812, the *Constitution* is the world's oldest commissioned naval vessel, launched in 1797. Free tours of this grand frigate are given by active-duty Navy personnel, who explain the inner workings of the ship with characteristic by-the-book precision and not a little dry humor—as one would expect from those familiar with captains' whims, sailors' gripes, and the toil of preparing a warship for all contingencies. While tour hours and off-season availability are entirely in the hands of the Navy commander, rather than the Park Service, you can always count on the daily morning raising and sunset lowering of the flag, accompanied by a booming broadside volley from the ship's cannon.

The adjacent **USS *Constitution* Museum**, tel. (617) 426-1812, supplements the actual vessel with exhibits tracing its history. Thumb through nifty "cruise journals" accompanying maps of the ship's globe-straddling missions, compare your crisis management skills with those of the captains, see what Boston was like when the *Constitution* was launched, and examine the craftsmanship that has gone into its restoration. Interactive videos put you aboard the ship during its maiden voyage or at the helm in battle (daily; free).

Located in the fairly modern brick pavilion on Constitution St. outside the Navy Yard's main gates, the National Park Service Visitor Center, tel. (617) 242-5601, has free information about both the Yard and the Boston National Historical Park as a whole. Ranger-led activities vary with the season, from year-round *Cassin Young* tours to summer programs focusing on lesser known parts of the yard. The center also has a small bookstore and some all-too-rare public bathrooms.

Bunker Hill Monument

As every student of American history must know by now, the Bunker Hill Monument and the battle that it commemorates are misnamed. The

marking the misnomer

bloody June 1775 confrontation between British regulars and colonial militia from Connecticut, Massachusetts, and New Hampshire actually took place on Breed's Hill, east of taller Bunker Hill. Colonial commander Colonel Prescott had been ordered to fortify Bunker Hill; while at least one map in circulation at the time mislabeled the terrain, the modern consensus is that Prescott chose Breed's deliberately (possibly because it was closer to Boston). Though the British won the day, it was a Pyrrhic victory; their nearly 50% casualty rate was a great morale boost to the colonists. It also proved that the militia's success against the Redcoats in Concord two months earlier had been no fluke—a fact not lost on either the French, who eventually sided with the Americans, or British General Burgoyne, whose prediction after the battle (that the Crown had as good as lost its colonies) was never brought to the attention of King George.

The 19th-century memorial obelisk marking the battlefield attracted great fanfare, with such celebrities as the Marquis de Lafayette laying its cornerstone and Daniel Webster giving the dedication speech, but insufficient financing prolonged construction over 17 years. The surrounding townhouses are a direct result: residential lots on the battlefield were sold off to raise much-needed cash. Though the windows at the top are small, their views are grand, well worth huffing and puffing up the 295-step spiral staircase. The base lodge explains the battle with artifacts, a large diorama, and quotes from participants on both sides; the attendant park ranger also gives talks and answers questions (daily; free; tel. 617-242-5669).

BACK BAY

The Esplanade
When the Back Bay was first enclosed, in the early 1800s, by a 1.5-mile mill dam, the thoroughfare on top attracted promenading couples fleeing the curiosity of their in-town neighbors. Romantic saunters are still possible along the **Charles River Embankment** (better known as the Esplanade), especially on warm evenings accompanied by the floodlit plume of the lagoon fountain and the city skyline painted in lights. Just don't expect much privacy: from sunrise until well after sunset, joggers, skaters, and cyclists fill the landscaped paths of this early-20th-century addition to Back Bay (notice the old 1821 seawall, still visible along Storrow Drive), while sunbathers insouciantly sprawl over the grassy open spaces whenever weather permits. Between spring and fall, the lower river basin is sprinkled with a confetti of sails, attended by an audience of ducks. On July 4, a zillion happy celebrants on beach blankets and boat decks listen to the Boston Pops perform at the Hatch Shell—one of many free concerts by the Pops and others, from jazz to alternative rock, offered at the Shell throughout July and August.

Four footbridges connect the Esplanade to Back Bay, from the coral pink Arthur Fiedler footbridge at Arlington Street to the ramp at the Boston side of the Harvard Bridge. The Harvard Bridge—on which Massachusetts Ave. crosses into Cambridge—is easily remembered as the bridge with absolutely no connection whatsoever to Harvard University; the bridge that *does*

go to the university is the Anderson Bridge, in Allston. Harvard Bridge instead links Back Bay to the Massachusetts Institute of Technology, which is why the span's sidewalks are calibrated in "smoots"—a length of measure based on the height of an MIT fraternity pledge, Oliver R. Smoot, Jr., who was rolled across the bridge in the late 1950s. Collectors of old Boston band trivia may also recognize the bridge and its terrific backdrops as the location of a mid-1980s music video by the Del Fuegos.

The Public Garden
Although considered part of his city-wide "Emerald Necklace," Frederick Law Olmsted did not design this formal English floral park (whose name is always pronounced as singular, not plural). Occupying a shallow Back Bay marsh originally filled for the benefit of Boston's fireprone ropewalks, the Garden was nearly nipped in the bud by a block of houses, but a sensible 1859 legislative act, backed by public referendum, forever set aside this horticultural jewel for the city and its people. Each year, 10,000 new tulip bulbs (old ones are recycled in other city parks) and an equal or greater number of annuals dispel all memory of gray December or ice-bound February so effectively that Bostonians are always genuinely perplexed by the following winter's first snowfall. In addition to the hothouse miracles performed by the dedicated park department gardeners, visitors may enjoy the summer shade or autumnal colors of over 400 trees representing 74 species, from oaks, beeches, maples, and elms to a giant sequoia, Amur cork tree, and three species of Japanese scholar tree. Among the garden's tallest trees are the three dawn redwoods, an ancient relic species thought extinct until a living grove was found in Japanese-occupied Manchuria in 1941 by Harvard botanists. When war broke out between the U.S. and Japan soon after, smuggling out seedlings became a major covert operation; therein surely lies a curious tale waiting to be told. To help ensure the species' survival, the specimens were propagated extensively at the university's Arnold Arboretum. If you notice the tree shedding its needles in the fall, don't be concerned—*Metasequoia glyptostroboides* is the only known redwood species that's deciduous.

The Public Garden is also a veritable outdoor art museum. Among its diverse collection of statuary and memorials is the Ether Monument, Lillian Swann Saarinen's *Jungle Book*-inspired "Bagheera" fountain, a 14th-century feudal Japanese warlord's lantern, and the city's most beloved public artwork, the *Make Way for Ducklings* group by Nancy Schön, from Robert McCloskey's children's book. The **Swan Boats** that ply the lagoon are nearly museum pieces, too: inspired by Wagner's *Lohengrin,* the two-ton pedal-powered boat concession has belonged to the same family since 1877, when Robert Paget built the first one out of copper, wood, and bicycle parts. Rides are offered daily mid-April through September ($1.75 adults, 95 cents kids).

A block from the Garden's western corner is the **Gibson House Museum,** 137 Beacon St., tel. (617) 267-6338, dedicated to the Victorian Age. Built the same year as its flowery neighbor, the Italian Renaissance Revival mansion wears its finery on the inside, behind thick drapes and stout double doors. With its low light and lush furnishings—all original, right down to the upholstery—the house and its tchotchkes are such a perfectly preserved time capsule that it needed no retouching before being used as a set for *The Bostonians,* the 1984 Merchant-Ivory film of Henry James's satirical Victorian novel. In addition to house tours, the museum presents a variety of seasonal programs illustrating life in the late 19th century, from period games and kids' parties to afternoon high tea and holiday decorating. Open Wed.-Sun. May-Oct., weekends only Nov.-March (tours hourly 1-3 p.m.; $4).

Commonwealth Avenue Mall

The massive project to fill in the tidal mudflats of Back Bay was built around the idea of a grand landscaped boulevard intended to rival the Champs-Elysées. That boulevard became Commonwealth Avenue ("Comm. Ave." to locals), and the fancy townhouses overlooking its center greenway went up about as fast as the gravel fill was put down. Of course, fashions changed over the 35 years it took to fill the flats from the edge of the Public Garden westward to what's now the Boston University campus, so Comm Ave. essentially became a life-size style guide spanning a third of a century. To anyone remotely interested in architectural ornament, a stroll past the alphabetical grid of cross streets—Arlington, Berkeley, Clarendon, and so forth—is like a birdwatcher's trip to Costa Rica: so many species in so small a space that it makes your head spin. Gothic dormers, corbeled and stacked chimneys, oriel windows, mansard roofs, rusticated arches, polychrome tiles, bow fronts, and conical turrets are among the features adorning the residences and private clubs along the Mall, each block containing some attempt to one-up the competition. The pièce de résistance is on the corner of Hereford Street a block from the end of Back Bay: the chateau-like Burrage Mansion is the limestone epitome of exuberance—gargoyles, griffins, and all. Among the avenue's registered historic landmarks is H. H. Richardson's first major work, the 1871 Church of the Holy Bean Blowers. Located on the corner of Clarendon, it's known to its congregation as the First Baptist Church. The nickname comes from the angels at the corner of the campanile's decorative stone frieze, carved by Italian artisans after a design by Frédéric Auguste Bartholdi, better known as the sculptor of the Statue of Liberty.

The Mall itself has plenty of fine statuary. Witness the likeness of historian and sailor Samuel Eliot Morison atop one of his beloved Gloucester boulders, gazing seaward over the tidal litter of bronzed shells, weeds, and scuttling crabs. Several of the pieces here are intriguing anachronisms; famous Yankees and war heroes are not so surprising, but why, you may reasonably wonder, is a statue of Argentine president Sarmiento here? (He copied Boston educator Horace Mann's K-12 grade school model when restructuring Argentina's educational system.) Another incongruity is Leif Friksson; 19th-century Harvard chemistry professor Eben Horsford, inventor of Rumford Baking Powder, practiced some alchemy over Leif's legend in a vain attempt at proving the mighty Viking explorer lunched here in the Back Bay. While historically unsound, his speculations *were* transmuted into a statue of the Norseman, now standing sentinel at the forgotten far end of the Mall.

Newbury Street

After spending days walking in the footsteps of dead patriots or studying the stone-cold legacy of dead architects, you are to be forgiven if you question whether Boston has a pulse. Come for a stroll down Newbury St. and such doubts will be quickly dispelled. If you wake up on the wrong side of an overpriced bed or get frazzled by the rush-hour crush on the T, come for a stroll down Newbury and feel the warm fuzzies take hold with each step. Rain or shine, day or night, summer or winter, Newbury puts Boston in its best light.

What's the secret? The continuity and elegance of the bowfront rowhouses help set a good stage. So does that comfortable scale: there are no overpowering buildings here. But the key is probably the simple fact that in addition to being a busy, chic commercial street, people still live here, above the shops, still do their laundry in the coin-op down the block, still buy their aspirin at the CVS and their hardware at the True Value. And while there's no shortage of classy apparel and pricey restaurants, secondhand stores and a smattering of genuinely lowpriced eateries help keep the street from becoming exclusively devoted to affluence and conspicuous consumption.

Initial appearances to the contrary, Newbury actually changes quite a bit between Arlington Street and Massachusetts Ave ("Mass. Ave."). The Public Garden end belongs to the Ritz-Carlton crowd, Burberry, Cartier, Versace, and art collectors. The first block alone accounts for about half the street's dozen contemporary art galleries (for a guide to all the street's galleries, stop in at Gallery NAGA, in the Church of the Covenant on the corner of Berkeley, and ask for a copy of the latest Artmap). Approaching the mammoth Tower Records overlooking the Turnpike at Mass. Ave., piercings and tattoos multiply, and Doc Marten boots outnumber Kenneth Cole loafers. But some constants *do* abide: expensive hair salons (about 80 in eight blocks) and Starbucks, at both ends and in the middle.

Many of the boutiques come and go like spring fashions, but the longevity of Newbury's bookstores happily suggests residents are as devoted to reading as to perfect coiffures and cappuccino. Up the street from DuBarry Restaurant's four-story mural of celebrity Bostonians is the flagship store of **Waterstone's Booksellers,** an Irish-English chain, the best in the Back Bay for just about everything new, from the latest popular fiction to foreign language literature, kids' books to cookbooks and architecture texts. Open until 10 p.m. most nights, it's located in the grand Romanesque rock pile at Exeter St., a can't-miss-it landmark still known to most as the Exeter Street Theater building. Up the next block, at No. 223, **Spenser's Mystery Books** specializes in used and newly published volumes. Be sure to let the owner know what you're looking for; not only will he point you to its precise location, he'll come up with a handful of additional suggestions to match your tastes. (For champagne truffles to die for, cross the street to **Teuscher of Switzerland,** at No. 230, makers of the best chocolate in the world—priced accordingly, of course.) Last but not least, the funkier block between Hereford and Mass. Ave. features not one but two purveyors of the printed word. **Trident Booksellers & Cafe** is your source for pop psychology, Eastern religion, some poetry and nonfiction, and a terrific magazine selection; and **Avenue Victor Hugo Books,** across the street, is the secondhand book lover's dream come true.

Boston is also a great place to shop for music, too—either recorded or in raw sheet form. For the widest possible range under one roof, the six-story, Frank Gehry-designed **Tower Records** casting its shadow over this last block is a good place for most CD and cassette shoppers to start. Don't think that just because you've seen one Tower, you've seen 'em all: unlike giant record stores elsewhere in America, Boston's retail music heavyweights stock a few copies of lots of titles, rather than whole bins full of a handful of titles. If your interest is radio-friendly alternative rock, or anything that makes parents and roommates slam doors in disgust, follow the pierced tribe into the **Newbury Comics** store at No. 332, above basement-level **Condom World.** Or, for a true sonic souvenir of Boston, check out **Mystery Train II,** back at 306 Newbury, tel. (617) 536-0216, which carries one of the city's best selections of consignment tapes and CDs featuring local artists. Solicit the expertise of the staff—almost all of whom are band members themselves—and you could save yourself months of clubhopping.

Copley Square

Architecture is, like history, one of Boston's strong suits, and numerous parts of the city have drawn an ace or two. A couple of spots, like Faneuil Hall, have even come up with a full house. But only Copley Square has been dealt a royal flush. Four superb 19th-century buildings in and around the square—a hotel, a library, and two churches—are juxtaposed with a dramatic 20th-century office tower (New England's tallest building). The prevailing ideologies of two centuries are played out in masonry and tempered glass: here the romantic medieval fascination of Ruskinian Gothic and Richardsonian Romanesque, there the classical poise of a pair of Italian Renaissance revivals, all under the reflective gaze of 1970s modernism. Arguably, it's a collection unrivaled in Boston.

Designed by Henry Hobson Richardson a year after his nearby First Baptist commission on Comm. Ave., **Trinity Church,** tel. (617) 536-0944, is recognized as a national architectural landmark. A definitive example of the Romanesque revival that became synonymous with Richardson, this early Victorian fixture in the heart of Copley Square also contains interior decoration by sculptor Augustus Saint-Gaudens and stained glass artist John LaFarge (daily; free). Fridays during the academic year, free organ recitals are presented just past noon. Outside, the square itself is host to special events throughout the year: New Year's ice sculptures, mid-April's Marathon, summer after-work concerts and twice-weekly farmers' markets. Skateboarders practice their moves on the upper level of the fountain, kids of all ages cool their heels in the lower level, and the real little tykes pose for snapshots on the Tortoise and Hare sculpture. Those for whom its verses are still fresh pause and recollect *The Prophet* at the Kahlil Gibran memorial near the Bostix discount ticket kiosk. A good time is generally had by all.

From the 60th floor of that mirror in which Trinity is forever admiring herself, the **John Hancock Observatory,** tel. (617) 247-1977, offers New England's highest indoor view over the region's largest city (daily 9 a.m.-10 p.m.; $5). Plagued after construction by problems with falling windows and unanticipated wind stress, the cloud-catching, sharp-edged Hancock Tower has earned local appreciation as one of Boston's most distinctive landmarks.

Also fronting Copley Square is the 1895 Renaissance Revival **Boston Public Library,** iden-

tifiable by its thorny Dr. Seuss-like cast iron lamps and the directory of the Western cultural canon inscribed around the frieze. Behind the big bronze doors' allegorical figures of Knowledge and Wisdom, Truth and Romance, and Music and Poetry is a beautifully rosy marble lobby with majestic lions guarding stairs up to the ornate vaulted-ceiling reading rooms. The library's architecture, history, and art are all thoroughly reviewed during the engaging free tours that start inside the Trinity-facing Dartmouth St. entrance (year-round Monday 2:30 p.m., Tuesday and Thursday 6 p.m., Fri.-Sat. 11 a.m., and, October through mid-May, Sunday 2 p.m.). Free copies of the artists' own explanatory essays are also available for several of the library's enormous murals, including *The Muses of Inspiration,* by Puvis de Chavannes, and John Singer Sargent's *Judaism and Christianity.* In warm weather, wet or dry, the quiet Italian courtyard is one of the best reading or postcard-writing spaces in the city.

On the corner of Boylston and Dartmouth opposite the library is the **New Old South Church,** built to house the congregation that outgrew downtown's historic Old South Meeting House. Boston being Boston, even this "new" church is older than the telephone (except for the bell tower—the 246-foot original started to lean so much it had to be dismantled; the shorter replacement was built in 1940). Like Trinity, New Old South is a national historic landmark, an ode to the European Gothicism popularized by the Victorian English art critic John Ruskin.

The Prudential Center and Vicinity

Up Boylston Street from Copley Square is the Hancock Tower's slightly older rival, the Prudential Center Tower, or "Pru," tel. (617) 236-3318. Some might consider the vista from its 50th-floor **Skywalk** better than the one from the Hancock's because . . . it includes the Hancock (daily; $4).

Between Saks Fifth Avenue at the base of the Pru and Neiman-Marcus, opposite Back Bay Station, dozens of shops constitute what amounts to a totally enclosed linear mall, the Shops at Prudential Center. You'll find such typical urban retailers as Warner Bros. Studio, Body Shop, Speedo, Ann Taylor, and Claiborne Men. Larger and more upscale Copley Place, anchored by Neiman-Marcus and a Marriott hotel, includes Tiffany & Co., Crabtree & Evelyn, Williams-Sonoma, Sharper Image, Gucci, Louis Vuitton, Rizzoli Books, and a branch of the Museum of Fine Arts' gift shop, among others. Not all of Copley's occupants are on the two main indoor levels: head down the escalators to the street-level Dartmouth Shops, nearly hidden beside the linear Southwest Corridor Park behind Neiman-Marcus, to find **Treasured Legacy,** tel. (617) 424-8717, where snazzy kinte cloth, striking masks and sculptures, and African-related books offer a welcome breath of diversity amid the high-priced chain stores. For another kind of shopping experience you won't find at your local mall, visit the **Women's Educational & Industrial Union,** 356 Boylston St., across from the Arlington Street Church back by the Public Garden. Founded over a century ago to leverage employment and educational opportunities for women (Amelia Earhart got job placement assistance here), the WEIU is supported in part through the sale of crafts, gifts, clothes, housewares, and antiques from its attractive quarters.

If you're in Boston attending a big trade show, there's a good chance you'll spend your days inside the **Hynes Convention Center,** on Boylston next to the Pru. If so, get one of your colleagues to cover for you and go check out the **Institute of Contemporary Art,** tel. (617) 266-5152, next to the Romanesque fire station across the street. Though small and underfunded, the ICA still mounts interesting and provocative shows and regularly showcases new film and video works in its comfortable little theater. Galleries open starting at noon Wed.-Sun. ($6), while the bookstore is open daily, noon-5 p.m.

The Mother Church
Properly known as **The First Church of Christ, Scientist,** the World Headquarters of the Christian Science Church has been a Boston landmark for most of the 20th century. The oldest part of the complex is the 1894 Romanesque building of gray New Hampshire granite, erected less than 30 years after the episode that led to founder Mary Baker "Mother" Eddy's discovery of Christian Science. When the huge Byzantine and Italian Renaissance basilica was added in 1906—atop 4,000 wooden piles driven into the Back Bay mud—it was (as it still is) the city's largest house of worship. Appropriately enough, it houses the world's seventh-largest working organ, an Æolian-Skinner "American Classic" with 13,595 pipes and 172 stops. A trio of huge poured-concrete additions designed by I. M. Pei and Araldo Cossutta has kept the Mother Church at the forefront of Boston architecture, punctuating the edge of Back Bay with a 15-acre plaza anchored by a dramatic 670-foot long reflecting pool and framed by neatly pruned linden trees. In winter, the downdrafts from the 28-story Administration Building seem to come straight from the Arctic, but come summer those strong crosswinds keep muggy weather delightfully at bay. (To cool off on *really* sweltering days, take a cue from the kids and skip through the fountain at the Prudential side of the plaza.) For a study in how much the world's political boundaries have changed since 1932, visit the **Mapparium,** a 30-foot diameter walk-through stained glass globe inside The Christian Science Publishing Society's neoclassical headquarters on Mass. Ave., beside the domed church. Up in the Administration Building, over a dozen rare and unusual Bibles—the oldest a 1546 Hebrew-Latin edition from Switzerland, the most recent a 1957 translation of the Eastern Orthodox *Peshitta,* the English interleaved with facsimiles of the ancient Aramaic script—are displayed in the tower's 22nd-floor library, where you may research the history of the thrice-married Mrs. Eddy and her church (visitors' passes are available in the lobby). For the schedule of free guided tours and the occasional organ concerts, call the church's recorded tour and event line, (617) 450-3790.

THE SOUTH END

The South End was originally intended, like Back Bay, to be an affluent residential neighborhood built on landfill, but it ended up nearly becoming a ghetto. State-financed Back Bay, with its minimum required housing values and proximity to upper-crust Beacon Hill, proved more appealing to wealthy prospective residents than the city-financed South End, which tarnished its potential exclusivity in the 1850s by promoting both affordable housing and charitable institutions. Besides the poor young wards of the Penitent

Female Refuge and Bethesda Society, poor Irish immigrants displaced to the South End by waterfront redevelopment further diminished the area's attractiveness to class-conscious Yankees. By the Depression, the blocks of attached brownstones and London-style squares had devolved into a district of densely packed rooming houses and apartments, separated from genteel Back Bay by large railyards. Southern black sharecroppers displaced by mechanized cotton harvesting settled in the neighborhood, many finding work as Pullman car porters or in other railroad jobs. That high concentration of porters inspired that statue of civil rights activist A. Philip Randolph in the Back Bay Station lobby, just within the dramatic wooden arched windows facing ritzy Neiman-Marcus on Dartmouth Street. Besides being a lifelong champion of fair labor practices—making him one of the first subjects of a J. Edgar Hoover dossier—Randolph founded the American Brotherhood of Sleeping Car Porters, the nation's first black trade union.

As the South End stretch of Mass. Ave. became a hotspot for jazz, the Savoy, Hi Hat, Roseland Ballroom (where Malcolm "Red" Little worked back before he replaced his last name with "X"), and other legendary hot spots along "the Avenue" attracted a jazz pantheon, from Pops Foster and Sidney Bechet to Duke Ellington and Lester Young.

Three decades of gentrification have brought the neighborhood back onto the radar screen for the rest of Boston, and though many lower-income residents suffered the usual fate of displacement, some affordable housing has been preserved amid the townhome renovations and condo conversions. A center for Boston's gay and lesbian community, working artists, and professional couples who find the suburbs too sterile and boring, the new South End has become a leading neighborhood for innovative food and theater, lively bars, and aimless urban walking through the nation's largest Victorian brick rowhouse district.

Walkers are never far from a tasty lunch. Options cover the gamut of new, old, and ethnic South End styles: from **Hazel's Cup & Saucer,** 130 Dartmouth facing the Copley Place Mall's back corner entrance, tel. (617) 262-4393, with its roast beef-with-horseradish mayo tortilla wraps, roasted veggie quesadillas, and luscious chocolate desserts, to Puerto Rican meat pies (*alcapurrias*) from hole-in-the-wall **Miami Cafe,** on Aguadilla St. by the corner of Tremont. For

ALAN ROHAN CRITE

The shuttered green awning at 410 Columbus Ave. in the South End is faded and broken. The old Victorian rowhouse rising above it seems almost as vacant as that storefront behind the shutters, where its blankets of dust have been gathering ever since the barbershop left many, many years ago. Actually, despite appearances, this house is a rather prominent neighborhood landmark: the **Alan Rohan Crite House Museum.** Never heard of him? Major metropolitan museums around the country have collected his drawings and paintings, churches have commissioned his carved and gilded altar panels, universities have bestowed honorary degrees, and he has traveled abroad as a cultural ambassador. Alan Rohan Crite, now approaching 90, is one of the nation's preeminent African American artists. Yet he also has difficulty keeping up with his utility payments. Turning his house into a museum is, in part, intended to help raise funds for conserving the works of this prolific lifelong artist, hundreds of which crowd the four floors of his home. "Museum" also bestows some formal recognition on a place that has long welcomed the public into its "galleries," intimate and unmuseumlike as they may be. Although he jokes about the odd sensation that comes with being the subject of a museum—"why would anyone be interested? I'm not even dead yet"—the gregarious Crite enjoys conversing about his artistic philosophy, neighborhood history, and the abilities of fellow members of the group known as the Boston Collective. Spending an afternoon with Crite is an immersion into a unique world—probably not something recommended for diffident browsers, or anyone looking for a tidy, 10-minute home-and-garden tour. Since age is robbing Crite of his ability to hear unexpected doorbells while at work in his top-floor studio, visits are by prearranged appointment only; tel. (617) 266-0488. And though he wishes it could be otherwise, the museum charges a $10 admission/donation.

perhaps the best possible combination of food and atmosphere, immerse yourself in an ever-lovin' true-blue South End institution: timeless **Charlie's Sandwich Shoppe,** 429 Columbus Ave., tel. (617) 536-7669, about five blocks from Copley Square. Admire the photo gallery of celebrity customers—from the pin-cushion star of *Hellraiser* to local pols—while chowing down on good burgers, cutlets, fish and chips, chili dogs, and the like (Mon.-Fri. till 2:30 p.m., Saturday to 1 p.m.). As befits a place that's been faithfully dishing up the South End's best turkey hash since 1927, breakfast is served until closing.

Here's a sample figure-eight stroll beginning from the Back Bay: take Berkeley St. over the Turnpike to the **Boston Center for the Arts** on Tremont St., passing the insanely overrated Hard Rock Cafe, attractive B&B-filled side streets like Chandler and Appleton, and artsy shops like **F. Kia,** 558 Tremont. From the BCA, walk away from downtown just a couple blocks, to Union Park Street, whose ellipse—one of several in the vicinity—is a throwback to the English elegance sought by the neighborhood's planners. At the east end of the park, turn left on Shawmut Avenue and enter a pocket that still betrays traces of the neighborhood's Lebanese and Syrian past (note the grocery—about the only place in town to buy a *couscousiere,* for steaming couscous). Return to Tremont by any of the next two or three streets that strikes your fancy, turn left and pass the funky shops, gay bookstore, cafes and crêperie around the BCA again, this time making a right at Rutland, about six blocks away. After enjoying another oval park, turn right on Columbus and walk back toward the downtown skyline. Return to where you began by taking any street on the left to the **Southwest Corridor Park,** running parallel to Columbus atop the underground Orange Line. Follow the skinny, well-landscaped park to Dartmouth Street and Copley Square, keeping an eye out for the poetry and prose engraved on the stele outside the Copley Place entrance, one of the many art installations above each of the Orange Line stations between Back Bay and Forest Hills.

FENWAY

Fenway is the schizophrenic neighborhood on the "other" side of Mass. Ave., a filled-in portion of Back Bay that's generally denied any modern right to share in the snob appeal that name now gives. The alphabetic ordering of street names persists here—Ipswich, Jersey, Kilmarnock—but Back Bay's orderly grid essentially evaporates west of Mass. Ave., riven in part by the meandering course of the Back Bay Fens, whose creation initiated Frederick Law Olmsted's seven-year relationship with the Boston Park System. The system of scenic carriageways Olmsted designed to accompany his parks begins here with The Fenway, whose pastoral curves proved irresistible in the late 19th century to a variety of educational and cultural institutions. Besides music conservatories, colleges, teaching hospitals, and art museums, Fenway also encompasses the exceptional acoustics of Symphony Hall, the rockin' nightlife of clubby Kenmore Square, and the delightfully old-fashioned Fenway Park, where the Red Sox toy with the affections of their long-suffering fans.

Back Bay Fens

The first of Olmsted's six contributions to what today is known as the Emerald Necklace, the Fens was conceived as the wild and picturesque introduction to nature, whose pastoral side would come later, at the end of the chain of parks. Subsequent alterations, total replacement of the original salt-tolerant plantings after the Charles was dammed in the 1900s, and the Back Bay skyline's encroachment over the background trees keep the Fens from sparking the same thrill as when it belonged to the nation's first generation of urban parks, but Olmsted's spirit is preserved here and there along the Muddy River's sinuous banks. Some visitors may in fact find the Pru a welcome addition to willow-framed views of rusticated stone arch bridges, and it's hard to be dismayed by the charming little **Rose Garden,** sheltered by a tall hedge.

Olmsted could hardly have anticipated the impact of foreign affairs on his intended oasis: WW II's original "Victory gardens"—still in use—were planted here, and memorials to Bostonians killed in WW II, Korea, and Vietnam are here, as well. Though no longer a great destination in its own right, the Fens certainly enlivens the stroll between Boylston Street and the art museums on The Fenway, and the pocket of casual neighborhood eateries cupped in the D-shaped bend of the park—the excellent and inexpensive Thai cuisine at the handsome **Brown Sugar Cafe** on Jersey St., for example, or the hearty Brazilian fare at **Buteco,** across the street—are generally less-expensive alternatives to the museum cafes.

Whether you arrive on foot via the Fens or aboard the Green "E" Line on Huntington Ave., you certainly couldn't miss the **Museum of Fine Arts,** tel. (617) 267-9300, even in the dark. Sprawling over an entire block, the MFA contains far too much to see in just one visit, so don't wear yourself out trying. Current temporary exhibitions, usually well touted around town, are always found in the modern West Wing, another of I. M. Pei's numerous contributions to the city. The strengths of the permanent collections are legion: 19th- and early-20th-century American painting, including scores of works by regional artists from John Singleton Copley to Edward Hopper; European painting from the Renaissance through the Impressionists; and extensive collections of decorative arts, including English silver, colonial American furniture, and European antique musical instruments.

If you like mummies, you'll love this place: by virtue of having co-sponsored numerous Egyptian archaeological digs, some of the museum's

DISCOUNT DAYS AND OTHER DEALS

CHEAP DATES
The following paid attractions around town offer free or discounted admission at certain times of the week, or offer special deals for anyone with a valid MBTA Passport or T Pass.

Thursday: The Institute of Contemporary Art: free 5-9 p.m.
Photographic Resource Center: free admission

Friday: The Children's Museum: $1 admission 5-9 p.m.

Saturday: Museum of Fine Arts: free admission until noon
Harvard University museums (all): free admission until noon
Franklin Park Zoo: free admission 10 a.m.-noon, first Saturday of the month only

Sunday: The Computer Museum: half price admission 3-5 p.m.

Bulk Savings
One of the best ways to save on museum admissions is to buy a **Boston CityPass,** good for single admission to six of the city's top attractions: the Museum of Science, New England Aquarium, Museum of Fine Arts, Isabella Stewart Gardner Museum, John F. Kennedy Museum, and John Hancock Observatory. The price of the pass—$26.50 adult, $13.50 kids 12-17—saves you 50% over the combined individual ticket prices (even if you just manage to fit in three of the first four on that list, you'll still be saving money). Buy the CityPass from the first of these institutions you visit, and use it for the rest of your stay—it's valid for nine consecutive days.

MBTA Passport Holders' Discounts
The Institute of Contemporary Art: two-for-one admission
Old State House Museum: two-for-one admission
Boston Tea Party Ship & Museum: 20% off adult admission
Museum of Transportation: 50% discount on individual admission
The John F. Kennedy Library and Museum: $2 off adult admission
Boston Duck Tours: $2 off adult ticket
Museum of Science, Museum of Fine Arts, and the Computer Museum: $1 off adult admission.

collections of ancient Near Eastern artifacts are unrivaled outside of Cairo.

Interested in textiles from Islamic Central Asia, early Chinese old master paintings, or swords and armor from feudal Japan? From its inception, the MFA has also maintained a strong interest in the Far East, as a result of which its Asiatic collections are among the finest to be found anywhere. Don't miss the room of Buddhas—meditatively dark, quiet, and furnished with benches—or the equally contemplative Japanese Tenshin-En ("Garden in the Heart of Heaven"), outside on the Fens side of the West Wing. And this isn't even to mention the classical Greek vases, gallery of ship models, costumes and textiles, prints and photographs, and room full of antiquarian musical instruments. Guided walks and gallery talks are offered most days, and an exceptionally good film series runs Wed.-Sun. evenings (admission extra). Open daily, sometimes till nearly 10 p.m. ($10 adults, $8 seniors and students, kids 17 and under free).

By comparison, the **Isabella Stewart Gardner Museum,** 280 The Fenway, tel. (617) 566-1401 (Tues.-Sun. and Monday holidays; $10), doesn't look very impressive from the outside. Like the Venetian-style palazzos it was designed to resemble, its most lavish decorative features are turned inward, reserved for its occupants and their circle of friends. Fortunately, in this instance the public has always been part of that circle: "Mrs. Jack" Gardner, a famous and outspoken socialite, built this palace a century ago to house her exceptional collection of European, Asian, Islamic, and American art, and then threw open her doors to the public while she lived upstairs. Much of the charm comes from her idiosyncratic arrangements, which her will stipulated must remain exactly as she left them. The interior courtyard is one of the city's best public spaces, bar none. A small gift shop and pleasant little cafe also grace the premises. On weekend afternoons Sept.-April, chamber and jazz music graces the upstairs ballroom ($15, including museum admission).

Kenmore Square

Ground Zero for Boston's biggest bunch of nightclubs and home of Red Sox Nation, Kenmore Square sits beneath the giant Citgo sign, whose prominent flashing red neon triangle is visible after sunset from points all along both banks of the Charles River. Erected in 1965 as a replacement for the City Oil Company's original four-leaf clover logo, the sign was too young to earn protection on the National Register of Historic Places when it was almost junked (in the early 1980s), but a grassroots petition drive to save it prompted the Oklahoma-based owner to restore and relight the vivid 60-foot beacon. The "Giant Delta" is only the most recent left-field target for Fenway Park batters to aim at: big billboards have occupied the roof of the building (now home to a Barnes & Noble superstore) almost since it was built in 1914, the same year Babe Ruth first wore a Red Sox jersey.

Kenmore Square also marks the eastern edge of the lengthy urban campus of **Boston University,** which stretches along Comm. Ave. and is served by seven stops on the Green B Line trolley. The trolley's first aboveground stop, Blandford Street, drops you virtually at the door of the **Photographic Resource Center,** 602 Comm. Ave., tel. (617) 353-0700, under BU's Morse Auditorium. Though small, the PRC's galleries are one of the few places around town to really get a well-curated taste of contemporary photography—high-quality noncommercial work way too fresh for most museums. Open Tues.-Sun., unless dismantling or mounting new exhibit; admission $3.

ROXBURY, JAMAICA PLAIN, AND DORCHESTER

These are not glamorous neighborhoods, outlined in brick sidewalks and wrought iron filigree. You'll find no shops selling tourist postcards and Boston-themed T-shirts. Corner storefronts sell cigarettes and soft drinks, not lattes and biscotti. Wandering these predominately residential areas with no destination in mind will not make good copy for letters home ("Wish you were here—today I saw lots of vinyl siding, cracked sidewalks, and apartment blocks with no yards!"). And downtown hotel concierges will ask where you think you're going if you request directions to the area. But despair not! The treasures here are worth searching out, if you have the patience.

Franklin Park and Vicinity

Frederick Law Olmsted's last major public park project was this 527-acre pendant at the end of his seven-mile Emerald Necklace of urban parkways. Intended as a "complete escape from the town," it was originally designed as a pastoral landscape, "a broad expanse of unbroken turf, lost in the distance under scattered trees." Financing came in part from a bequest made in Ben Franklin's will to an unnamed worthy cause to be chosen a century after his death. Boston convinced the executors of Franklin's estate that this park fit the bill—hence the name. Demands for active recreational facilities have wrought dramatic alterations to Olmsted's Arcadia: where sheep once grazed over rolling meadows, the public now comes to play golf, and other quarters have been pressed into service as playgrounds, a stadium, cross-country course, and the **Franklin Park Zoo,** tel. (617) 442-2002. In the process of a major long-term metamorphosis, the zoo's huge indoor African Tropical Forest and get-up-close-and-personal Lions of the Serengeti habitats are well worth a visit (open daily; $6 ages over 16, $3-5 kids and seniors).

Yet many thickly wooded areas remain, threaded with paths that take advantage of the naturally picturesque outcroppings of Roxbury puddingstone—an ancient conglomerate rock resembling petrified Silly Putty studded with gravel and chipped stone. Look for such other typical Olmsted touches as the 99 stone steps to

nowhere emerging from fallen leaves like a vestige of the Appian Way, and the rusticated stonework of footbridges and hilltop promenades.

Unfortunately, the park's scenic beauty has been threatened less by expanding soccer fields and fairways than by the city's neglect. Despite the fact that Franklin Park is as benign as Boston Common (and a lot safer than New Orleans's French Quarter), vast numbers of white Bostonians and suburbanites would sooner swallow goldfish than set foot in surrounding Roxbury—whose population is over 80% African-American, West Indian, and Latino, and disproportionately poorer than other city neighborhoods, not exactly a constituency with lots of friends in high places. Hidebound Boston's loss is your gain: the kite-flying, birdwatching, rockhounding, jogging, barbecuing, and Frisbee-throwing opportunities out here are unmatched by anything downtown—and free of the in-line skater congestion found along the Charles River Esplanade. And while Back Bay menus have only just started picking up on Caribbean flavors, this neighborhood has the real thing—visit on the second Sunday in July for the most concentrated dose, during the **West Indian Jamboree,** a pre-Carnival celebration featuring dance, costumes, arts, music, and all the goat curry, jerk barbecue, deep-fried patties, and sweet sorrel drinks one could ask for.

Franklin Park is one of those rare Boston places where parking supply usually exceeds

The Jamaica Pond Lantern Parade *mural* *by City Year, on* *Burroughs St. at* *Centre.*

demand, but it's also accessible by several subway-bus combinations. From the end of the Orange Line in Forest Hills, take either the free weekend and holiday shuttle to the zoo, or hop aboard the daily #16 JFK/UMass bus, which passes by the zoo entrance. More circuitous (but more frequent), the #45 Franklin Park Zoo bus runs daily from the bus platform of the Ruggles Orange Line station. It's also easy to get to Franklin Park by foot: take the Orange Line to Green St., turn right upon exiting the station, walk uphill four blocks, and you'll enter via a grassy old carriage road in the wooded northwest quarter. The path soon splits; both left forks end up at the zoo's driveway.

A short distance from the foot of Seaver St., on Franklin Park's north tip, is the **Museum of the National Center for Afro-American Artists,** 300 Walnut St., tel. (617) 442-8614. It's housed in a 19th-century Ruskinian Gothic mansion on a stone ledge with a V-shaped lot flanked by a low puddingstone wall; parking and entrance are from the Crawford St. side. Sculptures, including the aptly named *Eternal Presence,* an immense bronze head by John Wilson, dot the grounds. Inside the museum, three spacious galleries host a wide variety of excellent traveling exhibits, mostly by contemporary artists. There's also a permanent full-scale reconstruction of the 25-century-old burial chamber from the Nubian pyramid of King Aspelta, complete with golden sarcophagus. Besides the gallery openings that attend each new installation, occasional performances and other special events are held throughout the year (Tues.-Sun.; $4 adults, kids under 12 free).

Also near the park's north tip is the Boston Beer Company, better known as the **Samuel Adams brewery,** at Germania St. and Bismark, tel. (617) 368-5000, in Jamaica Plain, two blocks from the Stony Brook Orange Line station (turn left upon exiting and follow signs). Here on the premises of the former Haffenreffer Brewery (one of 17 long-vanished beer makers attracted to the now-buried Stony Brook), Boston Beer brews its lagers, ales, and seasonal specials for local draft accounts. Short but interesting tours and tastings ($1) are offered Thurs.-Fri. at 2 p.m. and Saturday at noon, 1, and 2 p.m.

A few blocks north of Franklin Park's Blue Hill Ave. entrance (outside the east gates of the zoo) is **Muhammad's Mosque of Islam #11,** 10 Washington St. at the corner of Blue Hill Ave., tel. (617) 442-6082. In 1954, Malcolm X founded Boston's Nation of Islam headquarters here, and served briefly as minister. His house at 72 Dale St., a mile away, is still ignored and in disrepair, despite the attention Spike Lee's biographical movie brought to the man.

Across from Franklin Park's southern entrance off Rt. 203 is the **Forest Hills Cemetery,** tel. (617) 524-0703, modeled after the better-known Mount Auburn in Cambridge. On its slopes are the final resting places of playwright Eugene O'Neill, poets Anne Sexton and e. e. cummings (whose flat headstone is engraved in capital letters), author and chaplain Edward Everett Hale, and suffragette Lucy Stone. The wealth of classical statuary, including numerous works by the nation's best-known sculptors of the late 19th and early 20th century, would be the envy of most museums. Among the most exceptional is *Death Staying the Hand of the Sculptor,* one of four major Forest Hills commissions by Daniel Chester French. His Lincoln Memorial has earned more permanent fame, but this piece—just inside the cemetery gates—was considered by contemporaries to be one of his best; the work of the sculptor it memorializes, Martin Milmore, is visible in the Civil War memorial located south of the lake, nearly opposite the fireman statue. (Milmore's contemplative soldier looking at the graves of his fallen comrades was so popular in its day that it was reproduced for Civil War cemeteries all over the nation.) A map identifying famous permanent residents is available from the office at the entrance, along with information about regular programs like birdwatching and historical walking tours. The office also sells copies of *Garden Memories,* by local historian and journalist Susan Wilson ($10), whose fact-filled pages will helpfully explain the stories behind two of Forest Hill's more unusual monuments, the Girl in the Glass Case and the Boy in the Boat. The cemetery's pedestrian entrance is at the end of block-long Tower St., opposite the Forest Hills Orange Line station. Also opposite the station is **The Dogwood Café,** a welcoming dinner-and-drinks spot whose inexpensive pastas, pizzas, salads, and specials put a fine finish to any afternoon spent amid Forest Hill's garden of stone.

Arnold Arboretum

While the 7,000 different shrubs, vines, and trees in its collection places this facility in the top rank of North American arboretæ, it doesn't take an academic interest to appreciate Jamaica Plain's botanical jewel, administered by Harvard University under a 1,000-year lease from the city. As with the rest of the Emerald Necklace, Nature is but a handmaiden to Olmsted's vision, which is preserved here more faithfully than in any of his other contributions to the Boston Park System. The great hilltop views to city and sea are best from Peters Hill, in the Arboretum's southern section. On this summit used to stand Roxbury's 18th-century Second Church of Christ. Remains of the church's burying ground—a smattering of markers from 1722 onward, including an unmarked stone for a group of Revolutionary War soldiers—is found among the tulip trees on the hill's steep west flank. Horticultural highlights include the continent's second-largest collection of lilacs; exceptional crabapple, maple, and conifer collections; and the small gazebo-size Bonsai House, near the maintenance offices. As harbingers of spring, nothing quite matches those lilacs (celebrated with Lilac Sunday, the third weekend in May), but the rhododendrons and azaleas are nothing to sneer at, either. It used to have the only tree in the entire Boston Park system on which climbing was permitted—an Amur cork tree—but, sadly, a group posing on it for a photo snapped the trunk in 1995; the remains—and a dedication plaque for its eventual replacement (now just a sapling)—are easily found along the lane not far beyond the Hunnewell Visitor Center.

The quickest way to get into the Arboretum is by walking up South Street from the Forest Hills Orange Line station, but the visitor center is actually closer to the route of the #39 Forest Hills bus (which departs from in front of the Copley Plaza Hotel). Ask to be let off in front of Arborway Natural Foods, at Custer St., just past "the Monument." Walk to the end of Custer and cross the busy Arborway at the pedestrian signal. The Arboretum entrance is on the right.

Kennedy Library and Museum

His name and legacy are routinely used as a lucky talisman by modern politicians, but what do you actually know of his presidency? Relive the 1960 campaign for the Oval Office and get an inside view on JFK's White House years at the museum attached to the National Archives presidential library. As media-savvy as Kennedy himself, the museum makes extensive use of videos to replay both key events—Jack standing up to anti-Catholic paranoia stoked by opponents Nixon and Lodge, the whole of his inaugural address, his famous "Ich bin ein Berliner" speech—and forgotten sidelights: Frank Sinatra's pro-Kennedy campaign jingle, Jackie's tour of the White House, Walter Cronkite's faltering composure as he reads the news of the Dallas assassination. Jutting into Dorchester Bay on windy Columbia Point (free shuttle bus from the Red Line's JFK/UMass station nearby), the dramatic I. M. Pei-designed building also affords great views of the downtown skyline from both inside and out. Open daily ($6; tel. 617-929-4523).

The eight-story library isn't solely the province of Kennedy researchers: Ernest Hemingway's papers are deposited here, too. Papa Hemingway is no stranger to Boston; his *Farewell to Arms* was one of the many books censored by bluenose moralists early this century.

BROOKLINE

Surrounded by Boston on three sides, Brookline (pop. 53,000) is nearly an island within the bigger city. Known for large Jewish and Russian populations, excellent public schools, and the only metro area ban on smoking in restaurants *and* bars, Brookline racks up points for being a desirable place to live (if you can afford it) but keeps a relatively low profile among tourists. The few attractions it *does* offer out-of-towners (besides kosher restaurants and bookstores carrying more than one kind of Haggadah—both most plentiful on Harvard Street) are rather scattered, and only the JFK Birthplace is less than a half-mile from the T. All sights and attractions are good destinations for cyclists, however.

Birthplace of Camelot

At 83 Beals Street, a block from Harvard St. and about 10 minutes' walk from the Green "C" Line, stands the natal home of the nation's 35th president, the **John Fitzgerald Kennedy Birthplace National Historic Site,** tel. (617) 566-7937. The

PUPPET PLAY

Given New England's unparalleled concentration of professional puppeteers, it comes as no surprise that the Boston area is home to one of the country's rare theaters devoted exclusively to puppetry. Brookline's **Puppet Showplace Theater,** 32 Station St., tel. (617) 731-6400, conveniently opposite the Brookline Village stop on the Green "D" Line, stages new productions every week, year-round, from classic fairy tales told by marionettes to original musicals featuring hand puppets. Selected performances are specifically designed for preschoolers, and many of the rest are ideal for children ages five and up, but the PST and the local puppetry guild also have teamed up to sponsor events specifically for grown-ups. These so-called **puppet slams** are essentially informal, inexpensively priced evenings of puppet cabaret, with a passel of puppet artists or groups performing adult-oriented works around a designated theme. The results are sometimes ribald, often both humorous and quite magical, and always highly entertaining, despite the occasional experimental piece that goes awry. Produced bimonthly at different venues in and around Boston, puppet slams are without a doubt one of the most unforgettable art events to be found in the city. Call the PST for schedule and ticket info, and reservations (recommended).

simple three-story house and its furnishings reflect the family's improving middle-class circumstances circa 1917, the year JFK was born. Though they moved four years later, the house was meticulously refurbished under the supervision of Rose Kennedy herself. Guided tours ($2) Wed.-Sun. 10:45 a.m.-4 p.m.

Home with a View

While by no means as famous as the slain president, Frederick Law Olmsted, the mastermind behind major urban parks in dozens of cities from New York to Los Angeles and San Francisco also resided in Brookline, and the house in which he lived and worked for nearly the last 15 years of his life is also preserved by the National Park Service. The **Frederick Law Olmsted National Historic Site,** tel. (617) 566-1689, a small estate named Fairsted, sits on exactly the sort of beautiful lot in exactly the sort of beautiful neighborhood you would expect of the grandfather of landscape architecture. Inside are displays that try to convey the magnitude of Olmsted's contribution to the look of the American built environment, from cemeteries to zoos, college campuses to city suburbs. Simply put, his legacy daily enriches the lives of city joggers, Frisbee players, dog walkers, bench sitters, and millions of other residents and institutional employees in 45 states, Canada, Cuba, Bermuda, Puerto Rico, and the Philippines. To see if you're among those unwittingly touched by his landscapes, check the master reference list in the bookshop. The Brookline Hills station on the Green "D" Line is the closest trolley stop—about seven-tenths of a mile through mostly residential streets. (Take a right on Cypress, another right on Walnut—the second light—and head up the hill past the burying ground and church, curving left onto Warren St.; Fairsted is a block ahead on the right, at No. 99.) Open (free) Fri.-Sun. only, but also, for researchers, by appointment.

Wheels of Fortune

Located even farther from public transit, in the even more affluent, country-club quarter of Brookline, on the historic Larz Anderson estate, the **Museum of Transportation,** 15 Newton St., tel. (617) 522-6547, documents America's favorite obsession in videos, photos, and cars, cars, cars. In summer, the 1889 Gothic carriage house hosts special celebrations sponsored by various car clubs, but in any season you will find plenty of hands-on displays and vehicles to climb around on (Wed.-Sun.; $5 adults, $3 kids).

CAMBRIDGE SIGHTS

Boston and its neighbor across the Charles River may seem inseparable to the visitor, but residents know better. Boston, often truculent about social and political change, tends to regard the other city as "the People's Republic of Cambridge." Though Boston would sooner elect Dumbo than vote for a Republican for mayor, it is equally unlikely to take a gay black candidate to the same office, as Cambridge already has. Before WW II, Cambridge was still a big manufacturing town, but most of the assembly-line workers have been replaced by software and soft money; while conservative Cantabrigians aren't unheard of, they're usually heavily outpolled by more liberal fellow residents. (How many other cities in the nation have a Peace Commissioner?) As dizzying rental rates force marginal residential and commercial tenants out of business or out of town, Cambridge finds itself in the process of discovering whether too much gentrification is a bad thing.

The principal axis of interest for out-of-towners lies between Harvard University and the Massachusetts Institute of Technology, although the Half Crown, Avon Hill, and Mid-Cambridge Conservation Districts are all worth a visit if you have a keen interest in residential architecture (or a desire to see the neighborhoods in which Julia Child and John Kenneth Galbraith live). Like competing superpowers, the two Ivy League schools carve up much of the city's riverside real estate into distinct spheres of influence; in practical terms, attractions may be spoken of as near one or the other, or in the buffer zone in between.

HARVARD SQUARE

Harvard Square has become a major tourist destination in its own right, much to the chagrin of locals who cherish its past. Popularity has brought skyrocketing property values, replacing mom-and-pop stores with national chains (Gap, Barnes & Noble, Tower Records, Structure, Sunglass Hut). Every year, returning students discover that another favorite grease pit has metamorphosed into a gleaming Starbucks. It isn't quite the Mall at Harvard yet—the pierced and punkish local teens still hang out in "The Pit" (the entrance around the subway), musicians and the homeless still play or plead for spare

Chemistry instructor Ellen Swallow Richards with her students at MIT, 1888

MIT MUSEUM

SUBWAY BUSKERS AND SIDEWALK VAUDEVILLE

Besides bringing budding trees, courting songbirds, and final exams, spring also marks the return of outdoor street performers to their usual roosts in and around Harvard Square. Friday and Saturday nights are busiest—a dozen or more musicians, acrobats, and magicians perform in doorways and on corner plazas—but almost any evening warm and dry enough for postprandial strolling is bound to attract at least a busker or two. (Inside the Harvard Square T Station, musicians perform year-round.)

The most famous alumna of the square's streets and subway is Tracy Chapman, but she's not the only busker to have ultimately landed a record contract—and it isn't uncommon to find many of these performers showing up on club stages around town. Among the current crop of regulars worth looking for are Jim the Juggler (whose finale involves balancing a shopping cart on his chin), unicyclist Peter Panic, slackrope-walking knife juggler Mark Farneth, and Ecuadoran musicians performing Andean folksongs.

JEFF PERK

Street performer Mark Farneth juggles on a slackrope in Harvard Square

change, and chessmasters still concentrate on their games in front of Holyoke Center. But developers seem intent upon stamping out all uniqueness, so don't be surprised if you arrive to find a Planet Hollywood or Nike Town in place of any of the landmarks mentioned below.

The kingpin of the Square is of course none other than **Harvard University.** With an endowment larger than Colombia's annual cocaine economy and an annual budget comparable to

WHAT'S WITH THOSE ADDRESSES?

For some reason, the area around Harvard Square abounds in addresses that begin with (or are) zero. Where else but Cambridge would the postal service respect a cipher, so to speak, as a valid address? Among the most notable zeroes are the Christ Church of Cambridge (0 Garden St.); Tealuxe (0 Brattle St.); and Out of Town News (0 Harvard Square).

the city of Boston's, Harvard looks and feels about as you would expect: big and powerful. Beginning in the 17th century with a dozen students—mostly candidates for the Puritan ministry—the university has grown to incorporate Harvard and Radcliffe Colleges and 10 other degree-granting graduate schools. Enrollment, drawing candidates from every state and half the world, comes to more than 18,000 students—with another 13,000 taking evening courses through the university's open-enrollment Extension School. Although it has eagerly joined the diversity bandwagon touted by every American college and university these days, this alma mater of six U.S. presidents, 11 Supreme Court justices, 30 Nobel laureates, and the Unabomber also has a well-earned reputation for being a handmaiden to wealth and privilege. Contrary to the perfervid declarations of Republican candidates, Harvard historically hasn't exactly been a den of card-carrying ACLU members and Kennedy liberals—even if having John Reed, William S. Burroughs, and FDR as fellow alumni probably makes a graduate like Antonin Scalia flinch. The school's intellectual trove of prize-winning faculty and their seemingly endless research triumphs is unimpeachable. But so is its steadfast resistance to organized labor (from busting up turn-of-the-century textile factory strikes with militia composed of the freshman class to an underhanded late-1980s campaign against its own clerical workers' efforts to unionize). Neither, mirroring the elite Boston society it served, did Harvard blaze any trails in admitting Catholics, Jews, minorities, or women—as either students or faculty. Barriers to all these groups have only been seriously discarded within the last generation or two.

A BOOK LOVER'S MECCA

Portland, Oregon, may sport some of the most prolific book buyers in the country, nourishing the success of a surprisingly large number of bookstores, but in the eyes of most publishing industry professionals Cambridge—and, more precisely, Harvard Square—is the true hotbed of American bookselling. Within a radius of half a dozen blocks is a concentration of bookstores unrivalled anywhere in the US. Not just any bookstores, either: the general retailers here are among the most successful in the nation, and many of the smaller specialty stores are nationally known leaders in their fields. So even though Borders Books & Music and Barnes & Noble have both blitzed the metro area with megastores over the past few years, qualitatively they're still sideshows to the scores of independents who specialize in almost anything you could want, from antiquarian and foreign-language books to mysteries, Judaica, and recycled student libraries.

While most of the following highly abbreviated list are in Cambridge, both Boston and Brookline have a few noteworthy bookdealers, too, such as **The Brattle Book Shop,** on West St. a block from Boston Common, tel. (800) 447-9595 or (617) 542-0210, and Coolidge Corner's **Israel Book Shop,** 410 Harvard St. in Brookline, tel. (617) 566-7113. But if you're simply enamored of browsing books—to midnight!—do not pass Go: head straight for Harvard. (For a complete list of 30 Cambridge booksellers, pick up a free Bookstore Guide from the information kiosk next to Out of Town News, at the main entrance to the Harvard Square T station.)

HARVARD SQUARE

Globe Corner Bookstore, 28 Church St., tel. (617) 497-6277, www.globecorner.com; open Mon.-Sat. till 9 p.m., Sunday till 6. The area's premiere travel bookstore, stocking all the guidebook series you've ever heard of and then some, plus travelogues,

handsome coffeetable travel books, atlases, globes, and other traveler's toys. Also carries a full line of domestic and international maps (including USGS topos, NOAA charts, DMA, British OS, and lots of difficult-to-find New England recreational maps), mapping software, and GPS receivers.

James & Devon Gray Booksellers, 12 Arrow St., tel. (617) 868-0752, e-mail nous@delphi.com; open Mon.-Sat. Been hankering to study Albertus Magnus in the original Medieval Latin? Or collect literature by Milton and his contemporaries? You've come to the right place: the Grays deal exclusively in books of the 17th century and earlier, including incunabula (books printed before the 16th century), in English, Latin, Greek, and other major Western European languages.

Grolier Poetry Book Shop, 6 Plympton St., tel. (800) 234-POEM or (617) 547-4648; open Tues.-Sat. in summer and Mon.-Sat. during the academic year. One of the brightest patches in the city's bookstore quilt is this cozy all-poetry store, unique in North America. The Grolier handles international mail orders as well as spoken word tapes for your next long-distance roadtrip.

Harvard Book Store, 1256 Mass. Ave., tel. (617) 661-1515; open daily till at least 10 p.m., Fri.-Sat. till midnight. Unaffiliated with the university across the street. Plenty of general-interest titles and bestsellers, but it shines brightest in academic categories, both new and used, and in university press titles. Also known for its highbrow hardback remainders.

Harvard University Press Display Room, Holyoke Center Arcade, 1354 Mass. Ave., tel. (617) 495-2625; open daily. Features every HUP and Belknap Press book in print, including the entire Loeb Classical Library.

Harvard Yard

Befitting its aristocratic English roots and the Oxford ties of its namesake and benefactor, Charlestown minister John Harvard, the campus is dominated by the tree-shaded quadrangles of Harvard Yard, beyond whose tall brick and wrought iron boundary swirl the buses and cars of Mass. Ave. Enter through one of the many ornate gates, named after their donors, and almost instantly the urban tumult fades, overpowered by the tranquillity of the Old Yard. Lending composure to the peaceful academy are many of the university's earliest buildings, including five that predate the American Revolution. Oldest is Massachusetts Hall, just inside the Johnston Gate, across from the First Parish

---

Schoenhof's Foreign Books, 76A Mt. Auburn St., tel. (617) 547-8855, www.schoenhof's.com; closed Sunday. Learning a foreign language? Shoenhof's dictionaries and grammar texts—covering over 300 languages and dialects—can surely help. Also features a wide array of foreign-language fiction and nonfiction in all the major European tongues. If that's not enough, the multilingual staff is expert at ordering just about anything in print, anywhere in the world.

Starr Book Shop, 29 Plympton St., tel. (617) 547-6864; daily till 6 p.m. or later. Used books covering all general subjects and many academic ones. A stalwart fixture of the Square for two generations.

WordsWorth Books, 30 Brattle St., tel. (800) 899-2202 or (617) 354-5201, www.wordsworth.com; open Mon.-Sat. to 11:15 p.m., Sunday till 10:15 p.m. One of the nation's top-selling bookstores, stuffed to the rafters with over 100,000 titles in nearly 100 subjects. Has a sideline in English imports from the UK, too. Better yet, all but the textbooks are discounted at least 10-15%. Within a block are two sibling branches, one for children's books and another for cards and gifts.

ELSEWHERE IN CAMBRIDGE

Kate's Mystery Books, 2211 Mass. Ave. (about five blocks north of Porter Square), tel. (617) 491-2660; open daily till 5 p.m. or later. All mystery books, all the time.

The MIT Press Bookstore, 292 Main St. (next to the inbound entrance for the Kendall Square T stop on the Red Line), tel. (617) 253-5249, mitpress.mit.edu/bookstore; open daily. Excellent source for The MIT Press books, MIT-related titles, and books by authors with ties to the MIT community. Don't come looking for paperback bestsellers, school texts, Moon Handbooks, or standardized test tutorials; those are across the street at the MIT Coop. But for titles related to science, technology, architecture, and political science, this place should be your first stop. Also has a good line of magazines—it's one of the few places around town, for example, to reliably stock that regular emission of the Mad Monks of the Road, *Monk* magazine.

New Words, 186 Hampshire St. (in Inman Square, opposite the Merit gas station at Prospect St.), tel. (800) 928-4788 or (617) 876-5310, e-mail new-words@world.std.com; open daily. Since 1974 New Words has been the region's leading resource for books and journals by and about women, in all the standard categories: fiction, biography, politics, health, art, and auto repair. Great posters, postcards, and bumper stickers, too, ideal for inspiring or awakening consciousness dulled by the mainstream.

Quantum Books, 4 Cambridge Center, on Broadway next to the Cambridge Marriott, tel. (617) 494-5042; closed Sunday. Hailed by *PC Computing* for having one of the nation's widest selections of computer-related books, this is the place to find that manual you always needed to integrated development tools and other technical issues. Also specializes in physics, math, and engineering titles.

NORTH OF CAMBRIDGE

Lucy Parsons Center, 259 Elm St., Somerville, tel. (617) 629-2649, e-mail lucyparsons@juno.com; open daily (till 10 p.m. Mon.-Sat.). Searching for children's books that don't assume the world is white, or straight? Look no farther. The local bookstore back home doesn't carry critiques of society, media, corporations, or foreign policy? Lucy Parsons does. From anarchism to *Z Magazine*, environmentalism to African-American parenting, if it makes Rush Limbaugh foam at the mouth, you'll probably find it here amid the "literature of liberation." Located inside the building opposite Papa Gino's, behind the nondescript lobby door next to the Dragon Garden Chinese restaurant, about a block from the Davis Square stop on the Red Line.

Church; while occupied in part by administrative offices (including the president's), it's also been a dormitory since it opened in 1720. Facing it is the 1764 Harvard Hall, built after a fire claimed its predecessor. Guides always tell an apocryphal story about this blaze destroying the entire library left by John Harvard—all, that is, except one book that had secretly been taken out by a student. Upon returning the volume to the college president, this student was first thanked most gratefully—and then expelled for unauthorized removal of the book. Whether such a hapless young man existed or whether he actually got off with just an overdue fine, *Christian Warfare* was indeed the sole survivor from the original Harvard bequest (although 403 other books, acquired after the bequest, also survived the fire).

Nearby stand two Federal-style contributions Charles Bulfinch (Class of 1781) made to the Yard. University Hall is the easiest to spot, behind the famous "statue of the three lies," around which tour groups often gather for photos. The irreverent nickname derives from the seated figure's wholly false inscription, "John Harvard, Founder, 1638." Conceived by an act of the Bay Colony legislature in 1636, the college officially existed before John Harvard had even left England, although it took two years to build a classroom and organize a curriculum. Shortly after classes commenced, the newly settled Puritan clergyman died in neighboring Charlestown, leaving his whole library and half his estate to the fledgling college; 1638 is the date the institution changed its name in gratitude for his gift. As for the young scholar in the buckle shoes, it's really the likeness of Sherman Hoar, a popular senior from the class of 1882, since sculptor Daniel Chester French could find no reliable likeness of Harvard himself.

Behind University Hall and bookended by the heavenly reach of Memorial Chapel's white spire and the bedrock mass of monumental Widener Library, is the Tercentenary Theatre—or "New Yard"—where commencement exercises are held, rain or shine, the first Thursday of June. Widener's broad granite steps lead only to the tip of the iceberg, for that is but one of 90 separate units constituting the complete Harvard Library, whose collective holdings outrank every other academic library on the planet and are second in

the U.S. only to the Library of Congress. Although the five miles of stacks are off limits to anyone outside the Harvard-Radcliffe community, you may take a look around inside, vicariously absorbing a little of the studious air and if nothing else examining the fascinating dioramas on either side of the inside stair. Depicting the evolution of Harvard Yard and Cambridge from 1667 through 1936, the models also illustrate the waterways whose vanished courses are still outlined by modern streets.

Guided tours of the Yard are offered by student volunteers, beginning at the Harvard Information Center in the concourse of Holyoke Center. During the school year, tours run Mon.-Sat., while during summer they run daily (four times Mon.-Sat., twice on Sunday). The info center also sells self-guided tour brochures in several languages, and a detailed map of the entire campus and the surrounding streets of Cambridge.

Beyond the Yard

Harvard Yard isn't the only oasis from the cascade of walkers and drivers streaming in and out of the Square's T station, ice cream shops, and ATM lobbies. Small greenspaces are scattered about just waiting to revive tired walkers on warm afternoons, or readers impatient to review their purchases from one of the many local bookstores, or anyone wanting to relax over an ice cream frappe or steaming cappuccino. Radcliffe Yard, off Brattle St. northwest of the T station, is one such spot: quiet, attractive, with perfectly

---

IVY LEAGUE ETYMOLOGY

These days, the phrase "Ivy League" is freighted with all the exclusivity and prestige of the eight universities that comprise its ranks: Brown, Columbia, Cornell, Harvard, MIT, Princeton, the University of Pennsylvania, and Yale. But the term was originally a mild pejorative, coined by sportscaster Caswell Adams in the 1930s as a put-down of these schools' athletic prowess. One day a pressbox companion favorably compared the league's teams to Fordham, then ranked number one in American college football. Adams utterly rejected the idea, dismissively rejoining, "Not a chance—they're just Ivy League."

JEFF PERK

JOHN FITZGERALD KENNEDY PARK

testing the waters in Kennedy Park

even lawns that invite cartwheel practice and squirrel watching. Stop by Brattle Street's old-fashioned **Billings & Stover** drugstore soda fountain for some refreshment on the way, and discover why New Orleans has no monopoly on living easy. If you return to the heart of the Square by Garden Street, you'll pass the Old Burying Ground and, just inside the iron fence at the corner, its colonial milestone. Bridges and landfill have more than halved the distance cited to Boston, but back then the only option from here was via the Great Bridge, through Brighton, and across narrow Roxbury Neck—currently a crosstown route you could roughly duplicate by hopping the #66 bus across the street and transferring to the inbound Orange Line at Ruggles, in Roxbury. It was avoidance of that eight-mile semicircle that motivated the British Redcoats to take boats across the Charles that night in 1775 when they marched for Lexington and Concord. Alarm rider and Revere sidekick William Dawes made no such shortcut when he took the land route by this stone—in memory of which, brass horseshoes are set in the sidewalk of that traffic island-cum-bus stop.

On the north side of the Old Yard is the **Science Center,** one of several International Style buildings designed for Harvard by Spanish modernist José Luis Sert, dean of the Graduate School of Design during the 1950s and '60s. Its plaza includes the attractive Tanner Fountain, whose dry outer stones are as fine a spot for people-watching or cloud-gazing as any in

the area. Grab a cup of joe from the Seattle's Best Coffee cart inside the Science Center lobby, or a student-priced polystyrene box of Chinese takeout from the lunch truck usually parked weekdays around the side on Oxford Street. For further diversion, check out the **Collection of Historical Scientific Instruments,** tel. (617) 495-2779, in the Science Center basement. Though small and open only Tues.-Fri. during the academic year (including summer school), the display cases present an imaginative jumble of polished brass, calibrated dials, intricate working models, and other oddities from as far back as 1450.

South of Harvard Yard lie the undergraduate dorms and dining halls of the residential "Houses," the Oxford-style colleges-within-the-College built along the Charles during Harvard's major pre-war expansion into a full-fledged university. From the Business School, across the river in Allston, the orderly Georgian brick and white-capped cupolas provide the most cinematic backdrop for the spectacle of crew rowers coordinating their swift daddy-longleg strokes. The elegant dorms also partly frame Kennedy Park, at the foot of JFK Street, whose broad lawn is regularly enjoyed by Frisbee players, sunbathers, and newspaper readers. Pick up a bargain pocket sandwich from **Stuff-It,** on Eliot St. opposite the Harvard Square Hotel, or a soup and butter-rich cookie from **Darwin's Ltd.,** a priceless little wine shop-deli at 128 Mt. Auburn, and join the office workers stretching out their lunch hours on the park's sunny benches. On Sunday afternoons during the academic year—or anytime Harvard beats Yale at anything—you may hear the pealing of the Lowell House carillon, a set of 17 bells acquired by an alumnus from a monastery in Stalin-era Moscow. Inscribed in Old Church Slavonic with such names as "The Sacred Oil," and "Pestilence, Famine, and Despair," the bells may sound slightly out of tune, unless your ear is accustomed to the untempered Eastern scale. The 18th member of the 26-ton bunch, "Hope, Felicity, and Joy," tolls by itself in the B-School belfry across the river.

Harvard Museum of Cultural and Natural History

The Harvard Museum of Cultural and Natural History, tel. (617) 495-3045 (daily; $5), comprises four distinct institutions, all physically linked by interconnected galleries in buildings between 26 Oxford St. and 11 Divinity Ave. behind the Harvard Science Center. The first three are such pure examples of the Victorian zeal for taxonomy—Harvard as Noah, gathering samples of all the world's animals, vegetables, and minerals into its glass-cased ark—that they invite reflection on the history and purpose of museums in general. **The Botanical Museum** is perhaps most popular of the four, thanks to its unique collection of **"Glass Flowers."** Properly known as the Ware Collection of Glass Models of Plants, the 3,000-odd specimens illustrating over 840 flower species represent nearly half a century of handiwork by Leopold and Rudolf Blaschka, brother artisans whose techniques went with them to their graves. Exactingly detailed—down to fuzzy stem hairs and pollen-covered stamen—the painted models actually look more like plastic than glass, but sonic booms and other accidents have amply proven that the fragile things are glass in all but appearance. Adjacent halls feature the vast rock, ore, gemstone, and meteorite collections of **The Mineralogical and Geological Museum,** and the great menagerie of fossils, dinosaur bones, preserved fish, insects, and 19th-century stuffed mammals belonging to the **Museum of Comparative Zoology.** Some of the formaldehyde-fragrant zoological specimens are historic in their own right: birds gathered by Lewis and Clark while Thomas Jef-

ferson was in the White House, for example, or spiders collected by Louis Agassiz before the Pony Express. Beyond the fantastical colors and crystalline geometry of the mineralogical collections is the **Peabody Museum of Archaeology and Ethnology,** whose displays draw upon the millions of artifacts the world-renowned Peabody has in its care. From Pacific Northwest totem poles to Andean gold and textiles, Easter Island effigies to Angolan figurines, four floors of exhibits represent indigenous cultures from every continent but Antarctica. In addition to occasional lectures, the combined Museum of Cultural and Natural History maintains modest gift shops at both the Oxford St. and Divinity Ave. entrances.

Across from the Peabody at 6 Divinity Ave. is the **Harvard Semitic Museum,** tel. (617) 495-4631, sponsor of archaeological excavations throughout the Middle East and Mediterranean since the late 19th century. Cuneiform tablets, pottery, coins, and other objects from the museum's field work are on display, along with a significant collection of 19th-century photographs of the Holy Land. Open 10 a.m.-4 p.m. Mon.-Fri. and 1-4 p.m. Sunday (free).

Harvard Art Museums

Harvard's artistic side is a couple blocks from its science; to find it, just locate the only North American building by the Swiss urban planner, architect, and Cubist painter Le Corbusier. (If you spot Henry Moore's appealingly organic sculptures on the eastern perimeter of Harvard Yard, you're close.) Fortunately for Cambridge, the man whose guiding dictum was "buildings are machines to live in" wasn't being asked to design one of his monumental cities-within-a-city; as it is, Corbu's raw concrete **Carpenter Center for the Visual Arts** seems an odd bedfellow among Quincy Street's staid red brick. Provocative installations of contemporary art usually occupy the ground floor, above the appropriately underground **Harvard Film Archive,** tel. (617) 495-4700 (schedule posted outside). The graceful ramp bisecting the building's angled mass allows passersby to peek into studio art classrooms within, too.

Spread along Quincy St. next to the Carpenter Center is the troika of **Harvard University Art Museums,** tel. (617) 495-9400 (daily; $5 for all three). The venerable **Fogg Art Museum,** at 32 Quincy, is oldest, its flamboyant swan's neck pediment over the entrance a foretaste of the treasures within. The Italian Renaissance, British Pre-Raphaelites, French Impressionists, and American landscapes are among the collection's highlights, arranged in galleries encircling the skylit replica of an Italian loggia. Stylishly modern Otto Werner Hall, grafted onto the back of the Fogg and sharing the same entrance, houses the **Busch-Reisinger Museum** collection of 20th-century art from Germany and its linguistic and cultural relatives. The legacy of the Bauhaus art and design school is strong: some of the museum's most significant works are by modernists who taught at this pioneering Weimar Republic school before it ran afoul of the Nazis in the 1930s, and the accumulated Bauhaus memorabilia and design materials—portions of which are routinely displayed—are unparalleled outside Germany. The archives of Bauhaus founder Walter Gropius, who, as Dean of the School of Architecture, spearheaded Harvard's immersion into the International Style, are also here.

Harvard alumnus Arthur M. Sackler must set some sort of high-water mark for art collectors: his hoard of Asian and Islamic art was vast enough to fill *two* museums. One is the Smithsonian's Sackler Gallery, in Washington, D.C. The other is Harvard's **Sackler Museum,** in an unusual postmodern edifice at the corner of Quincy and Broadway. Sackler's extensive bequest has been supplemented by additional collections of Korean ceramics, Japanese prints, Oriental textiles, Persian calligraphy, Indian paintings, and archaic Chinese Buddhist sculptures. The Sackler also houses the university's ancient Greek and Roman artworks.

As with the science museums, a gift shop may be found in the Fogg, but for a quick bite your best bet is to step around the corner to the **Broadway Market**, a block past the Sackler. There you'll find several deli counters and pay-by-the-pound salad bars, food court style, with indoor seating and a ubiquitous Starbucks on the side.

Tory Row

Beyond the "Washington slept here" parts of Harvard Yard and evocative slate markers of the Old Burying Ground, local history is perhaps most concentrated along Brattle Street. Shops and academic offices have crowded out most of the 18th-century houses on the low-numbered blocks by the T station, but past the busy orbit of Harvard Square, and past the historical marker to the village blacksmith, residential Brattle Street affords postcard views of Ye Olde Cambridge. While there are numerous contemporary homes between the 1882 Stoughton House at Brattle and Ash and the corner of Fayerwether Street, 10 blocks away, the overriding impression is of elegant historic houses. Some of the genuinely old mansions belonged to prominent Loyalists until the Revolution sent them packing to New Brunswick and Nova Scotia; it is on their account that this stretch of Brattle St. is nicknamed "Tory Row." On cloudless summer days, sandwiched between the cropped green lawn and majolica blue sky, the daisy yellow facade of No. 105 is especially photogenic. Its Tory owner was Major John Vassall, but the handsome 1759 Georgian mansion's most famous resident was America's first career poet, Henry Wadsworth Longfellow. Preserved as a museum to the man who penned the memorable lines, "Listen my children, and you shall hear/Of the midnight ride of Paul Revere," the **Longfellow National Historic Site,** tel. (617) 876-4491, is open Wed.-Sun. from mid-March to mid-Dec. ($2). Besides house and grounds tours, the staff conducts an annual "Troupe of Shadows" walk the first Saturday in July through nearby Mount Auburn Cemetery (final resting place of Longfellow and many of his contemporaries). Or sample Cambridge's bountiful literary history with the aid of *Footprints on the Sands of Time,* a 24-page walking-tour guide sold in the Longfellow House gift shop. And as a reminder that this is no mere mausoleum, the National Park Service sponsors an annual "Longfellow Summer Festival" of poetry and music each Sunday afternoon from June through early September. As for those who happen by on a Monday or Tuesday, when the house is closed, you should still visit the formal little garden at the back, where, seated at the bench with eyes closed, you can almost imagine the singing anvil of that blacksmith down the street, "Like a sexton ringing the village bell,/ When the evening sun is low."

One of the oldest houses in Cambridge (only a few years younger than the Revere House in

Boston's North End) is up the street at No. 159. Now headquarters to the Cambridge Historical Society, the **Hooper-Lee-Nichols House,** tel. (617) 547-4252, has been greatly altered since its 1680s construction as a two-story farmhouse, but original structural elements have been exposed for viewing, along with the 18th-century Georgian decorations, early 19th-century scenic wallpaper, early 20th-century Delft tiles, and other artifacts from the building's long and lively history (2-5 p.m. Tuesday and Thursday year-round; $5). Judge Joseph Lee, one of the Anglican founders of Christ Church, next to the Old Burying Ground, was a member of the colony's governing council appointed by the Crown as part of England's 1774 Coercive Acts, but an angry mob of fellow colonists persuaded him that resignation would be better for his health. Although forced to flee during the Revolution, Lee was the only Brattle Street Tory allowed to return home when the war ended.

Riverbend Park

On Sundays during summer and fall, the stretch of Memorial Drive between the start of the Alewife/Fresh Pond Parkway and Western Ave. is closed to traffic, making it ideal for skaters, strollers, and joggers. Throughout the summer, Riverbend Park itself, beside a pair of meanders in the Charles, is a favorite place for buff students to catch some Vitamin D and nap over their notebooks. Until the weather turns too cold, it's also an excellent vantage point for watching local crew teams skimming over the water in their fragile-looking, fly-weight shells. A Hong Kong Dragon Boat Festival adds a dash of the exotic on the fifth day of the fifth moon of the Chinese year (usually sometime in June), as the Charles hosts one of the international qualifying races for teams hoping to compete in Hong Kong (tel. 617-426-6500 ext. 778 for exact date). And in late October a sea of spectators lines the banks for the world's largest rowing competition, the Head of the Charles Regatta, but with a three-mile race course there's always space for everyone to comfortably relax and watch.

"Sweet Auburn"

Located west of Harvard Square on Mt. Auburn St. is one of the more attractive greenspaces on either side of the river: **Mount Auburn Ceme-**

tery, named after the opening line of a poem by author and playwright Oliver Goldsmith. Many illustrious New Englanders rest in its privately owned, 174 landscaped acres, from the founder of Christian Science to the inventor of the geodesic dome. The nation's oldest garden cemetery, Mount Auburn's arboretum landscape was widely acclaimed and imitated, igniting a great movement to bring "rural" spaces to the nation's teeming cities. Boston Common may get top billing as the nation's oldest public park, but it's more fair to say this cemetery is the forerunner and inspiration for America's greatest urban parks as we know them today. As popular today as ever, Mount Auburn still attracts the living with its sculpture, history, horticulture, and bird-watching—all just minutes from the underground busway in Harvard Square Station via the #71 Watertown or #73 Waverly trolley bus.

Every stone has a story, of course, and while you could comb local bookstores for the biogra-

crew practice on the Charles River

phies that cover the more famous few, most are more obscure. Take the grave of Swiss-born zoologist and Harvard professor Louis Agassiz, marked by a chunk of rock. Agassiz' landmark 1840 book on European glaciers, *Etude sur les glaciers,* fundamentally altered our understanding of glaciation, eventually overturning the prevailing scientific view that glaciers existed solely in the Swiss Alps. That tombstone is an erratic from the moraine of the Aar glacier—one of the keys that helped Agassiz unlock the true continental reach of ancient ice sheets, from the very place he'd conducted his research. You'll find a handful of similar tales in the walking-tour pamphlet available at the gatehouse, along with a map keyed to famous graves, tree and bird guides, translations of Latin epitaphs, and postings of what's currently in bloom. If all this literature whets your appetite for more, you may wish to join one of the special programs offered by the **Friends of Mount Auburn,** tel. (617) 547-7105; call ahead for current schedule (nominal fee).

CENTRAL CAMBRIDGE

Cambridge has no "downtown," but **Central Square** is the seat of city government, the halfway mark between its largest universities, and the focal point for nearly every bridge from Boston. Possibly the most racially and ethnically diverse part of Cambridge, it has long represented the Left Bank of the Charles at its most funky and affordable, although the latest development boom is chipping away at the neighborhood's unique character with new luxury condos, high-rent office buildings, and Starbucks outlets.

For the time being, though, Central Square is still rich in cheap ethnic eateries, colorful street murals, cool nightclubs, and unique mostly secondhand shopping opportunities. (It's also home to the Good News Garage, run by radio's most popular car guys, Tom and Ray Magliozzi.) Got an invitation to a black-tie event on your social calendar? Drop by **Keezer's,** 140 River St., the king of bargain-priced tuxedos and other high-quality, low-price used clothing (mostly for men).

Or, for less formal pre-owned apparel and costume jewelry, browse through the **Great Eastern Trading Co.,** 49 River Street. If you collect vintage 45s and other pre-CD music media, **Cheapo Records,** 645 Mass. Ave., next to the T station, has tens of thousands of old vinyl platters in every conceivable rock, pop, and R&B category. It carries tapes, too, and used CDs. Down the street, opposite Blockbuster Video, is the equally remarkable **Skippy White's Records,** 538 Mass. Ave., whose half-million vintage 45s should keep serious soul and R&B enthusiasts busy for a while. Skippy's is *the* place to go for gospel, funk, reggae, and rap—new or used, on record or hard-to-find CD. Folk music fans should mosey up a block past the YMCA to **Sandy's Music,** 896 Mass. Ave. Sandy's specializes in new and used folk and Celtic recordings and should also top the list of anyone shopping for an acoustic string instrument, be it a guitar, ukulele, banjo, or fiddle.

For slick arts and crafts boutiques, make tracks for Harvard Square, but if you share the opinion that art is best bought when fresh, check out the **Zeitgeist Gallery,** tel. (617) 623-1065, open Tues.-Sun., at the corner of Norfolk and Broadway, on Central Square's north side, halfway to Inman Square. There's no telling what you might find here: sculptures, drawings, or mixed media, by turns humorous, inscrutable, or, well, an acquired taste.

Like nearly every self-respecting neighborhood in Cambridge, Central Square also has a bookstore: the **Seven Stars,** 731 Mass. Ave., between City Hall and the Red Line station. This bookseller has carved out a unique niche in an otherwise crowded local field with New Age books, cystals, incense, meditation workshops, and psychic readings (open daily).

Central Square is easy to find: exit the eponymous Red Line T station and you're smack dab in the center of it. From Back Bay and Fenway, it's also accessible via a brief ride on the #1 Harvard Square bus, which runs the length of Mass. Ave. Subway riders shouldn't rush up from underground before taking a good look around at the ceramic art in the walls—not just the eye-grabbing enameled tiles, but the often humorous medallions atop the wall columns.

AROUND MIT

Occupying over a mile of riverfront real estate along the lower Charles River basin, the **Massachusetts Institute of Technology** may not be as universally recognized—or as lavishly endowed—as the school up the street, but within some circles it stands alone. In entrepreneurship, for instance: corporate America's roster of CEOs may be top-heavy with Harvard grads, but a growing slice of corporate America (about 150 new companies every year, to be precise) is founded by graduates of MIT. We're not talking about lemonade stands on the corner, either: 80% of the jobs created by these businesses are in manufacturing, and most involve cutting-edge technologies—no surprise, given that MIT is the nation's leading academic generator of new patents. In fact, unless you live on Neptune it's a safe bet someone with an MIT degree created something that's affected your daily life (consider Campbell soups, Gillette razors, aviation radar, and the World Wide Web, to name just a few). Harvard actually came within a hair's breadth of acquiring this prodigious fount of ingenuity back in 1904, when the presidents and trustees of the two schools voted to merge. Only a state Supreme Court veto of the sale of MIT's Back Bay land grant (and a student riot that injured 50) scotched the deal.

MIT also has a mischievous side, as evidenced by its rich culture of sophisticated pranks, or hacks. The hackers who make headlines for cracking into the Pentagon's computers or tying international databanks in knots are direct descendants of MIT's practitioners of collegiate cleverness, although in its purest form a true hack doesn't damage property and is always motivated by fun, not profit. The most spectacular hacks involve putting something outlandish atop the Great Dome, the campus centerpiece plain-

RAGS BY THE POUND

Surrounded by empty lots, unassuming residential streets, and a car-tire dealership, the nondescript building at 200 Broadway in Cambridge seems an unlikely major shopping destination. But observe for even a short while on weekend mornings and you'll witness a pilgrimage. New immigrants, students, urban survivalists, and others arrive and depart like leaf-cutter ants. The latter-day pilgrims come on bicycles, in cars, on foot, some pushing grocery carts, and all leave bearing bulging black trash bags. It's as if a ritual of yard-waste disposal is occurring within, and these people are acolytes of composting, dutifully carting away a mountain of dead leaves.

The building's most visible mark of identification is a sign (styled like the old Superman logo) reading The Garment District. That refers to the way-cool vendor of vintage clothing, ripped Levis, mod accessories, and Elvisiana—worth a gander, if not a pilgrimage, if only to get an eyeful of the decor (open daily; tel. 617-876-5230)—on the *second* floor inside.

But the trash-bag contingent operates *downstairs,* in the home of an outfit called Harbor Waste Textiles—makers of fine baled rags. What in Boston could make people line up for mere rags?

The pilgrims come not for rags in their finished form, but for rags in the raw—i.e., perfectly ordinary used clothes that haven't yet been shredded and bundled. Okay, maybe not *so* ordinary—in fact, often so outlandishly out of fashion as to be almost back in vogue again.

Half the pleasure of this place is that you might actually find something that (a) fits, (b) is in excellent condition, (c) is in a color you can live with, and (d) may even bear a designer label that still carries a cachet—a garment, in short, worth wading through a mountain of wide polyester ties, mawkish baby outfits, and unmatched vinyl-textured drapes. That wading is the other half of the fun. And wade you must, for the merchandise is literally (and liberally) strewn across the warehouse floor.

The name of this 9 a.m.-1 p.m. weekend textile circus is **Dollar-A-Pound** (the price is actually $1.50 per pound—with occasional items at 50 cents per pound—but the name predates a wave or two of inflation), which explains those Hefty bags handed out as you enter—and the big industrial scale used to tally your bill as you exit. It also explains the popularity of the place, since if you hit it lucky you can buy a fine wool vest or pure linen dress for less than it would (or will) cost you to dry-clean it.

ly visible from all over the lower Charles basin. A life-size plastic steer, a mockup of a dorm room and another of a campus police car (complete with flashing lights and box of donuts), and a working telephone booth are a few of the more memorable dome decorations, many of which are profiled in the Hall of Hacks at the **MIT Museum,** 265 Mass. Ave., tel. (617) 253-4444, about five blocks from either Central Square or the Charles River (Tues.-Sun.; $3). This main exhibition center is also home to selections drawn from the world's largest collection of holography, an installation of rather hallucinogenic touch-sensitive plasma globes, and a great gift shop for gizmo- and puzzle-happy shoppers. It's also strategically located between the fragrant New England Confectionery Company and one of Greater Boston's best ice cream shops, **Toscanini's,** on nearby Main St. opposite the Shell station. Though Cambridge is no longer the heart of the nation's confection industry, Necco still churns out its signature sugar wafers, conversation hearts, and varied other sweets in the massive 1927 plant across the street from the museum; to buy something fresh off the production line, simply follow your nose to the **Necco factory store** (Wed.-Fri. 11 a.m.-2 p.m.).

Several other museum collections lay scattered around campus; all are free. Along the ground floor corridor of Building 5 are the **Hart Nautical Galleries,** with 40 ship models illustrating nearly a millennium of maritime design. (With some exceptions, campus buildings are numbered rather than named, in chronological rather than geographical order. Most are physically connected to one another, too. Building 5 is adjacent to MIT's main entrance, at 77 Mass. Ave.; the Hart Galleries are down the hall to the right off the domed lobby, past the Information Office.) Changing exhibits devoted to the interplay be-

tween art and science are found in **The Compton Gallery,** in Building 10 (enter at 77 Mass. Ave. and proceed straight down "the Infinite Corridor" to the lobby beneath the Great Dome; closed weekends). On the east side of campus, near Kendall Square, is the **List Visual Arts Center,** in the Weisner Building at 20 Ames St., tel. (617) 253-4680, a set of galleries devoted to new works by contemporary artists from around the world (Tues.-Sun.). The I. M. Pei-designed Weisner—whose gleaming white, aluminum-covered facade is integrated with the enameled Minimalist tilework of Kenneth Noland—is famous among Internet digerati as the place where *Wired* pundit Nicholas Negroponte and his cohorts come to grips with the future in the legendary Media Lab. The List Center is also where you may purchase a copy of the campus walking-tour guide, an invaluable aid in locating MIT's excellent collection of outsized outdoor artworks by the likes of Henry Moore, Alexander Calder, and Pablo Picasso, as well as notable architectural contributions like Eero Saarinen's elegantly spare MIT Chapel, facing the concave-roofed Kresge Auditorium. Or for a more personal perspective, join one of the student-led tours of campus that depart from the Information Office inside the main lobby at 77 Mass. Ave. (Mon.-Fri. at 10 a.m. and 2 p.m.).

Like Harvard and Central Squares, MIT is served by the #1 bus along its Mass. Ave. front and the Red Line subway at its Kendall Square back. Subway riders should be sure to stop in the Kendall Square station and play "The Kendall Band," a set of three user-activated sound sculptures by Paul Matisse, grandson of the famous French Impressionist: *Galileo, Pythagoras,* and *Johann Kepler* (thunder-making sheet metal, tubular chimes, and resonating hammer-struck steel ring, respectively).

FUN IN THE HUB

The city of Boston offers entertaining diversions for residents and visitors alike. Perhaps you're an early riser. Then head straight for an island picnic on one of those jewels of the Boston Harbor. Or do you prefer to celebrate the midnight hours? Be entertained at one of the many classical venues for the arts—or choose to be the entertainer at the infamous poetry slams of the Cantab Lounge. The spirit of Boston has never been repressed by the clamor of blue-blooded ghosts, but thrives in a way that would make most of our forefathers and mothers proud. As the lively mix of activities below attests, the only problem is finding enough days in the week to play.

THE URBAN OUTDOORS

It's obviously no match for the open spaces of the West—or even western Massachusetts—but Boston is not wholly devoid of fresh-air activities. The finest involve the city's river and harbor: sailing, kayaking, and hiking around offshore islands. Fans of wooded walks and summit views should head out to the Holyoke Range in the Pioneer Valley, a two-hour drive west on the banks of the Connecticut River, or even to Wachusett Mountain, an hour west in central Massachusetts, but if leaving the metro area isn't an option, there's always suburban Milton's **Blue Hills Reservation,** the largest open space within 35 miles of the city and the highest coastal vantage point between Maine and Staten Island. The Blue Hills Trailside Museum and west entrance is on Rt. 138 at I-93 Exit 2; central and eastern trailheads are off I-93's Exits 3, 5, and 6. The center of the reservation is served by the #240 Avon Line and #240A Crawford Square buses, both of which depart from the Red Line's Ashmont station.

Boston Harbor Islands

No other city in the world has such a diadem sitting in its harbor as does Boston. Over 30 drumlins, oval hills of gravelly stone left in the Boston Basin by retreating glaciers, lie scattered within 10 miles of downtown, marooned by rising ocean levels after the end of the last Ice Age. These 10,000-year-old Pleistocene souvenirs, belatedly recognized for their geological, ecological, and historical significance, now make up the **Boston Harbor Islands National Park Area,** tel. (617) 223-8666, a partnership of a dozen public and private property owners and the National Park Service. Explore the ruins of a 19th-century farmhouse or the Civil War fort where Union soldiers composed the song "John Brown's Body." Hunt for wild berries and rose hips overlooked by the abundant bird population or for treasure washed up on shore; pirates are alleged to have used the islands, and a few old ships are known to have run aground on them, scattering 18th- and 19th-century military paraphernalia in the tide-shifted sands. Enjoy wildflowers, salt marshes, wooded trails, and fine views of the city skyline or Boston Light, the oldest lighthouse still in use in the U.S. (and the only offshore one still manned). Maybe you'll catch a glimpse of a shy muskrat, or hear rabbits rustling in the underbrush; in autumn you may spot an early arriving harbor seal spying on you from just offshore. Of the six islands accessible to the public, two have great sandy swimming beaches, and four allow camping (free, but permit required: call 617-727-7676 for details and reservations, and be sure to book ahead—the few dozen sites go fast). The park's gateway island has a snack bar, but neither it nor any of the others have fresh water; come equipped with a proper picnic from the mainland and you'll save yourself a lot of grief. (All six do, however, have composting toilets.) Campers, besides bringing plenty of water, should be sure to pack their food in sturdy animal-proof containers, or be prepared to suspend it from a tree—many critters have come to appreciate the convenience of humans delivering groceries directly to their door.

The park is open between May and mid-October, and access is by boat only. Daily scheduled ferry service is provided every hour 10 a.m.-5 p.m. by Boston Harbor Cruises, tel. (617) 227-4321, from Long Wharf to Georges Island (May-Oct; $8). From Georges, a pair of free water taxis loop around the other islands open to the public—Gallop's, Lovell's, Peddock's, Bumpkin, and Grape—but note that at the beginning and end of the season (before late June and after Labor Day) this service operates on weekends only. Self-guiding tour brochures to these six islands, plus a general map to the whole park and the latest scoop on ranger programs both around the waterfront and on the islands are all available from the ranger-staffed Harbor Island info kiosk at the foot of Long Wharf, immediately in front of the Boston Harbor Cruises Ticket Center.

As an alternative to departing from downtown Boston, South Shore visitors can catch a ferry to the islands from the commuter boat dock at Hingham Bay, where there's plenty of free parking (weekends May-June, daily late June-Labor Day, weekends until mid-October; $8).

If you have your own boat, Georges Island has 12 slips available on a first-come, first-served basis; the other islands have moorings and even provide ship-to-shore skiffs. Off season, the islands are accessible only by such special excursions as February's seal-watching tour of the outer islands, organized by park staff ($10 adults, $8 kids and seniors; tel. 617-727-7676). The Friends of the Boston Harbor Islands, an independent advocacy group, sponsors a half dozen annual sunset tours, each concentrating on a different island (bring a picnic for dining ashore). The visits to Boston Light are the most highly recommended, as no other organization has permission to land on the otherwise unapproachable Coast Guard-owned island of Little Brewster. (Be prepared to climb 92 steep steps from the landing dock to the base of the light.) For information and a schedule, call (617) 740-4290, or check out the Friends' Web page: www/tiac.net/users/fbhi.

The Charles River

Sailors and scullers aren't the only ones who get to enjoy the beauty of an afternoon among the mallards on the Charles. With the aid of the **Charles River Canoe and Kayak Center,** with locations in Brighton and Newton, you can take up a paddle and hit the water yourself. The Brighton location—in Christian Herter Park off Soldier's Field Road a short walk west of Harvard Square—offers access to the river's lower basin; drift downstream toward the busy realm of those athletic rowing teams and regatta racers to get an eyeful of Back Bay and Beacon Hill, or paddle upstream past yacht clubs and old industrial buildings toward the Watertown dam (weekends and holidays only, May through mid-Oct.). A short drive upriver at I-95's Commonwealth Ave./Rt. 30 exit is the center's headquarters, opposite the Newton Marriott on the edge of the river's more placid Norumbega Lake district (daily April through the end of October). The peninsula occupied by the hotel used to be the site of Norumbega Park, an 1897

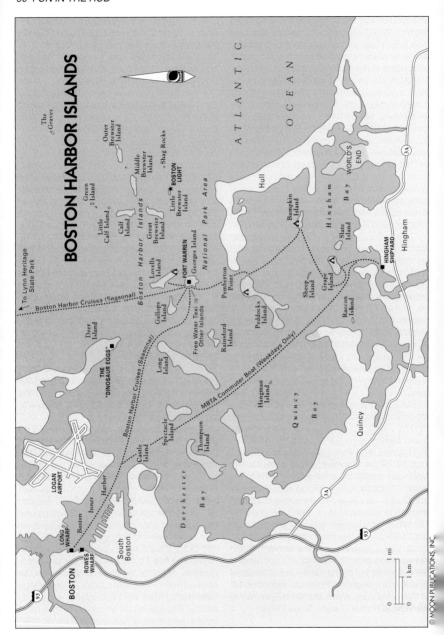

BOSTON HARBOR ISLANDS

amusement complex replete with bandstand, boating, and zoo. Its swan song was the Totem Pole dance hall, a once-famous destination for young fans of big bands, back before Elvis demonstrated what a pair of hips is really good for; canoeists will notice the old park's memory lingers on in the landscaping around the point. Rental rates at both locations are the same, and include everything but the sunblock: $9 per hour and $36 per day for canoes, $10-12 per hour or $40-48 per day for kayaks. Lessons and courses are also available; call (617) 965-5110 to inquire about details.

The Minuteman Bikeway

Along with the Esplanade and Riverbend Park, leisure cyclists and skaters would do well to consider the 11-mile Minuteman Bikeway heading westward out of Cambridge. Starting at the Alewife T station at the end of the Red Line, the paved rail trail follows the former route of the Boston & Lowell Railroad through the western suburbs of Arlington, Lexington, and Bedford, ending just a couple miles short of historic Concord. The scenery isn't all urban backyards: riders pass ponds, wetlands, wood-fringed meadows, and fields with rusting old farm implements, while Canada geese, chickens, and even a couple of horses enliven the view. The first daubs of color come with spring wildflowers; by summer, large patches of showy purple loosestrife emblazon weedy banks along bridge abutments and backyard fences. Another riot of color comes with autumn's turning leaves. Strewn in desiccated piles across the path, these also add a papery crunch under speeding bike tires. Arlington's **Old Schwamb Mill** museum and Lexington's **Battle Green** are among the historic sights just steps away from the Minuteman's route, and it passes straight through the Boston area's oldest railroad depot (now a bank), an unusual shed-sided 1846 structure later given the Colonial Revival makeover it still wears today. Given the bikeway's immense popularity and the fact that it passes within a block of two downtown commercial districts, quick refreshment is never far. Nor are bike rentals: shops are found at both ends and in the middle. To begin in Cambridge, head up to Porter Square's **Bicycle Exchange,** 2067 Mass. Ave., tel. (617) 864-1300

(closed Monday; rents bikes but no skates, and locks aren't included). In Lexington, try **Bikeway Cycle and Sport Center,** 3 Bow St., tel. (781) 861-1199, visible from Mass. Ave/Rt. 4. Contrarians and others who read the last page first—or cross-country skiers looking for a good day's workout close to Boston—should consider renting skates, bikes, or skis from **The Bikeway Source,** tel. (781) 275-7799, 111 South Rd., at the very end of the bikeway in Bedford.

Bike and Skate Rentals

Rental rates are roughly comparable around town, with all-day rentals running about $20 for bikes, $15 for in-line skates. With one notable exception, all safety gear is included free. Expect to plunk down a credit card or huge wad of cash for a security deposit. In general, rentals are made on a first-come, first-served basis, so be sure to show up early on any dry, warm weekend day between April and September. The shops listed are open daily in summer unless otherwise noted.

Downtown, Back Bay, and the South End are served by four shops, two with bikes, three with skates. Name notwithstanding, **Back Bay Bicycles,** 336 Newbury, next to the Trident Bookseller & Cafe, tel. (617) 247-2336, is a good choice for skate rentals, while its bike fleet depends on what used bikes are in stock. Conveniently, you can rent either 'blades or bikes for as little as two hours. Across the street next to the parking garage is an all-skate shop, **Eric Flaim's Motion Sports,** 349 Newbury, tel. (617) 247-3284, which, like Back Bay Bicycles, is less than five blocks from the Esplanade. A second all-skate shop is a block from the Common: **Beacon Hill Skate Shop,** 135 Charles St. South, tel. (617) 482-7400, which also has hourly rates and ice skates in winter. The South End's **Community Bicycle Supply,** 496 Tremont at Berkeley St., tel. (617) 542-6177, rents hybrid mountain bikes only, no skates, and charges $5 extra for helmets. While there are no bike rentals around Harvard Square, skates are available on summer Sundays, when Cambridge's Memorial Drive is closed to all but human locomotion; look for the itinerant skate shop vans parked along Riverbend Park by De Wolfe or Flagg Street.

SPECTATOR SPORTS

Many, many words have been written lamenting Boston's perenially unlucky home team, the **Boston Red Sox.** Come to a home game April-Oct. and decide for yourself whether Babe Ruth's being traded to the New York Yankees in 1920 permanently jinxed the Sox (the "Curse of the Bambino") as you watch another big lead evaporate in the final inning, or another pennant race fizzle in the final stretch. (The Sox won four World Series titles in the early 1900s, the last two with the aid of the Babe. Those were the last Series victories the Sox have seen.) If nothing else, come for the pleasure of baseball in **Fenway Park,** outside Kenmore Square, a small, odd-angled 1912 ballpark irresistibly unimproved by a retracting dome top, sushi vendors, Astro-Turf, or Sunbelt weather ($10-30; ticket charge tel. 617-267-1700).

Michael "King" Kelley, baseball player of the early 1900s

If the plans of the Red Sox front office come true, old Fenway and its infamous left-field wall (the intimidating "Green Monster") will be replaced soon—and, no doubt, eulogized, just as the humid old 1920s Boston Garden arena is reminisced about from the upholstered, climate-controlled comfort of its replacement, the 1995 **FleetCenter.** Built over the Commuter Rail's North Station, on Causeway Street at the foot of the North End, the 19,000-seat Fleet is palatial home to basketball's storied **Boston Celtics** and ice hockey's **Boston Bruins,** as well as host to annual visits from the Ringling Brothers and Barnum & Bailey Circus, Disney World on Ice, the Harlem Globetrotters, champion figure-skating revues, and major rock concerts. The Celtics season runs Nov.-April ($10-85; tel. 617-523-3030), the Bruins Oct.-April ($15-65; tel. 617-624-1000). Fans of pro football have to head south, to Foxboro, to catch the action of the New England Patriots (and pro soccer's New England Revolution), tel. (800) 543-1776, although you can see the legendary Ivy League rivalry of the Harvard-Yale game right at Harvard Stadium, across the river from Harvard Square, in November on even-numbered years (ticket office tel. 617-495-2211).

The Sox may draw crowds of 34,000 when they get on a roll, but that's peanuts compared to the crowds that turn up for the world-renowned **Boston Marathon,** tel. (617) 236-1652, whose finish line is in Copley Square. Over a million spectators typically turn out each April to cheer on the thousands of runners competing in America's oldest marathon, first run in 1897. The 26.2-mile event coincides with a state holiday, Patriot's Day, celebrated on the Monday closest to the April 19 anniversary of the American Revolution's opening salvos. (April was originally the month of Massachusetts's Fast Day, one of three holidays permitted by 17th-century Puritans—the other two were the Sabbath and Thanksgiving—but patriotism replaced penance three years before the first marathon.) VIP reviewing stands and media towers make it hard to get a front-row glimpse of the finish unless you have influential friends among the race sponsors, but Boylston Street in front of the Pru, Comm. Ave. between Mass. Ave. and Kenmore Square, and the entire aboveground route of the Green "C" Line all afford good sideline views of the final few miles.

A big turnout is always assured the third weekend in October, too, for the **Head of the Charles Regatta,** tel. (617) 864-8415, the world's largest rowing competition, which attracts thousands of athletes from around the world. Six bridges and miles of riverbank afford plenty of good vantage points from the Boston University starting line to the finish three miles upstream, beside Christian Herter Park in Brighton. Since Cambridge closes several major streets to traffic on the busier second day of the weekend event, you'll usually find Party Central along the riverfront by Harvard University—and anyone who gets claustrophobic in happy throngs of 300,000 should steer clear of Harvard Square then.

Followers of men's tennis may want to catch the **U.S. Pro Tennis Championship** tournament, tel. (617) 731-4500, held each August at the Longwood Cricket Club, 564 Hammond St. in Brookline, immediately adjacent to the Chestnut Hill stop on the Green "D" Line (third or fourth week of the month).

If racket sports are too refined for your tastes since John McEnroe retired, hop on the Blue Line to **Wonderland Greyhound Park,** tel. (781) 284-1300. There, you can cheer on the l'il doggies chasing Swifty around the track (daily year-round). It's the last stop on the line, on the V.F.W.

Parkway in Revere. Gamblers who won't bet on anything smaller than a horse need only get off the Blue Line a stop earlier to find themselves at **Suffolk Downs,** Waldemar Ave., recorded info and race results tel. (617) 568-3216, home to thoroughbred racing from the end of September through the first week of June.

TOURS

On Foot
There are scores of guided walking tours of the city, and they aren't confined to just the summer months. The **Boston Park Rangers** sponsor a broad and varying menu of weekly, monthly, seasonal, and annual walks (and rides) throughout the city park system, all free. Call the recorded Events Line (617-635-3445) to find out what's up, when, and where, or pick up a brochure from the Boston Common Information Center on Tremont Street. Among the regular offerings: one-hour walks around the Common and the Public Garden; a stroll along the Commonwealth Avenue Mall; hiking and biking tours of the entire Emerald Necklace, from the Common to Franklin Park; and several flora and fauna tours in Jamaica Plain's portion of the Necklace,

TOUR DE GRAVES

One of Boston's unique ways of welcoming fall is with the annual **Tour de Graves,** an all-day 25-mile bike ride around Boston's historic graveyards on a weekend in October. A fundraiser for the city's Historic Burying Grounds Initiative (coordinator of conservation and restoration work in 16 graveyards), each year's tour is slightly different. All include downtown burying grounds you could visit on your own, but most of the other stops are truly obscure—often hidden in residential neighborhoods behind brick walls or locked gates. At each site, local historians discuss gravestone art and its symbolism, trends in landscaping and urban settlement, and famous residents. The ride is such a popular way to visit neigh-

borhoods otherwise far removed from the usual tourist path that it's routinely booked to capacity, and advance registration is absolutely required (fee includes a picnic lunch). Call (617) 635-4505 ext. 6516 for entry forms (or to contribute to beautification and restoration efforts, or for information about the Initiative), or write to the Historic Burying Grounds Initiative, Boston Parks & Recreation Dept., 1010 Massachusetts Ave., 3rd floor, Boston, MA 02118.

For **bike rentals** near the tour's Boston Common starting point try **Back Bay Bicycles,** 336 Newbury, in Back Bay, tel. (617) 247-2336, or Community Bicycle Supply, 496 Tremont at Berkeley St., in the South End, tel. (617) 542-6177.

from Olmsted Park's ponds to the Arnold Arboretum's trees. The rangers also celebrate Black History Month (February) and Women's History Month (March) with appropriately thematic tours around downtown. Selected park tours are even conducted in winter—on cross-country skis.

A top contender among paid tours is the non-profit **Boston by Foot,** tel. (617) 367-3766 (24-hour recorded schedule), whose large repertoire includes separate architectural/historical walks for over half a dozen different downtown neighborhoods, plus an ever-popular "Underground Boston" tour, walks aimed at kids 6-12 years old, and an annual five-hour "Big Foot" Labor Day romp for serious urban hikers. The frequency of the walks ranges from daily to weekly, May 1-Oct. 31. Reservations are never necessary; just show up at the appointed time and place and off you go ($6-8). Promoting awareness of the city's heritage is also the mission of **The Historic Neighborhoods Foundation,** tel. (617) 426-1885, another nonprofit organization, which funds its extensive school programs with June-Sept. walks around Beacon Hill and the Public Garden/Back Bay ($5). It also does kids' walks around Chinatown, the Waterfront, and other downtown neighborhoods, and a couple of annual "neighborhood discovery" tours —no two are alike, and not all are on foot. Past examples: a tour of Boston churches with Tiffany stained-glass windows, an Irish pub crawl, and a visit to the Boston Harbor Islands. Call for prices and schedules.

For architecture and urban history specific to the mid- to late 19th century, join the walks conducted by **The Victorian Society in America,** at the Gibson House Museum, 137 Beacon St., tel. (617) 267-6338. Call or visit to obtain a calendar of upcoming tours, which range all over the metropolitan map, or to reserve a space on the next one (nearly year-round; $7).

If you have a group interested in Boston's social history, call **Discovering Boston Walking Tours,** tel. (617) 323-2554, for an insightful walk with Will Holton, a Northeastern University sociology professor. Holton weaves historical fact and contemporary observation to expose continuity here and evolution there, revealing Boston through a single church building's changing congregations, for example, rather than a who's who of prominent dead men. In addition to walks along the Freedom Trail, Holton conducts tours with such varied themes as Boston's ethnic diversity, sports history, and tabloid tales of infamous crimes and felons.

Across the Charles River, the **Cambridge Historical Society,** tel. (617) 547-4252, holds an appropriately eclectic series of walking tours over four spring weekends, beginning the last Sunday of April. Each is unique and concentrates thoroughly on the layers of social and architectural history within a relatively small section of the city. Call ahead to find out where to rendezvous with the tour leader ($10).

Other special walking tours on both sides of the river are sometimes highlighted in the "Cheap Thrills" and "Events" listings of the "Calendar" section in each Thursday's *Boston Globe.*

Chauffeured

Whether you're tired, in a hurry, or looking for a new perspective, several outfits stand ready to provide a Boston-in-a-day whirlwind tour without you having to either lift a toe or carry change for parking meters. The one with the best gimmick by far is **Boston Duck Tours,** tel. (617) 723-DUCK, whose vintage-WW II amphibious vehicles cut a distinctive and colorful swath through city traffic April-November. Departing from the Huntington Ave. side of the Pru, these streetwise steel tubs make a circle through Back Bay and downtown, plus a much-anticipated drive straight into the Charles River for a little cruise around the Esplanade. The quack-filled commentary is several notches above the rest, but sheer novelty is the big draw: nobody else can touch the Duck's-eye view of the city from out among the gulls and cormorants—neither do any other tours let kids take a turn at the tiller. Not surprisingly, it's the one tour guaranteed to sell out hours ahead of time, so plan accordingly. Tickets are all sold inside the Pru's main shopping concourse, with a limited number available up to two days in advance; departures are every half hour from 9 a.m. to an hour before sunset, rain or shine ($21, discounts for kids, seniors, and military).

More conventional, bus-style excursions are available year-round from Gray Line's **Beantown Trolleys,** tel. (617) 236-2148 ($20 adults, $16 seniors and students, $6 kids); **Old Town**

Trolley Tours, tel. (617) 269-7010 ($21 adults, $8 kids); and **Minuteman Tours,** tel. (617) TROLLEY ($23 adults, $9 kids). All three are narrated by drivers whose ability to keep cool and chatty in Boston traffic deserves more admiration than the depth and accuracy of their scripts. If it's door-to-door convenience you're after more than the color commentary, it's probably cheaper and faster to use taxicabs, since the trolleys are confined to wide and heavily trafficked arterial streets as far from specific attrac-

tions as any T station. Tickets are available from most major hotels, the "Trolley Stop" storefront at the corner of Charles and Boylston, and booths set up on Boston Common near Park Street Station; or just step aboard and the driver will help you.

Harbor Cruises
The cheapest way to see the city from the water —or to catch a closer glimpse of the city's resident porpoises—is to simply take **MBTA ferries**

BOSTON WHALERS

Both Gloucester and Provincetown are closer than Boston to the great whale feeding grounds of Stellwagen Bank, but if those towns aren't in your travel plans, you can hop a boat from Boston's waterfront and enjoy a brisk afternoon on the high seas and a powwow with whales. Unless otherwise noted, all boats accept credit cards and depart from within two blocks of the Aquarium T station.

New England Aquarium, Central Wharf. You'll pay more, but there's good reason. Passengers also have access to a fish finder, navigation radar, and weather instruments; a "wet lab" touch pool filled with tidal critters; and a CD-ROM terminal with a database of New England's known whales, identified by markings. Plus, narration on the voyage is provided by naturalists privy to the Aquarium's latest cetacean research. Tours run weekends only in April and the latter half of October, daily May through Columbus Day ($24 adults, $16.50-19 kids and seniors); recorded schedule and sightings tel. (617) 973-5277, reservations 973-5281. Final payment must be in cash or traveler's checks.

A.C. Cruise Line, 290 Northern Ave., in South Boston, past the World Trade Center, tel. (800) 422-8419. Tours run weekends only May-June, Tues.-Sun. from late June through early September ($19 adults, $14 kids and seniors). Pier is a 20-minute walk from South Station or the Aquarium T station, or a short bus ride on the #6 Boston Marine Industrial Park or #7 City Point

from South Station (no Sunday service). On weekends, A.C. also has free parking on its pier.

Boston Harbor Cruises, tel. (617) 227-4321, Long Wharf and Rowes Wharf. BHC's principal offering is its five-hour "safari" cruise, departing daily May through mid-October from behind their can't-miss ticket center on Long Wharf ($23 adults, $17-20 kids and seniors). For a few dollars more during the peak of summer they also offer a three-hour version aboard a high-speed catamaran, which spends the same amount of time out among the whales, but subtracts from the leisurely voyage there and back. This vessel departs daily July-Labor Day from Rowes Wharf, behind the Boston Harbor Hotel.

Boston Harbor Whale Watch, tel. (617) 345-9866, Rowes Wharf. Tours run weekends only the last two weeks of June, then daily July through early September ($21 adults, $18 kids and seniors).

Mass Bay Lines, tel. (617) 542-8000, Rowes Wharf. Daily departures late June through early October ($22 adults, $18 kids and seniors).

JEFF PERK

around the inner harbor. They're noisier up on deck than the tourist boats (they're smaller, so passengers are closer to the engines), and they don't make lazy detours to maximize photo ops, but the scenery is the same, and the price can't be beat: all are just $1. The only one that operates daily—and late enough in summer to catch sunsets—is the one that shuttles between the base of Long Wharf, next to the New England Aquarium, and the Charlestown Navy Yard. Weekdays, you have a couple more options: at the Navy Yard you can connect to a second ferry to Lovejoy Wharf, behind North Station and the FleetCenter; from Lovejoy, continue to the World Trade Center in South Boston, a scenic 20-minute journey down the length of the inner harbor (bring earplugs). Service is most frequent during morning and evening rush hours; middays, the South Boston boat operates only once an hour. Schedules for all these ferries are available at the Long Wharf gangway, or simply ask the crew.

For a more typically tourist-oriented ride, Long Wharf's **Boston Harbor Cruises**, tel. (617) 227-4321, and nearby Rowes Wharf's **Mass Bay Lines**, tel. (617) 542-8000, each offer basic 45- to 55-minute narrated trips around the inner harbor, ideal for a brown-bag picnic lunch on a hot day (it's always much cooler on the water). Both have multiple daily departures late May through early October; fares are $8. BHC also offers a weekday half-hour lunch cruise for a mere $2, plus sunset cruises, 90-minute outer harbor loops, and trips to the Boston Harbor Islands ($8-15). Mass Bay Lines runs evening party cruises with live bands (blues on Wednesday, rock on Thursday, June-Sept.; $15). For classy (if expensive) onboard dining and dancing, consider the sleek *Spirit of Boston*, tel. (617) 457-1450, or the sleeker *Odyssey*, tel. (888) 741-0275, for lunch and dinner cruises, sunset cocktails *(Spirit)*, or jazz brunch *(Odyssey)*. The *Spirit* departs daily year-round from Commonwealth Pier, next to the World Trade Center out on Northern Ave. in South Boston. The *Odyssey*, which looks like it belongs in a James Bond movie, has the more demanding dress code of the two (as well as the more contemporary food and music); it departs daily from Rowes Wharf, behind the Boston Harbor Hotel.

Perhaps more befitting Boston's maritime history are the S/V *Liberty* and its sister, the S/V *Liberty Clipper,* the only regularly scheduled cruise ships with masts. For atmosphere, it's hard to beat running under sail aboard an 80- or 125-foot schooner, especially at sunset. When the winds howl and small motorized craft head for shelter, join the "30-knot club" and find out what it means for a boat to have a "bone in her teeth." Besides weighing anchor ($25) several times a day from mid-May through early October at Long Wharf's Waterboat Marina, tel. (617) 742-0333, the *Liberty* sisters also play host to "Tall Ship Theatre" on weekends ($35), telling tales of Boston's shipwrecks and pirates with song, dance, rattling chains, and other swashbuckling mischief suitable for all ages—be prepared to salute the Jolly Roger and share your grog.

Brewery Tours

When it comes to beer-making, Boston is an old hand: its tradition goes all the way back to the Puritans, who brewed ales from malt and spice. In fact, until the triple whammy of Prohibition, Depression, and a postwar preference for Budweiser all but killed off the local industry, Boston's 26 breweries placed the city among the top rank of beer producers in the country. After a generation lost to insipid national brands, green-bottled imports, and that brief fling with Bartles & Jaymes, Bostonians are increasingly turning to microbrews from nearly a dozen new home-grown brewpubs and breweries. Of these, three offer public tours and tastings, so if you've got a huge thirst for beer that needs quenching—or simply want to learn about what goes into a fine, small-batch ale—consider paying a visit to these guys while you're in town:

Atlantic Coast Brewing Co., 50 Terminal St., Charlestown, tel. (617) 242-6464. A.k.a. the Tremont Brewery, this is the smallest of the lot, producing less than 8,000 barrels of beer a year. Tremont Ale is the signature brew in their line of fine English-style ales, produced with British barley malt and a Yorkshire strain of yeast. Seasonal offerings include a porter, bitter, strong ale, and the very special Old Scratch Barley Wine prepared just in time to improve your recollection of the lyrics to "Auld Lang Syne" and other holiday chestnuts. Tours Friday 4 p.m. and Saturday 1 p.m. year-round. For a great day of barbecue, beer, and local bands, check out the **Tremont Brewery Music Fest,** the fourth Saturday of June. The brewery's home is the hulking brick Charlestown Commerce Center, beside the Mystic River less than 10 minutes walk north of the Bunker Hill Monument, at the rear of Building 2 on the side facing the Tobin Bridge.

Boston Beer Co., 30 Germania St., Jamaica Plain, tel. (617) 368-5212, was begun in the mid-1980s by Harvard MBA Jim Koch. This producer of Sam Adams Lager spearheaded the city's modern craft beer revival, but has since leapfrogged out of the ranks of the microbrews and into the realm of the big national brands. Although none of its bottled product has ever, in fact, been made in Boston, its small Jamaica Plain brewery supplies local draft accounts, affording tour participants a chance to sample from the full range of Sam Adams styles. Tours are held year-round Thurs.-Fri. at 2 p.m. and Saturday at noon, 1, and 2 p.m., as well as Wednesday at 2 p.m. July-Aug. Tour donation $1.

Mass Bay Brewing Co., 306 Northern Ave., tel. (888) HARPOON or (617) 574-9551 ext. 33, is more familiarly known as the Harpoon Brewery. This outfit manages to project a happy-go-lucky air as it goes about producing barrels and bottles of its regular ales and pilsner, plus such seasonal offerings as the spring Maibock or year-end Winter Warmer. Tours Fri.-Sat. 1 p.m. year-round, except on holiday weekends. Tours are also suspended during special brewery festivities such as the mammoth **Harpoon Brewstock,** held in the parking lot the first Thurs.-Sat. in June, and featuring all-day party music from a raft of local bands (admission). Located in a plain two-story building on the South Boston waterfront, about a mile from the Financial District, the brewery may be reached on foot from Museum Wharf (15- 20 minute walk due east on Northern Avenue) or from the World Trade Center dock of the Lovejoy Wharf-WTC ferry (5-10 minute walk).

PERFORMING ARTS

For a general roundup of what's on stages and in clubs around town, pick up a copy of the *Boston Globe* (whose club listings are limited to Thurs-

day's "Calendar" and Sunday's "City" sections), the overpriced weekly *Phoenix,* or the free weekly *Tab,* in the red plastic newsboxes on streetcorners around town. If you know what you want to see, call **TicketMaster,** tel. (617) 931-2000, and charge by phone, or go directly to the box office if it's vital that you see what seats are available. If you want to scope out the menu of what's on stage around town tonight and at what price, visit a ticket agency. Best is **BosTix,** tel. (617) 723-5181 (10 a.m.-6 p.m. Mon.-Sat., 11 a.m.-4 p.m. Sunday), a cash-only discounter and TicketMaster outlet in the little round kiosks next to Faneuil Hall (closed Monday) and in front of Trinity Church in Copley Square, as well as on the ground floor of Harvard's Holyoke Center, among the Shops at Harvard Square. Its specialty is half-price same-day tickets to nearly everything from baseball to ballet, but it also sells full-price advance tickets. You can't beat the 50% discount by going in person to theater box offices—most day-of-sale rush tickets are reserved for students with valid IDs (the Boston Symphony Orchestra is an exception). While it doesn't do discounts, the **Hub Ticket Agency,** tel. (617) 426-8340 (9 a.m.-5 p.m. Mon.-Fri., to noon Saturday), in the trailer at the corner of Tremont and Stuart in the heart of the Theater District, does do credit cards—and covers the full panoply of concert, theater, comedy club, and sports events. If you're near Copley Square, try Back Bay Station's **Out-of-Town Ticket and Sport Charge,** tel. (617) 492-1900 or (800) 442-1854 (9 a.m.-5:30 p.m. Mon.-Fri.), on Dartmouth St., across from Neiman-Marcus. It accepts plastic and phone orders, and has the standard selection of tickets at its fingertips. All agencies charge fees for their services.

As for those occasional hot bands whose local appearances are guaranteed sell-outs, your best bet is to either call TicketMaster, tel. (617) 931-2000 (unless, of course, it's a Pearl Jam show or you're ethically opposed to the T-meister's monopolistic behavior), or visit the cash-only **Ticketron** counter at any Tower Records or Strawberries music store.

Theater and Opera

Most of Boston's major stages continue to maintain their historic attachment to Broadway, now as the first stop for blockbuster touring companies rather than as the tryout capital for new plays. As an alternative to hopping an express to Manhattan, the gilded palaces at Chinatown's perimeter do very nicely, although sometimes their meticulously restored Beaux Arts interiors outshine the action on stage. **The Wang Center for the Performing Arts,** tel. (617) 482-9393, at 270 Tremont, is the city's pride, its 3,700 seats and marbled decor ideally suited for Broadway's biggest musical extravaganzas. The smaller **Wilbur Theatre,** next door, tel. (617) 426-7491 ext. 13, and the Wang-affiliated **Shubert Theatre,** across the street, also book New York's boxoffice hits. The Shubert, whose pearly-white interior sports such flights of plaster fancy as to make a cake decorator swoon, is also home to the **Boston Lyric Opera** (Oct.-Mar.), whose productions may, like all Shubert events, be booked through the Wang box office. The dashing, gold-clad **Colonial Theatre,** tel. (617) 426-9366, two blocks away at 106 Boylston St., op-

posite the Common, hosts a mix of Broadway and off-Broadway plays, occasionally tempered by such performers as Penn & Teller, among others.

At the nether end of alley-like Warrenton St., behind the Shubert, is the intimate twin-stage **Charles Playhouse,** occupying an 1839 Asher Benjamin-designed church hemmed in by the broad brick backsides of its neighbors. It's best known as the 1980 birthplace of *Shear Madness,* tel. (617) 426-5225, an ongoing interactive comic whodunit that's been franchised to six other American cities and nearly a dozen international ones. Whether or not the Chicago, Budapest, or Buenos Aires versions are popular favorites, none quite compares to the original, whose thousands of consecutive performances have earned it a place in the *Guinness Book of World Records* as the nation's longest-running nonmusical show. The larger stage upstairs, tel. (617) 426-6912, is currently home to the slyly irrepressible Blue Man Group, whose nearly in-

---

ANNUAL MUSICAL EVENTS

A Joyful Noise, tel. (617) 495-4968, Saturday nearest January 15. A gospel concert in honor of Dr. Martin Luther King held at Sanders Theatre, in Harvard University's Memorial Hall, on the Red Line; admission.

Burns Night, tel. (617) 495-4968, Saturday nearest January 25. Celebrates the birthday of Scottish poet Robert Burns, at Sanders Theatre; admission.

WBOS EarthFest, tel. (617) 787-0929, the fourth Saturday of April. Celebrates Earth Day with a full afternoon of nationally known rock bands performing live at the Hatch Memorial Shell on the Charles River Esplanade; free. Note that the buses, trolleys, and subways of the T are also free all day long, also in honor of Earth Day.

Scottish Fiddle Rally, tel. (617) 271-0958, April or early May. Boston's large Cape Breton community (second in the U.S. only to Detroit) ensures a strong Nova Scotian showing among the guest artists at this festival held at the Somerville Theater, in Davis Square, on the Red Line; admission.

Blacksmith House Dulcimer Festival, tel. (617) 547-6789, in May. At the Cambridge Center for Adult Education, 56 Brattle St., in Harvard Square; admission.

Boston Globe Jazz & Blues Festival, tel. (617) 929-2649, June. At venues all around downtown, including lots of free outdoor performances at the Charles River Esplanade's Hatch Shell.

Celtic Festival, tel. (617) 271-0958, Saturday of Labor Day weekend. At the Hatch Shell on the Esplanade; free.

Sing-along *Messiah,* tel. (617) 262-1120 ext. 700, late November or early December. This New England Conservatory production—one of several renditions of George Frideric Handel's holiday chestnut that invites audience participation—is staged in Jordan Hall, 30 Gainsborough St.; admission.

HUNTINGTON THEATRE COMPANY/T. CHARLES ERICKSON

Huntington Theatre performers in Eugene O'Neill's Ah, Wilderness

describable blend of plastic tubes, art criticism, Cap'n Crunch, and toilet paper has acquired a cult following on par with the *Rocky Horror Picture Show.*

The district's second-oldest survivor is the 1903 **Emerson Majestic Theatre,** tel. (617) 824-8000, at 219 Tremont Street. (The oldest, the 1836 Bijou Theater on Washington St., is currently condemned to life as a video arcade.) The Majestic eschews Andrew Lloyd Webber and murder mysteries in favor of an eclectic mix by a variety of troupes. Originally built for opera, the crown jewel of adjacent Emerson College's Division of Performing Arts is known as an "empty house" in the trade, available to whomever has pockets deep enough to fill it. Any given season is guaranteed to include professionally assisted Emerson student productions, full-scale operatic works by the **New England Conservatory Opera Theater** (Feb.-April), and an annual Thanksgiving season Gilbert and Sullivan production by the **Boston Academy of Music.** Dance and music groups are also among its regular tenants.

Since crowd pleasers and good theater aren't always synonymous, there are a couple regional stages that take up where the pop musicals leave off. The **Huntington Theatre Company,** tel. (617) 266-0800, professionals in residence at Boston University, presents one of the best theatrical seasons in town at its well-appointed namesake on Huntington Ave. diagonally across from Symphony Hall. (Periodically, selected productions also appear in downtown venues such as the Shubert.) Besides reviving American classics and premiering recent works by top English-language playwrights from either side of the Atlantic, it's the only major Boston stage that consistently gives African-American playwrights their due (Sept.-May). And though the Huntington sticks to mostly traditional stagings, it's also produced such diverse fare as Anna Deavere Smith's *Twilight: Los Angeles, 1992,* pre-war style Berlin cabaret, and the musical *Nomathemba,* featuring Ladysmith Black Mambazo. By contrast, Cambridge's **American Repertory Theatre,** tel. (617) 547-8300, goes for more spectacle, contemporizing classic dramas (with mixed results), reprising past winners (Andrei Serban's version of Carlo Gozzi's *King Stag* is a perennial delight), and premiering new works by the likes of David Mamet, Derek Walcott, Dario Fo, Phillip Glass, and Robert Wilson. It's also a regular venue for performance artists. Established by Robert Brustein, founder of the Yale Repertory Theatre, the A.R.T. makes its home at the Loeb Drama Center, 64 Brattle St. outside Harvard Square, with occasional performances at other stages in the area (Oct.-June). Be advised that on-street parking for nonresidents is virtually nonexistent in these parts.

One of the virtues of **The Lyric Stage,** tel. (617) 437-7172, opposite the Hard Rock Cafe in the YWCA at Clarendon and Stuart (Sept.-May), is that it's so intimate; no seat is more than about 30 feet from the stage. It's also fairly affordable, although the lower ticket prices are off-set by an increased risk of winding up at a dud. The same holds true of the **Nora Theatre Company,** tel. (617) 495-4530, performing at various locations around town. Equally risky, but often buoyed by more artistic passion, are the various small troupes sharing Tremont Street's **Boston Center for the Arts,** tel. (617) 426-0320, in the South End between Berkeley and Clarendon. **The Coyote Theatre** and **Threshold Theatre** are two residents on the BCA's roster whose sharp-edged productions tend to be worth the walk across the MassPike from the Theater District or Back Bay. Finally, if you notice a current production by the **Beau Jest Moving Theatre,** tel. (617) 437-0657, buried in the small print of the theater listings, run, don't walk, to catch it. Though infrequent and often wacky, Beau Jest gives audiences some of Boston's best live entertainment for the money, usually in a small "black box" space at the South End's Piano Factory, 791 Tremont, four blocks from the Mass. Ave. Orange Line station.

Dance

Several top-ranked academic dance programs call Massachusetts home, making the state a hotbed of kinetic research, particularly in the Five College area of the Pioneer Valley. Although Boston's dance community is imperiled—as are all the city's artists—by a chronic lack of affordable studio space, for the time being Boston still benefits from many formally trained dance students sticking around after graduation, supplemented by professionals escaping New York's even higher cost of living and others drawn in from outside academia. With so many modern improvisers here—many of whom contribute choreography to nationally known dance companies—there's no reason why you should go home without a dose of good dance. Scan the listings in Thursday's *Globe* or the *Phoenix* for such sure-bet performers as the intergenerational, all-women Back Porch Dance Company, Caitlin Corbett Dance, the jazz-inspired Impulse Dance Company, or Paula Josa-Jones & Company. You'll also be fairly certain to get your money's worth at any performance at the **Dance Complex,** 536 Mass. Ave., tel. (617) 547-9363, or nearby **Green Street Studios,** 185 Green St., tel. (617) 864-3191, both in Cambridge's

Central Square. (The Dance Complex sponsors an open movement improv jam every other Monday night at 8 p.m. for $6, if you're inspired to do more than just spectate. All ages and abilities are welcome.) For a preview of modern dance's next generation of aspiring professionals, check out the **Boston Conservatory Dance Theater,** tel. (617) 536-3063, whose three faculty recitals and student productions take place between late October and early March at the Conservatory's own theater, 31 Hemenway St. near the Green Line Hynes/ICA station.

If you're leery of spending $12 on works-in-progress in church assembly rooms, or if you just don't want to be so close to the raw edge of alternative movement techniques, there's **Dance Umbrella,** tel. (617) 492-7578, presenting contemporary and multicultural dance. The company has done the hard work of sifting for the gold amid the gravel, not just locally but all over the world, so an Umbrella-sponsored performance is just about guaranteed to blow away your preconceptions about dance. The company's Oct.-June season is staged at well-appointed venues around Boston, from the Theater District's Wang Center and Emerson Majestic to the Tsai Performance Center at Boston University, 685 Comm. Ave. on the Green "B" Line.

Traditionalists will be relieved to know that Boston is also graced with not one but two ballet companies, including the critically acclaimed **Boston Ballet,** in residence at the Wang Center, tel. (617) 695-6955 box office, 482-9393 recorded info. Internationally respected for its sheer virtuosity and grand stagings, the company performs a half dozen classic works Oct.-May, punctuating its season in December with that perennial holiday favorite, *The Nutcracker.* José Mateo's **Ballet Theatre of Boston,** tel. (617) 824-8000, also bends to the popularity of Tchaikovsky's old chestnut in December, which launches the company's short Dec.-April season. Dedicated exclusively to its founder's choreography, the Ballet Theatre's singular magic may be enjoyed at the Emerson Majestic Theatre on Tremont St., a block from the Green Line's Boylston station.

Concerts and Recitals

When it comes to classical, early, and even avant-garde music, Boston boasts an embar-

ORGAN MUSIC

Boston is blessed with a number of fine pipe organs, and, since several downtown churches sponsor regular music programs, you don't have to sit through a sermon or a service to catch an earful of them.

On Fridays September through mid-June, **Trinity Church,** on Copley Square, tel. (617) 536-0944, holds half-hour noontime recitals (donations). Friend, if the voices of those 6,898 pipes don't get your mojo working, at least you came to the right place to ask for help.

On Thursdays Oct.-May, the **Cathedral Church of St. Paul,** 138 Tremont St., opposite Park Street Station, tel. (617) 482-4826 ext. 103, sponsors a more general weekly series of vocal and instrumental works, many of which showcase the church's huge 135-rank organs. Recitals start at 12:45 p.m. (donations accepted).

A couple of blocks away, at **King's Chapel,** on the corner of Tremont and School Streets, tel. (617) 227-2155, the baroque sounds of the C. B. Fisk organ are frequently featured either solo or as part of the chapel's eclectic series of classical, jazz, and pop music, offered every Tuesday at 12:15 p.m. year-round (donations).

On Tuesday evenings June-Aug., Boston's **Old West Church,** 131 Cambridge St., tel. (617) 266-2957, near the MBTA Bowdoin Station, hosts solo organ recitals on another excellent Fisk organ, starting at 8 p.m. (donations).

Across the river in Cambridge, the **Organ Recitals at Harvard,** tel. (617) 496-3192, showcase acclaimed national and international guest artists performing on the Adolphus Busch Hall's Flentrop organ, at 29 Kirkland St. behind Harvard Yard. Recitals begin at 3 p.m. every third or fourth Sunday Oct.-Nov. and Jan.-April ($5). The popular March event is always a tribute to E. Power Biggs, who commissioned the Busch Hall instrument (the organ donor, as it were). For a special gothic treat, there's also a free midnight concert every Halloween.

For a calendar of hundreds of organ concerts and recitals all over New York and New England, point your Web browser to http://www.cybercom.net/~tneorg, the homepage of *The Northeast Organist.* For a regular, printed subscription to the magazine, call (800) 841-4030.

rassment of riches. Devotees of PBS's "Evening at Symphony" broadcasts will recognize the city's preeminent musical institution, the **Boston Symphony Orchestra,** whose turn-of-the-century home, Symphony Hall, is considered one of the most acoustically perfect concert halls ever built in the U.S. The BSO's regular season runs from late September through early May; come summer, music director Seiji Ozawa and crew take up residence at Tanglewood, in western Massachusetts's Berkshire Hills. Wednesday evening and Thursday morning open rehearsals are a little over half the price ($14) of the cheapest regular performance ticket, but even better (if you can get them) are the $7.50 rush tickets to Tuesday and Thursday evening and Friday afternoon performances. Available only couple hours in advance, rush tickets must be purchased at the Huntington Avenue entrance. Also sharing Symphony Hall is the famous **Boston Pops,** which became America's most recognizable orchestra under the late, great Arthur Fiedler. Keith Lockhart, the latest Pops conductor, has brought them back to their old winning ways with sold-out world tours and chart-topping CDs. Catch the Pops in person May-July or alfresco at their Hatch Shell performances on the Charles River Esplanade from the end of June through July 4. For recorded info on BSO and Pops concerts and ticket prices, or to charge tickets by phone, call SymphonyCharge, (888) 266-1200, or (617) 266-1200. Tickets may also be purchased through the BSO's Web site, www.bso.org.

Boston is also home to the nation's oldest active performing arts group: the **Handel & Haydn Society,** tel. (617) 266-3605, founded in 1815—back when a Harvard education cost about $300 and there were only 19 states in the Union. Specializing in period performances—played on instruments and in styles appropriate to the selections—H&H presents chamber, symphonic, and choral works between October and early June, usually on a single Friday and Sunday each month. Handel's *Messiah,* which seems to have become the *It's a Wonderful Life* of choral groups, is a December staple, but the society is no newcomer on this fabulous oratorio's bandwagon: they've performed it annually since 1854. Concerts are usually held in Symphony Hall, across the street in the New England Conservatory's Jordan Hall, or occasionally at Sanders Theatre, in Harvard University's Memorial Hall, next to the Science Center. All are within a block of a T station. Jordan and Sanders are also home to the period instruments of the popular **Boston Baroque,** tel. (617) 641-1310, whose Nov.-April season of vocal and orchestral performances always includes a delightful "First Day" New Year's matinee concert—and, yes, the *Messiah,* too. Baroque is as *modern* as you'll get in the **Boston Early Music Festival Concerts,** tel. (617) 661-1812 or 262-0650, whose programs are as likely to feature medieval harps, Renaissance lutes, and a cappella court music as often as Bach and Vivaldi. Performances are held in chapels and churches when appropriate, as well as Jordan Hall and Faneuil Hall.

The **Emmanuel Music** chamber ensemble, tel. (617) 536-3356, is in the midst of a multi-year exploration (set to end in 2003) of Franz Schubert's major vocal, piano, and chamber works. Concerts are held late Oct. to early May at Suffolk University's C. Walsh Theatre, 55 Temple St., behind the State House. Musical appetites that enjoy blending 18th-century monody with 19th-and early 20th-century Romanticism should consider a date with the exceptional **Boston Chamber Music Society,** tel. (617) 422-0086 (Oct.-May in Jordan and Sanders), or **The Cantata Singers & Ensemble,** tel. (617) 267-6502 (Nov.-May in Jordan Hall exclusively).

Fans of the truly modern will be pleased to find the Boston area is also a hotbed for 20th-century music, from Stravinsky, Webern, and Varèse to the latest microtonal, minimalist, and electronic compositions—including frequent premieres and commissioned works. Several of the area's half dozen professional new music ensembles have been pushing the envelope for decades, including **Collage New Music,** tel. (617) 325-5200, in residence at Beacon Hill's C. Walsh Theatre (three concerts fall-spring); **Dinosaur Annex,** tel. (617) 482-3852, www.dinosaurannex.org, usually performing in Back Bay's First and Second Church, 66 Marlborough St. (October, February, and May); and **Boston Musica Viva,** tel. (617) 353-0556, www.camellia.org/bmv, in concert at Boston University's Tsai Performance Center and Longy School of Music outside of Harvard Square (five concerts Oct.-May). Look for these and other modern perfor-

mance groups in the newspaper listings at the head of the classical music page.

Several of the area's music schools present student and faculty recitals and concerts free of charge—truly the most underappreciated entertainment deal in the state. Don't for a minute think "student" and "free" adds up to an evening of dubious quality, either—many of these emerging talents are well on their way to professional careers; next time you want to see them perform, it's likely to cost you big bucks. **New England Conservatory,** tel. (617) 262-1120 ext. 700, is by far the most generous, with *hundreds* of free concerts each year, largely classical works with lashings of jazz and new music. Most take place in NEC's resplendent Jordan Hall, 30 Gainsborough St. diagonally across Huntington Ave. from Symphony Hall. Jazz, rock, and country are among the specialties of nearby **Berklee College of Music,** tel. (617) 747-8820—named after the founder's son, Lee Berk—whose free student and faculty concerts are usually held in a pair of recital halls at 1140 Boylston St. on the edge of the Back Bay Fens. And in Cambridge, classical, operatic, and early music are among the freebies at **Longy School of Music,** tel. (617) 868-0956 ext. 120, presented several times a week during the academic year. All concerts are at Edward Pickman Concert Hall, on Garden St. a block past the Sheraton Commander Hotel.

When Art Comes to Town

If there's a famous diva, instrumentalist, symphony orchestra, or dance troupe on tour in the U.S., he/she/they will likely appear in Boston as part of the **BankBoston Celebrity Series,** a local institution since before WW II. Information and tickets to the Oct.-May. performances (typically held at the Wang Center, Symphony Hall, and other major auditoriums) are available through CelebrityCharge, tel. (617) 482-6661. To get on the mailing list for the season brochure, call (617) 482-2595. A more rootsy potpourri of music and dance is imported by **World Music,** tel. (617) 876-4275, a local promoter that can be counted on for great shows nearly every week of the year (scope out the upcoming schedule on the Web at www.worldmusic.org). Among the many venues booked by World Music is the **Somerville Theater,** in Davis Square on the

Red Line, a former vaudeville stage whose year-round musical offerings also include folk, bluegrass, and Celtic music, plus annual extravaganzas like a Women in Folk-Rock Festival, Silly Songwriters' Festival, and Either/Orchestra's annual gig, tel. (617) 625-5700.

To find out if your favorite rock or pop bands are somewhere in town, consult the newspapers or ticket-selling music stores like Tower Records, or call the recorded info lines of the **Orpheum Theatre,** tel. (617) 679-0810, on Hamilton Pl. (the dead-end lane opposite Park Street Church downtown), the **Berklee Performance Center** on Mass. Ave. at Boylston St., tel. (617) 266-7455, or **The Paradise,** at 969 Comm. Ave., tel. (617) 562-8800, near the western end of the Boston University campus, on the Green "B" Line.

NIGHTCLUBS AND ACOUSTIC COFFEEHOUSES

Dance joints and live music stages are scattered all around both sides of the river, but clubland's major node is Boston's Lansdowne Street, in the shadow of Fenway Park outside Kenmore Square. With a solid block of neon-bedecked entertainment, clubhopping is as easy as walking next door (there are even occasional block parties, with multi-club admission). Other after-hours hot spots include downtown's Theater District, Central Square in Cambridge, and undergraduate-infested Allston, perhaps the most prolific breeding ground for Boston's independent music scene. Don't wait till midnight to start tearing up the town, as most clubs close early—Boston's by 2 a.m., Cambridge ones an hour earlier.

Everybody Dance Now

Kenmore Square's triple crown for the 20-something dance fiend includes **Avalon,** 15 Lansdowne, tel. (617) 262-2424, which doubles as a live stage for major-label bands a step shy of the stadium tour, or big-name musicians taking time out from giant concert-hall crowds; next-door, **Axis,** tel. (617) 262-2437, with its nightly segues among different themes, from techno-house and ultra-lounge to classic old soul; and **Karma Club,** 9 Lansdowne, tel. (617) 421-9595,

DANCING FOR GROWN-UPS

If you want to kick up your heels but feel too old for the barely legal college crowds hip-hopping around the floors of the major clubs, consider dropping in on one of the city's many traditional folk dances. Scottish, English, and Scandinavian country dances, lively Israeli, contra and square dancing, and catch-all international combinations are among the hidden pleasures found in alcohol- and smoke-free auditoriums, churches, VFW halls, YWCAs, and community centers throughout the metro area.

If you don't know a schottisch from a hey-for-four, have no fear: all welcome beginners and stress informality over competition (though dedicated regulars are numerous enough to satisfy experienced visitors, too). No partners are necessary, either (or big bankrolls—cover charges are typically $3-5 for hours of invigorating fun). Cambridge-based **Folk Arts Center of New England** has the most comprehensive recorded forecast of what's on and where, updated twice a week, tel. (617) 491-6084. Or consult the dance listings in the "Calendar" section of any Thursday *Boston Globe.* If you've already mastered English folk dancing, call the Country Dance Society's recorded calendar, (617) 354-1340, for a more select list of events catering primarily or exclusively to experienced dancers.

with the best decor and (mostly because of its high cover charge) the largest post-graduate clientele. Downtown dancers looking for a classier milieu than pierced college kids should check out **The Roxy,** tel. (617) 338-7699, on Tremont St. opposite the Wang Center. It's a large, rather elegant club popular with the Euro crowd and black urban professionals. The DJ-spun house, hiphop, and R&B is regularly supplemented by out-of-town headliners ranging from Brazilian samba queens to The Artist Formerly Known As Prince. Pierced body parts and backwards baseball caps are also notably absent from nearby **International Europa** and **Buzz,** a linked pair at 51 and 67 Stuart St., tel. (617) 482-3939, whose two floors and high-energy mix of house and Latin dance music attracts a diverse 21-plus crowd, including many snappily dressed youths from surrounding Chinatown. On the Piano Row edge of the Common is Boylston Place, a pedestrian alley off Boylston St. that's filled with clubs, including such dance joints as **The Big Easy,** the more barbecue-party casual **Alley Cat Lounge,** and chic **Club Mercury,** whose young limo-renting patrons seem to drink champagne as hard as they dance. Glamorous and free-spending night owls also consistently flock to **M-80,** 969 Comm. Ave., tel. (617) 562-8820, in Allston next to the Paradise rock club; to get there, take the Green "B" Line trolley to Pleasant St., the sixth surface stop outbound from Kenmore Square, and walk up the block toward the clot of double-parked cars.

If you're the hardcore kind who prefers deep techno grooves and black leather to cell phones and Italian silk, head to Cambridge and drop in on **Man Ray,** 21 Brookline St. in Central Square, tel. (617) 864-0400. Friday nights feature bondage and fetish themes; the midweek crowd is more relaxed, but the alterna-underground dance tunes are just as hot. For more of a mixed bill of fare—leaning toward reggae, hip-hop jazz, and good dance-able funk—take a 15- or 20-minute walk toward the river from the Central Square Red Line station and check out the **Western Front,** 343 Western Ave. in Cambridge, tel. (617) 492-7772. And if it's a Monday night and you're in the mood for some great kick-up-your-heels swing dancing to live music, head to Somerville's **Johnny D's Uptown Music Club,** 17 Holland St. in Davis Square, right on the Red Line. Preliminary dance lessons, if needed, start at 8 p.m.

Live (Mostly) Local Bands

Fueled by its vast student population, Boston is fertile ground for new bands, with what seems like millions of groups busy stabbing at musical immortality in bars, clubs, and mattress-padded basement practice rooms around town in any given week. If you want (or need) a preview before you actually immerse yourself in the sonic pleasures of clubland, call (617) 232-CITY for an automated excursion through sample tracks from some 300 of these local desperados. Keep a pen handy: band and club specifics are recited lickety-split.

Two of the best venues for local music are both in Cambridge's Central Square, within a couple blocks of the Red Line. **The Middle East,** 480 Mass. Ave., tel. (617) 497-0576 (press 1 for concert info and box office), earns the biggest raves for its exceptional, independent bookings on three stages—Upstairs, Downstairs, and The Corner—across a broad musical spectrum, from thrash guitar to African *soukous* so infectious it'd make Al Gore get down and boogie. Unplugged acoustic jams, belly-dancing lessons, poetry readings, no service fees on ticket-by-phone charges, and frequent benefit concerts for local organizations add to the club's distinction. It also serves good Middle Eastern food, as the name suggests. Next door on the Brookline St. side—adjacent to that great mural celebrating Central Square's cultural diversity—is **T.T. the Bear's Place,** tel. (617) 492-0082, an equally independent-minded place whose bookings principally mine the rich vein of local hard rock, although plenty of pop-minded songwriters and the occasional world-beat dance band roll through, too.

Another top spot for every flavor of rock, from radio-ready alternapop to heavy-grooving ska, is Boston's **Mama Kin,** on Lansdowne St. across from the mighty left-field wall of Fenway Park. Co-owned by Aerosmith (hence the band logo on the front stoop and framed concert photos above the bar), this intimate two-stage club has one of most reasonable cover charges in town—$5 weeknights, for example. Bookings lean toward the cream of the local crop. Every so often, one of the celebrity owners may drop by, but the staff has no more clue than you do as to when this will happen next. Besides such nice touches as stage curtains, and good draft brews (Anchor Steam, Red Hook ESB), this place has some of the best maintained bathrooms in clubland.

For solid roots music, from rockabilly, Cajun swing, and Afropop to Scottish fiddlers and surf guitarists, take the Red Line to **Johnny D's Uptown Music Club,** on Holland Ave. just steps from the Davis Square T station, tel. (617) 776-9667. With good food and draft beer to boot, this is an A-1 hangout. Before they land at Johnny D's, you can often find local singer-songwriters working out new or polishing their materials a subway stop away, in a pair of Cambridge clubs on Mass. Ave. Cover-free **Toad,** next to the Wok 'N' Roll restaurant opposite the Porter Square T station, tel. (617) 497-4950, is so small

IRISH PUBS

In addition to the downtown taverns and Boston's oldest Irish pub (Doyle's, in Jamaica Plain) cited in the text, the following selection constitutes a good beginning for anyone looking to crawl through Boston's stellar Irish pubs. All feature regular live music (often, but not always, Celtic). Cover charges vary from nothing at all to big bucks for big-name talent. Most host a weekly *seisiun,* a traditional informal Irish jam session (which is how it's pronounced in Gaelic, too); if the day isn't listed below, call to inquire.

AROUND NORTH STATION AND THE FLEETCENTER

The Irish Embassy, 234 Friend St., tel. (617) 742-6618. The varied musical bill of fare attracts a diverse young crowd, but the atmosphere is aided by lots of Irish accents on both sides of the bar (and better ventilation than most small places).

McGann's, 197 Portland St., tel. (617) 227-4059. Fancier than average, with lots of brass, varnished oak, a granite fireplace, and lighting that lets you see who you're talking to. Wednesday *seisiun.*

Grand Canal, 57 Canal St., tel. (617) 523-1112. Another place where antiques, wood trim, and draft microbrews are in far greater abundance than frat boys, baseball caps, and sports TV. Monday *seisiun.*

FARTHER AFIELD (AT LEAST A T RIDE FROM CENTRAL BOSTON)

Brendan Behan Pub, 378 Centre St., in Jamaica Plain, two blocks from the Perkins St. stop on the #39 Forest Hills bus, tel. (617) 522-5386. A tiny spot with a rich, juke-joint atmosphere, big 20-ounce Imperial pints, and, in keeping with its literary namesake, occasional poetry readings. Saturday and Tuesday *seisiuns.*

Plough and Stars, 912 Mass. Ave., in Cambridge, halfway between Central and Harvard Squares, tel. (617) 441-3455. More Cambridge than Dublin, it's still a venerable place as old as the hills.

The Druid, 1357 Cambridge St., in Inman Square, Cambridge, tel. (617) 497-0965. The epitome of a cozy neighborhood joint, the kind proudly adopted by a diverse but loyal crowd. Conversations among friends and bantering with Pedro, the energetic young owner, are never distracted by TV, because there is none. The well-poured Guinness is accompanied by a soundtrack of young Irish rockers, the Sunday early evening *seisiun,* and other occasional live or DJ-spun music, from Celtic to modern soul.

The Thirsty Scholar, 70 Beacon St., on the Cambridge/Somerville line, outside Inman Square, tel. (617) 497-2294. Attracts a convivial, energetic young crowd that appreciates the above-average pub grub (such as the roasted mussels in cream sauce), the poetry readings and book signings, and the great menu of over two dozen draft beers (including such imported delights as Old Speckled Hen and Bellhaven ales, plus regional microbrews like Magic Hat #9 and Pilgrim Ale). The exposed brick, book-lined shelves, large front windows that open to the sidewalk in summertime, and intimate one-table no-smoking nook (the "snug") also firmly set this place apart from the rest. The barkeeps tend to know their wares: at least one is willing and able to discuss their beers right down to their specific gravity.

The Burren, 247 Elm St., in Davis Square, Somerville, tel. (617) 776-6896. This capacious pub, well-appointed with wood and Irish brewery insignia, honors the heritage of its namesake—a picturesque limestone landscape in Ireland's county Clare, famous for its traditional music—with live Celtic *seisiuns* daily, including regular appearances by the owners, Tommy McCarthy and Louise Costello, a respected string duo in their own right. If that's not enough, there's also live country, blues, and folk music—Celtic *and* American—in the large Back Room, which features both a proper stage and a better sound system than you'll probably ever hear in any other pub on the East Coast. Monday night, come around 7:30-8 p.m. to catch the weekly set-dancing lessons in the back, and then try out your new *Riverdance* moves when the *seisiun* begins upfront between 9 and 10. If the Chieftains are in town for one of their regular concert hall appearances, come here later that night and you'll likely catch them in a more casual vein, jamming with their local musical friends. If you miss the real Irish breakfasts on weekends, never fear, traditional fare like white and black (blood) pudding are available anytime.

that most of its acts perform unplugged—and the audience often comprises fellow musicians taking a night off. **The Lizard Lounge,** tel. (617) 547-0759, in the basement of the Cambridge Common restaurant at 1667 Mass. Ave., between Porter and Harvard Square, is larger but equally intimate, its typically diverse audience drawn by great tunes, good vibes, and an atmosphere free of raging collegiate hormones.

Folk and Acoustic

Garage bands aren't the only scene happening in Boston. Folk music thrives in Cambridge. While rock fans gather in smoke-filled clubs and swill beer, folkies sip tea and cappuccino and nibble cookies at events called "coffeehouses"—typically held in church basements throughout the region. Most are weekly or monthly affairs, and many are partially or wholly open-mike—a true grab-bag experience in which anyone may sign up for three songs' worth of stage time. The grandfather of them all is the **Nameless Coffeehouse,** tel. (617) 864-1630, a Friday-night staple of the First Parish of Cambridge, the wooden 1833 Unitarian church facing Harvard Yard from the foot of Church Street. The Nameless (free) has been a home to up-and-coming acoustic musicians since the late 1960s. Thursday nights, the **Naked City Coffeehouse,** tel. (617) 731-6468, brings an open mike for music and poetry to the Old Cambridge Baptist Church on Mass. Ave. next to the Inn at Harvard. At the **Cantab Lounge,** 738 Mass. Ave. in Central Square, tel. (617) 354-2685, Monday features an open mike for folk, Tuesday for country and bluegrass. Not in the mood to gamble on untried talent? Head for the local kingpin of folk, Harvard Square's alcohol- and smoke-free **Club Passim,** under The Globe Corner Bookstore on Palmer St., tel. (617) 492-7679. Monday is for spoken word and Tuesday is open mike night, but the rest of the week Passim offers top-drawer folk and acoustic music from all over. Serious folk enthusiasts looking for a comprehensive listing of where and when to catch the next fix of acoustic music in Boston and around the state should visit the Folk Song Society of Greater Boston's Web site, www.world.std.com/~fssgb, and follow "other links" to "concerts in Massachusetts."

Jazz

Boston is no Manhattan (or even Hartford), and it was in the city's Symphony Hall that Benny Goodman's first appearance was dismissed by a newspaper critic as more fitting fodder for the baseball reporter. However, there *is* good jazz to be found around town, particularly at Harvard Square's nationally known **Regattabar,** in the Charles Hotel on Bennett St. (tel. 617-661-5000 recorded schedule, 617-876-7777 Concertix number for charge-by-phone tickets). January-May, the annual **Regattabar Jazz Festival** brings a who's who of celebrity jazz artists to the hotel's main ballroom. Other nearby spots to check out include **Ryles,** 212 Hampshire St. in the heart of Inman Square, tel. (617) 876-9330, dishing out jazz most nights, and **Scullers Jazz Club,** in the DoubleTree Guest Suites Hotel on the Allston side of the Charles River, a short cab ride or half hour walk from the Red Line's Central Square station, tel. (617) 562-4111. Also in Allston is the **Wonder Bar,** tel. (617) 351-COOL, a young hipster jazz bar at 186 Harvard Ave., a block from the Green "B" Line. Be warned that while you may feel out of place wearing sneakers at the two luxury hotel jazz spots, you won't even make it past the Wonder Bar's doorkeep without proper attire.

Wally's Cafe, a local jazz institution dating back to the 1940s, stands in a class by itself. Passed without a second glance by the unsuspecting, this tiny South End hole in the wall truly embodies the roots of jazz. Needless to say, there's no dress code or stuffy attitude here, just cheap beer and damn good music from mostly homegrown groups, including plenty of students from nearby Berklee College of Music. Look for the telltale Bud sign among the brick rowhouses at 427 Mass. Ave. a few dozen yards from the Orange Line and only two blocks from Symphony Hall.

Blues

True blues hounds should make a beeline for Allston's **Harper's Ferry,** 158 Brighton Ave., tel. (617) 254-9743, Boston's preeminent spot for catching both local and national acts. Besides being right on the route of the #66 bus from Harvard Square or a short walk from the Green "B" Line's Harvard Avenue surface stop, Harper's lies within five minutes' walk of a half dozen Vietnamese restaurants. Big-name bluesmen and -women also often headline at the **House of Blues,** on Winthrop St. in Harvard Square, tel. (617) 491-BLUE (general info) or 491-BABY (tickets), the original flagship of this ever-expanding nightclub chain. Despite the great music lineup and nifty collection of southern folk art, the place is more of a marketing concept than anything else, and on weekend nights most of the audience could probably care less about who's on stage so long as they think it shows good taste to be there. Needless to say, it seems there's never a slow night. On Sunday, a series of brunch seatings is accompanied by live gospel music. It's no surprise that the founder of this Gap-like merchandiser of blues music, soul food, and logo-stamped blueswear was also responsible for giving the world the Hard Rock Cafe; more unusual may be the fact that in addition to celebrities like Blues Brother Dan Aykroyd, financial investors include that rockin' local cat Big Crimson (a.k.a. Harvard University). For a Sunday **gospel brunch** that *doesn't* feel like a cattle call, check out **Dick's Last Resort,** a Texas chain of party-hearty restaurants with a local outpost on the Huntington Avenue side of the Pru. Or, for some serious raise-the-roof gospel singing, try and squeeze in the doors of the always-overflowing Sunday morning services at the **New Covenant Christian Church,** 340 Blue Hill Ave., in Dorchester, tel. (617) 445-0636.

To check out the local blues scene thoroughly, arm yourself beforehand with the blues concert calendar assembled by WGBH-FM "Blues After Hours" diva Mai Cramer. Send your e-mail request to mai_cramer@wgbh.org, or send a stamped, self-addressed envelope to Blues After Hours, WGBH Radio, 125 Western Ave., Allston, MA 02134. *BluesWire,* a well-crafted broadsheet on the regional blues scene, also publishes an excellent listing of blues and R&B concerts around New England; order a copy from P.O. Box 657, Bedford, MA 01730.

Gay Nights

A number of otherwise straight clubs feature at least one night a week on which they cater to gays, lesbians, or both. Among these, Sunday at Avalon, on Lansdowne St., has reigned supreme since the late '70s. Lansdowne's Queer Circus

at Axis (Monday), Fenway's unabashed Ramrod (1254 Boylston, beside the Latin music lounge, Sophia's), the Theater District's gay hotspot Chaps (100 Warrenton St.), Northern Avenue's H2O (a lesbian-favored weekend dance club in Mark's Crab House), and Cambridge's Man Ray and Ryles (featuring a mixed lesbian and hetero crowd), also merit mention.

Boston's tiny Bay Village neighborhood, wedged between Park Square and the South End, boasts a range of gay nightlife, from the full-out drag queen and transvestite dance bar **Jacques,** at Broadway and Piedmont behind the Radisson Hotel on Stuart St., to the **Napoleon Club,** 52 Piedmont St., a gay piano bar (allegedly a favorite of Liberace) dating back to 1952. To get the full scoop on gay nightlife, pick up a free copy of *Bay Windows,* the newspaper for Boston's gay community, from coffee shops and laundromats around the Back Bay, South End, and Fenway neighborhoods.

MORE TREATS FOR EYES AND EARS

Poetry

While poetry readings have become a fixture at hip coffee shops and cafes around Boston and the nation over the past few years, the local poetry scene actually has deep roots. The **New England Poetry Club** has presented regular readings for longer than most of today's barstool poets have even been alive. Founded in 1915 by Amy Lowell, Robert Frost, and Conrad Aiken, the NEPC presents free Monday-evening poetry readings Oct.-May at Harvard's Yenching Library, on Divinity Ave. off Kirkland St., a block from the university's Science Center, tel. (617) 643-0029. For over 15 years, the club has also co-sponsored a summer series at the Longfellow National Historic Site, 105 Brattle St. outside of Harvard Square, tel. (617) 876-4491 (free). So long as friend-of-the-Beats and general poetical torchbearer Jack Powers draws a breath, **Stone Soup Poets,** tel. (617) 227-0845, will also give audiences a taste of verse—as it has each and every week for over a quarter century. Get a serving of this iconoclastic stew of raw and established voices every Monday night at T.T. the Bear's Place, 10 Brookline St., in Central

Henry Wadsworth Longfellow

BOB RACE

Square, Cambridge, next to the Middle East Restaurant and Nightclub ($3). The Monday night poetry readings at the Cambridge Center for Adult Education's **Blacksmith House,** 56 Brattle St. in Harvard Square, tel. (617) 354-3036, have also been steadfastly reveling in the power of language for over 20 years ($3), with local and visiting poets in regular attendance.

The more recent phenomenon of **poetry slams** involves poets competing head to head and being judged, Olympic-style, by a panel of volunteers from the audience. Catch the leading local example of these highly topical performance events ($3) every Wednesday night at the "Third Rail"—the downstairs room of the **Cantab Lounge,** 738 Mass. Ave. in Central Square, tel. (617) 354-2685. If you're fortunate enough to drop in during the spring championships, which determine who represents Boston and Cambridge at the U.S. Grand National poetry slams, you'll hear some of the country's top-ranked slammers.

Check the bulletin board of the **Grolier Poetry Book Shop,** 6 Plympton St. behind the Harvard Book Store, tel. (617) 547-4648, for other poetry-related events, including the shop's own reading series.

Film
Showtimes for the latest commercial releases may be found in any of the local daily and weekly newspapers, or with a touch-tone call to Boston's Moviephone, tel. (617) 333-FILM—an automated menu-driven service that will even give you directions to particular theaters if you navigate through the prompts correctly. But Boston also abounds in films that will never make it to any mall multiplex. Harvard Square's **Brattle Theatre,** on Brattle St. next to the HMV music store, tel. (617) 876-6837, and Brookline's nonprofit **Coolidge Corner Theatre,** on Harvard and Beacon Streets at the Green "C" Line, tel. (617) 734-2500, are stalwarts of the national art-house circuit. The Brattle—one of the first repertory cinemas in the U.S., whose '50s revivals of Humphrey Bogart films are credited with making Bogie an American classic—also sponsors the annual Boston International Festival of Women's Cinema, while the Coolidge carves a unique niche with plenty of local premieres, animation festivals, occasional silent films shown to live orchestral accompaniment, and autumn's annual Jewish Film Festival, co-hosted with the Museum of Fine Arts. The **Harvard Film Archive,** in the Carpenter Center for Visual Arts on Quincy St., tel. (617) 495-4700, has even more freedom to explore noncommercial filmmaking; its schedule regularly includes obscure, neglected, and experimental cinema, film classics reprised for curricular purposes, and perennial showings of Dusan Makavejev's work. It's easy to be lulled into thinking Hollywood and western Europe have a monopoly on producing compelling films, but a sampling of the films shown at the **Museum of Fine Arts,** tel. (617) 267-9300, ext. 800, will open your eyes to the rich and varied storytelling found outside the mainstream, from Iceland to Iran to documentary filmmakers here in our own backyard. The MFA screens its winning picks from contemporary world cinema mostly Wed.-Sun. in the West Wing.

COURTESY OF THE BOSTON PUBLIC LIBRARY, PRINT DEPARTMENT

ACCOMMODATIONS

If you won't settle for anything less than the sort of place that routinely earns a fistful of diamonds and stars from Mobil and AAA, know that local hotel rates are entirely out of proportion to the city's size. It's a case study in low-supply—high-demand economics: there are more rooms in Las Vegas's four largest hotels than in all of Boston and Cambridge combined, and the year-round occupancy rate here is close to 80%; consequently, the Hub's average room rate is exceeded only (in this country) by New York City's. Well-appointed downtown rooms—with double beds and private baths, enough room to permit morning calisthenics without moving furniture into the hall, and with views of something other than utility shafts—will almost without exception cost you well over $200. Per night. Parking, 12.45% tax, tips, and breakfast are additional. Sound like highway robbery? Wait till you see what $100 gets you.

Don't expect your trusty economy chain motels to come to the rescue of your pocketbook, either: in Boston, brands like Best Western and even Days Inn are luxury-priced lodgings. In fact, count on all the national chains here to

charge two or three times what they would for an almost identical room out in Michigan or Arizona.

Savvy high-end travelers will use corporate discounts, weekend packages, or a discount hotel broker (see chart) to take the edge off the high-priced business-oriented hotels, but for anyone on a more modest budget there's precious little relief during a high season that stretches from early spring through November. Unless your child is valedictorian, for heaven's sake avoid visiting during Harvard Commencement (the Thursday after Memorial Day)—any Boston or Cambridge room that won't make mom squeamish will have been booked years in advance, and room rates—with a few praiseworthy exceptions—will look uncomfortably similar to the tuition bill. Indicating that somebody's community relations must be falling short of the mark, most local innkeepers target only Harvard parents (and MIT's by default, due to identical scheduling), while ignoring the other graduation dates on the spring calendar. As a general rule, lodgings throughout Greater Boston start high and are priced in direct proportion to their distance from either Harvard Yard or the downtown waterfront. If you seek a standard motel room for under $60, consult the sidebar on more affordable accommodations outside the city.

Almost the only oasis of even moderate prices ($60-85) is Brookline, which is also nearly immune from price gouging aimed at college parents. B&Bs around the city mostly occupy the middle ground between plain guest houses and fancy hotels, but, while some offer exceptional hospitality and spacious, comfortable quarters at rates reasonable enough to more than offset their extra distance from high-profile attractions, others seem to assume their prime locations will blind you to claustrophobic rooms, threadbare decor, and outrageous four-day minimum stays.

Boston first-timers should remember that most small inns and guest houses, particularly in historic neighborhoods, sport signs not much larger (or better lit) than your average phone book—if they have signs at all. In fact, gas stations are about the only businesses in the metro area that advertise with neon.

Lastly, if you let a travel agent who is unfamiliar with Boston geography handle your hotel bookings—or you use the Internet yourself to scour hotel Web sites—be forewarned that a few familiar national chains located in the industrial and commercial sprawl north of Logan Airport will, to the untutored eye, look temptingly close to Boston and its attractions. In simple mileage terms, this is true, but for sheer conve-

DISCOUNT HOTEL BROKERS

Before hunting for a hotel in Boston on your own, consider making your first call to the following companies, which either contract with certain hotels to provide preferred rates (just like any big corporation will negotiate), or act as booking agents for unsold rooms. Discounts, generally available on properties whose rack rates are $250 and up, run 10-50%. The two Boston-based services can steer you to accommodations under $100, but not at any discount. While there are times when a broker's discount (typically locked in by yearly contracts) may be exceeded by a promotional rate temporarily available from the hotel itself, double-checking with the host property typically is for soothing doubts rather than for uncovering additional savings. Comparison shoppers are better off checking rates from other discounters.

Keep expectations in line with the calendar, as the savings inevitably dry up when occupancy rates peak during late spring graduation weeks, summer, and fall.

The first two names on the list below are based in Boston, and given the sheer depth of their knowledge about properties they represent—and even those they don't—they should top your call list. Most of the rest will also simply make a booking in your name, payable when you check in, but depending on the hotel, the broker may act as a wholesale "owner" of blocks of rooms, in which case prepayment is made for a room voucher that's either mailed to you or held for check-in. In either case, pay attention to

cancellation policies, or, just as with any hotel reservation confirmed with a credit card, you could end up paying for a night you can't use.

Central Reservations Service of New England, tel. (800) 332-3026 or (617) 569-3800, www.bostonhotels.net. Besides advance discounts, Central also specializes in same-day bookings, either by phone or in person for travelers arriving at Logan Airport: look for their desks in Terminal E, next to the info booth outside of Customs, and Terminal C, on the baggage claim level.

Citywide Reservation Services, tel. (800) 468-3593 or (617) 267-7424, www.cityres.com, In addition to arranging discount stays at high-end properties, Citywide can book you into just about any hotel, motel, inn, or guesthouse in the whole metro area.

Accommodations Express, tel. (800) 444-7666 or (609) 391-2100, www.accommodationsxpress.com

Central Reservation Service, tel. (800) 548-3311 or (407) 339-4116, www.reservation-services.com

Hotel Reservations Network, tel. (800) 964-6835 or (214) 361-7311, www.180096hotel.com. The only broker that occasionally is able to resell vacant rooms at the Club Quarters Boston, an exclusive members-only club that functions like a hotel, smack in the heart of the Financial District.

Quikbook, tel. (800) 221-3531 or (212) 779-7666, www.quikbook.com

nience (plus that intangible satisfaction that comes from waking up to something other than potholed highways lined with shopping plazas and oil storage tanks), you may want to pass on such establishments as the Howard Johnson Lodge in Revere, and the Econo Lodge in Malden.

BUDGET: UNDER $35

Boston's only budget options are hostels, offering dorm-style accommodations with shared baths. Anyone who thinks such places are untidy hives of chain-smoking slackers barely out of high school has obviously never been to either the immaculate and friendly **BeanTown Hostel,** on Friend St. above the Hooters Restaurant one block from North Station, tel. (617) 723-0800, e-mail BeanTown@aol.com, or adjacent **Irish Embassy Hostel,** upstairs of the eponymous pub at 232 Friend St., tel. (617) 973-4841, e-mail EmbassyH@aol.com. Designed by experienced budget travelers to be the best of all possible hostels, this pair delights the most jaded backpackers with its bounty of freebies, including full linen service (no smelly sleeping bags, no regulation sleep sacks), pack storage, earplugs (rooms are shared, after all), free barbecues at nearby pubs under the same ownership (four nights a week, including a vegetarian one), and free admission to all live music events at these same establishments. All this and no membership requirements! The fully skylit, well-soundproofed BeanTown caters to morning people—those early to bed, early to rise types—while its sister is more appropriate for those who take most advantage of the free club hopping available to its guests. In winter, some rooms in each may be rented as private doubles if demand is slack. All beds are $15 all the time—unequivocally the best hostel deals in all of New England. Needless to say, advance reservations strongly advised.

If you can't land a space at Friend St., there's always **Hostelling International Boston,** 16 Hemenway, a few minutes' stroll from Mass. Ave. and the Green Line's Hynes/ICA station, tel. (617) 536-1027. Besides the standard hostel self-service kitchen, HI-Boston has some private rooms for couples and families (starting at

$54), sponsors a range of special programs, and is open around the clock. During the May-Oct. busy season, its nearly 200 beds (never more than five to a room) are supplemented by an additional dormitory building a few blocks away on Beacon Street. Rates are $19 members, $22 nonmembers, plus a refundable $10 deposit for linens and room key. Given the dearth of other cheap accommodations around town, reservations are encouraged.

INEXPENSIVE: $35-60

While singletons and winter visitors will find inexpensive rates at some of the places mentioned under the "Moderate" category below, couples traveling in summer aren't nearly so lucky. Other than the hostels, only two *rooms* in the whole city-suburban metro area—out of some 22,000 in over 140 guest houses, motels, hotels, and B&Bs of all shapes and sizes—cost less than $60 for two people in high season, after taxes (and those rooms, in a South End B&B, are booked so solid that the owner asked not to be identified, so she won't have to turn people away). The only runner-up is seasonal: the **Boston YMCA,** at 316 Huntington Ave. near Symphony Hall and Northeastern University, tel. (617) 536-7800, whose rooms are only available late June to September ($60 d, $39 s, almost all with shared baths). Better rooms at a higher price are available from the city's other YMCA, in Charlestown, below.

MODERATE: $60-85

Several establishments have "Beacon" in their names. All are closely related in price, and several in location, but the one to burn into your memory is the **Beacon Street Guest House,** 1047 Beacon St. in Brookline, tel. (800) 872-7211 or (617) 232-0292. The large, simply furnished rooms in this graceful, elevator-less brick townhouse have enough oak trim, paneling, and now-disused hearths to lend it the air of a vintage Ivy League alumni club. Rates are $55-69 d for rooms with private baths (subtract $10 for shared baths, another $10 if you're alone). The front rooms' big bowfront windows overlook one of

TIME VS. MONEY: CHEAP SLEEPS FOR COMMUTERS

Throughout eastern Massachusetts the average tourist looking for a decent and inexpensive place to sleep will find precious little relief in either city or suburbs, since most accommodations strung along the Rt. 128/I-95 loop around Boston cater heavily to the office parks and corporate headquarters that give this road its "Technology Highway" nickname. Truly desperate travelers may resort to the smattering of chain motels stuck in various semi-industrial sprawls along the city's radial highways (particularly north of the airport), all priced appealingly below downtown competitors but still close enough to $100 to make them generally a poor value. (Any nominal savings on the room rate will easily be expended on city parking, as inconvenient locations will force you to rely on your car more than you should have to.) Quite simply, if you want something for $60 or less, look to the outer interstate ring, I-495, at least a 30-mile commute from downtown Boston. Counterclockwise from north to south, the choices are as follows:

Tage Inn–Andover, at I-93 Exit 45, just north of I-495, tel. (800) 322-TAGE or (978) 685-6200. This flagship of a small, family-owned chain has rooms and amenities comparable to nationally known upmarket brands (indoor pool, tennis court, exercise facilities, modem ports, guest-room voicemail), at a price $90-200 lower than comparable Boston hotels ($58 d to be exact). Such savings may more than compensate for the half-hour drive into the MBTA commuter parking at Lechmere, at the East Cambridge end of the Green Line, and walking distance to the Museum of Science. (Get off I-93 Exit 30 and follow Rts. 38 and 28—the McGrath Hwy.—till you see the trolley terminal on your right; the $2.50 commuter parking is opposite, next to Bernie and Phyl's Furniture Discount.)

Friendly Crossways Conference Center, about 15 miles southwest of Lowell, tel. (978) 456-3649 before 9 p.m., e-mail friendly@ma.ultranet. com, or visit its Web site at www.ultra-net.com/~friendly. Occupying a large white clapboard farmhouse in the rural town of Harvard (no relation to the university), this friendly and informal Hostelling International affiliate features dormitory beds or semiprivate rooms in a pastoral setting ($12-17 per person for HI members, $15-20 pp nonmembers), although private rooms for couples ($25) and family rooms ($40-50) are also available. Take I-495 Exit 29B to Rt. 2 west, immediately getting off at the next exit, Littleton/ Boxborough. Make a series of three lefts from the end of the ramp—onto Taylor St., then Porter Rd., and finally at the stop sign, Whitcomb Ave.—and proceed another 1.5 miles to the signposted drive on the right.

Tage Inn–Milford, beside Rt. 109 immediately west of I-495 Exit 19, tel. (800) 322-TAGE or (508) 478-8243. Like its Andover cousin, this economy-priced property offers standard motel rooms at a very nonstandard rate ($58 d). Conveniently located just two interstate exits north of the Forge Park station at the end of the Commuter Rail's Franklin line, with up to 16 daily departures to Boston's Back Bay and South Station, about an hour away. You couldn't drive into the city any faster, even if there wasn't another car—or cop—on the road, and the roundtrip fare of $7.50 plus $1 for parking at the commuter lot is still a better deal than most city parking, hands down.

Motel 6, off Rt. 140 near the southern junction of I-95 and I-495 in Mansfield, tel. (800) 4MOTEL6 or (508) 339-2323. The $52 d price may seem high for this budget chain, but given the $80-plus tariffs at other so-called "economy" motels in the region, it's still a bargain.

Bunk & Bagel, Plymouth, tel. (508) 830-0914. A backpackers' B&B of sorts whose owners retired from many years of operating Friendly Crossways, above. Located just a couple of blocks from downtown, it features beds in one of three shared, single-sex rooms for $15-25 pp (the best deal in southeastern Massachusetts for single travelers). Couples should inquire about the availability of a room of their own. As the name suggests, a modest breakfast is included in the rate.

the city's early Victorian-era boulevards near Boston University, a tree-lined design after the French manner then in vogue. With the convenience of both fine restaurants and the Green "C" Line trolley stop at Audubon Circle just a stone's throw down the block (on the Boston city line), this place is arguably one of Greater Boston's best lodging values.

But for the lack of private baths, almost as good a bargain stands just up the street at **Anthony's Town House,** 1085 Beacon, tel. (617) 566-3972: $55-75 d or $35-60 s, *including* tax (cash only). The ample rooms are quite comfortable and display a quirky charm with their glazed-tile hearths (purely decorative now), painted furniture, lime green carpet, and well-preserved oak woodwork. Reserve parking ahead if you'll need it.

For proximity to downtown, look across the water to the year-round **Constitution Inn at the Armed Forces YMCA,** 150 Second Ave., in the Charlestown Navy Yard, tel. (800) 495-9622. If it weren't equipped solely with twin beds, its rooms would be superior to the Harvard Square Hotel's in size and amenities, for well under half the price ($69 d, $79 with kitchenettes, discounts for military personnel or veterans). Being a full-service Y, the modern, flag-draped granite edifice comes with Olympic-sized pool and fitness center (free to guests) and is just a few minutes' walk from the $1 MBTA water shuttles to Long Wharf and, on weekdays, North Station. Several good restaurants within walking distance cater to the waterfront condo dwellers and office workers who now inhabit the Navy Yard's renovated brick and granite buildings, including an excellent Italian bistro, **Gabriele's,** only a block away (closed Sunday), and **Biga Breads,** a delectable breakfast-lunch bakery-cafe, at the end of Eighth St. in the Navy Yard's Flagship Wharf building (open daily).

Single travelers unable to land a spot at any of the above, or who are looking for a kitchen-equipped alternative to the hostels, might consider sharing modestly renovated, fully furnished apartment units with three or four other strangers at the **Farrington Inn,** 23 Farrington St. in Allston, tel. (800) 76-SLEEP or, from the U.K., (0800) 896-040, for $40-60 (note, though, that if you don't like nicotine dreams, you may be out of luck, given how much the European clientele would rather smoke than breathe). The Farrington—actually a series of rooming and apartment houses in a small residential pocket a block off Allston's commercial Harvard Avenue, 10 minutes by bus to Harvard Square—has tiny, closet-size singles sharing a bath on a hall, too, for the same rates, but Brookline's Beacon St. lodgings are a much better value, and more convenient to most of Boston. (There are also double rooms with private baths and small kitchenettes, vastly overpriced at $95-120 in high season, unless you have a weakness for acoustic tile, mismatched dorm-quality furniture, and old cast-iron radiators.)

Don't even think of finding moderate-priced rooms in Cambridge. Unless you visit in winter, when expensive rooms at properties described below take a temporary dip, bargains simply don't exist here.

EXPENSIVE: $85-110

If you enjoy B&Bs, one in Cambridge offers a good value: Central Square's **Prospect Place,** tel. (800) 769-5303, a few minutes' walk from the Red Line ($88-105 d, surcharge for single night stays most of the year, but no tax). Carefully restored to exhibit the Victorian craftsmanship that went into its original construction, this Italianate home features delicately rippled cylinder glass and marble fireplaces. It's appropriately furnished with antiques, too, but a genial host and genuine lived-in warmth dispel any sense of being in a museum.

If proximity to beautiful Arnold Arboretum or the pleasant jogging path around Jamaica Pond is more appealing than being in the heart of Cambridge—or if you're traveling with a dog, or need a dedicated modem line for your laptop—try the beautifully restored 1855 **Taylor House B&B,** in Jamaica Plain, tel. (888) 228-2956, e-mail taylorbb@ziplink.net, near the Emerald Necklace and within a block of the #39 bus to Copley Square. Rooms that share a bath are as low as $80 d during the week; those that have private baths run as high as $120 d for weekends.

Unless you value room service, handicap access, or multistory atriums, the best deal going next door to Harvard University is **A Friendly**

Inn at Harvard Square, 1673 Cambridge St., tel. (617) 547-7851. Though neither large nor oriented to receive much natural light, all rooms have private baths and phones, and most have small TVs; light continental breakfast is included, and parking is free. Most of the year rates run $88-107 d ($10 less for a single), but inquire about their sharp winter discounts in January and February. If you aren't picky about price or quality as long as you're next to Harvard, refer to A Friendly Inn's next-door neighbor, the Irving House, under **Premium,** below. Alternatively, try the **Susse Chalet Inn—Cambridge,** 211 Concord Turnpike (Rt. 2), tel. (800) 258-1980, the local outpost of an East Coast economy motel chain. The principal drawback (besides that annoying tendency chains have of charging for local phone calls) is its location, a quarter mile west of Alewife station at the end of the MBTA Red Line, in a pedestrian-unfriendly realm of highways and faceless office parks at the very fringe of North Cambridge. May-Nov., rates start at $92.70 d; in winter they drop by about a third (kids *don't* stay free). At least the parking is free, and the morning sweets and coffee are, too.

Across the river in Boston, one of the few decent choices in this price range is the **Hotel Buckminster,** 645 Beacon St. in bustling Kenmore Square, tel. (800) 727-2825. The least expensive double rooms are small, but larger sizes

BED AND BREAKFASTS

Visitors who have a preference for staying at B&Bs rather than in hotels will find the metropolitan area host to a broad range of these private accommodations, from cozy rooms that share a bath to virtually self-contained studio apartments furnished for your maximum comfort. Although by no means inexpensive, rates and amenities may prove quite attractive when compared to the shoot-the-moon pricing that now grips most city hotels and inns. A few standout B&Bs are featured on the following pages, but most prefer to let one of several independent agencies handle inquiries and bookings. Although none of these services is free (rates start at about $15), using them carries a couple advantages over simply scouring the Internet for referrals from other travelers. First, these agencies are practiced matchmakers: describe the particular experience you seek—romantic oasis in the city's heart, historic digs convenient to a specific attraction, or just a quiet and budget-friendly place to flop down at the end of a busy day—and they'll steer you there. Second, they'll save you the time and expense of making 20 phone calls or e-mail messages trying to find that one room available where and when you want, at a price you can afford. Beside reservation fees, be advised that single-night surcharges or minimum-stay requirements in high season may apply. Deposits are usually also required, and take those cancellation policies seriously—they aren't just for show.

Most city B&Bs have found their clientele has little or no interest in full breakfasts. If you're a purist who doesn't consider boxed cereal and Thermos coffee synonymous with breakfast, be sure to inquire closely about what's really meant by such terms as "hearty" or "gourmet continental."

Diabetics and other travelers with special needs will find most owner-operated B&Bs willing to handle special breakfast requests if you give them clear guidance. Anyone keeping kosher, on the other hand, has but one choice: the **Four Seasons B&B,** in the Boston suburb of Newton, within a pleasant walk of the Green "D" Line to downtown Boston, tel. (617) 928-1128. It's the only kosher B&B in the whole state (at $70 d, including a full homemade breakfast, it's also an excellent value no matter what your dietary restrictions).

Despite the fact that most of the following reservation services have e-mail and Web sites, all unanimously suggest that old-fashioned phone calls will yield the most rapid and, ultimately, most personalized service.

Bed & Breakfast Agency of Boston, tel. (800) CITY-BNB or, from the UK, (0800) 895-128, or (617) 720-3540; www.boston-bnbagency.com

Bed and Breakfast Associates/Bay Colony, Ltd., tel. (800) 347-5088 or (781) 449-5302; www.bnbboston.com

B & B Reservations North Shore/Greater Boston/Cape Cod, tel. (800) 832-2632 outside Massachusetts, or (617) 964-6016; www.bbreserve.com

Host Homes of Boston, tel. (617) 244-1308

are available, and some even come with kitchenettes ($99-229 d in high season). Though furnished like an average chain hotel, the historic Buckminster has a certain *je ne c'est quoi*—stemming, perhaps, from the odd angles and spaces created by modernizing an older building, or the big bay windows with their urban views. Or maybe there are just benign ghosts from the deal to rig the 1919 World Series—the seed of what was to became known as the Black Sox scandal—which was made in the hotel's small lobby. Three of the T's four Green Lines converge virtually beneath the hotel entrance, and despite the hubbub of activity in the Square, the Buckminster's massively overbuilt masonry walls keep the din firmly at bay.

PREMIUM: $110-150

Some of the city's most comfortable rooms at any price are found in the incomparable **Mary Prentiss Inn,** 6 Prentiss St. in Cambridge, tel. (617) 661-2929. May through mid-November, rates are $129-209 d, depending on size of room (Jan.-Feb., rates drop as low as $89-119), including full or continental breakfast and free parking (limited, so reserve ahead). Like a Chopin etude, the beautifully restored 1843 Greek Revival building exudes the artist-owner's strong command of style and obvious appreciation for grace and comfort, from freshly baked afternoon cookies and personable staff to good-sized rooms with wet bars discreetly built into cabinets—even a couple in-room fireplaces. As for convenient location, the Porter Square Commuter Rail and Red Line station is a few minutes' walk away, Harvard is seven blocks, and plenty of good restaurants are around the corner along Mass. Ave.

A block from Boston's Public Garden, **The College Club,** 44 Comm. Ave. at the corner of Arlington, tel. (617) 536-9510, offers a lucky few travelers a taste of the elegance for which the fashionable Back Bay is renown, in a TV-free Victorian brownstone belonging to a 19th-century women's club. The six rooms with private baths are perfectly enormous, with 14-foot ceilings, pleasant decor that blends reproductions with true antiques, and ornamental old fireplaces. Given the location alone, the rate of $112 d on

these is a real steal; the free continental breakfast is simply gilding on the lily. Some significantly smaller single rooms, all sharing baths on the hall, are also available for $70, which again is hardly a price to be sneezed at, in this overpriced town.

Another good deal in Boston proper is **The Copley Inn,** tel. (800) 232-0306, a small 21-room guesthouse tucked into a South End Victorian rowhouse at the corner of Garrison and St. Botolph St., just steps away from Huntington Ave. and the Green Line's Prudential station, and a few short blocks from the heart of Back Bay. Though free of period frills, the light and comfortable rooms all include kitchenettes and phones with voice mail, which partly explains the regular clientele of businesspeople staying by the week. They also recognize good value when they see it: rates are only $125 d (or $85 off season, typically late Dec.-Feb., holidays excepted). Medium- to long-term visitors who'd take kitchen privileges over room service any day may also want to consider a fully furnished studio apartment or guesthouse efficiency suite from **Copley House,** 239 W. Newton St., two blocks from the Prudential Center, tel. (800) 331-1318. This firm maintains apartments in three historic brick rowhouses around the Symphony Hall edge of the South End and Fenway neighborhoods. Imagine—all the modern conveniences and a generic hotel-Victorian look for only $85-130 per night, with a three-night minimum (parking $8 extra per night). Weekly rates are even more reasonable: $475-675.

For those who prefer to be in the absolute thick of fashionable Back Bay rather than at its edge, the consider the **Newbury Guest House,** 261 Newbury St., tel. (800) 437-7668. More a small hotel than guesthouse, the Newbury swaddles its guests in faux Victorian trimmings from hardwood floors and Oriental runners to four-poster beds and ornamental fireplaces in the larger front rooms. (If you're a light sleeper who turns in early, you'll prefer the smaller but quieter back rooms.) For "only" $110-150 d, the comfort and value of even the smallest compares favorably to nearby chains. (Parking is $15 at a nearby garage.) The tradeoff is space and room service: if you need more of either while remaining within central Boston, you require a luxury-priced hotel.

Matching the Back Bay's cachet brick for exclusive brick is the Beacon Hill address of **The Eliot & Pickett Houses,** 6 Mt. Vernon Pl., tel. (617) 248-8707, e-mail P&E@uua.org, 19th-century brick townhouses sitting so close to the State House and the Common that its roof deck overlooks both. (Mt. Vernon Place is a three-car-length dead-end lane off Joy St. between Mt. Vernon St. and Beacon.) More a plain, institutionally simple inn than fancy B&B—there are no in-room TVs or daily maid service, and guests prepare their own breakfasts from the eggs, bread, cereal, and other fixings left for them in the fridge—these residences are owned by the Unitarian Universalist Association, whose headquarters are a few doors away. Rooms not booked for church business are available to the public mostly for $140 ($120 off season), with twin double beds and private baths, although small, under-the-gables queen rooms with shared baths are as low as $85. Parking is available in the Boston Common Garage for $19 on weekdays, $7 on Saturday or Sunday.

Once privately run for the benefit of families visiting patients at nearby hospitals, the friendly **John Jeffries House,** 14 Embankment Rd., tel. (617) 367-1866, now also welcomes the world at large. Though standard doubles are minuscule, each room comes with a kitchenette that gives it the feel of a tiny city pied-à-terre. The exceptional location faces the Charles Street Red Line station at the foot of Beacon Hill, within easy strolling distance of fine shops, restaurants, the Museum of Science, and the riverfront Esplanade, almost within earshot of the Boston Pops' outdoor concerts if the brick walls weren't virtually soundproof. Rates begin at $105 d; oversized rooms and suites run $120-145; and validated parking is $15 at an adjacent garage.

If you need to be closer to Boston University, or to the Longwood Medical Area (where many of the city's hospitals are clustered), or are traveling with a small pet; if you want a base convenient to both city transit and out-of-town drives (without fighting downtown traffic or paying downtown hotel parking rates), or simply want more than a plain carpeted box for $100, **The Bertram Inn,** in Brookline, tel. (800) 295-3822, Web site www.bertraminn.com, is a sure bet. Named after a hostelry in an Agatha Christie novel, the Tudor-style Victorian at 92 Sewall Ave. (one block from

the Saint Paul St. surface stop on the Green "C" Line) combines well-appointed, "casually elegant," antique-filled rooms with modern amenities and service-oriented staff, as personable and dedicated as any B&B owner. Two of the rooms in this former private mansion have working fireplaces, too. Summer rates are $99-209 d, with free parking and continental breakfast; off-season rates drop to an absolute bargain at $79-129.

If a refrain of "no vacancy" is all you hear from any of the above, a couple more options at this price range are worth checking out. Consider, for example, the **Shawmut Inn,** 280 Friend St., nearly opposite North Station, tel. (800) 350-7784 reservations, (617) 720-5544 information. Rooms come in all shapes and sizes, but most are more spacious than those at twice their price only 15 minutes' walk away in the Financial District. While furnished as cleanly and simply as a modern hospital (and with about the same degree of charm), each room at least has a mini-refrigerator and microwave, and hacker tourists can request a room with a modem-compatible phone. There's also a health club across the street available to guests for a nominal fee. Rates start at $116 d May-Nov., $89 off season.

Even more lacking in uniformity are the rooms of the **Irving House,** 24 Irving St., right at the periphery of Harvard, four blocks from the Science Center and Graduate School of Design, tel. (800) 854-8249 out of state, (617) 547-4600 locally. Despite the dramatic variation in size, condition, and comfort, this establishment provides a vivid example of what I dub the Harvard Effect, as most of its rooms are priced $140 d and up (with private baths and modest continental breakfast) in the high Sept.-Nov. season. (Dec.-Feb., doubles with private baths are as low as $100.) Single rooms with shared baths run $75-95. For Commencement Week, the rates jump to $185 d. Despite the steep Ivy League prices, it's still cheaper than the full-service hotels around Harvard; this fact and its European *pension* atmosphere keep it chock full most of the year. For newly constructed, more uniform (and even *more* expensive) rooms in a similarly large and graceful clapboard house, inquire about the Irving's sister B&B inn outside Central Square: the **Isaac Harding House,** 288 Harvard St., tel. (617) 876-2888. Both properties have free but limited parking, available on a first-come, first-served basis.

If you need a handicap accessible room—or prefer lodgings with that national-chain-motel look and feel—your most convenient choice is in East Cambridge on the Somerville line at the **Cambridge Inn**, 250 Monsignor O'Brien Hwy. (Rt. 28), tel. (888) 887-7690 or (617) 441-9200. It's just two blocks from the Lechmere end of the Green Line, not far from the Museum of Science; high season rates begin at $139 d, including free morning coffee and danish. Slightly more economical choices are found in Allston-Brighton, a few miles west of downtown. One is the **Best Western Terrace Motor Lodge**, 1650 Commonwealth Ave. in Brighton, tel. (800) 528-1234. Outside of winter's low season, rates start at $119 d, including free parking and continental breakfast. Although the hilltop location near St. Elizabeth's Hospital is in an unremarkable neighborhood of apartment blocks, the Green "B" Line trolley from Boston College to downtown stops just out front (avoid riding it during rush hour—it's arguably the T's most crowded trolley line, and if you're bound to or from downtown, you'll be standing for almost 20 stops). On the bright side, Allston's plethora of cheap and delicious ethnic eateries are just a few T stops down the hill. Equally off the beaten path is the **Days Inn**, 1234 Soldiers Field Rd., in Allston, tel. (800) 325-2525, with an outdoor pool, free parking, and a decent Italian restaurant-nightclub on the premises; $119-139 d in high season, or as low as $79 d in winter. Though hedged in by such charming neighbors as a roller rink and the city transportation department sandlot, it's right across from some nice jogging paths along the Charles River, and is only about a 20-minute walk through riverside Christian Herter Park to Harvard Square and the T.

Alternatively, consider the **Howard Johnson Inn—Boston/Fenway,** 1271 Boylston St., within a Mo Vaugh grand slam of Fenway Park, tel. (800) I-GO-HOJO. The least expensive of the three HoJo properties in the city, its April-Oct. rates start at $140 d, with free parking, outdoor pool, and free shuttle to the Longwood Medical area.

LUXURY: $150 AND UP

If cutting corners isn't in your vocabulary, why settle for anything less than either the townhouse-styled **Ritz-Carlton,** 15 Arlington St., tel. (800) 241-3333, or the more modern **Four Seasons,** 200 Boylston St., tel. (800) 332-3442. Overlooking the Public Garden a block apart, these are routinely ranked as Boston's finest hotels, earning their garlands by waiting on you hand and foot. Consider such niceties as a room-service kitchen on every floor, so you don't have to wait to sate any sudden cravings for caviar

and toast (the Ritz), or a ready supply of duck food for your young children to disburse among the Lagoon residents across the street (the Four Seasons). An evening at the Four Seasons' outstanding restaurant, **Aujourd'hui,** is a way to sample that hotel's attentiveness for only about a third of the room rate. Afternoon tea at the Ritz (jackets no longer required for men) offers a similarly luxurious foray into high society at a fraction of the regular admission price.

If these two are the rival princes of Boston's hotels, the undisputed queen mum is **The Fairmont Copley Plaza,** on St. James St. next to the John Hancock Company's 65-story headquarters in Back Bay, tel. (800) 527-4727. Appropriately lavish in its marbled, coffered, and antique-filled interior, the Copley is a grande dame indeed—the sort of place where, if you spend the afternoon in your large, high-ceilinged room, you'll be fussed over to distraction by gracious housekeepers bringing you another pile of fluffy towels, mints to stash by your bedside, fresh flowers, an extra dusting here, a plumping of the pillows there; but what do you expect from a place that stamps its crest into the sand in its lobby ashtrays? Be sure to inquire about package deals ($189-379 d, plus $26 parking).

For one of the best values in its class, look no further than **The Eliot Hotel,** 370 Comm. Ave. on the edge of Back Bay, a block from the Green Line, tel. (800) 44-ELIOT ($195-325 d, $20 parking). Often characterized as European—meaning it doesn't have thousands of rooms, or a giant lobby to park your kids in—the Eliot provides exceptional comfort in all 90 of its two- and three-room suites, from refrigerators and modem-compatible dual-line phones to the tasteful furnishings, house plants, and large marble-appointed baths. For corner views overlooking both Massachusetts and Commonwealth Avenues ask for an "04" room.

At the edge of the Back Bay—or, more accurately, on its cusp with the South End—is **The Colonnade Hotel,** 120 Huntington Ave., tel. (800) 962-3030. Spacious, well-furnished rooms with views of either the Prudential Center across the street or quiet South End patios and pocket gardens, a Green Line T station virtually beneath the front door, and a very knowledgeable concierge give this place a discernible edge over the Sheraton and Hilton a block away, for about the same high season rack rates ($295 and up, plus $22 for parking). Very often the discounted rate available from the local hotel brokers is markedly better than those offered by its neighbors, too.

The Lenox Hotel, at the corner of Boylston and Exeter streets, tel. (800) 225-7676, is a great little oasis of civility. Classical music wafts gently across the spacious lobby with its chandeliers, cathedral ceiling, and French Provincial decor. Attentive staff prompt you with Sirs and Ma'ams from registration up to your room ($265-295 d depending on size), which, if you've planned far enough in advance, could be one of the dozen with working fireplaces ($345 d). Be sure to inquire about package deals. The Sam Adams Brewhouse is conveniently located at street level,

and the Green Line's Copley station is a block away; hotel parking starts at $22 per day. On Huntington Ave. a block away is the Lenox's sister property, the **Copley Square Hotel,** tel. (800) 225-7062, a venerable old place that once hosted William McKinley's campaign headquarters during his successful 1895 run for the White House. With a third fewer rooms than its sibling, it makes up in personal attention whatever it may lack in size and opulence. Rack rates are $175-215, or $325 for family rooms (two bedrooms sharing a full bath), but skip the low end "moderate" rooms—they're too small to justify their price. Parking is another $20 daily. Off season (Jan.-Feb.), package rates may be available for as low as $149, and discounted rates for Entertainment Card members or other eligible groups may be as low as $107.

Standard business-class hotel rooms at a luxury price are available from several Back Bay chains. **The Westin Hotel, Copley Place,** 10 Huntington Ave., tel. (800) 228-3000, offers a full range of amenities, including fitness room, sauna, and a 34-foot indoor lap pool. Besides great city views from upper-story rooms, it's one block from Amtrak's Back Bay Station and the T. Three blocks west stands the **Back Bay Hilton,** 40 Dalton St., across from the Hynes Convention Center, tel. (800) 874-0663. Rooms are about the same as the Sheraton across the street, but since there are about one quarter as many, you're much more likely to land one with a view of the city, rather than of the neighboring block of rooms. Far quieter public areas, too ($185-290).

Besides having enough gilded lobby decorations to rival Versailles, the **Boston Park Plaza Hotel,** 64 Arlington St., tel. (800) 225-2008, is also known for its annual sponsorship of summer's quartet of live swans at the Public Garden a block away (hence the swan logo on the brass door pulls). Though regular rack rates for the hotel's cozy, agreeably furnished rooms top off over $270 d, off-season rates are as low as $149 (parking is $23 extra). Though the place is enormous, the staff keeps it from feeling impersonal, while a bunch of fine restaurants and dessert shops on the ground floor ensure that you need not walk out of doors to obtain some of the city's finest comestibles.

When hospitality with a personal touch is more important than proximity to the Public Garden

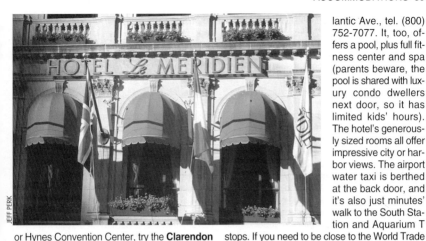

JEFF PERK

or Hynes Convention Center, try the **Clarendon Square B&B,** tel. (617) 536-2229, e-mail Clar SqrBnB@aol.com ($135-200 d, generally a two-night minimum), a South End gem located on W. Brookline St. near the Boston Center for the Arts and Tremont Street's vibrant restaurant row. The lavish continental breakfast buffet serves equally well for early risers and late sleepers, and though guests are encouraged—rather than forced—to be social, if it's utter privacy you want this place can give you that, too. Annotated city maps, suggested itineraries for short stays or rainy days, a roofdeck, modem lines for laptop-toting e-mail junkies, and informed opinions about neighborhood dining are among the extra touches. Romantic types looking for a cosmopolitan winter lair will be gratified to find working fireplaces in each guest room.

Downtown and along the waterfront are several additional choices for those to whom money is no object: standard double-occupancy rack rates nearly all begin at about $300. For extra-large rooms and superlative service, try **Le Meridien Boston,** 250 Franklin St., tel. (800) 543-4300, in the heart of the Financial District. Among the other amenities found at this former Federal Reserve Bank are a 40-foot lap pool, health club, and, not surprisingly, early morning delivery of the *Wall Street Journal* to your door. Its central location is within a few blocks of Amtrak, the airport water shuttle, and the T. Nearby, framing the waterfront with its stunning 80-foot arch, is the **Boston Harbor Hotel,** on Rowes Wharf off Atlantic Ave., tel. (800) 752-7077. It, too, offers a pool, plus full fitness center and spa (parents beware, the pool is shared with luxury condo dwellers next door, so it has limited kids' hours). The hotel's generously sized rooms all offer impressive city or harbor views. The airport water taxi is berthed at the back door, and it's also just minutes' walk from the South Station and Aquarium T stops. If you need to be close to the World Trade Center on Northern Ave., consider the **Seaport Hotel & Conference Center,** tel. (800) WTC-HOTEL, just across the street. Features include pool, fitness center, van shuttle to South Station, water taxi to airport, hotel-wide intranet, and many high-tech communication capabilities. On the other side of downtown at the edge the Theater District stands the **Radisson Hotel Boston,** 200 Stuart St., tel. (800) 333-3333, whose standard rooms are among the city's largest, all with balconies overlooking busy Charles Street or the hidden warren of residential streets known as Bay Village ($245-295 d). The T is conveniently within a couple of blocks, and if walking the city proves insufficient exercise, there's an indoor rooftop pool and weight room. A block away in the center of the Theater District, across from the Wang Center for the Performing Arts and Tufts/New England Medical Center, is the **Tremont House Boston, a Wyndham Grand Heritage Hotel,** 275 Tremont St., tel. (800) 331-9998. Although the hotel name is bigger than its standard rooms, their interiors are possibly Boston's most bold, with sleek modern furnishings and colors drawn from David Hockney's palette ($259 and up).

Cambridge seems to regard luxury as a perquisite of the executive rather than leisure class, given that its finest hospitality is found in modern, efficient, business-oriented establishments. While "business hotel" is often a synonym for "boring," that's certainly not the case at

The Charles Hotel, just outside of Harvard Square, tel. (800) 882-1818. Easily one of the region's top hotels (and a favorite of visiting film and music stars), the independently run Charles distinguishes itself from the crowd with such thoughtful touches as high-end Bose Wave radios in every room, professionally narrated children's stories at the touch of a button on every bedside phone, a direct search-and-deliver phone line to nearby WordsWorth bookstore (purchases are automatically charged to your room and delivered within minutes), and some of the city's best dining in both its restaurants. The contemporary decor is softened by design motifs echoing the collection of American quilts—some dating back to the early 19th century—that adorn many of the hotel's public spaces. Standard rates run $225-329, with super-saver packages as low as $179—all in all, a vastly better value than the nearby Inn at Harvard, whose charming four-story atrium masks undersized, underwhelming rooms at prices that betray a uniquely Harvard interpretation of Ludwig Mies van der Rohe's dictum, "less is more."

Hard-working business travelers may also want to consider the **University Park Hotel at MIT,** tel. (800) 222-8733, on Sidney St. a block off Mass. Ave., by the Necco candy factory outside Central Square. Larger than average rooms, ergonomic furniture, excellent task lighting, and customized desks with built-in power outlets and modem jacks on top not only spare you from moving furniture or crawling around hunting for plugs in order to check your e-mail, but may actually make you productive enough to take time to savor Central Square's vibrant food and live music scene. Rack rates are in the high $200s, but as always, inquire about special rates for which you may be eligible, or check for deals via local discount brokers.

Overlooking the mouth of the Charles River and the Museum of Science is East Cambridge's

Royal Sonesta Hotel, tel. (800) SONESTA, on Land Blvd. opposite the Cambridge Galleria mall, a short walk from the Green Line's Lechmere station or complimentary van ride from Harvard ($250-300 d in high season, $195-250 d in low; parking $17). The modern aesthetic here leans toward comfortably sized rooms whose unobtrusive decor won't distract from those views of sailboats and the State House dome. More interesting is what's outside the rooms: the Sonesta chain is known for its exceptional patronage of 20th-century art, some 70 pieces of which are on display in this flagship property's public spaces, including a Jonathan Borofsky figure suspended over the entrance, a Frank Stella opposite the registration desk, a series of Andy Warhol flowers facing the West Tower elevators, a Sol LeWitt across from the lobby shop, signed Buckminster Fuller "blueprints" along the connecting corridor to the next-door headquarters of IBM's Lotus Development division, and numerous works by local and regional artists. Pick up a free guide to the whole collection at the lobby Guest Services counter and take a walk through the mini-museum.

If you want to keep one foot outside the city, the better to escape on daytrips, consider North Cambridge's **Best Western Homestead Inn,** 220 Alewife Brook Parkway, tel. (800) 528-1234, next to the Fresh Pond mall and within a short walk of Alewife station on the Red Line. Rates vary depending on season and demand, but start at $169 d spring-fall and $119 in winter. Free parking and complimentary breakfast, plus an indoor pool. If your preferred escape hatch is the airport, you'll find comparable prices at either the **Ramada Inn Logan Airport,** on the airport grounds, tel. (800) 228-3344, or the **Holiday Inn Boston—Logan Airport,** 225 McClellan Hwy. (Rt. 1A), adjacent to Blue Line subway, tel. (800) HOLIDAY.

COURTESY OF THE BOSTONIAN SOCIETY/OLD STATE HOUSE

FOOD

If you think Boston dining consists of clam chowder, baked beans, broiled cod, and boiled beef, you'll either be surprised or disappointed at the truth.

Sure, seafood is a staple, and two local chains —**Skipjack's** and **Legal Seafoods**—will handily slake your need for chowder, but things with fins and shells are so common that you don't have to confine yourself to these or the big-ticket waterfront places in order to enjoy a good fishy meal.

Traditional New England boiled dinners are a little more rare, but they, too, can be had if you're really, really adventurous: **Amrhein's,** on W. Broadway in South Boston, tel. (617) 268-6189, is the undisputed winner in this category—and it's only a block from the Broadway T stop. Baked beans, too, are something of a novelty outside of the Maxwell House-and-white-bread circuit, but Faneuil Hall's **Durgin-Park** does serve a toothsome traditional pork- and molasses-flavored version of the dish.

But most Boston meals worth your dollar reflect a far more varied set of idioms: the 1980s influence of California seen in local bistro menus,

for example, or the decade-old Pan-Asian invasion—Thai, Vietnamese, Korean, Japanese—which provides an alternative to their Chinese forerunners all over town. Sicilian pizzerias and Greek-American homestyle eateries are fixtures predating JFK, and the latest restaurant revival has returned Boston to the Mediterranean, this time to Tuscany, Provençe, Perpignan, Spain, Portugal, North Africa, and the Levant. India, Brazil, the Caribbean, and continental Europe are never far away, and both inexpensive burrito bars and upscale brewpubs are common. Irish pubs, roast beef, sinfully rich chocolate desserts, ice cream parlors, and leisurely Sunday brunches are all local institutions. Many places cater to vegetarians and healthful eaters with one or two meatless, but macrobiotic cooking is far more difficult to come by; **Masao's Kitchen,** in the Porter Square Exchange, Cambridge, tel. (617) 497-7348, and **Five Seasons,** on Beacon St. in Brookline, tel. (617) 731-2500, are your best bets for this specialty.

Kosher restaurants, both the meat- and milk-free varieties, are found primarily on Harvard St. in Brookline (home to the only American Hasidic community outside of New York), but downtown's **Milk Street Cafe,** in the Financial District, is an excellent fish-and-dairy kosher lunch spot. Since this *is* a student capital, you won't have to dress up for dinner except at the trendy spots frequented by the Armani-wearing Euro-crowd and their local imitators. Even the Ritz has dropped its jacket requirement (in its cafe, anyway).

Many of the best eats are in residential neighborhoods, not downtown near the major hotels, so don't be shy: go where real Bostonians go when their employers aren't picking up the tab. Nearly all the restaurants cited below are within easy walking distance of both public transit and other restaurants, so no venture off the tourist track need be in vain if your first choice has taken the day off. Mind the time, though: due to the political clout of resident associations vigilant about their nightly peace and quiet, extraordinarily few restaurants serve later than 9:30-10 p.m. Exceptions are primarily in the South End, where a few kitchens remain open till 11 p.m. or midnight, and Chinatown, where a handful of places stay open till 3 or 4 a.m.

BEACON HILL AND DOWNTOWN

Charles Street

Just steps away from the civilized bustle of Beacon Hill's main drag is the cozy basement home of **Lala Rokh,** 97 Mt. Vernon St., tel. (617) 720-5511. It's intimate enough to make diners speak in library whispers, but the Persian cuisine is worth shouting about ($12-16). Try leg of lamb stewed in a sauce of fenugreek, scallions, cilantro, chives, and dried lime—or chicken, tomato, and saffron with fragrant basmati rice seasoned with cumin, cinnamon, rose petals, and tart barberries. Even the simple-sounding grilled sirloin kebabs are richly marinated to bring out flavors you might never have thought beef capable of. Add a couple vegetable side dishes and pickles and you'll have the makings of a shah's feast. Everything's as good as it sounds, and the waitstaff expertly advises anyone reduced to indecision by the exotic-sounding choices. Literally translated as "tulip face" (meaning rosy cheeks), this gem of a restaurant takes its name from a romantic 1817 best-seller by poet

ONE FISH, TWO FISH: DINING ON SEAFOOD

When it comes to dining, most out-of-state visitors to Massachusetts come looking for seafood. It's understandable: clams, oysters, mussels, scallops, lobster, monkfish, bluefish, striped bass, shad, yellowtail flounder, bluefin tuna, mackerel, and, yes, even cod are among the native denizens of the sea whose appearance on local menus is almost always worth the tariff. (It should be noted that scrod, though occasionally seen on fried-fish menus, isn't actually a species of fish—it's a catchall term at the Boston fish auction for baby cod, haddock, and any other flaky white-flesh fish under 2.5 pounds in weight.) Don't be fooled, however, into thinking that Massachusetts seafood restaurants exclusively serve Massachusetts seafood. Given the collapse of offshore fisheries due to overfishing, rendering numerous species commercially extinct, the state is actually a net *importer* of seafood. Which means there are restaurants whose scallops may be flash-frozen product from Asia or Iceland, and whose de-

licious-sounding salmon du jour is probably raised on the same aquaculture farm up in Maine that express-ships its product to Atlanta and Chicago. But in this age of overnight cargo, don't let such caveats obscure the more relevant fact that this city draws on such a deep *tradition* of seafood preparation that you could give many local chefs a frozen fish stick and they'd still make something so wonderful and tasty of it that you'd never know or care where it came from before ending up on your fork.

A couple of cases in point: **Kelly's,** on the coast north of the airport, and the **East Coast Grill,** in Inman Square, Cambridge. The former—whose full name is actually Kelly's World Famous Roast Beef—is by all appearances a lowly take-out joint on Revere Beach, a legendary strip of ocean-front real estate known for its summer population of guys in muscle cars and babes with teased hair. But there's nothing lowly about Kelly's glorious fried clams, heaped up beside monster mounds of french fries and fried

Thomas Moore, a copy of which is on display (despite not even knowing the difference between Egypt, Persia, and India, the book was such a success that it made Moore a Persian expert in the West).

Dip into old-fashioned sensual excess at **75 Chestnut,** tel. (617) 227-2175, a block off Charles St. in the "flatlands" below Beacon Hill. Embroidered upholstry, oil paintings of Edwardian cityscapes framed by forest-green walls, and fringed draperies imbue the place with the distinct air of a luxurious private club. It's an impression reinforced by the hefty portions of wood-grilled and charbroiled dishes, such as a slab of tuna smothered in puttanesca sauce, chicken breast with portabello mushroom gravy, or roasted pork loin with candied shallot glaze, not to mention one of the city's better New York sirloins (entrees $12.95-22.95). The house breads are excellent, as are the desserts—the chocolate mousse-and-meringue Concorde cake alone will banish boredom from your evening. The beer and wine list lacks luster, but that doesn't stop customers from gathering four deep at the bar even on early weekday nights. Service is impeccable, too, right down to the doorman who

politely greets every passerby, including—to their continual surprise and delight—all the scruffy young Emerson College students trudging to class nearby. The only missing element is a portly gaggle of plutocrats settled in wing chairs sipping brandy and puffing expensive cigars.

Given neighbors like these, it should come as no surprise that Charles Street's best market, **Savenor's,** carries lobster-gorgonzola ravioli, wild boar sausage, and farm-raised zebra steaks. Needless to say, the local pizza chain is also anything but ordinary. So when you're in the mood for the paper-thin Roman variety, wood-fired with toppings like fresh-shucked clams, caramelized leeks, or fig and balsamic jam, get thee to **Figs,** 42 Charles, tel. (617) 742-FIGS. It's no slouch with the pasta dishes, either, or the beautiful salads ($10.50-16.95).

If diner fare suits your taste more than all that gourmet stuff, check out **The Paramount,** next door to Figs at 44, tel. (617) 720-1151, whose broiled chops and burgers have been lubricating Beacon Hill digestive tracts since the Great Depression. Another mostly yuppie-free dining option is **Buzzy's Fabulous Roast Beef,** a very modern takeout shack nestled in the shadow of

---

onion rings. And no day is so perfect that it can't be improved by Kelly's lip-smackingly delicious lobster rolls. A basic commodity of New England fast-food from beachfront snack shacks to local McDonalds, it outwardly resembles tuna salad served on a hot dog bun, but with lobster meat instead of tuna. Fish and chips, fried scallops, and New England clam chowder are also staples of Kelly's menu. (Although clam chowder is nearly ubiquitous in the region, diligent chowderheads will find almost no two versions alike. Middlebrow theme restaurants that come in from outside the region, like the Elephant and Castle in downtown Boston, often mistakenly assume that New England clam chowder should have the texture of wallpaper paste, but don't be fooled: proper "chowda" never requires a spackling knife. Nor does it have tomatoes: that's Manhattan's recipe.) And yes, as the name suggests, Kelly's also does roast beef sandwiches (they claim to have invented them, back in 1951—but that's another story). Open daily year-round—tel. (781) 284-9129 for current hours—Kelly's can be easily reached from the end of the Blue Line (last stop Wonderland): after exiting the

station, walk toward the ocean (one block) and stroll north (left) about a third of a mile to where the line of eager clam-eaters stand waiting for their orders.

At the opposite end of the spectrum is the East Coast Grill, 1271 Cambridge St., Cambridge, tel. (617) 491-6568, about 15 minutes' walk from the Central Square station on the Red Line. Though its owner, Chris Schlesinger, has made a national name for himself with his *Thrill of the Grill* barbecue cookbooks and television shows, top-notch straight-off-the-boat seafood is a specialty of the house, typically prepared with bold sauces, colorful accompaniments, and portions that would satisfy a hungry doryman (except for the vegetarian specials and the slow-cooked smoke-pit barbecue, entrees average about $20). Underutilized fish species from local waters are featured nightly, and the restaurant's raw bar is easily one of the city's best. Casual and loud, with cocktails as hot as the "live" volcano in the side room, the EC is one big live wire most nights, so make reservations or be prepared to wait (Sun.-Thurs., reservations only taken for parties of five or more).

at the Haymarket

JEFF PERK

the old Charles St. jail's impenetrable stone walls, beside the busy rotary under the Charles St. T station. Heart-stopping sandwiches of blushing beef top the menu here, but there's a mean roast turkey with Dijon mustard, too, and even a half-decent vegetarian hummus wrap. The hand-cut french fries are among Boston's best. Always open, it's a favorite of both cabbies and insomniac residents from nearby hospitals, but the juicy bargains draw a good lunch crowd, too; sit at the picnic tables inside or out and you get free entertainment from drivers playing roller derby a few yards away.

Faneuil Hall and the Financial District
The Faneuil Hall Marketplace is nothing for diners to seek out; in general better value can be had elsewhere in the vicinity without having to contend with either the dizzying crowds or food that's been congealing under heat lamps. For a start, try the Haymarket area across North Street. **Marshall's,** 15 Union St., tel. (617) 523-9396, next door to the Union Oyster House, is a great spot for fresh shellfish. Order a plate of oysters on the half shell and the bartender shucks them for you then and there, instead of plucking them out of a pan of ye olde crushed ice. The place's barstools may not have been polished by Revolutionary breeches, but are you looking for history or a meal? If you want a little of both, nip into the **Green Dragon Tavern,** around the corner on cobblestone Marshall St., tel. (617) 367-0055, a cozy watering hole named for the

spot where Paul Revere, Dr. Joseph Warren, and other thirsty Freemasons active in the American Revolution plotted against King George. Wash down the simple fare with what some say is the best Guinness in town—a fiercely competitive honor, given the city's legion of Irish pubs. Additional doses of fish and chips or lamb stew can be had on the downtown side of Quincy Market, in **The Black Rose,** on State St., or the intimate and less-touristed **Mr. Dooley's Boston Tavern,** at the corner of Broad and Batterymarch, deeper in the Financial District. These blocks are home to a thick cluster of Irish taverns and Japanese sushi bars, all catering to thirsty office workers in need of a little unwinding, or the occasional group of Fidelity employees testing trickle-down economics with their bonus checks. Besides Mr. Dooley's, the short stroll between State St. and the Big Dig sports at least four places to swill beer with your fish and chips and two more for the sake-and-sashimi crowd, including **Nara Japanese Cuisine,** tel. (617) 338-5935, coyly tucked down a veritable alley (Wendell St.). Small and intimate enough to resemble a private dining club, its size may belie its namesake—in Japan, Nara is known for the world's largest bronze statue, the 500-ton eighth century Great Buddha of Todai-ji Otera—but the gracious ambiance proves fittingly temple-like, especially before or after the principal lunch and dinner crush. Open Mon.-Fri. only, 11 a.m.-2:30 p.m. and 5-10 p.m.

Palates that shudder at the mere mention of pub grub or raw anything may prefer the classic French cuisine of the unflappable **Maison Robert,** in the grandiose Second Empire-style Old City Hall on School St., tel. (617) 227-3370. If your per diem doesn't cover such splurges—or if you left your dinner jacket at the dry cleaners—**Ben's Cafe,** downstairs, offers less expensive renditions of similar fare in more casual surroundings.

Chinatown

Chinatown's narrow sidewalks and congested one-way streets never quite seem to sleep. From morning until long after sensible people have gone to bed, visitors to the short stretch of Beach Street between the Leather and Theater Districts are never more than a few steps from a good meal. Among the best are **Grand Chau Chow Seafood,** 41-45 Beach, and **East Ocean City** at 25-29 Beach, in whose fish tanks perhaps swims your next meal. Both offer page after page of inexpensive choices and stay open until at least 2 a.m. weekdays, 4 a.m. weekends. Yet another top contender is the **Jumbo Seafood Restaurant,** 7 Hudson St., tel. (617) 542-2823. It, too, greets patrons with tanks full of live fish, as well as eels, shrimp, and lobster, just so there's no doubting the freshness of your seafood dinner. It's also one of the cleanest, most attractive, least tacky Chinese restaurants in downtown, despite the huge velvet painting of the Hong Kong skyline at night.

While every menu in the neighborhood has vegetarian choices, **Buddha's Delight,** 5 Beach St., tel. (617) 351-2395, is *entirely* vegetarian. In keeping with traditional Chinese Buddhist cookery, many dishes are named as if they had meat, even though seitan (wheat gluten), braised tofu, and other substitutes are used instead.

Harder to find (but worth the effort) is the **Chinatown Eatery,** on the second floor of 44-46 Beach St., at the corner of Harrison. With their menus crowding the walls above each small counter, half a dozen hole-in-the-wall vendors representing several Asian cuisines ring a large room filled with communal school-cafeteria-style tables. Sample from one or all, claim a seat amid the crowd, and enjoy the busy stew of foreign accents and fragrances as you sip spicy hot-and-sour soup from one or dine on the pad Thai from another. Dirt-cheap prices complement the minimal decor but belie how good the food usually is. Open until 2 a.m. Several blocks away from Beach Street's beaten path is the equally fast-food-simple **Chinatown Cafe,** 262 Harrison, at the base of the Tai Tung Village high-rises overlooking the MassPike. It isn't the finest Chinatown has to offer, but it's an unsurpassed value given that most menu items handily feed two people—for under $6. The only catch: no late dining (closing time is 8:30 p.m.).

If you're just looking for something sweet, **Hing Shing Bakery,** at Beach and Hudson, is a good first choice for sweet bean cakes and melon buns, while animal-cracker lovers shouldn't miss the giant zoological figures at **Kam Lung Bakery,** two blocks away on Harrison, which has also added a Chinese touch to many standard American treats, too—in case you have a taste for cross-cultural chocolate chip cookies and the like.

Chinatown is also host to a half dozen Vietnamese *pho* kitchens, fluorescent-and-Formica specialists in bargain-priced soups, as well as

JEFF PERK

THIS IS BOSTON, NOT MANHATTAN

Displaced or visiting New Yorkers seem dumb-founded that a city of Boston's stature should lack a good New York-style deli. Los Angeles, after all, has its deli barrio, down on Fairfax Avenue; Ann Arbor, Michigan, has Zingerman's. You can find Dr. Brown's sodas even in Oberlin, Ohio. So why not in Boston, already?

In fact, New York-style deli ventures just flat fail here. Boston has no shortage of delis, but it seems to stubbornly resist homogenization with New York (even if New Yorkers have bought up our newspapers and department stores).

The Manhattan purist will scoff, but, folks, we're not talking the difference between dish-water and seltzer. Unless you were weaned on Zabar's silken smoked Nova Scotia salmon, there's no reason to let debate among scholars of the deli *schul* spoil your Boston bagel with lox. And, if nothing less than a Brooklyn bialy or big fluffy Brighton Beach knish will stop your kvetch-ing, get on the MassPike westbound, hang a left at I-84, drive for four and a half hours, and start looking for parking.

one of the best (and busiest) Japanese restaurants in the city, **Ginza,** on Hudson St. near the Chinatown Gate, tel. (617) 338-2261 (open Sun.-Mon. till 2 a.m., Tues.-Sat. till 4 a.m.). Although the unfiltered cigarettes preferred by its Asian customers often overwhelm the ventilation, few other places offer handrolls quite as big, sushi quite as fresh, or maki quite as inventive. Cooked entrees ($9.25-25) provide an alternative to the sushi menu without any sacrifice in quality or presentation. (Nonsmokers should try the sister restaurant in Brookline, listed below under **Fenway and Kenmore.**) More miserly raw fish lovers—or those who prefer smoke-free sur-roundings—should save their appetites for the Sun.-Thurs. 5 p.m.-2 a.m all-you-can-eat sushi nights at Korean-Japanese **Suishaya,** on the corner of Beach St. and Tyler, tel. (617) 423-3848. For $25 per person you have your choice of all but the most expensive nigiri and special maki selections. Plan on taking your time and making an extended evening of your meal—not only because it gets fairly busy, but because

you'll be charged for what you don't eat, so it's best to keep ordering modest amounts until you reach your limit.

Even trendy Malaysian cuisine is represented at **Penang,** 685-691 Washington St., the local outpost of a New York-based chain ($4.50-16.95; tel. 617-451-6373). If the varnished *Gilligan's Island* decor—tree trunks with mesh roof, cor-rugated metal over the kitchen, rope room di-viders—doesn't tempt you to leap straight for fish in *belachan* sauce (a salty minced-shrimp paste) or chicken in a yam pot (a retaining ring of cooked yam, flash-fried crisp on the outside, soft as minced crab inside), the menu also fea-tures more familiar Chinese, Thai, and Muslim In-dian dishes.

Theater District and Park Square

West of Chinatown's bargains, a number of restaurants showcase ambiance and prices skewed more to theater-goers and luxury hotel guests—although the eateries in the Trans-portation Building on Stuart St. offer a relatively inexpensive oasis, particularly if you're hankering for a thick juicy burger from the likes of **Fud-druckers'.** More typical of what this area aims for, though, are the sourdough crostini, smoked duck, and garlic mashed potato sprinkled around the menu at **Brew Moon,** on the corner of Tremont and Stuart Streets, one of a high-con-cept brewpub chain whose flashy grub, slick decor, super-loud music, and shiny, happy clien-tele almost—but don't quite—obscure the medi-ocrity of the place.

Several of the city's most highly regarded chefs ply their trade in the surrounding blocks—to enough acclaim that reservations are neces-sary for dinner most nights. One such hot spot is tiny little **Galleria Italiana,** 177 Tremont St. on the Common, tel. (617) 423-2092 ($16.50-26), whose menu varies continually with the seasons and never disappoints. The restaurant serves dinner nightly, buffet lunch Tues.-Saturday. Two long blocks away, on the Public Garden, is one of Boston's gastronomic landmarks, **Biba,** 272 Boylston St., tel. (617) 426-7878, whose chef-owner, Lydia Shire, has trained what seems like half the city's culinary vanguard. An evening at the font of such creative gourmandizing easily tops $100 for two with wine and dessert. If smoke and crowds don't bother you, though, you can graze on appetizers at the bar for about half the tab of a full dinner. Dress as if you own a Porsche or Jaguar and you'll fit in.

Behind Biba, in the Park Plaza Hotel, is that Boston warhorse, **Legal Seafoods,** tel. (617) 426-4444, whose quality and popularity are reflected in the menu prices ($11.95-28.95, lobsters up to over $50). If you'll pay whatever it takes to get your socks knocked off by New England seafood, try Legal's catch of the day or lobster casserole; otherwise check out the North End and Cambridge for less expensive seafood options. Closer to the narrow pointy end of the same building is the **Legal C Bar and Grille,** tel. (617) 426-5566, putting a Caribbean spin on whatever's fresh from Neptune's realm at a slightly more palatable price ($10.95-19.95). Don't let a dislike of spicy hot food keep you from enjoying a delicious meal here: while the Jamaican jerked items almost live up to their fiery billing, most of the menu's other "hot hot hot" boasts are simply for show. Make reservations or expect a wait after 6 p.m.: a short children's menu, casual atmosphere, and kid-friendly waitstaff make this a busy family destination in the early evenings, while food service daily till midnight, a busy bar, and late-night live Caribbean dance bands once a month are all proven attractions to the adults-only crowd.

On Stuart St. next to the Radisson Hotel, a stone's throw from the C Bar—if that parking garage wasn't in the way—is **Jae's Korean Grill,** tel. (617) 451-7788, a three-story restaurant with a different theme to each floor. You could try the sushi bar on the first, or the dining room on the second, but I'd strongly suggest you answer the greeter's question with "third floor, please." When the elevator doors open at the top, you'll be ushered to a seat around one of the many gas grills, on which meals are made to order right before your eyes. Actually, all the menu items from the first two floors are also available on the third, but if you've never experienced true Korean barbecue—a delicious feast of marinated meats accompanied by a rich palette of sweet and spicy pickles and condiments, sticky rice, and thick and thin sauces, all of which are to be mixed on fresh lettuce leaves, rolled up, and eaten by hand—it's definitely the way to go. Open daily till 10 or 10:30 p.m., and Thurs.-Sat. till 1 a.m.

THE NORTH END

Some unwritten book governing North End restaurants seems to stipulate that portions must be inversely proportional to the size of the establishment. Or maybe North End restaurateurs all believe in giving you your money's worth; at any rate, more often than not, when you order for dinner you get the next day's lunch, too. The principal streets for restaurants are Hanover and Salem, but hardly a block seems bereft of something good to eat, be it a bakery, *salumeria* (Italian market), cafe, or restaurant.

Travelers who rely on credit should note that the North End is one of the city's last bastions of cash-only dining. Even where some types of plastic are accepted, your corporate AmEx card may not be one of them.

Just across from the can't-miss Mike's Pastry marquee on Hanover St. is **The Daily Catch,** tel. (617) 523-8567, where calamari is king. This tiny joint is so warm and inviting that a meal here is like eating in the kitchen: the cook could shake hands with half his customers without leaving his stove, and the menu's mainstay, seafood over linguine, is served in frying pans instead of on plates. Reasonable prices and robust house vino round out the pleasant atmosphere. Since the place only seats 20, bring something to read or someone to talk to if you arrive after 6 p.m. (Cash only, no reservations.) Taking a page out of the same book, next-door **Pomodoro,** 319 Hanover, tel. (617) 367-4348, is also so tiny that the warmth and fragrance of the open kitchen contribute to the ambiance of the room as much as the sponge-painted caramel-toned walls and back-to-back intimacy of the tables. The bathroom, meanwhile, is in a cafe two doors down. Of course, in defiance of the puny stage, the chef acts only on a grand scale—evident in the Mt. Etna of littlenecks over linguine, the slab of beef tenderloin, the plump chicken with artichokes and capers—so if you can't make good use of leftovers, seriously consider choosing an appetizer and splitting an entree, rather than vice versa. Since big portions are so common in this part of town, and so many of the menus sound so similar, you may wonder why the prices are a tad high. Taste the food and you'll quickly appreciate that you pay on a merit system here—

and by almost any measure you're getting a great value. The seafood fra diavolo alone will wipe out any memory of having waited for a table. (Cash only, and it serves no desserts or coffee—if you want to linger over cannoli, head down the street to the excellent **Modern Pastry Shop,** 257 Hanover, and pray one of its two tables is empty).

Around the corner from these two restaurants is **Artú** 6 Prince St., tel. (617) 742-4336, whose extensive trattoria menu offers dozens of robust selections, all served in outsized portions at remarkably low prices, which is why families often outnumber students and young couples ($6.95-15.95, credit cards accepted). For something slightly fancier, step into **Ristorante Saraceno,** 286 Hanover, tel. (617) 227-5888, and go to town over the excellent spectrum of traditional Neapolitan dishes ($10.95-25.95) safe in the knowledge that your credit card will be welcome when the bill comes. Reservations are also accepted—and downright essential on weekends if you have no patience for waiting.

Parallel Salem St. is more intimate—effectively just a narrow, one-way back street leading up to the famous Old North Church on Copp's Hill. Dining options here run the gamut from the cozy and reliable—and very pink—**Nicole Ristorante** at No. 54, tel. (617) 742-6999 (closed Monday), to the contemporary exposed brick of **Marcuccio's** at No. 125, tel. (617) 723-1807, whose nouveau greens, garnishes, and plate

BREAKFASTS OF CHAMPIONS

If coffee and donuts, latte and muffins, or $10 hotel fruit plates comprising mostly unripened cantaloupe aren't your ideal eye-openers, consider starting the day out right with a real sit-down breakfast.

Beacon Hill

The Paramount, 44 Charles St., tel. (617) 720-1152. Though spruced up in recent years and a bit upscale at dinner, the breakfasts at this generations-old neighborhood favorite still hew to the diner-style origins of the joint. Order the spinach-feta omelet and you'll get a slab of cheese large enough to satisfy your feta cravings for a week.

Chinatown

Fans of that Chinese point-and-eat cuisine, dim sum, should try the **Golden Palace** or **China Pearl,** both on Tyler St. between Beach and Kneeland, or the **Emperor Garden Restaurant,** in the spacious former theater upstairs of 690 Washington St. All are reasonably priced, with above-average brunches and a good variety of offerings. All three serve dim sum from 8 or 8:30 a.m.-3 p.m. daily; on weekends, expect a wait around peak brunch hours (10-noonish).

Back Bay

Steve's Greek & American Cuisine, 316 Newbury St., tel. (617) 267-1817. Within a few blocks of the Copley Square and Hynes Convention Center hotel clusters, Steve's swank Newbury address belies the fact that it's essentially an honest-to-goodness diner, with menu and prices to match. Open daily.

South End

Charlie's Sandwich Shoppe, 429 Columbus Ave., tel. (617) 536-7669. Western omelets, hamsteak and eggs, and turkey hash are complemented by more newfangled notions like French toast with cranberry compote, Cajun omelets, and strawberry griddle cakes at this reliable neighborhood favorite. Just three blocks directly behind the Prudential Center, Charlie's makes a good alternative for anyone staying in the Back Bay. Open Mon.-Sat., cash only, serves breakfast until closing (i.e., 2:30 p.m. weekdays, 1 p.m. Saturday).

Jamaica Plain

Sorella's, 388 Centre St., at the Hyde Square rotary, tel. (617) 524-2016. For more omelet choices than Baskin-Robbins has flavors and an equally exotic array of pancakes and French toast, there's no topping this two-room little eatery on the edge of JP's Latino half. The menu may feature ingredients like oyster mushrooms, boursin, and Gran Marnier, but the humble prices are more in line with the mismatched silver- and glassware. Open daily, cash only.

Cambridge

Cafe of India, 52A Brattle St., tel. (617) 661-0683. Unlikely as it may seem, one of Harvard Square's nicer Indian restaurants is also one of the best places to enjoy a reasonably priced morning repast of your favorite omelets, French toast, and the like, seven days a week.

presentation are as stylish as anything in the city (cash only). In between is a pair of jointly owned restaurants whose chefs cloak great food in what feel like relaxed neighborhood spots: the light and airy **Terramia,** tel. (617) 523-3112, whose dinner-only menu ($9.50-25) sounds more upscale notes with truffles, wild mush-rooms, foie gras, and 25-year-old balsamic vine-gar (but no dessert or coffee); and the intimate **Antico Forno,** across the street at No. 93, tel. (617) 723-6733, whose lunch and dinner menus are weighted toward the rustic delights of wood-fired dishes from southern Italy ($7-16.50). Seafood lovers take note, when it comes to *pesce* and *frutti di mare,* both these places put the high-priced waterfront joints around the World Trade Center to shame. (Both stay open till 11 p.m. Mon.-Sat., too, and until 10 p.m. Sunday.) All but Marcuccio's take at least MasterCard and Visa, and all recommend reservations for Fri-day and Saturday nights—up to a week in ad-vance in the case of Marcuccio's.

For a take-home dessert, step into the **Bis-cotti Pasticceria,** next door to Antico Forno, or head up the street to **Bova's Bakery,** at the cor-ner of Salem and Prince, which conveniently re-mains open to 1 a.m.

Think I've forgotten something? For the oblig-atory pizza, try the place that's been making them longer than anybody else in town: **Pizzeria Regina,** 11$^1/_2$ Thacher St. between N. Wash-ington and N. Margin. There are others in this local chain—in Faneuil Hall Marketplace, for in-stance—but none can touch the first for either at-mosphere or food.

BACK BAY AND THE SOUTH END

Back Bay is good grazing territory for fans of fu-sion cuisine, that interesting and funky *mesclado* of colorful, fresh ingredients with south-of-the-border or Pacific Rim flavorings, served in casual but design-coordinated surroundings and often accompanied by microbrews. Places prized for their social cachet more than their food tend to be found along fashionable Newbury Street, itself a fusion of bowfront townhouses and high-end boutiques; you might find decent things to eat at **Sonsie** or **Armani Cafe,** but that's not the point of going there. When it's finally time to give your

gold card a rest, Back Bay's boundary with the lower-rent Fenway neighborhood comprises a string of inexpensive ethnic restaurants dishing up great Asian, Middle Eastern, Indian, and even Cajun food.

The South End, full of food-savvy single men and women, has become one of the city's best dining areas. Many of the chef-owned neigh-borhood joints spearheading the Boston res-taurant revival are found here, either on Tremont Street near the Theater District or spread out on Columbus Avenue parallel to the Orange Line. Fusion happens less in individual dishes than on menus as a whole—chefs demonstrate their skill in preparing creative but authentic dish-es combining elements from two or more conti-nents. It comes to exceptional food in cozier quarters with less glitzy veneer and more per-sonality than Back Bay, all for about the same prices—which is to say, not cheap, though ex-ceptions do exist.

Both neighborhoods are within walking dis-tance of subway lines, although nether parts of the South End may be more suited to a short cab ride if you don't like wandering quiet resi-dential streets at night. The restaurants below are listed roughly as one would find them while strolling—or sometimes zigzagging—outward from downtown, despite evidence of street num-bers to the contrary; keep in mind that parallel streets in Boston rarely have corresponding numbers from one block to the next, since they rarely begin at the same place.

Back Bay
To share in the kind of sandwich Boston's top chefs put together when set loose in the kitchen after hours, step over to the **Parish Cafe,** 361 Boylston near the corner of the Public Garden, tel. (617) 247-4777. A sandwich and scoop of salad costs $8-10—and service during the late-night see-and-be-seen parade can border on rude—but the food is an inspiration (grilled steak with blue cheese bread and pickled onions, or tortilla-wrapped smoked turkey with cranberry chipotle sauce), perfect for tired city walkers or finicky midnight snackers (yes, the kitchen serves until 1 a.m.). If you didn't come to coastal New England to eat yuppie designer food, you should try **Skipjack's,** tel. (617) 536-3500, one of the city's seafood kings. Reigning over the corner of

Clarendon and Stuart Streets, behind Trinity Church, this local chain isn't content until it can offer a couple dozen choices of the freshest seafood anywhere, even if it means flying orange roughy in on the red-eye from Auckland. (If importing fish to Boston seems like shipping coals to Newcastle, stick to the steamers and cod.) The flash of creativity in sauces is matched by the dash of neon amid the Art Deco interior of this popular establishment, which also features live jazz during Sunday brunch.

Copley Square's **Small Planet Bar and Grill,** 565 Boylston St., tel. (617) 536-4477, is one of the neighborhood's better culture blenders ($5.95-15.95). Designed for maximum aesthetic stimulation, it's good for internationally influenced appetizers, vegetarian dishes, cheap gourmet pizzas, rich desserts, microbrews and eclectic wines, and speedy service—all at moderate prices. The fancier dishes aren't such good value, though; jazzy presentation alone doesn't merit the higher price, and the chefs aren't *that* ready to go head-to-head with San Francisco. Open until midnight most nights.

If you like Middle Eastern, make a beeline for **Cafe Jaffa,** 48 Gloucester, near the Hynes Convention Center, tel. (617) 536-0230 ($3.95-9.25). Exposed brick, a high black ceiling, copper sconces, and lots of gleaming wood fit the off-Newbury address, but prices fit the budgets of Fenway's numerous music school students a few blocks away. As for quality, you won't find a better falafel and hummus plate in town. Israeli and Lebanese beer and wine are available, too. Marching to the Zydeco beat of a completely different drummer is the tasty and affordable **Dixie Kitchen,** 182 Mass. Ave., tel. (617) 536-3068 ($5.95-9.95), next door to the Berklee College of Music. It's one of New England's rare outposts of New Orleans cookery—although lacking the kind of sophistication found in the NOLA kitchens of Emeril Lagasse or Susan Spicer. Come here instead for the timeless simplicity of po' boys, catfish fry, shrimp etouffeé, sausage gumbo, even a passable version of that Big Easy cornucopia of meat, the muffaletta. Cajun tunes, red-checkered tablecloths, and tattooed young waitstaff add to the authentically insouciant atmosphere.

Dixie Kitchen's neighbors along the stretch of Mass. Ave. between Berklee College of Music and Symphony Hall are predominantly Asian, including the all-you-can-eat Korean steam-table buffet at **Arirang,** 162 Mass. Ave. ($5.99 lunch, $7.50 dinner; tel. 617-536-1277), and the first-in-New-England **Bangkok Cuisine** across the street, whose quality has never rested on its laurels ($7.95-13.50; tel. 617-262-5377).

Also in the heart of Berklee territory, at 1124 Boylston St. a few doors past Jack's Drum Shop, is the irresistibly kitschy **Mucho Gusto Cafe & Collectibles,** tel. (617) 236-1020, dishing up meaty Cuban comfort food for breakfast, lunch, and dinner amid endearingly overdone Lucy 'n' Ricky decor. The food is good, but it's those collectibles that shouldn't be missed, an amalgam of '50s and '60s home furnishings and cha-cha-tchotchkes recalling an eight-cylinder streamlined era of limbo dancing and hi-fi leisure.

At the edge of this neighborhood, Symphony Hall sits beside a large cluster of fast-food burger, pizza, and ethnic eateries on Huntington Ave., catering more to nearby New England Conservatory and Northeastern University students than to BSO ticket holders pouring out of their taxis and limos. Slightly hidden from the crowd, around the back of Symphony Hall, is a perfect alternative to Burger King or Pizzeria Uno: **Cena,** 14 Westland Ave., tel. (617) 262-1485, opposite the Bread & Circus supermarket a block west of Mass. Ave. Proximity to the Symphony, Jordan Hall, and the Huntington Theatre make this casual spot an excellent choice for the après-theater crowd, especially given that it's open till midnight Tues.-Sunday. The one-page menu concentrates on flavors of the Mediterannean, from Iberia and North Africa to the Middle East, although a dash of India and the Far East is occasionally thrown in for kicks ($12-15). Vegetarians will be in their element here, as half the choices are meatless. Good selection of microbrews, too, in bottles and on draft.

South End

Within a couple blocks of Copley Square is a budget-friendly riff on a West Coast theme: the **Baja Mexican Cantina,** tel. (617) 262-7575, 111 Dartmouth St. near the corner of Columbus ($6.95-12.95). It consistently does best with dishes you'd wash down with beer rather than wine, although the spicy duck fajitas or mussels in

JEFF PERK

parchment cooked in Corona beer go down well with either beverage.

A rich vein of restaurants is found around what's known as Tremont Street's restaurant row, anchored by the Boston Center for the Arts and **Hamersley's Bistro,** on the BCA's Clarendon St. corner, tel. (617) 423-2700. It's consistently judged one of the city's top dining spots, a "destination" featuring bold, French-influenced cuisine. Reservations are strongly recommended (entrees $21-30). If you didn't plan on making an early withdrawal from your IRA simply to afford dinner, there's always **Emilio's,** 536 Tremont St., a popular pizza counter and sub shop that stays open late enough to feed hungry cast members from BCA performances across the street. Inexpensive is a word that also applies to the breakfast, brunch, lunch, or post-theater snacking amid South End cafe society at little **Mildred's,** 552 Tremont, tel. (617) 426-0008, although most of its regulars would probably prefer to call it funky, irreverent, or delicious. Both make appealing casual choices for anyone staying at a B&B in the vicinity.

Another cook who, like Gordon Hamersley, knows his sauces and uses eye-catching presentation to complement rather than conceal holds forth a couple of blocks up the street at **Tremont 647,** tel. (617) 266-4600. Hints of Asia, the American South, and the South American weave harmoniously through the menu, along with a missionary's dedication to reviving underutilized legumes like the monk pea and appaloosa bean. The results—a sirloin appetizer with monk pea hummus, steamed mussels in a lemongrass broth, succulently grilled and glazed duck breast over hand-cut pappardelle with cob-smoked bacon and broccoli rabe—are distinctive, assertive, and wholly satisfying ($14.50-18.50). Excellent desserts include a signature banana cream pie that redefines the genre.

One of the city's favorite places for intimate dining is the **Metropolis Cafe,** tel. (617) 247-2931, at 584 Tremont St., next to Geoffrey's Wine Bar. Though quite small, the high ceiling, light decor, odd corners, and handful of high-backed booths lend the room a rare blend of privacy and space amid the close quarters. Impeccable service, beautiful and flavorful Italian-influenced dishes like proscuitto-wrapped cod or risotto with wild mushrooms and chicken, and portions perfectly sized to leave room for a first or last course all add up to a consummate evening of fine dining. Though expensive (entrees up to $19.95, appetizers up to $8.95, and desserts $6.95), there's always at least one dish priced for those with less than infinite means. Don't think it's all hushed whispers and doe-eyed couples, either: the background sound is as likely to be funk or fusion as often as Tony Bennett-style crooners, and the crowd includes both denim-jeaned neighborhood regulars and designer-dressed suburbanites notching another well-known hot spot into their belts. Open nightly till at least 10 p.m., with reservations advisable for Fri.-Sat. nights.

If you're in the mood for something unfancy (but appetizing), head for the corner of Columbus Ave. and Braddock Street. There on Columbus, under the faded purple awning next to Charlie's Sandwich Shoppe, is **Anchovies,** tel. (617) 266-5088, a seemingly generic bar which actually dishes up belt-stretching portions of delicious Italian comfort food (even the nachos are made with mozzarella) in a small dining area in back ($5.95-8.95). It's one of the South End's hippest hangouts, though, so you'll escape the heavy smoke and loud din only if you come early. A lively, less smoky, kick-back-with-your-buddies atmosphere reigns at nearby **Jae's Cafe & Grill,**

520 Columbus a few blocks from the Mass. Ave. Orange Line or Symphony Hall Green Line stations, tel. (617) 421-9405 ($7.50-24.00). Its across-the-menu excellence, friendly service, and prime summer sidewalk seating make this a top dog—best for sushi lovers and Korean hotpot fans. It carries fine Belgian ale, too. Outdoor tables sprout up in front of neighborhood cafes all over the South End as soon as warm evenings become the rule rather than the exception, but few make as pleasing a destination as the **Claremont Cafe,** 535 Columbus, opposite the Cha Cha Cha! hair salon, tel. (617) 247-9001. Its upscale New American entrees are all proportioned for a bricklayer's appetite, making the $13.95-21.95 prices a relative bargain in this neighborhood. The seasonally fresh menu also welcomes light eaters with its multi-ethnic variety of tapas, some of which betray a hint of the chef-owner's native Peru. Dinner is served until at least 10 p.m. Tues.-Sat., while breakfast, lunch, or brunch are available Tues.-Sunday.

Iceberg salads and meatball subs fit the plastic table and paper napkin style of the **Mass Cafe,** 605 Mass. Ave., tel. (617) 262-7704, a few blocks from both the Claremont and Symphony Hall, but try one of the hearty Eritrean-Ethiopian dishes on the other half of the menu instead and you'll be blissfully transported into the world of the travel posters on the wall. Big portions and low prices make this a steal; open daily ($4.95-7.65). If your palate would be happier with something a little closer to home (but not as close as those meatball subs), check out **Bob the Chef,** 604 Columbus Ave. a block west of Mass. Ave., tel. (617) 536-6204. This is soul food territory, and if you don't know chitterlings from chicken livers, here's where to learn. All the quintessential dishes of the Deep South are here ($5.95-14.95), from "glorifried" chicken to collard greens, but even vegetarians or abstainers denying themselves any truck with fried food will find a few menu items to savor. If these prospects inspire expectations of greasy Formica and shiny metal napkin dispensers on the middle of each table, guess again: Bob's is casual, but the warm, kinte-cloth colors, lofty black ceiling, and original art put it closer to some trendy Chicago or L.A. bistro than to any Mississippi lunch counter or Tennessee "meat 'n' three" family restaurant. Live jazz combos take over a corner of the restaurant on Sat.-Sun. evenings and during Sunday brunch ($2 cover).

FENWAY AND KENMORE

From the Back Bay Fens residential pocket across the park from the Museum of Fine Art to nightclub-rich Kenmore Square, these large and amorphous neighborhoods are endowed with cozy little local favorites offering good, inexpensive meals in mostly simple settings. A prime candidate: the **India Quality Restaurant,** 536 Comm. Ave., in the heart of Kenmore Square, tel. (617) 267-4499, an aptly named eatery tucked into a tiny nook across the hall from a used record shop and next to a convenience store. After sunset, the delicious Northern Indian dishes and extensive multinational beer list are accompanied by the neon dance of the giant Art Deco Citgo sign on the roof of the Barnes & Noble bookstore across the square.

Kenmore Square also sports one of the many McDonald's franchises around the city, as well as a 22-hour **IHOP,** if pancakes up until 4 a.m. suits your taste. But for dining worth a ride in from elsewhere in the city, look to the higher-priced cluster of ethnic restaurants at Audubon Circle, where the Green "C" Line comes up from underground, just across the MassPike from Kenmore Square. Although not entirely unique—it's a clone of a restaurant across the river in Somerville—the French-Cambodian **Elephant Walk,** 900 Beacon St. at Park Dr., tel. (617) 247-1500, is unquestionably unusual. Exotic Asian and classic continental are separate on the menu, but judicious border-crossing keeps even the most familiar-sounding dishes deliciously out of the ordinary ($9.50-14.95). The desserts can be quite stunning, although if it's lunchtime or early in the evening you might prefer to take out a magnificent little *gateau* from **Japonaise,** a French-Japanese bakery a block up the street at 1020 Beacon, across from the T stop. (The Boston city line lies beside Elephant Walk, so both Japonaise and its neighbors are technically in the town of Brookline.) If you're more in the mood for straight Japanese or Chinese cuisine, look to either the sushi and seafood of **Ginza,** tel. (617) 566-9688, or the Szechuan and Mandarin fare at **Chef Chang's House,** tel. (617) 277-

4226, both within the 100 yards separating Elephant Walk and Japonaise. Back toward Kenmore Square you'll find a very sleek bar with above-average eats at **Audubon Circle Restaurant,** 838 Beacon, tel. (617) 421-1910 (look for the sign with the red circle around the letter "A"). Though not sized for large appetites, sandwiches are well-made, cod cakes are wonderfully crisp and piquant, the Tuscan bread is delicious, and the vegetables all perfectly fresh (appetizers $3.50-7.50, sandwiches and entrees $5.50-12). Libations, from the handful of beers to a generous sampling of single-malt scotches, are equally well chosen. Open 11 a.m.-1 a.m. weekdays, and 5 p.m.-1 a.m. weekends.

CHOW DOWN 'N THE HOOD: ALLSTON AND JP

Several of Boston's residential neighborhoods have become dining destinations in their own right. Allston and Jamaica Plain ("JP" to locals) are two of the most accessible, with direct trolley or subway service to downtown and several bus connections to Back Bay, Cambridge, Brookline, and each other. Few tourists venture here—the land of 10-year-old Hondas, where chain link is more common than prim white pickets—though a few B&Bs cater to the intrepid travelers who do. Try it yourself and you'll discover a more

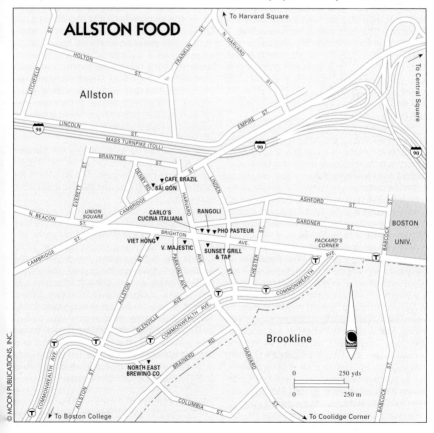

ALLSTON FOOD

honest depiction of where citizens live, shop, and eat than at either Faneuil Hall or the gaslit, cobblestoned cloister of Beacon Hill.

Cheap Eats Mecca: Allston

Within a handful of blocks around "downtown" Allston—the large, ever-congested "H" formed by the intersection of Commonwealth, Harvard, and Brighton Avenues, bounded on one side by the Green "B" Line trolley—lay more than a dozen inexpensive restaurants. Several are worth a trip in from outside the neighborhood. Reflecting Allston's diverse demographics, the cuisines in this densely populated area include Chinese, Brazilian, Indian, Middle Eastern, Thai, Vietnamese, Italian, Greek, Tex-Mex, Chicago (pizza), Seattle (espresso), jazz bar, and yuppie brewpub, all within a 10-minute walk of the Harvard Ave. T stop. A high concentration of nightclubs keeps parking scarce, but the neighborhood is less than 30 minutes from downtown via the Boston College-bound trolley, or barely an eight-minute bus ride from Harvard Square in Cambridge (via the #66 Dudley) or Coolidge Corner in Brookline (via the #66 Harvard).

For Indian food, **Rangoli,** 129 Brighton Ave., tel. (617) 562-0200, should be a top candidate. Presentation earns as much thought as preparation, and the menu features a number of specialties from southern India—crepe-like dosas, broth-like sambhar—not often found in the northern-dominated Indian restaurant trade. Though priced about the same as its brethren around the city, Rangoli is a bargain given the quality and attractiveness of its meals ($4.95-9.95).

Vietnamese may be the neighborhood's best-represented food group. **Pho Pasteur,** on Brighton Ave. next to Rangoli, specializes in the giant bowls of soup, or *pho.* **V. Majestic,** a block up Brighton, next to Harper's Ferry blues bar, is best for its cheap "special noodle" dishes, its rolling beef, and anything in caramel sauce. **Viet Hông,** farther up at 182 Brighton Ave. opposite the Osco Drugs plaza, tel. (617) 254-3600, is known all over town for the mountain of piping hot vegetables piled atop most of its entrees, for its pungent seafood soups, and for its generous fresh spring rolls (closed Monday). Behind the Osco plaza, next to the delicious and inexpensive **Café Brazil** on Cambridge St., **Sài Gòn,** tel. (617) 254-3373 carves a niche with its

ground shrimp with fresh sugarcane, salmon served sizzling in clay pots, and omelet-like *bánh xèo* (daily to 10 or 11 p.m.). Sài Gòn also has the most attractive decor, ideal for lingering over chicory-laced Vietnamese coffee sweetened with condensed milk. The others have as much charm as any Chinese takeout joint, but who's complaining: at any of these places, $15 will get you a good dinner, possibly a carton of leftovers, and probably more than enough change to catch the trolley or bus back to your lodgings.

None of its regulars was surprised to see **Carlo's Cucina Italiana,** 131 Brighton Ave., tel. (617) 254-9759, end up on the top of Zagat's list of best southern Italian spots in the city. A favorite hangout of young city chefs on their nights off, Carlo's demonstrates that sometimes traditional comfort food can beat the pants off fancier fare. The professionals know honest talent when they see it, and their patronage is a mark of respect. Try the homemade tortellini, any seafood dishes, or the veal. Despite upscale appearances—the dark wood wainscoting, linen napkins, trompe l'oeil paintings on the walls—the prices recall the room's former life as a takeout pizzeria, so expect to wait for a table most nights ($7.95-11.95).

In a category by itself, there's the **Sunset Grill & Tap,** 130 Brighton Ave., tel. (617) 254-1331, next to Fern Cleaners. The food leans toward nachos, BBQ ribs, and the like; if you want something ritzier than fish and chips—pan-seared cod with shaved fennel, for example, washed down with fresh beer made on the spot —try the **North East Brewing Company,** tel. (617) 566-6699, a few blocks away at 1314 Comm. Ave. But for a global perspective on the brewer's art, don't miss the Sunset. With nearly 80 beers on tap and another 400 or more in bottles—lagers, bocks, Belgians, Lambics, ESBs, wheats, porters, stouts, Irish reds, ambers, IPAs, Scotch ales, potato ales, cream ales, barley wines, seasonal brews, and many, many more, plus mead, sake, hard ciders, nonalcoholic beers, and root beers—no other bar in New England comes close to providing so many hours of enjoyable globetrotting in a glass.

Jamaica Plain

Centre Street is this neighborhood's main thoroughfare. From the Orange Line T station at

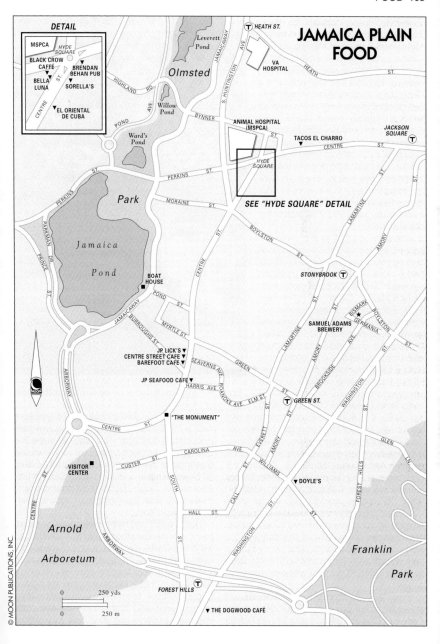

JAMAICA PLAIN FOOD

DETAIL

MSPCA
HYDE SQUARE
BLACK CROW CAFFE
BELLA LUNA
BRENDAN BEHAN PUB
SORELLA'S
EL ORIENTAL DE CUBA
CENTRE ST.

HEATH ST.
Leverett Pond
JAMAICAWAY
S. HUNTINGTON AVE.
VA HOSPITAL
HEATH ST.
Olmsted
HIGHLAND RD.
Willow Pond
BYNNER
ANIMAL HOSPITAL (MSPCA)
ST.
TACOS EL CHARRO
CENTRE ST.
JACKSON SQUARE
Ward's Pond
POND AVE.
PERKINS ST.
HYDE SQUARE
PERKINS ST.
MORAINE ST.
SEE "HYDE SQUARE" DETAIL
Park
BOYLSTON ST.
LAMARTINE ST.
AMORY ST.
Jamaica Pond
CENTRE ST.
STONYBROOK
PARKMAN DR.
PERKINS ST.
PRINCE ST.
BOAT HOUSE
LAMARTINE ST.
AMORY ST.
BISMARK
GERMANIA
BOYLSTON ST.
SAMUEL ADAMS BREWERY
BROOKSIDE AVE.
POND ST.
MYRTLE ST.
JAMAICAWAY
BURROUGHS ST.
JP LICK'S
CENTRE STREET CAFE
BAREFOOT CAFE
SEAVERNS AVE.
GREEN ST.
ARBORWAY
JP SEAFOOD CAFE
HARRIS AVE.
ROANOKE AVE.
ELM ST.
GREEN ST.
WASHINGTON ST.
"THE MONUMENT"
CENTRE ST.
CAROLINA AVE.
EVERETT ST.
AMORY ST.
WILLIAMS ST.
GLEN LN.
VISITOR CENTER
CUSTER ST.
SOUTH ST.
CALL ST.
DOYLE'S
FOREST HILLS ST.
CENTRE ST.
HALL ST.
Arnold
Arboretum
ARBORWAY
WASHINGTON ST.
Franklin Park
0   250 yds
0   250 m
FOREST HILLS
THE DOGWOOD CAFÉ

© MOON PUBLICATIONS, INC.

Jackson Square through the Hyde Square rotary at Perkins Street to "the Monument," south of the fire station, Centre reflects JP's diversity: most of Boston's Cubans and Dominicans, many of its gays and lesbians, and a rising class of young homeowning families reside along its length. JP's eateries span an equally broad range, from American diner to Korean-Japanese sushi shop, Mexican roadhouse to Lebanese cybercafe. Unless noted otherwise, the best access is via the #39 Forest Hills bus from in front of the Copley Plaza Hotel, a 20-35 minute ride, depending on which end of the neighborhood you want and what hour of the day you travel.

Transport yourself to the *criolla* village of San Luis, south of Santiago de Cuba, with *bistec encebollado* (steak and onions) and *mofongo* (plantain mashed with pork rinds and garlic) from **El Oriental de Cuba,** tel. (617) 524-6464, Formica-booth and fluorescent-light casual at 416 Centre St., opposite the Hi-Lo supermarket. Meaty simmer-all-day seafood, chicken, and tripe soups and rich fruit *batidos* (smoothies) are among the many other specialties ($4-10.50). If cheery tropical decor is key to your food enjoyment, cross the street to the **Bella Luna,** 405 Centre, tel. (617)

detail from a Centre St. mural by the Boston Youth Corps

524-6060, a gourmet thick-crust pizzeria with low prices, big portions, uniquely painted dinnerware, service to at least 10 p.m., and seductive live jazz or flamenco many nights and weekends (closed Monday; $6-12).

Stroll around the curving facade of small shops to the **Black Crow Caffé,** at 2 Perkins, tel. (617) 983-2747, a cozy, colorful cafe whose short, ever-changing menu might include such tempting dishes as peppery collard greens soup, hoisin-glazed grilled salmon, or turkey lasagna with eggplant. Beer, wine, and pricey but superb desserts are also available ($10-14). Open for dinner Mon.-Sat., plus weekend brunch 9 a.m.-4 p.m.

Solid, Mexican-style blue-plate specials are the order of the day a couple blocks away at **Tacos el Charro,** 349 Centre, tel. (617) 522-

2578, a popular plastic-chairs-and-big-mirrors hole in the wall whose chiles rellenos and mole poblano will dance off your plate when the live mariachi band rocks the joint on weekend evenings (entrees $4.95-16.95). Open Fri.-Sat. till midnight, too, and to 11 p.m. Sun.-Thurs. (closed Tuesday), but don't cut it too close: if business is slow, the kitchen can close up to almost an hour early.

Half a world and half a mile away in "downtown" JP, the **Barefoot Café,** 697 Centre, tel. (617) 983-CAFE, dishes up such Lebanese specialties as red-bean *fassoulya,* diced potato *yakné,* and a vegetarian version of Lebanon's national dish, *kibbe,* made with pumpkin instead of ground beef. Meat kebabs, falafel, stuffed grape leaves, and other Middle Eastern standards are available, too, all at such rock-bottom prices ($3.25-6.49) that it doesn't matter that the place feels like a Domino's. Leave room to sample the incredible phyllo pastries (open to 11 p.m. daily). Comforting Korean food beckons from across the street at the modest storefront **JP Seafood Cafe,** 730 Centre, tel. (617) 983-5177, open to at least 10 p.m. nightly. The mean chili-laced beef-and-rice *bibimbop* has caught the palates of local reviewers, but from grilled salmon to vegetarian pan-fried noodles, it's all tasty, sparklingly fresh, and reasonably priced ($7.95-14.95). Dozens of great sushi choices, too.

Some of Jamaica Plain's most affordable and flavorsome meals are found at the **Centre Street Cafe,** 669A Centre St., tel. (617) 524-9217, a casual neighborhood fixture whose California-style menu pairs bright, bold flavors with whatever poultry, fish, and vegetables are in peak season ($7.95-13.50). Perhaps you'll catch some fresh bluefish with black beans and avocado-caper salsa, or a riot of summer veggies and spicy chicken sausage ladled over a bed of lemon and spinach linguine. Vegetable stir-fry, hefty burritos, big salads, and from-scratch soups round out the standard daily fare, and citrus lovers feeling lost amid Boston's chocolate hegemony will want to come for the key lime pie alone. Folks who love flea-market Americana mustn't miss the collection of salt and pepper shakers on the tables, either. The Centre Street also serves up a mean weekend brunch; expect to have to wait for a table, especially on beautiful summer mornings.

When it comes to brunch, don't forget to check out **Sorella's,** 388 Centre, at the Hyde Square rotary, another spot drawing loyal patrons out in force. While both Centre Street and Sorella's still count as a bit of a neighborhood secret, weekend brunch at **Doyle's,** a mile away, at 3484 Washington, tel. (617) 524-2345, is a bona fide city-wide institution. (Upon exiting the Orange Line's Green St. station, turn right and walk uphill to the traffic light at Washington. Turn right again; two blocks ahead, at the corner of Williams St., you'll see Doyle's on the left, behind a brick facade misleadingly labeled Braddock Restaurant.) From huge omelets and gravy-soaked turkey to pumpernickel bagels and veggie quiche, you'll get good food at a good price (cash only), accompanied by one of the best

beer menus in town, in a setting redolent of cigar-chomping ward heelers scratching backs and passing fat envelopes full of something the color of the shamrock. With its high, 19th-century coffered ceilings and dark wooden booths like tall-backed pews, Doyle's is a church of good cheer whose guardian angel is no less than the late Mayor Curley himself.

BROOKLINE

Fueled in part by attractively upscale demographics, Brookline teems with neighborhood restaurants, mostly small, casual eateries with devoted local followings. If you're staying at one of the Brookline inns or guest houses, visiting the local historic sights, or shopping for Judaica among the Harvard Street shops, you'll find a significant family-friendly, budget-priced cluster of eateries at Coolidge Corner, the intersection of Beacon and Harvard Streets (and a stop on the Green "C" Line). Most of Boston's major food groups are replicated in Brookline, from international to traditional American and the inescapable McDonald's. But the standouts are Middle Eastern places, bagel bakeries, and kosher spots catering to the town's large Jewish population. Brookline is certainly unique in one respect: since 1995 it has banned smoking completely in both restaurants *and* bars, unless fully separate ventilated rooms are available.

Within Harvard Street's first two blocks south of the Coolidge Corner T stop is a typical mix. Choose from reliable Chinese at **Chef Chow's House,** a bountiful menu of Northern Indian favorites (including many wonderful breads) at the **India House,** or Middle Eastern flatbreads and *sanbusaks,* a Syrian calzone, at the fast-food **Zaatar's Oven.** Next door, the dashing **Pandan Leaf,** 250 Harvard St., tel. (617) 566-9393, serves up a broad menu of Malaysian cuisine, from noodles to curries, vegetables to seafood ($6.50-17.25). Experienced Southeast Asian diners will appreciate that for the most part the exclamation marks signifying spicy hot dishes are well earned. Open till at least 10:30 p.m. nightly.

Beefeaters should turn north from the T stop and proceed past the golden arches to **The Tam O'Shanter,** a well-known music club-bar-restaurant diagonally across from the Coolidge Corner Theatre. Sure, a Big Mac may be cheaper, but the indelible brand of the charcoal grill on the Tam's hefty 10-ounce burgers makes them worth darn near every penny of their $6.45-7.45 price tag. Now, if only Ronald McDonald could teach the Tam's grillmeisters the secret to good french fries. . . .

Anyone looking to keep kosher should continue up the street to **Rami's,** a shoebox-sized Middle Eastern counter-service joint whose limited menu is as delicious as it is cheap (and, man, is it cheap), or walk a few blocks farther to the more commodious glatt kosher **Jerusalem Café,** next to Kupel's Bagels at JFK Crossing, tel. (617) 278-0200 ($3.50-13.95). The same few blocks have a pair of quite decent Japanese restaurants and the vegetarian Chinese **Buddha's Delight Too,** for those in an Asian frame of mind, but if you want kosher dining *and* chopsticks, you'll have to take a 15-minute hike (or the #66 Dudley bus) back down Harvard St., across the C Line, past the gas station and supermarket, and down the hill to **Shalom Hunan,** tel. (617) 731-9760, on the corner of Harvard and School Streets.

Additional cheap ethnic eats may be found on either side of the trolley tracks above Coolidge Corner, from plastic-cup and paper-napkin places that stay open until at least 11 p.m. daily. Lebanese **Shawarma King,** 1383 Beacon, is the most spacious, but **Anna's Taqueria,** 1412 Beacon, and **Rod Dee Thai Cuisine,** 1430 Beacon, are also worth the squeeze if you want a good meal for just a few bucks. At Rod Dee, for example, well over half the menu's 80-plus entrees are $6 or less, and only two items (both versions of fried whole fish) break the $9 mark.

For more upscale dining, albeit still casual enough welcome anyone in jeans and t-shirt, hop aboard the (free) outbound Green Line trolley at Coolidge Corner and get off four stops later at Washington Square. There at the corner of Washington St. and Beacon is **Five Seasons,** tel. (617) 731-2500, whose eclectic menu places a special emphasis on wholesome, natural foods, from macrobiotic soba or udon noodle dishes to fresh seafood and free-range chicken ($8.25-17.95). Organic wines, dairy-free and maple-sweetened dessert options, and purified water are among the many other touches ap-

preciated by its devoted regulars.

CAMBRIDGE

Dining options in Cambridge cover the spectrum—from swish, upscale places that prompt normally conservative restaurant critics to effervesce like tipsy guests making toasts at a wedding, to chipped-Formica-and-paper-napkin joints where the Fryolator is king. Almost every ethnic cuisine available in the region can be found here, too. Among the specialties that entice people over the river or out of the suburbs: the minimall of Japanese sushi bars in Porter Square; the Indian, Creole, and Korean restaurants of Central Square; four-star hotel restaurants in Harvard Square; the brewpubs; and the coffeehouses. Nearly every named square has numerous choices within a small walkable radius. Cambridge's Harvard, Central, Porter, and Kendall Squares and—just over the line in adjacent Somerville—Davis Square are all easily accessible by the Red Line. Inman Square is a short hop by bus (#69 Lechmere) or cab from Harvard, or an easy 15-minute walk from Central.

Harvard Square
Student staples like pizza, sandwiches, espresso, and wraps (upscale, anything-goes burritos —a far cry from rice and beans) are well represented around the square—you'll find everything from local-gone-national establishments like **Bertucci's** and **Au Bon Pain** to more familiar names like **Pizzeria Uno** and **Starbucks.** The Garage, on the corner of JFK St. and Mt. Auburn, is home to multiple fast-food options, from bagels to burritos, plus one of the more attractive examples of the growing **Pho Pasteur** chain of Vietnamese restaurants. A block behind The Garage at **The Wrap,** 71 Mt. Auburn, diagonally across from Schoenhof's Foreign Books, you'll find such multicultural fare as grilled chicken with jasmine rice, Asian slaw, and Thai peanut sauce in a spinach tortilla, along with equally fashionable fruit smoothies. Health-conscious eaters will appreciate the full nutritional breakdown of the menu of tasty sandwiches and pasta salads at tiny **Santa Barbara Cafe,** 1 Arrow Street. Readers wanting to grab a good burger should follow their noses to **Mr. and Mrs.**

Bartley's Burger Cottage, 1246 Mass. Ave., next to the Harvard Book Store. One of the last remaining off-campus haunts familiar to folks attending their 35th reunion, Bartley's and its grilled burgers have few peers in or out of eastern Massachusetts. Inhale the heady aroma, enjoy the whimsical menu and time-capsule bumper-sticker decor, and then take a bite out of one of the fat, perfectly seared burgers—under $4 plain, over $6 "gourmet"—and see if you don't agree (closed Sunday).

Inexpensive ethnic food runs the gamut from Spanish **Iruña,** an unassuming but heartfelt little soup-and-paella cafe at the rear of 56 JFK St., tel. (617) 868-5633, to **Bangkok House Thai,** a good find in the basement of 50 JFK St. opposite the Galleria mall, tel. (617) 547-6666. Several northern Indian restaurants inhabit the Square and environs, but none quite matches the Galleria's **Bombay Club,** tel. (617) 661-8100, a spacious and elegantly underlit second-story spot overlooking JFK St. and small Winthrop Park. The food, too, is a flight above most of the competition, and while the menu leans toward Kashmiri and Punjabi cuisine from the north, dishes from central and southern India are also represented ($6.95-14.95). A more sustained dose of southern Indian cooking is featured around the corner at **Tanjore,** tel. (617) 868-1900, occupying an attractively decorated storefront on Eliot Street. The menu encourages sampling among the regional specialties with its score of tapas-like *nashta,* which fall between appetizers and full entrees in both portion and price (entrees $9.50-12.75, nashta $3.75-8). If you like Indian food but have limited tolerance for hot and spicy, the **Cafe of India,** 52A Brattle St., tel. (617) 661-0683, is for you—even its so-called hot selections are relatively mild, and the extensive bread selection greatly appeals to American palates. Lustrous copper goblets, individual chafing dishes brought to keep your food warm, and intricately carved chairs lend an air of sumptuous comfort ($8.95-17.95).

Harvard alumni who haven't returned for years will remember Brattle St.'s **Casablanca,** tel. (617) 876-0999, as a dim hangout with basic pub grub, superlative martinis, and signature murals of Bogart, Bergman, and other cast members from the movie. While it still occupies the lower level of Brattle Hall beneath the Brattle Theatre, still has the murals and martinis, and still seems relaxed enough for jeans to be as acceptable as professorial tweed—especially at the bar in the rear—the expanded restaurant now boasts one of Cambridge's most creative menus, prepared by one of the region's star chefs. Local seafood, ever-popular poultry, and reliable steaks are tinged with hints of the sunny Mediterranean, from North Africa to Turkey, and served with seasonal vegetables from the area's top organic farms. It's certain to be unlike almost anything you've ever tried before ($10-21).

Another stellar local chef holds forth at **Rialto,** in the Charles Hotel at the edge of the square, tel. (617) 661-5050, a darling of restaurant critics and cosmopolitan gourmands with excess disposable income. To find out what the raves are about, it's best to book a reservation a couple weeks in advance ($20-29). The hotel's main dining room, **Henrietta's Table,** tel. (617) 864-1200, is Rialto's well-bred rural cousin, creatively interpreting traditional New England cuisine with the absolute freshest regional products available, in a creamy white clapboard decor reminiscent of fine old country inns. Grilled smoked pork chops with apple sauce, fillet of sole stuffed with Maine crab and asparagus, braised lamb, or a meatless entree of grilled native vegetables might be among the day's selections, which vary depending on what's available and in season; separate pricing for entrees (mostly $10-13) and side dishes ($3.25) allows diners to mix and match to personal taste. The wine list is exclusively West Coast, but the "fresh and honest" support-the-locals theme is maintained in the beer department, which features tasty wares from over half a dozen Massachusetts microbreweries (if you enjoy a good stout, try Henrietta's exclusive "Big Pig" brew, custom-made in Boston). A produce market at the front of the restaurant nearly completes the illusion of being close to the farm rather than in the heart of a teeming metropolis.

While fish in some form is featured on the menu of nearly all the Harvard Square restaurants above, anyone wanting to sample local seafood at its simplest—fried, baked, or broiled—should make a beeline for reliable old **Dolphin Seafood,** 1105 Mass. Ave., tel. (617) 661-2937. Tucked into the upper end of a modern little shopping arcade, opposite the Typotech copy

detail from The Potluck, *a mural by David Fichter, behind the Tandoor House in Central Square*

JEFF PERK

and print shop, this plain lunch-and-early dinner eatery conjures up waterfront dining with such specialties as stuffed scrod, baked bluefish with mustard sauce, mussels marinara, clam chowder, and of course live lobsters, steamed and served whole or baked and stuffed with scallops ($8.95-11.95, lobsters market price). Open Mon.-Thurs. 11:30 a.m.-9:30 p.m., Fri.-Sat. till 10:30 p.m.

Central Square
Through Central Square, Mass. Ave. seems strewn with half a dozen casual Indian eateries—sort of a less cohesive Cambridge version of lower Manhattan's 6th St. Indian restaurant row. Differences exist between them, but more apparent at first glance are the similarities: mostly northern Indian cuisine, mostly averaging around $10, and mostly served quickly by polite, quiet men in fairly simple storefront restaurants. **Gandhi,** at No. 704, is one of the better of the lot, with South Indian *dosa* added to the usual curries, korma, and vindaloo, and a good variety of vegetarian specialties. For good tandoori dishes, try the **Tandoor House,** 569 Mass. Ave., or the **Indian Globe,** 474 Mass. Ave. Across from Gandhi is Central Square's other inexpensive exotic, **Asmara,** tel. (617) 864-7447, serving Ethiopian-Eritrean cuisine. For timid companions who aren't attracted to the tender stewed and sautéed meats and richly sauced vegetables—all served on the crepe-like *injera* bread that doubles as your flatware—there's a side

menu of Italian dishes, a legacy of Ethiopia's colonial rulers ($6.75-8.95).

Although Chinese food hardly seems exotic anymore to American palates, **Mary Chung Restaurant,** 464 Mass Ave., tel. (617) 864-1991, has the highly unusual distinction of having its own Usenet chatgroup (alt.fan.mary-chungs). A favorite of generations of Internet-savvy MIT students, it sometimes seems as if those not currently residing on campus down the road seem to plan their get-togethers solely around Mary's peerless dun dun sesame noodles and steamed *suan le chow show.* These and the 150-plus other items on the Sichuan and Mandarin menu constitute a good, grease-free alternative to a trip into Chinatown. Prices are within reach of those hungry scholars, and everything is efficiently served in spotless, casual digs ($4.50-9.50).

While there's no law requiring Central Square eateries to make generous use of chili peppers and complex spice blends (the fast-food burger chains and donut shops provide proof), it seems that most do. **Rhythm & Spice,** 315 Mass. Ave. about a block past the Shell station, tel. (617) 497-0977, applies Caribbean heat in jerk-rubbed barbecue, curries, and marinated fish dishes, with relief provided by fruit chutneys, ice-cold island beers, and home-brewed sweet sorrel. The tropical palm-fringed decor and lively (often live) music seem to keep the sun shining even in the depths of a winter night.

One of the metro area's best Korean restaurants is found a few blocks north of the Central Square T station. **Koreana,** 154 Prospect St., tel. (617) 576-8661, is worth a trip just for its extensive menu of hotpots and sushi accompanied by the usual array of beautifully pickled vegetables and blazing *kim chi* (fermented chili-laced cabbage). Groups interested in sharing Korean barbecue can reserve one of the tables with built-in grills. Also on Prospect halfway between Mass. Ave. and Koreana is **Carberry's Bakery & Coffee House,** tel. (617) 576-3530, an ideal spot for a little elevenses, relaxing over tea and monster-sized scones while planning your next move, or for picking up tomorrow's breakfast. The great baked goods include Scandinavian pastries and about 30 varieties of traditional European-style breads, including hearty Icelandic *grøn,* a fiber-laden whole-wheat variety (open to 8 p.m. daily).

North of Harvard

Until refrigerated rail cars in the late 1870s undercut local abattoirs with cheaper processed meat from Chicago, the district north of Harvard Square was one of several cattle markets serving New England in the 18th and 19th centuries. One legacy of that era is the porterhouse steak, a cut named after a hotel that once stood in Porter Square, near the Red Line T station. Today, the Mass. Ave. neighborhood a mile north of Harvard is renowned even in Tokyo as a center of Japanese shops and restaurants. Aside from Sasuga, the Japanese and English bookstore on Upland Road just across Mass. Ave. from the T station, the biggest cluster of Japanese shops is inside the cream-colored art deco Porter Exchange building a block back down Mass. Ave. from the T. A string of open-kitchen, market-style eateries lines an inside hall, offering the sort of menu specialization common in Japan but rare among Japanese restaurants in the United States. Among the selections, try fried tempura at **Tampopo,** noodles at **Sapporo Ramen,** *wasoku* (Western dishes reinterpreted for Japanese tastes) at **Cafe Mami,** macrobiotic fare at **Masao's Kitchen,** and sushi at **Kotobukiya.** There's also a Kotobukiya supermarket toward the rear of the building for cooks interested in trying some of these dishes at home.

Half a mile and one stop farther outbound along the Red Line, in the adjacent city of Somerville, is Davis Square, Somerville's answer to Harvard Square. Although lacking as many bibliophiliac attractions, Davis in many other respects recaptures the spirit of old, pre-chain-store Cambridge. The excellent Somerville Theatre and a couple of Irish bars and clubs draw numerous people in from outside the neighborhood, but diners looking for distinctive meals have reason to come, too. **Redbones,** 55 Chester St., tel. (617) 628-2200, off of Elm St. two blocks south of the Somerville Theatre, is a prime example. It has the hands-down best two-fisted open-your-mouth-when-you-laugh Dixie ambiance of any barbecue joint in Greater Boston, if not all New England. Arkansas travelers, Texan tourists, and Memphians missing a taste of pork amid all the multicultural highfalutin' New American fusion stuff should park themselves at the back counter by the mesquite cooker and breathe deeply for proof that New England isn't a complete lost cause. The advantage to this place over those back home is a superior beer selection, including a fluctuating set of two dozen fine microbrews on tap. It even manages to out-Cambridge Cambridge, by offering valet bicycle parking. The kitchen is open until 10:30 p.m. nightly, while the bar stays open until 1:30 a.m. (cash only, $5.95-13.95).

Davis Square is also home to one of the area's few classic diners. Serving decent meals and accessible to the T, just off Elm St. a block past Redbones, **The Rosebud Diner,** tel. (617) 666-6015, is a handsomely restored 1940s semi-streamliner from the Worcester Lunch Car Company, the state's preeminent diner manufacturer. Steak tips with honey barbecue sauce, char-broiled chicken breast sandwiches, pasta and meatballs for two, and other renovated standards fill the bill, along with great fluffy omelets and other breakfast dishes ($4.50-10.95; cash only). Tucked discreetly behind the smoked-glass storefront between the Rosebud and Picante Mexican Grill (a better-than-average burrito parlor) is one of Somerville's better upscale restaurants, **Gargoyles,** 215 Elm St., tel. (617) 776-5300. The intimate space, busy little bar, and snappy background tunes make this a hot spot for impressing that special date, but for those whose first love is fine food, the top-notch, seasonally adjusted New American menu will sweep you off your feet. Open for dinner only, Tues.-Sun. till 10 p.m. ($14-19). Less expensive creative cookery is found on the north side of the Somerville Theatre, including **Johnny D's Up-Town Restaurant & Music Club,** 17 Holland St., tel. (617) 776-2004, with modestly inventive comfort food and good vegetarian selections. There's also a half-price early bird menu Tues.-Friday.

If you do come by T, as you enter or exit Davis Square, be sure to look closely at the bricks beneath your feet. You'll find 11 poems inscribed on the subway platform, including ones by Emily Dickinson, Walt Whitman, and Elizabeth Bishop, and this favorite:

> *At 7 am watching the cars on*
> *the bridge*
> *Everyone going to work, well*
> *Not me, I'm not*
> *Going to work.*
> —James Moore

Millions of scuffing shoes and grit are causing them to fade, but they're worth the effort of deciphering.

CITYWIDE SPECIALS

Ice Cream
On average, New Englanders consume nearly twice as many quarts of ice cream and frozen yogurt as anyone else in the country—despite spending half the year clad in wool sweaters and long underwear. But there's no mystery behind this passion—sample the quality of local ice cream makers and you'll double your consumption, too. **Steve's,** at the east end of Faneuil Hall Marketplace, isn't a bad place to start—use it to establish a baseline for comparison. After selling out to a major corporation, the founder, Steve Herrell, founded **Herrell's,** which is a decided improvement over his now-franchised first creation. Found in Allston at the corner of Harvard and Brighton Avenues and on Dunster St., in Harvard Square, Herrell's is particularly good for dense, chocolatey flavors. If there were any more chocolate in the chocolate pudding flavor, for instance, and it would no longer legally be

---

CELEBRATION OF ICE CREAM~ IT'S THE SCOOPER BOWL!

If you've graduated to the expensive super-premium dairy desserts in your grocer's freezer, you won't want to miss the annual **Scooper Bowl,** tel. (617) 632-3300, on City Hall Plaza, across Congress St. from Faneuil Hall and the Haymarket area. Tuesday through Thursday the first full week of every June, tens of thousands of Bostonians reschedule work and suspend their diets in order to head down for their daily recommended dose of dairy products. Over the course of the three days, more than three dozen vendors scoop and serve 11 *tons* of ice cream, sherbet, frozen yogurt, and everything in between for the happy hordes.

Your selfless participation in the all-you-can-eat frenzy also helps two worthy causes: first, all proceeds are donated to the Dana-Farber Cancer Institute's Jimmy Fund, which supports research into childhood cancer; second, if you get hooked by the quality and flavor of what you taste, maybe you'll go out and buy more—and thus help preserve New England's dairy farmers from extinction (given the greater profit in houses than Holsteins, it's probably a losing battle, but every little bit helps—so stop counting calories and eat more ice cream!).

---

ice cream. For liqueur-flavored ice creams, deceptively rich-tasting but low-fat hard yogurts, and a true chocolate-lover's hot fudge sauce, **J P Licks** is the place to go, in Jamaica Plain, Coolidge Corner, and Back Bay. The JP location at 659 Centre St. is easy to spot—just look for the life-size cow over the entrance (even more irresistible is the upper Newbury St. parlor, by Tower Records, with tilework à la Antonio Gaudi). Farther down Newbury, between Hereford and Gloucester St., **Emack & Bolio's** makes the definitive Oreo ice cream, while **Ben & Jerry's** (between Exeter and Dartmouth St.) does the best job of matching flavors to pop cultural icons. But for the true pinnacle of the local ice cream scene, cross the river to Cambridge and find one of the three **Toscanini's** along Mass. Ave. (The one opposite Harvard Yard is easiest to find but is also the most expensive and limited in its selection; better are the original parlor, at the corner of Main St. and Mass. Ave., in Central Square, and the one in the MIT Student Center, opposite MIT's 77 Mass. Ave. entrance.) Toscanini's specialties are intense flavors like nocciola (hazelnut), burnt caramel, malted vanilla, and seasonal fruit flavors, plus the occasional bit of whimsy. (Guinness ice cream, anyone?)

If you want a milkshake from any of the above, order a "frappe" (rhymes with trap), or you'll get nothing more than milk and flavored syrup.

For those who find ice cream a poor substitute for the processed form of *Theobroma cacao,* all your chocoholic cravings will meet their most formidable challenge at the Chocolate Bar, an all-you-can-eat buffet of over 30 chocolate desserts presented each Saturday afternoon 1-3 p.m. Oct.-May at Le Meridien's **Cafe Fleuri** in the Financial District, tel. (617) 451-1900.

Coffeehouses and Hangouts
Boston once had its own distinctive high-end coffeehouse chain, but Starbucks, that Microsoft of the espresso bean, bought it, and thereby defused a much-anticipated East Coast-West Coast coffee war. Taking up where Boston left off, in fact, have been two more West Coast chains, Seattle's Best Coffee and Peet's. The former sells through suburban storefronts and campus pushcarts, the latter through a strategic alliance with Au Bon Pain bakery-cafes. Coffee (and tea) drinkers interested in sparks of individuality in the local market should look in either Cambridge or Boston's North End—although Back Bay's smattering of hangouts provide equally piquant alternatives to the sip-and-run storefronts.

A well-established trend in college-saturated and computer-savvy Boston is the Internet cafe, a place where you can browse the Web, cappuccino in hand, for a fee that's generally competitive with those charged for renting desktop computer time at copy shops like Kinko's. Defining the high end of this genre is **Cybersmith,** upstairs from the Border Cafe on Church St. in Harvard Square, tel. (617) 492-5857. Cybersmith's snaking neon, suspended halogen lamps, and scores of built-in terminals make it just your average corner patisserie designed by Braun and furnished by MacWarehouse. It's chosen some of the area's best sandwich,

dessert, and coffee bean suppliers, though, so even if you feel like a Jetson you certainly don't have to eat like one. As an alternative to a computer arcade, check out any of the following places gathered around Harvard and within walking distance of one another: **Cafe Paradiso,** facing the Harvard Square Hotel, with gelati and shots of Italian syrups; **Cafe Algiers,** on Brattle St., one of whose specialties is a bracing Turkish coffee you can almost eat with a fork; or **Cafe Pamplona,** on Bow St. between Baskin-Robbins and Arrow St., with uniquely intimate low-ceiling philosophers-club ambiance.

Although the Algiers' pot of sinus-clearing mint tea is warmly recommended, tea lovers may prefer the singleminded dedication of **Tealuxe,** a "tea bar" at Zero Brattle St., next to Urban Outfitters. Although a hip place for sipping and socializing, it's too cramped to be truly relaxing. On the other hand, it's a darn sight more affordable than either the posh high tea served at the Ritz in Boston (often to the accompaniment of of a live harpist), or the equally ritzy tea service at the neighboring Four Seasons Hotel, overlooking the Public Garden.

The most Berkeley-like of Greater Boston's java joints is at Central Square, a stop away from Harvard on the Red Line. Named in honor of a long-vanished local jazz club (the actual street number is 757 Mass. Ave.), the **1369 Cafe** is a favorite haunt of local Moon authors, as the mellow staff, good tunes, giant scones, smoke-free atmosphere, and quality house joe all lend themselves to writing away an afternoon. Another tasty and laid-back spot to linger is **Carberry's Bakery & Coffee House,** 74 Prospect St., within two blocks north of the T station, open nightly till 8 p.m. If nicotine is critical to your caffeine enjoyment, try the smoker-friendly **Phoenix Coffeehouse,** 675 Mass. Ave., virtually atop the outbound side of the T station, whose hazy atmosphere helps mask the rather sterile plate glass and exposed brick of its former-video-store quarters. Good coffee and baked goods, if you can taste them through the carbon cloud.

No rundown of one-of-a-kind coffee stops would be complete without mention of the **Someday Cafe,** in the heart of Davis Square, in Somerville. Just steps from the Red Line station, the Someday welcomes its predominantly younger patrons with a "Sorry, we're open" sign, thrashing music (to keep cell phone-packing Sharper Image types away), no-nonsense espresso, and top-notch biscotti. Don't take the attitude personally, sit in the back room away from the stereo speakers, and you'll enjoy one of the hippest hangouts inside Rt. 128.

Across the river, in Boston, the self-conscious antidote to Back Bay's self-conscious yuppiness is **The Other Side Cosmic Cafe,** 407 Newbury St., on the forgotten side of Mass. Ave., kitty-corner from the giant Tower Records store atop the Hynes/ICA Green Line station. Here, the Joe Camel generation balances tar and nicotine with fruit and vegetable smoothies, wheatgrass shots, sandwiches, soup, veggie lasagna, decent desserts, and all manner of espresso drinks. It's a well-established hangout, and you'll enjoy it most if you like listening to Cranes or other college radio alternative music.

A block away, at 338 Newbury, the **Trident Booksellers & Cafe** offers a more clean-cut slice of Bohemia—the kind you'd feel safer introducing to your mother. Against a backdrop of a very literary and political magazine selection and art and new-age books, readers in solitary reverie or couples in animated conversation linger over coffees, herbal teas, light meals, and lovely desserts. If you're in downtown's Theater District, you might mosey over to the very foot of Columbus Avenue, opposite the rounded point of the Statler Building (home to the Park Plaza Hotel), and check out the **Tar Bar,** a dark hangout favored by Emerson College performing arts students and other theater types. There's no sign out front, but if you enter the door to the left of the Hub Pub, and end up in a joint with "LIQUORS" in giant neon at the back, you've found the right place.

Finally, there's the North End, whose main artery, Hanover Street, has a number of good cafes serving cappuccino and cannoli, chased perhaps with Sambuca or grappa. For a cross-section of what's available within a radius of thirty yards, sample the ever-lively mirror-covered **Caffè Paradiso,** modern **Cafe Graffiti,** or soccer-crazy **Caffè dello Sport.**

FROM THE COLLECTIONS OF HENRY FORD MUSEUM & GREENFIELD VILLAGE

DAY TRIPS BEYOND BOSTON

Several of the state's highlights for visitors lay within a short distance of Boston, accessible by car or mass transit. The North Shore, stretching up the coast from Boston to Cape Ann and the mouth of the Merrimack River near New Hampshire, is home to several 19th-century coastal resort communities whose legacy of handsome mansions, yacht clubs, and beautiful beaches has largely withstood the Hub's virulent suburban sprawl. In recognition of its rich history, the National Park Service has designated the surrounding county a National Heritage Area, and has established a regional visitor center in Salem as an interpretive gateway to the many small museums, historic sites, and scenic attractions that dot the region. Northwest of Boston, Jack Kerouac's hometown of Lowell is a living monument to the Industrial Revolution that reshaped the state and the nation throughout the 1800s, as well as host to such colorful annual events as the nation's largest free folk music festival and a long weekend celebration of all things Kerouac. To the west, along the Battle Road between Lexington and Concord, the violent birth of nationhood and later flowering of American literature have left their strong imprint, whether in the Revolutionary War battlefields now grown up in woods, the annual reenactments of those fateful April 1775 events, or the homes of authors like Emerson, Alcott, and Hawthorne, preserved for generations of new readers touched by their words. South of the city, history again springs up in Quincy, "City of Presidents," and Plymouth, the eventual landing place of the Pilgrims. And while the remembrance of things past is obviously one of Massachusetts's favorite occupations, parks, wildlife sanctuaries, and art museums—particularly in the Charles River watershed region west-southwest of Boston—offer other, utterly history-free incentives to explore beyond the city's bright lights.

SALEM

In light of the infamous Witch Trials of 1692, it may seem a tad ironic that Salem derives its name from the Hebrew word for peace, shalom. In fact, the village in which those 17th-century persecutions occurred erased the irony long ago by changing its name to Danvers. That's right, modern Salem isn't really the scene of the crime, so to speak. It isn't entirely disconnected from the trials, either—a judge lived here, and most of the victims were hung here. But fact and proportion are flimsy restraints, and given Danvers's renunciation of its dark past, it stands to reason that Salem's merchants would adopt the story of those old witches as their own. Contemporary ones are welcomed, too, so watch out for low-flying broomsticks and plenty of costumed phantasmagoria in October, when the city pulls out all the stops for Halloween.

History

The offspring of an abortive fishing venture, Albion, established in 1623 further north at Cape Ann, the Salem area was among the earliest sites of English settlement in the northeast. When the backers in Albion pulled the plug on the unprofitable plantation, some of its members chose to move south to the Pawtucket Indian village of Naumkeag, whose scant survivors of European epidemics welcomed their new neighbors as protectors from hostile tribes to the north. By the time the Massachusetts Bay Colony was officially chartered in 1628, the newly rechristened town of Salem was a viable settlement. Its "Old Planters" were accustomed to both autonomy and relative religious freedom, from Church of England faithfuls to Separatist (e.g., Pilgrim) dissenters relocated from Plymouth. Both of these traits made Salem a very sharp thorn in the side of the fundamentalist Puritans, who alighted in Salem only long enough to depose Governor Endicott before moving south and making their capital in Boston under the rule of John Winthrop. The conflict came to a head when Salem chose Roger Williams as minister. Williams criticized as "a National sinne" the Puritan doctrine of total disregard of Native American land rights. Boston ultimately brought Salem into line by banishing the heretical Williams in 1636, on pain of death; but before being carted back to England, he escaped and founded the Providence Plantation—now known as Rhode Island.

Salem's 17th-century affair with witchcraft, a fever pitch of finger-pointing and snitching neighbors and veritable lynchings, seems to comprise the town's most enthralling historical episode, judging by the sheer quantity of commercial attractions based on it. The impact of the trials is disturbing: 19 men and women were hanged; one man was crushed under heavy stones; and an untold number died in jail, or, like the five-year-old child imprisoned for a year, were psychologically crippled for life. The shame lasted for generations. Nathaniel Hawthorne added a "w" to his family name to distance himself from his ancestor, trial magistrate John Hathorne. Embarrassment may yet be a reason the town of Danvers to this day doesn't publicize trial-related sights within its boundaries.

After the American Revolution, Salem rose to prominence in seaborne trade. Ships from Salem sailed east, monopolizing Africa, Arabia, India, Malaysia, Indonesia, and the Philippines, multiplying profits geometrically by trading at each port en route. The local fleet of nearly 200 "East Indiamen" traded Yankee rum, chocolate, salt cod, furniture, and flour for coffee, indigo, cotton, sugar, and a major slice of the Indonesian pepper crop. But Salem's days as a pepper potentate and coffee kingdom were numbered: President Jefferson's 1807 embargo on American overseas trade and "Mr. Madison's War" with England in 1812—foreign policies ostensibly designed to punish England for violating American neutrality at sea—cut off Massachusetts maritime trade at the knees. Sea trade began again after the war's end in 1814, but Salem's port never regained its former stature. By the middle of the 19th century, manufacturing overtook trade as Salem's economic breadwinner.

SIGHTS

Peabody Essex Museum

With over two dozen galleries in two buildings and nine historic houses, this is one of New England's largest museums, and the oldest continuously operating one in the nation. Reflecting both Salem's past and the activities of its 18th-century founders, the strengths of the collections lie in maritime art and history, Asian and Pacific ethnographic art, New England architecture and decorative arts, and a peerless collection of Asian export art specifically crafted for foreign trade. Salem's globe-spanning commerce is amply illustrated with artifacts from every imaginable trading partner and then some. The legacy of indigenous New Englanders is also extensively documented within the museum's collections. You can study the infamous Witch Trials here, free of the dramatics that attend their description elsewhere in town, and examine some of native-born Nathaniel Hawthorne's personal effects. The two main buildings, on Essex and Liberty Streets near East India Square, tel. (800) 745-4054, www. pem.org, are open daily between Memorial Day and Halloween, and Tues.-Sun. the rest of the year. The museum's historic houses are mostly in the block adjacent to the Essex Street building, although one, the Ropes Mansion, is at 318 Essex St., in the McIntire Historic District. Six are open seasonally to guided tours only, including the stately 14-room **Gardner-Pingree House,** whose three stories of red brick are widely regarded as the zenith of Samuel McIntire's work. Some architecture critics even consider it the definitive example of the Federal style. Admission to the museum and the houses is $8.50 adults, $5 kids (discounted family rates available).

Maritime and Literary Sights

Over a half dozen historic structures along the city's old commercial wharves have been preserved as part of the **Salem Maritime National Historic Site,** including Derby Wharf, the Custom House, and other buildings related to the East Indies trade. The sites are united by a waterfront park whose centerpiece is the *Friendship,* a functional replica of a 1797 sailing vessel. Start at the two-room Central Wharf Orientation

figureheads from the ship Talma, *the bark* Western Belle, *and the ship* Indian Princess, *in the Peabody Essex Museum's East India Marine Hall*

Center on Derby Street for a video introduction to the site and a menu of ranger-led tours ($2).

The Custom House at the head of Derby Wharf is another of the many Massachusetts buildings Nathaniel Hawthorne helped put firmly on the map, this one by lampooning its functionaries in his prefatory sketch to *The Scarlet Letter.* The inspiration for Hawthorne's vinegary satire derived from his short term as a government surveyor, a patronage appointment wrung from his friend and Bowdoin College roommate, President Franklin Pierce, whose fawning campaign biography Hawthorne penned.

The National Park Service operates a spacious **Salem Visitor Center** in the old brick armory at the corner of Essex and New Liberty Streets, tel. (978) 740-1650, between the two halves of the Peabody Essex Museum grounds. A few displays and a very good film presentation put Salem's maritime pursuits into the wider context of surrounding Essex County, whose historical riches have earned it designation as a

MARK SEXTON/COURTESY, PEABODY ESSEX MUSEUM, SALEM MA

National Heritage Area. Pick up free guides to the county-wide Heritage Trails, or a walking tour brochure to Salem's own Heritage Trail, marked by a red line on downtown sidewalks. Restrooms, gifts, a wall full of well-selected books, and the chance to query the friendly ranger staff for suggestions or opinions about sights, restaurants, or the fastest routes out of town are all further reasons to visit the center, which is open daily 9 a.m.-6 p.m.

Four blocks east of Derby Wharf stands **The House of Seven Gables,** 54 Turner St., tel. (978) 744-0991. Celebrated as the setting for Nathaniel Hawthorne's eponymous novel, parts of this rambling waterfront mansion date back to 1668. Period gardens and several other 17th-century buildings, including the Salem house Hawthorne was born in on the Fourth of July, have been relocated here and are included in the guided tours (open daily; $7).

Witches, Wretches, and Pirates

Salem leads the state in cheesy sideshow-style entertainment venues masquerading as museums. Kids love 'em, and if you need to plan a birthday party for a bunch of 12-year-olds, you could do a lot worse than booking it at one of these. With one exception all are seasonal, generally open daily from April or May through Halloween or Thanksgiving. Admission fees are about $4-5 each; several knock off a dollar if you buy admission to their companion attraction. None are hard to find: stroll west along Derby and New Derby Streets from the wharfside Orientation Center and you'll pass a handful— **Salem's Museum of Myths & Monsters,** in the Pickering Wharf shops, and the **New England Pirate Museum,** the **Salem Wax Museum of Witches & Seafarers,** and **Dracula's Castle,** on the pedestrian-only Marketplace. On the other side of downtown Washington Street is the **Witch Dungeon Museum,** 16 Lynde St., which at least gives you some live theatrics (loosely based on an actual witchcraft trial transcript) for your money. The **Salem Witch Museum,** on Washington Square across from the common, purports to be the most popular, but behind the photogenic stone facade, the amateurish diorama-with-lights show is truly the biggest disappointment of the whole lot. Stick to the gift shop. Despite the long swirling cape and tall, wide-

brimmed hat, the statue in front is neither witch nor judge. It's Roger Conant, Salem's first European settler.

The *Real* Witchcraft Sites

Besides the graves of two of the witchcraft trial magistrates—John Hathorne's in Charter Street's old Burying Point behind the wax museum, and Jonathan Corwin's in the Broad Street burial ground—modern Salem has very little remaining that's truly related to the infamous trials. The courthouse in which the proceedings were held is long gone; the site, beneath Washington Street in front of City Hall, is marked only by a plaque on the Masonic Temple. The jail, or gaol, in which the accused were incarcerated was also felled in the name of progress. Its site now belongs to a telephone company building. The location of Gallows Hill has never been conclusively identified, although a couple candidates are west of downtown off Boston Street. The principal surviving site from 1692 is Justice Corwin's home,

---

SAMUEL McINTIRE'S LEGACY

Charles Bulfinch gets (and deserves) the lion's share of the credit for originating the Federal style of architecture. But he was never its sole practitioner. In fact, some of the finest Federal structures in existence are the work of Samuel McIntire—a *Salem* builder.

A homegrown American variation on the prevailing English decorative style, Federal architecture emphasizes symmetry and two-dimensional ornament—square facades framed on the sides by flat pilasters, for example. The center doorway gets the most lavish treatment—a columned portico, perhaps; fanlight windows; sidelights sometimes. A distinguishing feature of most Federal houses is that the third-story windows are much smaller than those on either of the first two floors. Roofs are flat, rather than pitched, and usually have fancy railings running along the edge.

Ranger-led walking tours of McIntire's legacy start at the National Park Service's Salem Visitor Center. Or, to wander on your own, pick up a free Park Service guide to the McIntire District (centered in Chestnut St.), a couple of blocks west of downtown.

A Modeſt Enquiry

Into the Nature of

Witchcraft,

AND

How Perſons Guilty of that Crime
may be *Convicted* : And the means
uſed for their Diſcovery Diſcuſſed,
both *Negatively* and *Affirmatively,*
according to *SCRIPTURE* and
EXPERIENCE.

By **John Hale,**

Paſtor of the Church of Chriſt in *Beverley,*
Anno Domini 1 6 9 7.

When they ſay unto you, ſeek unto them that have
Familiar Spirits and unto Wizzards,that peep,&c.
To the Law and to the Teſtimony ; if they ſpeak
not according to this word, it is becauſe there is no
light in them, Iſaiah VIII. 1 9, 2 0.
That which I ſee not teach thou me, Job 3 4 3 2.

BOSTON in N. E.
Printed by *B. Green,*, and *J. Allen,* for
Benjamin Eliot under the Town Houſe: 1702

the title page from a 1702 manual on witchcraft

popularly mislabeled **The Witch House,** 310 Essex St. at the corner of North, tel. (978) 744-0180. Tours focus on the First Period architecture, furnishings, and the life of the building's infamous owner.

It takes a car, but if you are determined to see where most of the Salem uproar really occurred, you'll have to drive west to neighboring Danvers. Although houses that belonged to people who testified at the witchcraft trials and the tavern in which preliminary hearings were held are now almost all private residences, there are a couple of notable exceptions. Foremost is the 1678 **Rebecca Nurse Homestead,** 149 Pine St., tel. (978) 774-8799, the house and farm of a devout septuagenarian whose standing within the community was high enough to give the witch trial magistrates pause before accepting the accusations against her. Although initially found not guilty, the fits of her accusers prompted judges and jury to reconsider their verdict; in July of 1692 she was hanged with four other alleged witches. Tours of the property are the most historically accurate of all the witch-related attractions, and do not pander to popular superstitions or the public thirst for over-simplified histrionics. Open Tues.-Sun. 1-4:30 p.m., June 15-Labor Day, plus weekends through the end of October. Admission is $4. Tours begin in the replica of the Salem Village Meetinghouse built for the TV movie *Three Sovereigns for Sarah,* which shares the homestead grounds with other farm buildings. The original meetinghouse, in which some of the pretrial examinations took place, sat on Hobart Street opposite Danvers's present pale granite memorial to the witchcraft victims.

The 1692 witch hysteria all began at yet another Danvers locale, the home of Reverend Parris. He lived there with his oddly behaving daughter and niece, and Tituba, one of the family's two slaves and the children's alleged guide to satanic arts. Though long gone, the home's foundations may still be seen at the **Salem Village Parsonage Archaeological Site,** now a town park with a few interpretive signs to tell the tale. Despite billing itself one of the most significant historical sites of colonial America, it is nearly inaccessible, located behind a private home at 67 Center Street. Foliage nearly obscures the only streetside sign, and no real safe or legal parking is available. (Parallel park with two wheels a foot or so over the curb and leave your emergency flashers on if you do pay a visit.) To get there from the Nurse Homestead, continue north on Pine and make a left on Hobart (at the flashing yellow signal), and then a right where Hobart intersects Center. Number 67, a yellow-clapboard house whose owner doesn't take kindly to visitors, will come fairly quickly on the right after the bend.

PRACTICALITIES

Food and Drink

Being a tourist hot spot hasn't overloaded Salem with witch-themed restaurants or fast food franchises. Downtown has its share of bar-restaurant combos, where buffalo wings and steak tips reign supreme, but there are also some fine upscale New American places, and great ethnic spots. Folks desperate for an espresso fix will find a less-expensive alternative to Starbucks in the **Cafe Bagel Co.,** on Washington St. just south of Essex.

Popular with locals and tourists alike is Derby Street's **In a Pig's Eye,** tel. (978) 741-4436, a cheerful den a couple of blocks past the Custom House. The eclectic fare is a good match for the ambiance; skip the Mexican items (too far from the source) and you won't leave disappointed or hungry. It's open to midnight Mon.-Saturday. A slightly more '90s menu of brick oven pizzas, lots of things laced with chipotle peppers or dry-rubbed spices, and plenty of fresh veggies is found up the street at the **Salem Beer Works,** 278 Derby, tel. (978) 741-7088 ($10.95-15.95). All this is accompanied, of course, by a passel of beers brewed on the premises.

The **Thai Place,** inside the Museum Place shops on the Essex Street pedestrian mall, tel. (978) 741-8008, is Salem's reliable Southeast Asian offering. Everything's well-spiced, swiftly served, and reasonably priced ($8.75-12.95). Another prime Asian contender is **Asahi,** 21 Congress St., tel. (978) 744-5376, a very informal, often quite busy spot next to Pickering Wharf. Besides the usual sushi and sashimi—some of which arrives in lacquered bento boxes like little treasure chests—the fine tempura and a number of hotpot entrees are also deservedly popular ($9.50-18.95). Closed Monday. Across the street at 26 Congress is one of the area's best restaurants, **Grapevine,** tel. (978) 745-9335. An elegant, relaxed oasis of mostly northern Italian cuisine, its chef spices up the menu of familiar dishes with unexpected flavors from other continents ($12.95-18.50). Dinner nightly; lunch Wed.-Saturday.

Several blocks south of the touristy Pickering Wharf area is **Red Raven's Love Noodle,** 75 Congress St., tel. (978) 745-8558. The scene behind the little maroon, flowery facade could teach Boston a thing or two about the cutting edge of cool. Open daily 5-10 p.m., the Noodle attracts a young, loud crowd hip to ethnic noodle dishes, lots of boldly seasoned appetizers, an extensive list of under-$20 wines, lots of dark sweet beers, ginseng elixirs, and fruit-based concoctions (entrées $10-15). Beware: "no credit cards or yuppies," and it's located in an urban edge neighborhood that draws customers into complicity with the owners' spirit of adventure. Though more upscale, **Red Raven's Havana,** tel. (978) 740-3888, the second sibling in the growing Raven family, almost manages to make Love Noodle look tame. The purple awning and heavily draped windows at 90 Washington St., downtown, conceal an interior approximating a bordello designed by Pedro Almodovar—beaded curtain at the entrance, animal print upholstery, artwork ranging from the Renaissance to Cubism, and a ripe, Batista-era big-band sound pouring out of the house stereo. The mixed drinks are named with such undisguised double entendre that if they were funded by the National Endowment for the Arts, Congress would pillory the artist who concocted them. The menu is divvied into three categories: spa (non-or low-fat), bourgeois, and gastronomique. The simplest entrée might be a vegetable paella with cumin-scented crisp bulgur bread; a more self-indulgent patron may prefer a spiced walnut-crusted rack of lamb. As you could guess, such a rich sensory experience doesn't come cheap: entrées run $14.75-24.75. If you feel any slight vibrations under your feet, it's only Salem's Puritan founders spinning mightily in their graves.

Finally, though it's a drive from downtown, the **Salem Diner,** 70 Loring Ave. (Rt. 1A) near the intersection with Canal St., tel. (978) 744-9776, is well worth a detour for a good square meal or fine short-order breakfast (open to 7:45 p.m. weekdays, and to half past noon on weekends). Come for fluffy pancakes, tasty omelets and home fries, steak tips, fried seafood, and all the excitement of watching the masterful staff juggle a score of meals in the aisle behind the Formica, with barks of "Order's up!" punctuating the bacon-sizzle and plate-clatter. Sit at the counter and Alex and Pete will show appropriately gruff concern for whether you enjoy your meal, but don't pay the guys any strong compliments. Too much praise and they might get some swell ideas, raise their rock-bottom prices, and start adding French accents to the menu, heaven forbid. Diner fans won't want to miss this place: it's one of a handful of Sterling Streamliners still in use, a 1941 model rounded at both ends in the sleek, aerodynamic style pioneered by their maker, the Massachusetts-based J. B. Judkins Company.

Getting There
Although only 16 miles from Boston, with bridge or tunnel traffic it'll take a good 40 minutes to drive to Salem from the Hub, and parking is free in city lots only on weekends and holidays. Alternatively, hop aboard a train or boat, and let someone else do the driving. Catch any train bound for Rockport or Ipswich on the MBTA **Commuter Rail** from Boston's North Station; in half an hour or less you can step off at Salem's Bridge Street depot, at the end of Washington St. on the edge of downtown. Roundtrip fare is $5; for daily schedules call (617) 222-3200 or, toll-free within Massachusetts, (800) 392-6100. Or, choose the **Harbor Express** high-speed cata-maran, with multiple daily departures from the north side of Boston's Long Wharf (behind the Marriott) to Salem's Blaney Street pier, a couple blocks east of the House of Seven Gables, for $16 roundtrip (bikes free). The ride up takes 80 minutes, due to a stopover at Logan Airport en route, but the return is a scenic one-hour ride; call (978) 741-3442 for schedule.

LOWELL

Over a century ago when Lowell was the envy of weavers worldwide, its factories and canals earned flattering comparisons to Venice and became a compulsory stop on any foreign dignitary's American tour. A marvel of the Industrial Age, Lowell became one of its casualties, too, when the industry it long monopolized fled south. Today, the vast 19th-century mills and their working class neighborhoods have many interesting tales to tell now that they've been renovated into a city-sized museum, which highlights the nation's transformation into an industrialized society. And it's more than just a nuts-and-bolts story of technical innovation or shrewd capital management: the lives of the early "mill girls," the changes wrought by massive immigration, and the struggles for decent working conditions are given as much attention as the engineering and financial wizards whose names are on street signs and building facades.

Lowell may seem to be an old Rust Belt city that's rather well preserved but otherwise unremarkable. Look closely, though: the galleries and condos occupying those 19th-century factories, the Cambodian and Laotian influence in store windows and on local menus, *two* professional minor league sports teams, and the extensive calendar of local cultural offerings hint at how much more there is to this place than first meets the eye. Car-free travelers needn't miss out, either, as Lowell is a reasonably cheap and easy commute from Boston.

History
The city straddles a sharp bend in the Merrimack River between Pawtucket Falls and the confluence with the diminutive Concord River, an area that was a vital salmon fishery and trading site for the area's indigenous people thousands of years before either Christ or Columbus. When Samuel de Champlain sailed up the Merrimack in 1605, the two sides of the falls were occupied by a pair of Algonquian-speaking tribes in northern New England's Pennacook confederation—the Pawtucket and Wamesit tribes. The frequent presence of the Pennacook's supreme leader, Passaconaway, suggests the falls were a seat of government. Ravished by European plague and lethal raids by Mohawk and Abenaki warriors from the west and north, the confederation was in no position to resist the English who soon came in Champlain's wake. By 1644 Passaconaway had signed a covenant with Boston's colonial government pledging fealty, unleashing a rash of laws regarding dress, behavior, religion, and just about everything else that could possibly distinguish Native Americans from Bible-thumping Puritans. After 16 more years of losing land to court-favored colonists, the once-great sachem and shaman, rumored to be over 100

years old, abdicated his power to his eldest son Wannalancit with warnings to followers that quarreling with the white man would bring certain destruction. The advice was misdirected: the Pennacooks were soon so decimated in a retaliatory raid against the Mohawks that they couldn't have joined King Philip's War even if they'd wanted to. A village of Christianized Indians was established briefly after the war, but the encroachment of colonial farmers forced Wannalancit to sell the land and move most of his band north well before the end of the 1600s.

East Chelmsford, as the township was then known, tilled the soil for nearly a century. As population outgrew arable land, residents turned to cottage industry and trade. East Chelmsford's transformation in particular was spurred by transportation improvements begun in the 1790s to provide access to New Hampshire timber. The 1.5-mile Pawtucket Canal was financed by shipbuilders at the Merrimack's mouth to circumvent the town's hazardous falls, and the 27-mile Middlesex Canal was built largely to bring logs from the upper Merrimack directly to Boston. In 1821 some Boston-area industrialists looked at these canals and saw horsepower waiting to be har-

JACK KEROUAC

San Francisco may have named a street for him, and Greenwich Village wouldn't have been the same without him, but Jack Kerouac always considered himself a Lowell boy. Patron saint of the Beat Generation—whose name he coined one long-talking night in 1948—and poster boy of bohemian excess, Jean-Louis Kirouac was born March 12, 1922, to a French-Canadian family living in the Centralville (say "Cennerville" if asking directions) part of town.

At the **Kerouac Commemorative,** on Bridge St. downtown, excerpts from several of the author's more prominent works are inscribed on granite monoliths. When the golden late afternoon sun burnishes the red-brick backdrop of the Massachusetts Mills, this is one of Lowell's nicer urban oases.

After his alcohol-related death on October 21, 1969, in St. Petersburg, Florida, Kerouac came home for good. He's buried in Edson Cemetery, on Gorham St. (Rt. 3A), a couple of miles south of downtown. Altar-like pile of offerings mark the flat gravestone beside the cemetery's Lincoln Ave., between 7th and 8th St., or follow the tracks if there's snow.

Lowellians have had their share of ambivalence toward Kerouac, and some—with personal memories of his self-destructive lifestyle—

Jack Kerouac, 44, and his third wife, Stella Sampas, 48, at home after their wedding, in Hyannis, in November 1966

COURTESY OF THE BOSTON PUBLIC LIBRARY, PRINT DEPARTMENT

question paying lofty tribute to such a role model. But if you're around during the first weekend of October, check out the **Lowell Celebrates Kerouac!** festival, with photo exhibits, walking tours, literary symposia, poetry readings, music, and much more—and judge for yourself what epithets or eulogies are worthy of the guy. To receive a festival calendar of events (which actually begin midweek), call the Greater Merrimack Convention & Visitors Bureau, tel. (978) 459-6150, or write to Lowell Celebrates Kerouac!, P.O. Box 1111, Lowell, MA 01853, or e-mail mhemenway@drc.com, and ask to be added to the mailing list.

nessed and a shipping lane for both raw materials *and* finished products. Within a year the Boston Associates began building a company town named after their founder, Francis Cabot Lowell. Though he himself didn't live long enough to enjoy the rewards, this Boston cloth merchant's successful development of a power loom (based on a mechanical design memorized during tours of English mills) was the final step to automating the whole textile manufacturing process under one roof, from cotton bale to bolts of finished cloth. Implementing the "Lowell system" on the Charles River at Waltham, just west of Boston, proved so hugely profitable that Lowell's partners quickly sought a place suitable for a massive expansion. They found it by the bend in the Merrimack at Pawtucket Falls; within a generation "Spindle City" was the second most populous community in Massachusetts, its 10 giant mill complexes employing over 10,000 workers. Lowell remained the nation's leading textile producer until almost 1880, when it was finally surpassed by Fall River in southeastern Massachusetts.

By the end of the 19th century, the success of the mills stopped trickling down to the workers. Massive immigration permitted wages to drop as competition among mills intensified, and both racism and the all-important need to uphold satisfactory profit margins forestalled any concern about worsening health and living standards. At various times throughout the 1800s, Lowell's mill workers went on strike for shorter work hours or to protest pay reductions, but each time some pool of poor newcomers was effectively used as strikebreakers. Cooperation across ethnic lines was finally acheived during the 1912 general strike, begun downstream in Lawrence, but victory was not sweet. By the time the Great Depression hit, those among Lowell's cotton capitalists who were deaf to innovation went bankrupt. The rest took their profits and ran to the South, which actively courted manufacturers with cheaper labor, lower taxes, and a hands-off attitude toward working conditions. With mills quiet and a fifth of its population gone in search of work elsewhere, Lowell eked by, down but never quite demoralized. A couple of short-lived reprieves during WW II and the early '80s heyday of computer-maker Wang Labs helped preserve the immense facade of its former industrial glory, now recognized as a major physical, cultural, and historical asset to the city's future. The city's economy has even returned to a semblance of prosperity—*without* becoming dependent on a single major industry or employer.

LOWELL NATIONAL HISTORICAL PARK

Begin a visit to Lowell at the National Historical Park's **Market Mills Visitor Center,** on Market St., tel. (978) 970-5000, across the canal and trolley tracks from the neon mule at Haffner's "It Kicks" gas station. With free introductory slide show, helpful and well-informed park rangers, ticket desk for canal boat tours, self-guided walking tour brochures (ask about the Canalway and Riverwalk), local cultural events calendars, and an excellent bookstore/gift shop that even carries Kerouac, it's the best place to orient yourself to what's happening and where. Free ranger-guided walking tours are always worthwhile, but if at all possible call ahead and reserve a space aboard one of the boat trips through the city's historic waterways. Narrated tours offered almost daily between early June and mid-October range from the 75-minute trips along Pawtucket Canal to a wonderful series of two-hour excursions between the canals and the Merrimack, which may include helping test water quality, exploring the water-diverting gatehouses, or simply enjoying a sunset cruise. All are $4 ($7 with combined admission to the Boott Cotton Mills Museum). Due to enormous popularity advanced reservations are essential.

One could easily spend all day visiting the park's holdings, which are scattered around downtown—the map from the visitor center shows where—along with a variety of public artworks celebrating the city's heritage. Most exhibits are free and share the visitor center's schedule of staying open daily year-round. An impressive working example of the water-powered flywheels that drove a whole company spins mightily amid a whiplashing of leather belts and pulleys at the Suffolk Mills, several blocks away on the banks of the Northern Canal. The human side to the lost factories, the original Yankee farm daughters who labored in them and Lowell's many successive waves of immigrant workers

mill workers, 1911

LEWIS HINE/LOWELL NATIONAL HISTORICAL PARK

are the subjects of exhibits at the **Mogan Cultural Center,** 40 French St., tel. (978) 934-4998, appropriately ensconced within a reconstructed 1830s boardinghouse dating back to the Boott Mills' paternalistic early days. With its octagonal clock tower and gilded yarn shuttle weathervane rising behind Boarding House Park, the 19th-century Boott complex is one of the most handsome of the sprawling brick edifices around town. Inside, the **Boott Cotton Mills Museum,** 400 John St. ($4), features the dramatic sight and sound of 88 vintage power looms clanging away like a mad mechanical version of the Anvil Chorus, along with interactive exhibits on the Industrial Revolution and the labor movement's rocky road to unionization. Take the elevator up to the **Tsongas Industrial History Center,** whose regular hour-long family programs ($3 per person over age 5) give young inventors and hydro-engineers props and guidance in practicing their professions, or ride to the fifth floor to visit the **New England Folklife Center,** tel. (978) 970-5193, showcasing traditional folk arts through both changing exhibits and an ethnic foodways program in their demonstration kitchen (Mon.-Fri., $1.50). Be sure to inquire for the free *Cambodian Neighborhood Walking Tour* brochure, too, if you want to get beneath the city's working-class veneer and witness how

Lowell's latest—and largest—immigrant group has established a community.

While the National Historical Park's constituent parts are within walking distance of one another, from March to November you can hop aboard the park's trolleys—meticulous reproductions of vintage 1901 and 1912 electric street railway cars used in eastern Massachusetts—for a step-saving free shuttle between the visitor center and the Boott Mills.

Visitors equipped with their own bikes or willing to purchase the necessary $5 permit for bringing a Boston rental bike up on the Commuter Rail should consider joining the National Historical Park's **Spindle City Bike Tours.** In spring and fall these two-hour ranger-guided rides around Lowell are scheduled each Saturday morning at 10 a.m.; come summer they begin on Thursday at 6 p.m., neatly avoiding the dehydrating afternoon heat. All tours are free, and each is different: one may venture into the city's 19th-century park-like cemetery; another may hit local Kerouac-related landmarks. Others visit historic city neighborhoods with a good anecdote or two to add to the Lowell story. Group size is limited, so register in advance at the Market Mills Visitor Center or by calling (978) 970-5000. Helmets required.

OTHER LOWELL ATTRACTIONS

Museums

The art and history of quilting, a classic New England domestic industry, are showcased at the **New England Quilt Museum,** 18 Shattuck St., tel. (978) 452-4207, a block from the Market Mills Visitor Center. Both antique and contemporary quilts are displayed, with galleries devoted to both the museum's permanent collection and changing exhibits highlighting the work of modern practitioners (would you believe photorealism in fabric?). Open Tues.-Sun. May-Nov. and Tues.-Sat. in winter ($4). For something totally unrelated to mills, textiles, or water power

check out the local branch of the multistate **New England Sports Museum,** tel. (978) 452-6775, across the street in the former 1886 W. A. Mack stovemaking shop, behind an eye-catching statue of Portuguese soccer star Eusebio. Offering interactive and seasonal exhibits on professional and amateur sports, the museum is open Tues.-Sun. till 5 p.m. year-round; admission is $3 adults, $2 kids, or $10 for a family of up to five.

George Washington Whistler was in charge of the locomotive and railroad works for the city's mills when his son, James McNeill Whistler, was born here in 1834. Although baby James never returned to Lowell after the family moved abroad (his father was hired to build a railroad for the Russian czar), the **Whistler House Museum**

THE LOWELL FOLK FESTIVAL

The largest free folk festival in the nation takes hold of Lowell on the final weekend (Fri.-Sun.) of July. A score of music and dance performers appear on half a dozen stages set up all over downtown, from Boarding House Park on French St. and the JFK Plaza beside City Hall to smaller open spaces in and around Market Mills, on Market Street.

The event is truly international in scope. Past festivals have included gospel, zydeco, bluegrass, klezmer, tap dancing, Celtic button accordion players, Swedish fiddlers, Mexican-American mariachis, traditional West African kora music, ancient Vietnamese imperial court music, and Yup'ik (Eskimo) music and dance.

young members of the Ankgor Dance Troupe

You can also count on being tempted by tons of ethnic food, homemade food, fast food, and more food. An outdoor concourse of craft demonstrations includes masters of traditional arts—Puerto Rican gourd carving, German *scherenschnitt* paper cutting, and Russian lacquer painting, for example—and local occupational artisans in such fields as bookbinding, pipe organ restoration, brick carving, plaster molding, and locksmithing.

Despite the fact that the festival enjoys an attendance of hundreds of thousands of people, you

won't feel like you're stuck at some huge stadium concert: the large number of venues and the grand scale of Lowell's mills promote a big, happy, block-party ambiance. Boston visitors can follow a Saturday morning parade from Faneuil Hall to North Station to catch the special noontime Festival Train up to Lowell (or hop any of the other hourly Commuter Rail connections to the Spindle City for only $7 roundtrip). Call festival co-sponsor Lowell National Historical Park, tel. (978) 970-5000, for schedule or information, or visit the Web site www.nps.gov/lowe and follow the "Special Events" links to the latest Folk Festival homepage.

of Art on Worthen St. near towering City Hall, tel. (978) 452-7641, embraces Lowell's "native son" with examples of the expatriate artist's lesser-known prints and memorabilia. The collection also includes works by Whistler contemporaries, as well as artists with modern ties to Lowell. Open Wed.-Sun. March-Dec. (closed Jan.-Feb.); admission $3.

A very long block south of the Whistler home is the **American Textile History Museum,** 491 Dutton St., tel. (978) 441-0400, occupying the enormous premises of the former Kitson Machine Shop. Don't worry about needing a map: there's only one way to circulate through the nearly 100 displays covering the history and diversity of American-made woven cloth and period clothing up through the mid-1900s. The museum, which relocated here in 1997, also houses one of the nation's largest and possibly most advanced labs for textile conservation. Given the modern installation and expert staff, it's a mystery why display labels aren't more informative; some even allow readers to infer that satin and damask are types of material like cotton and wool, rather than correctly identifying them as styles of weave. Nevertheless, the collection of fabrics, costumes, and tools is unparalleled, and walking through the display of spinning wheels is alone worth the $5 admission (Tues.-Sun.). Among the museum store's many gifts, books, and other textile-related wares are replicas of exhibit pieces, including some produced with the working machinery on display. A pleasant little cafe mercifully saves footsore visitors from having to walk back downtown to slake thirst or sate hunger.

Parks and Sanctuaries

Two nearby state parks also invite exploration by mountain bike or foot: **Lowell/Dracut/Tyngsboro State Forest,** straddling the northwest corner of Lowell and its two neighbors about three miles west of downtown, and **Great Brook Farm State Park,** about eight miles due south in the town of Carlisle, signposted off Rt. 4. The state forest, located on Trotting Park Rd. off Varnum Ave., offers six miles of trails for hiking and biking, plus a swimming beach on modest-sized Althea Lake. Most of its 1,150 acres were once included within the boundaries of the 17th-century

"praying Indian" village of Wamesit, established by a compact with English colonists. Native American powwows are still held in it; the Greater Lowell Indian Cultural Association, P.O. Box 1181, Lowell, MA 01852, tel. (603) 878-1368, can provide information on these.

Great Brook Farm, tel. (978) 369-6312, is both state park and working farm, with farm buildings, farm animals, and farm stand selling fresh sweet corn in summer and cranberries from the county's last working cranberry bog, among other things. Miles of paths trace through the property's meadows, wetlands, and woods, looping around a canoe-able pond, low hills laced with wild berries, and over brooks both great and small. Seasonally there's an ice cream stand at the farm, but the product it sells is a commercial brand from southeastern Massachusetts, not homemade; for a more authentic farm-fresh summer treat visit the summertime **Kimball Farm Ice Cream** stand on Rt. 225 about 2.5 miles south of park headquarters and east of Carlisle center.

If a day in Lowell has whet your appetite for fascinating relics of our nation's industrial past, make tracks about 10 miles west to the town of Westford, at I-495 Exit 32. Hidden there in the **Russell Bird Sanctuary** is a beautifully well-preserved 1872 stone arch bridge over duckweed-covered Stony Brook, once part of the Red Line, a.k.a. the Nashua, Acton, and Boston Railroad. The mortarless 60-foot arch is one of the finest of its type remaining in the region, and despite being favored by adolescent smokers, hasn't been seriously defaced. Though the sanctuary is totally unmarked, the bridge trailhead is posted with a small sign on a tree in a pine grove on Cold Spring Road at the corner of Forge Village Road. (Turn north toward Westford at the bottom of the interstate ramp, then turn left a mile later at the corner of Main St. by the town common; Forge Village Road is the continuation of Main, and Cold Spring is just over a mile.) The bridge is unmistakable—it's half a mile from the trailhead and the town's huge buried reservoir. From the main path atop the abandoned old railroad bed, additional trails run around the sanctuary's wetlands; one even has strategically placed benches for spying on the many migrating waterfowl that frequent the place.

PRACTICALITIES

Food

One Lowell dining landmark is the **Southeast Asian Restaurant,** 343 Market St., tel. (978) 452-3182. A place that offers Laotian, Thai, Cambodian, Vietnamese, and Burmese food is rather rare even before considering that the owner is Italian, but this Vietnam vet and his Laotian-born wife know of what they cook. Whether or not the large Southeast Asian community in Lowell helps keep them on their toes, the net result is a casual place with great city-caliber ethnic dining at a small-town price ($5.95-11.95). The specialty of the **Công Ly Restaurant,** 124 Merrimack St., tel. (978) 970-0740, is Vietnamese beef soup, or *pho.* It's very good and extra large, just as the menu says, and cheap—a complete meal for under $6. Besides the soup, the menu is full of inexpensive exotica: clay pot combos with seafood or poultry, spicy salads such as "tiger's tear" or "jumping squid," big bowls of vermicelli with grilled meats, and plenty of vegetarian treats. Lunch buffet and dinner Mon.-Sat. till 10 p.m.

Besides Southeast Asian places Lowell is enviably endowed with several gems of the dining car era, such as the 1930s **Club Diner** on Dutton St. nearly opposite the Market Mills Visitor Center, or the equally antique **Paradise Diner** on Bridge St. next to the Boott Cotton Mills Museum (open for breakfast and lunch only). But best of all is the **Four Sisters' Owl Diner,** a classic Worcester Lunch Car Company model on Appleton St. between the Commuter Rail station and downtown. Square meals don't get much better than this, which is why you may have to wait in line, particularly for Sunday brunch. Such a well-maintained setting deserves huge Western omelets, perfectly browned hash, silken turkey gravies, and decent coffee; happily, the masters of the short order grill deliver on all counts.

An abundance of history hasn't restrained the city from acquiring such modern accoutrements as the brewpub restaurant, the mulitplex, or the video arcade. In fact, someone has efficiently wrapped all of these under one giant old mill roof, throwing in a billiard parlor, sports bar, and indoor miniature golf course for good measure. It's **The Brewery Exchange,** 199-201 Cabot St., tel. (978) 937-2690, off Father Morissette Blvd. in the great limbo of parking lots and underoccupied buildings over the Northern Canal from downtown. Take a tour of the Mill City Brewing Company, sampling its wares in the taproom or at the **Brewhouse Cafe & Grille,** whose menu ranges from wild mushroom fettuccine and salmon en croute to the more dependable burgers, beefs, scampi, and chicken parmesan, all reasonably priced ($5.95-19.95). Wildly popular, with frequent live music and lots of dating rituals, the Exchange is open daily.

"Cooking Just Like Mom Makes"—the Club Diner, a 1930s Worcester model

For fancier fare, try the French-influenced cuisine of intimate little **La Boniche,** tel. (978) 458-9473, in the beautifully renovated old Bon Marché Building at 143 Merrimack St., an Art Nouveau landmark shared with Barnes & Noble. It's not cheap, but don't you deserve something special now and then? The appetizers are generous enough that almost any two will make a meal, especially if you wisely choose to leave room for dessert (entrees $15-21). Open Tues.-Sat. for lunch and dinner.

Getting There

Lowell's only passenger trains are those of the MBTA **Commuter Rail** from Boston, offering daily service from North Station ($7 roundtrip). Travel time is about 45 minutes; for a recorded schedule, call (617) 222-3200 (or toll-free 800-

392-6100) and work through the touch-tone prompts. Lowell is also a stop on the Boston-to-Burlington, Vermont, interstate buses of **Vermont Transit Lines,** tel. (800) 451-3292, departing Boston's Logan Airport and South Station several times a day. From New York City, **Peter Pan Bus Lines,** tel. (800) 343-9999, makes two trips a day to Lowell via Hartford, Connecticut, and Worcester. Whichever option you choose, you'll arrive at the Gallagher Transportation Terminal on Thorndike St. opposite the South Common. Though barely six-tenths of a mile walk from the Market Mills Visitor Center, Thorndike's particularly pedestrian-unfriendly interchange with Routes 3A and 110 will make it seem much farther; alternatively, catch the regular public shuttle bus to downtown (Mon.-Sat. only, and no evening service; 30 cents).

CRADLE OF REVOLUTION

On April 19, 1775, a British expedition to confiscate a suspected cache of colonial arms touched off the American Revolution. The magnitude of what that day wrought indelibly marks this upland region west of Boston, so much so that it's hard to speak of Lexington without Concord, or to think of either without recalling bits of America's collective national legend about bold minutemen, daring midnight rides, and those stiff-necked Redcoats put to flight by American marksmanship. A passel of historical sites help place the spark and its kindling in a wider context; see also the **Booklist** at the end of this guide for background readings about the Revolution and its origins.

Concord's contribution to the region also includes America's first native literature, transcendentalism, and that feisty iconoclast Henry David Thoreau. If you stayed awake through high school English class you'll recognize the other men and women, such as Emerson and Alcott, who gathered in this little town, a generation of writers whose homes now comprise the other half of Concord's tourist landmarks.

Minute Man National Historical Park

You can retrace the most eventful leg of the British troops' day in the country "alarmed and assembling," from Lexington to Concord and

back again, by visiting some of the homes and taverns whose occupants played a role that April morning, by walking or cycling along nearly six miles of the "Battle Road" itself, by surveying key skirmish sites on foot, or by studying the exhibits in the two visitor centers at either end of the Minute Man National Historical Park. Descriptions of the highlights are divvied up across town lines, just as they are on the ground, from Lexington's Battle Green to Concord's North Bridge. For best results orient yourself in advance to the lay of the land and the Revolution's chronology at the **Minute Man Visitor Center,** off Rt. 2A just west of Rt. 128/I-95 Exit 30. While there, consider joining one of the many ranger programs offered throughout the year.

The third Monday in April is observed as **Patriots Day,** a state holiday. The precipitous events of April 18 and 19, from the lanterns being hung in Old North Church in Boston to the confrontations between armed colonial militia and British Redcoats, are commemorated with lots of costumed finery, musket volleys, speeches, and hot beverages to ward away the predawn chill of the earliest events. Lexington scrupulously observes the timing of the actual skirmish on its town green at daybreak; plan to arrive well before 5:30 a.m. if you hope to find both parking and a good position near the front lines of the large,

a minuteman being called to battle

sleepy-eyed crowd. Concord has tended to be a stickler about reenacting the North Bridge battle at 9:30 a.m. on the 19th, if it falls during the weekend, rather than on the observed Monday holiday, so don't assume everything is coordinated around the same day. Schedules for the weekend's events are usually known to rangers at the Park Service visitor centers by the first week of April; tel. (978) 369-6993, ext. 6.

The respective centers of Lexington and Concord are accessible via public transit from Boston, albeit with some difficulty outside of commuter hours; see **Getting There,** below, for guidance. Cyclists, on the other hand, enjoy nearly direct access to nearly all the attractions of the national historical park—and then some—via the Minuteman Commuter Bikeway from North Cambridge. It runs right beside Lexington's small visitor center opposite the Battle Green, and connects to the Battle Rd.'s paved 5.5-mile parklike path via Hartwell Ave. and Wood St., on the west side of the bikeway's bridge over Rt. 128.

LEXINGTON

Now a largely residential suburb on Boston's western edge, Lexington was the original destination of Paul Revere's famous ride, since two important leaders of the colonial independence movement happened to be in the parsonage a

short distance from the town common. The town has preserved everything even remotely associated with the morning that royal British infantry inflicted the day's first casualties on the town's militia, killing two outright and six more as they fled. The common—now smaller, sown with a broad lawn, and renamed the Battle Green—is still watched over by Buckman Tavern, where Revere and fellow courier William Dawes took a thirst-quenching break. The Hancock-Clarke House, in which Sam Adams and John Hancock slept until Revere awakened them, also still stands. And if Lexington's sturdy mansions and tall church spires make gunfire between militia and Redcoats difficult to imagine, step into the chamber of commerce visitor center for a little prompting from its small diorama of the scene.

Museum of Our National Heritage

At the hilly junction of Rt. 2A and Rt. 225 east of downtown Lexington sits the northern headquarters of the Scottish Rite of Freemasonry. Adjoining the Masons' large, modern inner sanctum is a set of galleries featuring a permanent exhibit on Lexington's attitude toward the prospects of a rebellion against Mother England, plus changing exhibits on American history and contemporary culture. Past examples include exhibitions of Navajo weaving, fly-fishing, the history of the diner, the Vietnam Veterans' Memorial,

Shakers—in short, a pleasantly eclectic variety, always well curated, and often accompanied by equally diverse lecture and live music programs. Open daily, the museum itself is always free, although special events may not be; tel. (781) 861-9638.

Around the Battle Green

Until cherishing American myths became such a major civic preoccupation, the Battle Green was the plain old village common. H. H. Kitson's statue, *The Minuteman,* now prominently marks the site where advancing British Regulars fired upon the three or four score armed militiamen gathered under Captain Parker by Paul Revere's call to alarm. The **Buckman Tavern,** in which militia members debated how to greet the approaching threat, stands across the street from the musket-toting bronze figure. It's open to visitors daily from Patriots Day through Halloween, one of three historic houses whose role in April's drama is recounted by Lexington Historical Society guides (single house admission $4, or $10 for all three; $1-2 for kids 6-16). The other two are the **Hancock-Clarke House,** 36 Hancock St. about a block from the Buckman, and the **Munroe Tavern,** 1332 Massachusetts Ave., a few blocks east of the Battle Green, in which the retreating British ministered their wounded while Lord Percy's artillery-equipped reinforcements temporarily staved off the swelling colonial regiments. For more info on hours or occasional special programs, call the historical society at (781) 862-1703.

CONCORD

The steady headlong rush of traffic on Rt. 2 belies the sedate character of Concord's main village, in which small boutiques and gourmet coffee shops nestle near homes whose parlors have hosted the men and women who presided over the "flowering of New England," as critic Van Wyck Brooks put it. Such a well-preserved small town doesn't need Little Women T-shirt shops or Minuteman Motels, but occasional historical plaques, readily available tourist brochures, and busloads of tourists paying pilgrimages to the place all serve as frequent reminders that you can't throw a stick without hitting something associated with Thoreau, Emerson, or the Revolution.

Conservation land around the town captures some of the spirit of that earlier time, when transcendentalists looked for guidance in the simplicity of the natural world. The extent of wooded land also lends a peaceful air to the former battlefields, although in fact much of what is now tree-covered was wide open pasture, cleared for colonial farms that have long since gone the way of buckskin coats and horse-drawn plows. For a relic of this rural past of apples and asparagus, peaches and black cherries, look no further than the old drystone walls running through Concord's fields and forest.

By the North Bridge

Everybody who comes to Concord stops by the **North Bridge** off Monument St., and so should you. Lexington may demur politely about whose act of resistance can be called the Revolution's start—even nearby Acton stakes a claim, since its minutemen were the first on the colonial side to return British fire—but here in Concord is unarguably where the first British casualties were inflicted. Over 500 well-trained colonial minute- and militiamen, assembled in regimental companies from Concord and three surrounding towns, advanced across the original "rude bridge" over the Concord River with a smart military precision that surprised the British. Though under fire from the Redcoats, these colonial "irregulars" displayed more order, taking aim before shooting and specifically targeting officers. To the surprise of all concerned, the king's troops broke ranks and ran. By sundown the British column limped across Charlestown Neck into the protective range of Boston Harbor's naval guns with over 270 killed, wounded, or missing. The colonial losses were about a third of that.

That first wooden trestle is long gone. Despite sometimes being called the "old" North Bridge, this one, the fifth, was built in 1956. At the western end downhill of the North Bridge Visitor Center stands the iconographic *Minuteman* bronze by Daniel Chester French (of Lincoln Memorial fame), the young Concord artist's first statue. On its base is the first and most memorable stanza of Ralph Waldo Emerson's "Concord Hymn"—a celebrity endorsement, so to speak, of Concord's claim that the war began on her turf:

By the rude bridge that arched the flood
Their flag to April's breeze unfurled
Here once the embattled farmers stood
And fired the shot heard round the world.

The old colonial parsonage next to the North Bridge predates the Revolution by six years. Its builder, the Reverend William Emerson, supposedly stood in his fields rooting for his neighbors that fateful April morning while his family and his African slave, Frank, witnessed the skirmishes from an upstairs window. But the house derives most of its recognition from literature. Like most of the other historic homes open to the public around town, **The Old Manse** is known for the authors who lived under its weathered slate roof. The reverend's grandson, Ralph Waldo Emerson, briefly lived here after becoming a widower, penning his essay *Nature* before remarrying and moving across town. Nathaniel Hawthorne and his honeymoon bride Sophia rented the place for several years, scratching all sorts of love-tinged grafitti into the window panes with her diamond and writing the story collection from which the house got its name, *Mosses from an Old Manse*. The inscribed panes are still to be seen, along with rooms of 18th- and 19th-century furnishings, household artifacts, and hobby collections. The Trustees of Reservations, current owners, give guided tours daily from mid-April through October ($5.50; tel. 978-369-3909).

Other Historical Attractions

At the busy junction of Lexington Road and the Cambridge Turnpike, about 10 minutes' walk east of the town common, is the **Emerson House.** Here from 1835 until his death in 1882, Ralph Waldo Emerson wrote essays, organized well-attended cross-country lecture tours, and entertained scads of visitors. Here, too, the nascent Transcendental Club convened and created a wholly American literary movement. Knowledgeable guides conduct intimate tours of the prosperous-looking home Thurs.-Sun. and on Monday holidays between mid-April and the last full weekend of October ($4.50; tel. 978-369-2236). As you might expect, a small shop purveys copies of Emerson's works and related souvenirs.

The house isn't totally intact. Harvard University has most of Emerson's library, for example, while his original study is across the street at the **Concord Museum**, 200 Lexington Rd., tel. (978) 369-9609 (open daily; admission $6 adults or $12 for families). The museum's wide-ranging historical collection also includes one of several incarnations of Thoreau's cabin, artifacts from his sojourn in the Walden woods, and plenty of Revolutionary War relics—including the only extant member of the "one if by land, two if by sea" pair of signal lanterns that some might say precipitated the wake-up shot to the world on the other side of town.

On Lexington Road about a half mile east of the Concord Museum stands **The Wayside,** home at one time or another to nearly all the town's leading literary figures. Bronson Alcott and his family—including young Louisa May—moved into the Lexington Road house in 1845, when it was already over 150 years old. Nathaniel Hawthorne bought the property, then called Hillside, from the financially strapped Alcotts, enlarged it, and lived in it until his death. As with several other houses around the state, it's his name for the place that has stuck. Later it belonged to children's book author Harriet Lothrop, known pseudonymously as Margaret Sydney. Now owned by the National Park Service, the house offers excellent tours every day but Wednesday from mid-May through October ($4; tel. 978-369-6975). The dreamy utopian (and perpetually vagabond) Bronson Alcott eventually returned as Hawthorne's chatty neighbor next door in the **Orchard House,** whose appearance will be familiar to any reader of his daughter Louisa's *Little Women.* Among the remnants preserved from the Alcotts' 20-year residency are drawings "Amy" left in her room at "Apple Slump." Come on the weekend closest to May 23 and be a guest at eldest daughter Anna's wedding to John Pratt, or visit the week before Christmas and enjoy the living tableaux of family life, all in period costume. House tours are scheduled daily until 4:30 p.m. (except on weekdays Nov.-March, when the last is at 3 p.m.) mid-January through the end of December ($5.50 adults or $16 for family with up to four kids; tel. 978-369-4118). Advance same-day ticketing *is* available. Besides thematic knickknacks and crafts, the small gift shop stocks every Louisa May Alcott book in print.

Concord's place in American letters even extends to its burial grounds. **Sleepy Hollow Cemetery,** on Bedford St. a short walk from the town common, is the final resting place for the Alcotts, Nathaniel Hawthorne (but *not* his wife—curiously, she's in England), the Emerson clan, and Henry David Thoreau. All are up on Author's Ridge, back against the cemetery's north side. For a little contrast to the disarming simplicity of these graves keep an eye out for the classical beauty of *Mourning Victory,* a memorial sculpture by Daniel Chester French, who was tutored in drawing as a lad by Louisa May Alcott's sister May.

Walden Pond

A deep kettlehole formed by a melted chunk of glacial ice, Walden Pond State Reservation has become a mecca for Henry David Thoreau readers, who are often spotted on the circumferential path deeply engrossed in dog-eared copies of *Walden,* Thoreau's philosophizing account of

the writer's tombstone, Sleepy Hollow Cemetery

two years spent in the surrounding woods. The pond's reputation as a good swimming hole is well known to three million Bostonians, so you'll have to come at the crack of dawn or off season if you want to park anywhere remotely within walking distance, or to find any hint of the solitude Thoreau enjoyed. A Commuter Rail line from Boston borders one side of the reservation, across the pond from the bath house and the most accessible (and therefore most crowded) part of the shore; between screaming kids and rumbling trains Thoreau fans may recognize some sort of ironic proof of Henry's critical foresight. (To be fair, it's worth noting that the railroad actually predates Thoreau's Walden days.)

A replica of Thoreau's cabin may be found by the reservation's parking lot; here in summer daily ranger talks are held. The original house site, 15 minutes' walk into the woods on the pond's north side, is identified by an inscribed stone marker and an accretion of rocks representing over a century's worth of visitors. Ranger-led programs are offered in every season, from summer's regular living history interpreters or guided saunters with a Thoreau scholar to January's celebration of Martin Luther King's birthday with a walk drawing parallels between the civil rights leader's strategy and Thoreau's *Civil Disobedience.* Swimming, canoeing, and fishing are allowed, but mountain biking is not; May-Oct. the parking fee is $2. No more than 1,000 vehicles are allowed at any one time, so be prepared to be turned away at the gate if you drive up after 10 a.m. on any warm, sunny, summer weekend. Call (978) 369-3254 to find out if the lot's full or to ask questions of the friendly, patient park staff.

Whether you have a high school paper to research or simply a modicum of curiosity about the man behind the American myth of rugged individualism, consider dropping by the new multimillion-dollar home of the **Thoreau Institute,** the Thoreau Society's successor to its cramped little lyceum formerly located in Concord. Handsomely situated on an 18-acre wooded estate just over the town line in Lincoln, the institute welcomes the public to programs and exhibits drawn from the world's most comprehensive collection of anything and everything related to Thoreau. Since it's located at the end of a private road with limited parking, the institute's good-neighbor policy (contractual agreement, in fact) obliges people to call ahead before arriving; call (978) 259-9411 or drop by **The Shop at Walden Pond,** the Society-run gift and bookstore on Rt. 126 beside the state reservation parking lot, for directions and dibs on a parking space.

BACK TO NATURE

Sandwiched between and slightly to the south of Lexington and Concord is the beautifully rural and stunningly wealthy town of Lincoln. Along its rolling, wooded roads are several gems worth a detour. A cyclist can visit them all over the course of an eight- or nine-mile loop from Walden Pond, where one can finish with a swim. The supermarket in the back of the Mall at Lincoln Station on Lincoln Rd. makes a convenient refreshment stop, and **Lincoln Guide Service,** tel. (781) 259-1111, across the street rents mountain bikes, road bikes, tandem bikes, even high-end full-suspension bikes to those in need (rates start at $10 for two hours, $25 a day). For folks totally without their own wheels, MBTA **Commuter Rail** provides regular service from Boston's North Station to the whistle-stop platform that's shouting distance from the bike shop; for details see **Getting There,** below.

Attractively nestled among the farmlike estates along Sandy Pond Road, the **DeCordova Museum and Sculpture Park,** tel. (781) 259-3628, Web site www.decordova.org (open Tues.-Sun.; $6 for the museum, sculpture park free), consistently presents challenging exhibitions by New England contemporary artists to complement its permanent collection of 20th-century art, newly housed in the modern wing cascading down from the original benefactor's hilltop castle. Overlooking a large pond, the 35-acre grounds are a favorite destination of weekend cyclists, families, and picnickers who spend the afternoon amid the sometimes whimsical, sometimes interactive outdoor sculptures. Ceramic artist Robert Arneson's irreverent *Bench Head,* Sol LeWitt's conceptual *Incomplete Open Cubes,* and George Rickey's kinetic *Three Lines* are among the park's varied treats. A wooded open-air amphitheater hosts a popular summer music series; the entrance is near *The Musical Fence* by Paul Matisse, a work no man, woman, or

child can resist. Adjacent Sandy Pond features circumferential trails through its surrounding public conservation land, including the Three Friends Trail historically enjoyed by Thoreau and his boon companions William Ellery Channing and Sterns Wheeler. The trail is thought to pass close to the place where Wheeler, another natural philosopher, built a hut in the woods for use during college vacations between 1836 and 1842. Thoreau wanted to try his experiment here by Sandy Pond, too, and for many years after begrudged the owner who refused to give permission. Fortunately for posterity, his friend Ralph Waldo Emerson owned a woodlot beside another pond in the area, and was much more favorably inclined toward Henry's experiments.

A short distance west of the DeCordova sits the **Gropius House,** 68 Baker Bridge Rd., tel. (781) 259-8098, one of 45 unique properties under the care of the Society for the Preservation of New England Antiquities (SPNEA). Built in 1937 by Walter Gropius, founder of the original Bauhaus school in Weimar, Germany, this personal residence introduced the then-revolutionary Bauhaus design precepts to the American landscape. Boston-born skyscraper architect Louis Sullivan may be accorded the credit for declaring "form ever follows function"—a pithy summation of a millennia of architectural desires—but thanks to the profound impact of Bauhaus's modernism he and his predecessors have been roundly usurped by a new standard for functional design. That we now take sharp machine-tooled lines, planar surfaces, and mass-produced building materials so for granted can be traced back in part to this modest structure. Some of the furnishings are by Marcel Breuer, a fellow Bauhaus proponent and founding member, with Gropius, of The Architects Collaborative, one of the most influential practices in its field. Tours begin on the hour 11 a.m.-4 p.m., Wed.-Sun. between June and mid-October, and Sat.-Sun. the rest of the year ($5).

Another SPNEA property in the vicinity is the **Codman House,** a.k.a. "The Grange," on Codman Rd., tel. (781) 259-8843. The contrast to the Gropius House, a half-hour stroll through the woods to the north, is striking: the Grange is a 16-acre estate with English country gardens. The main house is a veritable dictionary of major 19th-century architectural styles, from

Georgian to Colonial Revival. Interior furnishings are less eclectic; mostly they reflect the neo-classical tastes of Ogden Codman Jr., the last owner of the place. In his day Codman and collaborator Edith Wharton guided the tastes of upper-class England and America as profoundly as Emily Post would later influence etiquette; their book *The Decoration of Houses* was required reading in mansions on both sides of the Atlantic. Tours begin on the hour 11 a.m.-4 p.m., Wed.-Sun. from June through mid-October; admission is $4.

Drumlin Farm

Outside of a farmstay out in the western Massachusetts towns of Charlemont or Colrain, **Drumlin Farm Education Center and Wildlife Sanctuary,** tel. (781) 259-9807, is about as close as you can get to that increasingly rare Massachusetts artifact, the working farm. Doubling as headquarters for the Massachusetts Audubon Society (which is older than, and quite independent of, the national Audubon Society), Drumlin specializes in kids' programs of all sorts. Hayrides, baby animals, and Harvest Days are among the seasonal highlights that appeal to families, while adults are drawn to the regular birdwatching and nature walks. As avid birders know, the combination of both wooded and open habitat—and the edges between the two—promotes a diverse set of species within what is a relatively small area. Located on Lincoln's South Great Rd. (Rt. 117) slightly east of Rt. 126, the farm is closed Monday. Admission $6 adults, $3 kids and seniors.

Garden in the Woods

Wildflowers are the star attraction of this woodsy acreage, owned and operated by the New England Wild Flower Society, a conservation advocate and partner in maintaining a seed bank for endangered wild flora. A lily pond, pine barren, wetland bog, and rock garden are among the habitats replicated in the garden, incorporating some 1,500 plant varieties. Two acres are also set aside to showcase over 100 rare and endangered species native to New England, nearly a third of which

are found almost nowhere else on earth. The garden and its shop—which sells plants and books along with small gifts—are open year-round, daily from mid-April through Oct., Tues.-Sun. the rest of the year. In May, when many flowers are in bloom, the hours are extended to 7 p.m.; otherwise plan to arrive by 4 p.m. to gain admission ($6). The easiest approach is from US 20 in Sudbury; look for the signposted turn south on Raymond Rd., between Wayland's attractive Congregational church at the Rt. 27 junction and Sudbury's heap of quaintly misnamed shopping plazas.

Appetites made large by nature walks may appreciate a detour to the sandwich and barbecue counter at **Gerard Turkey Farms,** tel. (508) 877-2300, on Water St. in Saxonville less than two miles southeast of the Garden in the Woods. The poultry in the turkey burgers and barbecue chicken certainly beats US 20's fast food for flavor and freshness, and the salads aren't half bad, either. Open Mon.-Fri. to 6:30 p.m., Saturday to 4 p.m.

Canoe or Kayak

Paddle in the gentle wake of Henry David Thoreau's journey down the Concord River, or simply get the fish-eye view of where the embattled farmers fought in 1775 by the North Bridge when you rent a canoe or kayak from **South Bridge Boat House,** Main St. in Concord, tel. (978) 369-9438. Open daily April-Oct.; rates run from $7.75 an hour weekdays to $8.85 an hour weekends. The rental dock is on the Sudbury River just a few minutes away from where the Assabet joins in to form the Concord River, so from South Bridge you have your pick of placid waters. Downstream

to the north, the Concord flows through the Great Meadows National Wildlife Refuge. Upstream to the south, the Sudbury broadens out into lake-like Fairhaven Bay, beneath the brow of Lincoln's Mount Misery, an attractive parcel of conservation land whose public trails connect through to Walden Pond. If you're ferrying your own boat around, use the excellent put-in next to the Rt. 117 bridge over the Sudbury, on the eastern, or Lincoln, side of the river (Concord is on the western bank). The parking area is signposted discreetly enough that you may only spot it as you pass it; from the east it's about a mile from Rt. 126 (Concord Road).

PRACTICALITIES

Food

Top-drawer restaurateurs in nearby Cambridge and Arlington needn't be afraid of Lexington trying to lure away their customers, but if you're content with such staples as pizza, somewhat Americanized Thai, or Chinese, you won't have to venture out of downtown. **Bertucci's,** 1777 Mass. Ave. (781) 860-9000, is the top pizza contender, solidly upholding this regional chain's reputation for wood-fired brick-oven pies with ample fresh toppings on thin, smoky crusts. Hearty salads, pasta, and calzones are also available, along with a kids' menu that stretches the umbrella of Italian cuisine to include peanut butter and jelly sandwiches. Across the street **Lemon Grass,** (781) 862-3530, offers a safe introduction to Southeast Asian food, with a top-40 approach to delicious Thai dishes and a conservative hand on the chili peppers.

In Concord the best fine dining—and essential stop for garlic lovers—is at **Aïgo Bistro,** 84 Thoreau St., (978) 371-1333, in the festively colored upper floor of the former Concord depot. Whether dressed to kill or slumming in your jeans, the staff will treat you to impeccable service, while the chef prepares excellent Mediterranean and Provencal-influenced cuisine. Prices are a tad on the high-side compared to the competition for this level of quality from suburban places closer to Boston—most entrees are $18 and up—but if you're not counting change it beats hunting for a parking space in Harvard Square. Open daily. Even more Dockers and

fewer ties are in evidence at casual **Walden Grille,** 24 Walden St., tel. (978) 371-2233, the town's other high-end choice ($14.95-21). Enjoy a hearty Tuscan-influenced menu with all the arugula and sun-dried tomato a gourmand might expect, yet enough grilled meats and potatoes for traditionalists. Like the Aïgo, Walden Grille has a broad selection of wines by the glass, and locally brewed Concord Junction beer.

With so many attractive spots for picnicking—Revolutionary battlefields, Walden Pond, the banks of the Concord River, even Sleepy Hollow Cemetery—a well-stocked gourmet store such as **The Cheese Shop,** 31 Walden St., (978) 369-5778, makes a picnic hamper a viable alternative to sit-down dining. From raw ingredients to fully prepared deli meals-to-go, this place will furnish everything but the sunshine. Open Tues.-Saturday. In a similar vein across Rt. 2, **Concord Teacakes,** 59 Commonwealth Ave., (978) 369-7644, opposite the West Concord Commuter Rail platform, is ideal for high-quality sandwiches, soups, and sweets for eat in or take out.

If basic burgers and fried fish would suit you more than smoked turkey and escarole on multigrain sourdough bread, head straight away to **The Willow Pond Kitchen,** on Lexington Rd. (Rt. 2A), the only small dingy-looking place with a Schlitz sign between Concord Common and the Minute Man Visitor Center. Inside under the glassy stare of a mangy stuffed cougar, the clock seems to have stopped somewhere in the decade after this place opened in 1944. The food won't earn any awards, but it's got character in spades, and nobody in town can beat its prices.

Getting There

Both Lincoln and Concord are on the Fitchburg line of the MBTA **Commuter Rail,** which departs Boston's North Station eight to twelve times a day; fares are $6-6.50 roundtrip. Call (617) 222-3200 for recorded schedule info, or toll-free (800) 392-6100 from anywhere in North American outside Greater Boston. Of Concord's two stops, the first is the closest to the town's many literary and historic sights, although not so close that you won't regret forgetting to wear comfortable walking shoes. (The Old North Bridge and the Emerson House are each a mile from the rail depot, as well as from each other, while the

Wayside and Orchard House are a half mile beyond Emerson's place.) The historic center of Lexington is accessible year-round by two MBTA buses, the #62 Bedford V.A. and the #76 Hanscom Field, departing from the busway atop Alewife Station at the end of the Red Line. Unfortunately for tourists, neither bus operates on Sundays, and when they do run it's with infrequent, mostly hourly service.

THE CHARLES RIVER VALLEY

"Valley" may conjure up visions of a great V-shaped topographical feature with a river coursing down the middle like an oversized drainage ditch, but this watershed is nothing if not subtle. Rising in wetlands in the town of Hopkinton, the Charles River practices every dilatory move known to water as it wends its way to the sea. By the time it reaches Boston Harbor it has covered a full 80 miles, testing every point of the compass along the way. Any self-respecting crow could cover the same ground in about 26 miles (which is why the Boston Marathon coincidentally begins and ends where the Charles does).

This is the most densely populated watershed in New England, shot through with highways and houses and such a jumble of shops and signage that for the most part you'd never notice a river runs through it unless you knew where to look. Seek, and ye shall find: a general theme among the parks and sanctuaries highlighted in this section is that they abut, overlook, or include portions of the Charles River or one of its tributaries. As a happy consequence of waterways being superseded in importance by roads and rails, these rivers have become in modern times some of the region's best urban wilds, rich in flora and fauna. Several lakes and reservoirs in the area are also good for boating and swimming. If you're unimpressed by all the water-related activities, how about some long country walks?

Broadmoor Wildlife Sanctuary

East of Hopkinton, Rt. 135's semi-rural quality quickly evaporates as large houses set well back from the road are supplanted by a checkered array of multifamily dwellings, quick lube garages and car dealerships, gas stations and tire stores. Until Wellesley's obvious wealth restores a semblance of landscaping, Rt. 135 wallows in enough petroleum products and doughnut shops to make a wildlife sanctuary not only unlikely, but inconceivable.

Yet south of the Boston Marathon route, the Charles River flows implacably onward amid a corridor of lush green. Once upon a time a pair of small mills used its waters to produce flour and lumber; now the long-abandoned site and its surrounding forests and fields are preserved for your enjoyment in the Massachusetts Audubon Society's Broadmoor Wildlife Sanctuary, tel. (508) 655-2296. Trails offer visitors a chance to catch a glimpse of many feathered and furry residents, from great blue herons nesting by the pond to field mice scampering around the meadow grasses. Don't miss the long bridge over Indian Brook, either. Programs are offered most of the year: natural history walks, canoe trips, bird counts and banding, and the ever-popular Mother's Day "Birds & Breakfast." Admission to the sanctuary is $3; special programs are extra (closed Monday). If you left your Peterson's at home, the small nature center and gift shop can sell you a new one, along with all the other field guides you might want. Located on Rt. 16 in South Natick near the Sherborn line. Call ahead for program reservations.

WELLESLEY

This small bedroom community straddling Routes 9, 16, and 135 also happens to be the most affluent college town in the state. The most widely known of its three institutions of higher education is **Wellesley College,** one of the nation's top-ranked liberal arts schools, whose graceful, hilly campus lies between Rt. 135 (Central St.) and Lake Waban at the west end of town. Often confused—in name only—with Connecticut's Wesleyan University, Wellesley has been an all-women's college since its doors opened in 1875, although men enrolled within a

Mother and Child, *by Fernand Leger*

from the college is a six-acre Italianate topiary garden on the private Hunnewell estate. H. Hollis Hunnewell coined "Wellesley" from his wife's family name, Welles, when he acquired the property in the 19th century. The post office branch and college adopted the name, too, and his fellow townsfolk followed suit when they split from Natick in 1881. The tiers of neatly shaped trees and shrubs are thought to be the nation's oldest such garden. Equally exotic are the tropical and desert fauna in the college's **Margaret C. Ferguson Greenhouses** by the Science Center, tel. (781) 283-3094, open to the public daily until 4:30 p.m., year-round. While there's next to nothing in bloom in summer, the spring perennials and bulbs will enliven any visit Feb.-May. As for the tree collection, simply look about as you stroll the campus: the entire grounds constitute an arboretum, and nearly all specimens are tagged for easy identification. Free tours for prospective students and others are generally offered Mon.-Fri. year-round plus Saturday mornings during the academic year. Tours depart from the Board of Admission at Green Hall, whose square, cathedral-like tower dominates the campus. To confirm that student guides will be available the day of your visit, call (781) 283-2270.

regional consortium of 12 colleges are accepted as exchange students for a semester or two. Marathon runners know they're reaching the halfway point of their ordeal when they hear the sound of students lining the race course, whose traditional tunnel of screaming encouragement lifts flagging spirits and speeds contestants into the marathon's toughest part—the Newton Hills.

Generally overlooked on the periphery of museum-rich Boston is the college's excellent—and free!—**Davis Museum and Cultural Center,** 106 Central St., tel. (781) 283-2051 (Tues.-Sun.), near the campus physical plant. Reflecting its benefactors' diverse interests, the Davis collection includes everything from classical antiquities and African art to works by Warhol and de Kooning. The world-class holdings are shown to further advantage by the building interior itself—a dramatic and light-filled space designed by the Spanish architect José Rafael Moneo. Aside from the museum and nearby science building, the campus is dominated by Gothic architecture, lending it a European air. This is reinforced by the view over Lake Waban: across

Food

In Wellesley, dining out generally means a casual counter-service cafe, pizza, or Asian food. The cluster between campus and Wellesley Square, the oblique intersection of Central and Washington Streets (Routes 135 and 16), gives a good taste of what's in store. Closest to campus is **Figs,** 92 Central St., tel. (781) 237-5788, an upscale Boston-based pizza and pasta joint highly recommended for its thin crusts, woodfired oven, and gourmet toppings. On parallel Linden St. across the Commuter Rail tracks—turn off Central at Crest St. and you'll find it—is a more local favorite, **Jimmy's Cafe,** 151 Linden, before the Roche Bros. supermarket, tel. (781) 431-7616. Behind the flower-filled window boxes and dark awnings is a place whose down-home spirit infuses the menu, which has plenty of high-toned toucheswild rice and fresh fruit chutney, garlic mashed potatoes and Dijon glaze—without either the attitude or the price. For ingredients as fresh as these, the under-$10 average is a steal. No corkage fee for folks who bring their own beer or wine, either. Closed Sunday and Monday. If it's lunchtime and you just want something to go, consider the fine fresh fare available up the street past the VW-Mazda dealer at **Captain Marden's Seafoods,** 279 Linden, suppliers to some of Boston's finest restaurants. Try a sandwich with whole clams or lobster salad for a proper bit of New England flavor.

Back in the center of the square is another great inexpensive option, **EatSmart,** 555 Washington St., one of a new breed of cafes serving fast food with flair (open only to 9 p.m. most nights). Blonde maple decor, gourmet coffee, fruit smoothies, fresh vegetables, and ethnic flavors are the standard here, with items such as Jamaican jerk chicken or poached salmon and veggies in a spinach tortilla, or maybe just a generous helping of pasta tossed with pesto. Everything's under $10, and the staff doesn't make you feel like you're the billionth customer they've served. A block away is the local Thai contender, **Amarin,** at 27 Grove St. just off the square, tel. (781) 239-1350. All your favorite curries, seafood sautés, beef with macadamias and watercress, and a smattering of vegetarian selections are served up with quiet alacrity in an attractive space at reasonable prices ($6.75-14.75).

Getting There

Wellesley College is relatively easy to reach via the MBTA **Commuter Rail** from Boston's South Station. Multiple departures are available daily (tel. 617-222-3200 for recorded schedule, or 800-392-6100 within Massachusetts); board trains serving the Framingham/Worcester line, and get off at Wellesley Square ($5 roundtrip). Campus is on Central Street (Rt. 135), about a 10-minute walk west from the rail platform (take a left at the top of the stairs, a right on Central, and you'll see the college entrance past the next set of traffic lights).

ROUTE 109~
ROAMING WESTERN NORFOLK COUNTY

As most commuters who ride this spoke to Boston know, Rt. 109 is often a forgettable claptrap of commercial signage, but don't let inauspicious beginnings keep you from delving beyond the clutter. The gentle hills of the area are the trailing edge of the eastern Massachusetts uplands; south of I-95 and the Norfolk County line the land flattens out into the sandy-soiled, pine-covered coastal plains. Historically this section of tripartite Norfolk County, whose southern edge marks the boundary between the old Puritan and Pilgrim colonies, was a leading supplier of straw bonnets for the northeastern United States.

Noanet Woodlands

Protecting the headwaters of Noanet Brook (no-ANN-it), a tributary of the Charles River, are extensive woodlands with over 30 miles of trails through tall white pines and mixed hardwood forest, around four ponds, and to the 387-foot crown of namesake Noanet Peak, whose 20-mile vista includes Boston's skyline. By late spring the pond lilies have put forth their showy white blossoms, painted turtles sun themselves on branches, and warblers trill among the trees. Slough away summer's heat-induced lethargy with shaded walks beneath rustling birch and oak, or explore the rebuilt stone-faced dam whose original incarnation helped power the Dover Union Iron Company's forges back when Illinois still belonged to Indians and machine-made cotton cloth was a novelty. After September's broadwings migrate past eager hawk-watchers atop that hill, autumn's bright chemistry paints the woodlands with maple-leaf reds and beech yellows, and squirrels have a field day hiding acorns for the winter. Although the property is split between The Trustees of Reservations (TTOR) and privately managed **Hale Reservation,** mountain bike permits ($15 for a calendar year) are available for the whole woodlands from either Noanet's ranger station (staffed on weekends and holidays only), or from the Hale main office (open 8 a.m.-8 p.m. daily, late May to early Sept.), or by calling The Trustees of

DAY HIKES:
THE BAY CIRCUIT

In the late 1920s, advocates of setting aside undeveloped land for the enjoyment of Boston's burgeoning population created an ambitious plan for a great semicircular park outside the city—a great green ring looping from north of Cape Ann clear to the South Shore. Events—including the Crash of 1929, world war, urban population loss to the suburbs, and construction of the Rt. 128 beltway—intervened and spoiled any chance that this "Bay Circuit" could ever be implemented as originally conceived. But the idea was never scrapped.

Finally, in 1984, a precedent-setting state bond, floated to finance conservation projects, revived the Bay Circuit's prospects. Bond money leveraged land acquisition and led to an overall plan, but economic recession and top-down intransigence on environmental initiatives (financing the purchase of open space was derided as "elitist" by the state's most recent Republican acting governor) has put the Bay Circuit in the position of being heavily outgunned by politically influential real estate developers. Still, the 200-mile trail is slowly being stitched together through the tireless efforts of grassroots proponents, town conservation agencies, and the Bay Circuit Alliance—the trail's dedicated cheerleader.

When completed, after the year 2000, the Bay Circuit will encircle Boston from Plum Island—at the mouth of the Merrimack River—in the north to the South Shore's Kingston Bay. Some 80 parks, forests, and sanctuaries and 50 towns will be connected by paths across rural, residential, and institutional property, along river banks, on paved rail trails, and even on roads. The result will be an English-style cross-country ramble through towns and farms, meadows and woods, over hills and across highways, along gravel lanes and over wetland boardwalks. Sights are as varied as you can imagine: hidden forest parcels, Thoreau's famous Walden Pond, sleepy villages with welcome little stores selling cold drinks, downtown Lowell and its historic textile mills.

Bay Circuit trailheads are identified with medallions of the Bay Circuit logo, but the route is mostly marked by white blazes roughly the size of a dollar bill (where the route follows a road shoulder or street for a ways, look for these on telephone poles). In places where the trail crosses a school campus or other private property, maps are usually posted at either end of the unmarked section directing walkers to where blazes resume.

Though the Bay Circuit around Boston is still very much a work in progress, you'd never guess that from a hike through its completed MetroWest sections. In large part, this is because the route incorporates so many well-established conservation properties. Here are three of the best local bits, with directions to the trailheads.

Acton-Sudbury (17 miles) runs south through Concord's beautiful Estabrook Woods, an ecological study area partly owned by Harvard University, around Walden Pond, and through a small but very attractive corner of Lincoln. Maps covering portions of the trail include the Lincoln Land Conservation Trust's guide to all Lincoln walking trails and the New England Orienteering Club's map of Estabrook Woods—both available from the Shop at Walden, the Thoreau Society's store, at the entrance to Concord's Walden Pond.

For the **Sherborn** (11 miles) section, hike either south from Barber Reservation, whose entrance is signposted from Western Ave., or north from the TTOR Rocky Narrows Reservation. Perfectly beautiful section, this. If you want to carry a natural history guide, pick up a copy of *Sherborn Walks*, by Arthur Schnure ($10), at the gift shop at the Massachusetts Audubon Society's Broadmoor Wildlife Sanctuary, Rt. 16 in South Natick, tel. (508) 655-2296.

Begin the **Medfield-Sharon** (9 miles) from the north at TTOR's Noon Hill Reservation, in Medfield (signposted off Causeway St. a little over a mile south of Rt. 109), or from the south at Massachusetts Audubon Society's Moose Hill Wildlife Sanctuary, on the east side of I-95 between Exits 10 and 8. From Exit 10 catch Rt. 27 north to Walpole, and turn on Moose Hill St. before crossing over the interstate; from Exit 8, head east on Main toward Sharon, and turn, within a mile, on Moose Hill Street. Includes a primitive campsite (you must notify the Walpole police and fire departments before using).

Additional information about the Bay Circuit and a list of available trail guides may be found on the Internet at www.serve.com/baycircuit. Or drop in on **Moor & Mountain,** 3 Railroad St. in Andover, tel. (978) 475-3665, for a sample of the most complete guide and map inventory for the entire route.

Reservations regional office at (781) 821-2977. Admission for hikers is free; parking and trailhead access is at Caryl Park in the town of Dover, on Dedham St. between Dover center and the Charles River. The main office for Hale Reservation, tel. (781) 326-1770, is signposted from Dover Road, off Rt. 109 in Westwood. Hale Reservation is a privately run tract that operates day camps on a large pond, with water sports and a swimming beach available by membership only ($565 per year).

Rocky Woods Reservation

Immediately east of Noanet over the Medfield town line is one of TTOR's most popular holdings, nearly 500 acres of forested wetlands and hills aptly known as Rocky Woods. Hike for an hour or an afternoon on the dozen miles of paths and trails that wander into every corner, or visit in winter for wonderful cross-country skiing. A self-guiding nature trail interprets the reservation's geology, flora, and fauna. Admission is free weekdays, $2.50 weekends and holidays; entrance and parking is off Hartford St. about half a mile east of where it intersects Rt. 109 in Medfield.

Gates of the Charles

For most of its length the Charles River winds through a broad floodplain, but at the boundary between Middlesex and Norfolk Counties it cuts between sharp granite cliffs backed by wooded hills. These "Gates of the Charles" are protected as part of TTOR's **Rocky Narrows Reservation,** along with gravelly eskers, a wonderful picnic spot known as King Philip's Overlook, and some of MetroWest's prettiest Bay Circuit mileage. Spring is unmistakable for the migrating songbirds that fill the forest and wildflowers that fill the open pasture. Summer vacation brings the usual complement of hot weather, late afternoon mosquitoes, and the occasional radio-controlled airplane hobbyist to the fields across

the river from that high overlook. As days grow shorter the buzzing aerobatics are replaced by the dry rustle of unseen mammals scampering about in the fallen leaves; come winter's snow and cross-country skiers will at least see tracks of those that don't hibernate. The reservation's trailhead is in a tiny parking area off Rt. 27 in Sherborn, on the Dover-Medfield line 3.5 miles north of Rt. 109.

Noon Hill

Despite appearances, The Trustees of Reservations aren't the only stewards of open land in this region, but they certainly do the best job of providing access to what land they do own. Medfield's Noon Hill Reservation is akin to their other properties within the Charles River watershed, with its shade-tolerant, moisture-loving birch and beech below a tall canopy of pine, general topography of hills abutting floodplains, and miles of trails fit for peaceful wandering. But the wetlands here are truly extensive, augmented by a sizable acreage maintained as a natural floodwater storage basin by the Army Corps of Engineers. This reservation also shows more evidence of its early agricultural use, with old drystone walls encompassing long-overgrown fields made fertile by the seasonal whims of the Charles and Stop Rivers, back before dams were built at the mouth in Boston. In addition to its autumnal display of colorful foliage, the property is the scenic access point for a quite varied stretch of the Bay Circuit. Parking and trailhead are signposted off Causeway St. a little over a mile south of Rt. 109. Also off Causeway St. just south of Rt. 109 is the marked parking area for TTOR's **Medfield Rhododendrons,** a small parcel on the north side of the Stop River with a short trail through a colony of native rosebay rhododendrons. Though familiar as a garden ornamental, in the wild this gaudy July bloomer is one of New England's rarest shrubs.

QUINCY

Spread along the South Shore between the Neponset and Weymouth Fore rivers, Quincy (QUIN-zee) has essentially been a Boston suburb since the early 1600s. It certainly has that satellite look: lots of residential neighborhoods, shopping plazas, edge-city-style executive office parks on the perimeter, a modest downtown, and stores that cater mostly to the immediate community.

When it comes to history, Quincy's page in the books is guaranteed, largely by virtue of being the birthplace to much of the great Adams dynasty, wellspring of several generations of prominent public figures. The Quincys, relatives and neighbors of the Adamses as well as descendants of the city's namesake settler, also merit notice, having produced three generations of influential Boston mayors. (They were among the last of the blue-blooded Yankees to hold the job.) With such a pedigree one might think that the "City of Presidents" butters its bread with patrician grace, but actually its industrial history is about as long as the Adams family tree, and filled with as much distinction.

The city's exposed bedrock helped make Quincy a leader in the nation's granite industry for nearly 200 years. At the height of the business, its high-quality hard stone was known to builders and pavers worldwide. Quincy also built ships: wooden ones for the local fishing trade in the 1700s, and eventually steel ones for the Navy during and after WW II. The mighty Fore River Shipyard, now slated for building supertankers rather than destroyers or aircraft carriers, has the distinction of being Massachusetts's last significant heavy industry.

Quincy is the location of several of New England's earliest colonial settlements—fishing and fur-trading enterprises begun in the 1620s. All were short-lived, and they illustrate how the colonists were often their own worst enemies. The first, Wessagusset, comprised 60 indentured servants and a handful of overseers sent over in 1622 by one of the original financial backers of the Pilgrims to the south. The disputatious bunch fell apart over Indian relations (some robbed and abused them, some lived with them quite amicably) and finally went back to England after the Pilgrims came and "rescued" them by killing local sachems (which naturally invited retaliations). Six months later another group came to Wessagusset, and while the leader lacked the endurance for a New England winter, the remainder either stayed behind or scattered themselves around the north and west rim of Massachusetts Bay. (Reverend Blaxton, who was an influential farmer, was one such pioneer.)

The decade's most notorious lot of would-be homesteaders was the third settlement, another group of indentured servants with but four masters, who arrived in 1625. After two years of no profits, *their* leader, a Captain Wollaston, left for Virginia with his lieutenant to traffic more rewardingly in servants for the Jamestown settlers. One of the principals left behind, Thomas Morton, booted out the fourth overseer by appealing to the servants to cast off their bonds and join him in a community of equals. Morton mischievously christened their settlement Ma-re Mount, erected a maypole for traditional English festivities, and became successful enough in civil and trade relations with neighboring Indians that the Pilgrims no longer could find anyone to barter with for corn or furs. Furious at the unorthodox disregard for class differences, unholy Mayday revels, and—perhaps most important— the liberal-minded friendship with the Massachusett tribe, Plymouth raided Morton's settlement and deported the "Lord of Mis-rule" back to England. Morton soon returned, this time scandalizing his new Puritan neighbors to the north. After a second deportation, the righteous English of Boston and Plymouth were rid of their disruptive, free-thinking competitor. It's perhaps unfortunate that Quincy's forerunners couldn't prevail over their nervous neighboring countryfolk; as one scholar has noted, it's interesting to speculate how New England would have developed had a more secular community free of religious zealots established a successful foothold in the region.

The Adams

Home to four generations of Adamses, including two American presidents and their heirs, the **Adams National Historic Site,** 135 Adams St., tel. (617) 770-1175, is brimming with history. This large 1700s-era Georgian Colonial with its lovely flower beds and orchard was christened "Peacefields" by George Washington's vice president and successor, John Adams—but was known as "The Old House" to his family. The property retains traces of the lawyers, diplomats, politicians, and academics who

John Adams

occupied it for a century and a half. John's wife Abigail mockingly called the place a "wren's nest" after returning from ambassadorial life abroad. Come, and decide for yourself whether her criticism was warranted. Among the free special programs offered at the site are condensed reenactments of historical events in which Adamses took part, including defending the British soldiers accused in the Boston Massacre (program held on Patriots Day, the third Monday in April); passage of the Declaration of Independence (July 4); Congressional debates over southern secession (Gettysburg anniversary, mid-August); and passage of the Constitution (Constitution Day, September 17, and the nearest Saturday). Visitors are supplied scripts to take part and are rewarded with refreshments.

The grounds are open year-round, but the house is only open for scheduled tours between Patriots Day (the third Monday in April) and Veterans Day (November 11); tickets are sold at the small National Park Service visitor center a short walk away on Hancock Street, in the Galleria shops of Presidents Plaza. The $2 admission includes validated parking in the plaza's garage, guided tours at both the Old House and the two presidential birthplaces (a mile away on Franklin Street), and free connecting transportation between them all by trolley—a real bargain. If your appetite for early American decorative arts and architecture isn't sated by these, ask the rangers for directions to the historic

homes in which Abigail Adams was born, in neighboring Weymouth, or to the two homes of the Quincy family (the Dorothy Quincy Homestead and the Josiah Quincy House), all of which are seasonally open to the public for a price.

If driving from the north, take I-93 Exit 8 and follow the National Park Service arrowhead logo to downtown Quincy, a circuitous route past homes, an overgrown hillside, and a couple of shopping plazas. The logo signs unfortunately disappear, but at the foot of the eight-story Stop & Shop office building, turn left and follow traffic around the gold-domed, gray-granite First Parish Church, turning left again at the Harvard Community Health Center. The park visitor center is in the multistory building next door; parking is at the rear. From the west or south take Rt. 3 Exit 18 and follow the Burgin Parkway north; in just under two miles and a little ways past a large T station, make the indicated right turn at the sign for the visitor center, and then the next unsigned right onto downtown Hancock Street. The visitor center will be on your left. By T from Boston or Cambridge, take any Red Line Braintree-bound train (*not* an Ashmont one) to Quincy center (*not* Quincy Adams) and follow signs out the Hancock Street exit. The visitor center is on the ground floor of the six-story building straight ahead. The Park Service's site maps, available to visitors, have clear pedestrian directions to all the historic Adams houses.

USS *Salem*

As an anodyne to all the decorum and decorative arts of that Adams clan, follow the signs from Rt. 3 or Rt. 3A a couple of miles south of downtown Quincy to the berth of the vintage *USS Salem* at the Fore River Shipyard, tel. (617) 479-7900. Over 40 years old and over two football fields long, this huge successor to the battleships of WW II is the nucleus of a hoped-for museum to U.S. naval shipbuilding, a business with which Quincy is intimately acquainted. From late May to Oct. 1 the ship is open daily 10 a.m.- 4 p.m.; wander at will during the week or join the guided tours on weekends. Since the vessel is staffed by volunteers year-round, off-season visitors won't be turned away; just ring the bell if nobody's on the quarterdeck, and someone will come and let you aboard. Keep in mind that the amount of indoor heating is very limited. Admission is $6 adults, $4 seniors and kids ages 4-12.

The shipyard may inadvertently have been the source for arguably the most widespread piece of graffiti ever produced: "Kilroy was here." Throughout WW II an equipment inspector named James J. Kilroy allegedly scrawled that famous tag on war materiel inspected by his work gang.

If you don't have a car, the shipyard is accessible from downtown Boston via the **Harbor Express** Quincy commuter ferry, operating daily (except Thanksgiving and Christmas) from the north side of Long Wharf, behind the Marriott Hotel. Travel time is about 30 minutes, and the ferry puts you within steps of the USS *Salem*. The one-way fare is $5.

Food
Destination dining is certainly not one of Quincy's strengths, although visitors to the Adams sights will find at least as many eateries downtown along Hancock Street as salons for doing your nails. From donuts and bagels to pizza and gyros, most of the choices are local variants on fast-food, although Mando's Italian Cafe, Siam House Thai Cuisine, and the Blackboard Cafe offer some worthwhile variations within the blocks immediately south of the National Park visitor center.

Getting There
Since the principal connection to Boston from the south, Rt. 3, suffers some of the most intractable rush hour traffic tie-ups in eastern Massachusetts, truly the smartest alternative is to hop aboard a Braintree-bound train (*not* Ashmont-bound) on the T's Red Line, which run from Cambridge and downtown Boston to within blocks of Quincy's main historic sights.

GETTING TO THE SHORE ON TIME

Every city and town from Boston south to Cape Cod has some sort of public beach. The ones worth a visit—those with fine sand, nearby parking for nonresidents, and enough breadth to accommodate the crowds that flock to them—are in

COURTESY OF THE BOSTON PUBLIC LIBRARY, PRINT DEPARTMENT

fun in the sun

the towns of Hull, Marshfield, and Duxbury, all about 45-75 minutes' drive south of the Hub via Rt. 3 and local roads. There is no direct public transit from downtown Boston to any of these. The weekday ferry from downtown Boston to Hull only serves suburban residents commuting into the city, meaning its earliest departures *to* Hull are at the end of the day, with no return until morning. As a result, the MBTA is only useful to beach-going bicyclists. For example, cyclists have the option of taking the Boston-Hingham MBTA commuter ferry from Rowes Wharf (weekdays only, $10 each way, bikes free), which at least cuts the distance to Hull's beaches to under five miles. Similarly, riders may reach the other two beach towns with a head start on Commuter Rail. For only $8 roundtrip, the Old Colony Line from South Station will put you at either Kingston or Plymouth station—within a 6-12 mile ride of every public beach from Duxbury to Marshfield. Bike permits (they're good for four years) to bring your wheels aboard the train are available from all of Boston's Commuter Rail terminals for $5. Alternatively, disembark at the Plymouth end of the line and walk half a mile south on Rt. 3A to **Martha's Bicycles & Fitness**, tel. 508-746-2109, the region's only rental shop remotely close to public transit. Along with sunscreen, remember to pack a copy of the *Eastern Massachusetts Bicycle and Road Map* from Rubel BikeMaps, available at better bookstores (and bike shops) throughout Boston, Cambridge, and the rest of the region (or from P.O. Box 1035, Cambridge MA 02140, for only $5.25, postpaid). Not only is it indispensible for identifying the most bicycle-friendly route to your final destination, it'll also show you where to find both bike repair shops and—more importantly—local ice cream stands.

PLYMOUTH

Historic Plymouth, where New England's first successful English settlement took root in December of 1620, didn't draw serious interest in its preservation until the 1800s. Now, after another century of practice, this town could teach Walt Disney a thing or two about marketing Pilgrim-related trinkets and mementos. While history may be the town's trump card, it has a good hand of other activities, including water sports, whale-watching, and antiques. Appropriately enough for the home of America's first Thanksgiving, Plymouth is also one of the leading lights in the cranberry industry, processing tons of the tart fruit from bogs found along many of the more rural state roads in the surrounding county. Great blooms of red dot the autumn-browned landscape during the year-end harvest as bogs are flooded with water and millions of floating berries are corralled for trucking to Plymouth.

Pilgrims Progress

On sloping ground overlooking Plymouth Bay from beside Rt. 3A south of downtown, some 20 thatched structures sit within the stockade of the **Plimoth Plantation,** a carefully studied reproduction of the early 17th-century Pilgrim village. Within the timber walls time is frozen at 1627 as costumed interpreters replicate the quotidian lives of actual villagers, English dialects and all. Though recounted in modern terms, an equally thorough view of 17th-century Native American life is provided at **Hobbamock's Homesite** along the adjacent Eel River. The interpretive staff are very well informed, and while they understandably don't waste their capabilities on those who simply try to trick them into confessing how much time they spend watching TV, anyone who shows the least bit of genuine interest in the lives of their characters is treated to bravura performances.

If you were raised on the usual pabulum served up in school, you may be quite surprised by what the Saints and their Merchant brethren really believed. (Abandon all political correctness ye who enter here-it has no currency in the 17th century.) It's also pleasantly challenging to answer *their* questions about *your* life, when you must resort to analogies or concepts familiar to someone who predates nearly every technology you know by over 350 years, but do try; it doubles the fun. Elsewhere in the complex are museum exhibits, a crafts center wherein artisans produce colonial-style works for sale, food service, and a well-stocked gift shop with quite

The Mayflower II

the comprehensive book selection. Open daily April-Nov.; admission to the Plantation alone is $15 adults, $9 for kids 6-17. If you intend to visit both the village and the *Mayflower II,* it pays to buy a combined general admission for $18.50 adults, $11 kids. With validation from the Plantation Visitor Center, tickets may also be used for a second day. Call (508) 746-1622 for more information, including a schedule of such upcoming special programs as the popular harvest dinners, prepared according to 17th-century recipes and techniques.

Two and a half miles away on the harbor waterfront, the **Mayflower II** stands at anchor. Since no detailed description has ever been found for the ship that brought the Pilgrims to New England—even its name went unmentioned until three years after landing—this vessel is a generic rather than specific reproduction of a 17th-century sailing ship. The costumed interpreters who greet you on board, on the other hand, like their Plantation counterparts, are modeled after passengers and crew known to have made the 1620 voyage. Admission, if separate from the Plantation, is $5.50 adults, $3.75 children. Days and hours of operation are the same as at the village.

While there isn't any public transportation shuttling between the downtown and the Plimoth Plantation, weekday commuter buses of the **Plymouth & Brockton** line stop off at the Plantation weekdays on their run from Boston's South Station. You can effectively use them as shuttles if you catch 'em at their stop in front of the CVS pharmacy in downtown Plymouth. Only two departures allow enough time to take it all in without being stranded; call (508) 746-0378 for automated schedule and fare info.

Other Pilgrim-Related Sights

In the shoreline park beside the *Mayflower II* stands a grandiose columned vault, inside of which lies one of most famous thresholds in American history: **Plymouth Rock.** The claim in favor of this surprisingly diminutive stone (which "isn't worth, at the outside, more than 35 cents," cracked Mark Twain) being the welcome mat for some reconnoitering Pilgrims back in 1620 rests on the secondhand recollections of a 95-year-old gent who identified the artifact in 1745. Both the surrounding park and "Brewster Gardens," a block south and across the street along Town Brook, are good spots to ponder the ironies of hanging so much American myth on such a small hinge. That brook, barely more than a little freshet for ducks, and its accompanying path run west to the Jenny Grist Mill, a replica of the Pilgrims' 1636 wind-driven cornmeal grinder anchoring a tiny "village" of shops, including an ice cream stand and the aptly named Run of the Mill Tavern.

Rising sharply above Plymouth Rock is Cobb's Hill, on which the earliest Pilgrim settlement was built. Plaques on the houses along Leyden Street and its neighbors tell the early Pilgrims' tale in bite-sized morsels of names and dates. If piecing them all together, adding the Massasoit statue at the hill's seaward edge, and salting with the inscriptions from the adjacent Pilgrim burial marker is still too flavorless for your tastes, check out the **Plymouth National Wax Museum,** there behind Massasoit at 16 Carver St., tel. (508) 746-6468. This, too, is entirely a matter of taste, but at least it leaves nothing to the imagination. Open daily March-Nov.; admission is $5.50, but be sure to inquire about AAA and other discounts, or look for coupons in the various tour brochures at the nearby waterfront visitor information center.

When **Pilgrim Hall Museum** first opened its doors, James Monroe was in the White House and Thomas Jefferson was still throwing parties at Monticello. With the largest extant collection of Pilgrim-related artifacts, it's the town's second must-see for anyone seriously interested in the lives of those 17th-century European immigrants, though it also makes an honorable effort at accurately interjecting a dose of Native American history, too. Among its treasures are the only portrait of a *Mayflower* passenger—Edward Winslow—and the hull of the *Sparrow-Hawk,* one of several vessels that carried the immigrants to these shores, its frame a collection of improbably bandied and spavined tree trunks. The museum's granite Greek Revival facade can't be missed at 75 Court St., tel. (508) 746-1620, where it's open daily till 4:30 p.m. Admission is $4.

Be sure not to pass up on a visit to **Burial Hill,** rising steeply west of Main St. behind the First Church in Town Square. Besides being the one place where the Pilgrims identified their dead, it offers a fine panorama of town and harbor. Plymouth also has a half dozen 17th- and 18th-century homes open seasonally to the public, including one from 1667 that actually housed some Pilgrims. The friendly folks at the visitor information center on Water Street can supply directions and information on each one.

Prevents Scurvy, Too

Everything you always wanted to know about cranberries—and then some—is found at **Cranberry World,** sponsored by industry-dominating Ocean Spray, 225 Water St., tel. (508) 747-2350. Daily from May-Nov. the visitor center offers displays on the plant's life cycle, the history of its cultivation, and examples of products made from cranberries through the years. Try samples and take home recipes, too. Like everything at Cranberry World, it's all free.

Of course, to really taste the full potential of that bright red berry head over to the **Plymouth Colony Winery,** off Rt. 44 three miles west of Rt. 3 Exit 6, tel. (508) 747-3334. As you could probably guess from the acres of fertile bogs surrounding the place, cranberry wines are the specialty, but other locally grown fruits are featured in the lineup, too. Free tours and tastings are available daily April-Dec., and weekends in March. Massachusetts blue laws regarding beer and wine sales apply only to retailers, not producers, so you may arrive on a Sunday confident of being able to buy whatever strikes your fancy.

PRACTICALITIES

Food

Eating out in Plymouth is like voting in a Congressional race: outside of a few exceptions most of the choices are either unremarkable or downright disappointing. This is the home of the BLT, veal parmesan, chicken fingers, seafood Newburg, and shrimp scampi. Do you miss your Stovetop stuffing and glossy squares of Velveeta? Rejoice, you can quench all such homesickness right here, with a waterfront view no less. No-surprise dining is also available at a variety of fast-food places familiar from home and on the road; besides those along Rt. 3A through town check out the food courts at the huge Independence Mall beside Rt. 3 Exit 8 in adjacent Kingston.

When it comes to fried or broiled fruits of the sea, head for Plymouth's town wharf, home to several seafood-in-the-rough places, each of which has a loyal following that will only grudgingly admit to the strengths of the opposition. Trading its lack of waterfront tables for a slight edge on price, **Souza's Seafood,** tel. (508) 746-

5354, is at least equal to its neighbors on the fried shellfish front, but the dish that dusts the competition is the lobster bisque: thick, rich, flavorful, and not to be missed. Open daily in summer till 10 p.m., cutting back in winter to Thurs.- Sun. until late afternoon or early evening, depending on business. Alternatively, a few miles south of Plimoth Plantation on Rt. 3A is **Star of Siam,** tel. (508) 224-3771, a Thai takeout joint of surprisingly good quality.

Getting There

Although any glance at a Commuter Rail map will temptingly show a nice direct line southward out of the Hub, Plymouth's station is actually some

two miles north of downtown at the Cordage Park Marketplace on Rt. 3A. Furthermore, service is strictly off-peak: for maximum appeal to Boston-bound commuters doing the 9-5 thing, rush-hour service skips Plymouth entirely and substitutes the Kingston station, near the Independence Mall on Rt. 3. However, if you sensibly avoid rush hour, upon arrival at the Cordage Park depot you can catch the **Liberty Link,** an hourly bus that loops into downtown (to return to the station, catch the **Freedom Link,** the Liberty's twin that follows the same route in the opposite direction). Call (800) 392-6100 or (617) 222-3200 for Commuter Rail schedules and fares.

FROM THE COLLECTION OF NORMAN B. LEVENTHAL, BOSTON, MASSACHUSETTS

BOSTON BASICS

Visiting Boston is more than just fun and games. What's the best way to get here, and once here, around? When do the subways stop running? When do you not need to pay to ride the streetcar lines? How do you recover your car if it's been towed for a parking violation? What doctors make house calls to hotels? Where can you exchange foreign currency, or purchase pre-paid phone cards? What do you tune your portable radio to if you want to catch "Car Talk" while working out in your hotel fitness center? Relax! The answers to these and other vital questions are provided in detail below.

TRANSPORTATION

Whether you come by train, plane, or automobile, getting to Boston is easy. But driving around its historic labyrinth of one-way streets can put an unnecessary strain on any vacation, especially if you don't realize that, unlike most of North America, Boston is not a car-friendly place. (If you doubt this, see what happens to your travel budget after a single day of either renting a car or paying to park your own.) Lucky for you, the secret Tantric text to hassle-free touring around Boston is now in your very hands. So read on, and become enlightened in the impenetrable mystery of transporting yourself to, and around, the Hub.

GETTING THERE AND AWAY

Planes

All the major domestic airlines, many smaller regional ones, and over 15 international carriers fly into **Logan International Airport,** making it one of the busiest airports in the nation. Competition is strong enough to keep most domestic fares on par with New York—about as low as it gets for transcontinental travel. Unfortunately, the cost of doing business at either city's airport has prevented cut-rate airlines from making more than minor inroads, robbing New York- and

Boston-bound passengers of the significant competitive benefits associated with such short-haul and no-frills fliers as Southwest Airlines. To enjoy Southwest's savings, you must fly into T.F. Green Airport in Providence, Rhode Island—a $13.50, 90-minute bus ride from downtown Boston via Bonanza Bus Lines, tel. (888) 751-8800 or (401) 751-8800. Depending on the value you place on your time, you may be glad to ride that bus: on selected routes, *all* airlines flying into Providence will match or beat Southwest's fares, which can translate into literally hundreds of dollars of savings off a comparable flight into Boston. Similarly, Boston is often a significantly more expensive destination for international passengers than nearby New York. However, connecting from New York to Boston is either so expensive ($89-129 one-way via the hourly airline shuttles) or time-consuming (minimum seven hours by bus or train, counting transit time from airport to the respective stations) as to thoroughly negate any savings.

Airport Transportation: Although few large cities boast such a major airport so close to downtown as Logan is to the heart of Boston, nobody inching through rush-hour tunnel traffic takes comfort in the fact that downtown and the airport are little over a mile apart.

On the other hand, having the Inner Harbor lapping at the ends of the runways also means that no ground transportation quite matches the **Airport Water Shuttle**—for speed or sheer fun. (Unfortunately, none match it in price, either: even taxis are cheaper.) From the Logan dock, it's just a seven-minute ride to Rowes Wharf at the edge of the Financial District (every 15 minutes weekdays, 30 minutes on weekends; $10 pp one-way, $17 roundtrip, kids under 12 free). Specially marked buses (#66) serve stops outside each terminal's baggage claim area and the Logan dock.

Any hour of day or night, the latest fares and schedules of all the buses and boats available to transport you—plus up-to-the-minute traffic reports on airport roadways—are just a touch-tone call away: Massport Ground Transportation Information Service, tel. (800) 23-LOGAN.

For other harborside destinations, from South Boston's Black Falcon Cruise Terminal and World Trade Center to the North End's Fleet-Center or even Charlestown, consider the **City Water Taxi,** on call daily from April to mid-October ($10 pp to or from Logan, $8 pp for parties of two or more, $5 between any two off-airport stops). Ask the driver of dock-bound bus #66 to radio ahead for a boat to meet you, or call (617) 422-0392 to schedule a pickup. If you're bound for the South Shore, **Harbor Express,** tel. (617) 376-8417, offers up to 20 daily sailings from Logan to Quincy, a 45-minute cruise ($10), or connect to the MBTA's equally frequent—albeit weekdays only—**Hingham Commuter Boat** via the Water Shuttle (discounted joint fares available; inquire aboard the shuttle or call 617-23-LOGAN). Harbor Express also schedules some half-dozen daily sailings from the Logan dock north to Salem, an hour away.

If you choose to travel via road, **taxi** rates for up to four people from Logan to downtown and Back Bay typically run $13-20; Brookline, Allston, or Cambridge drop-offs may set you back $18-24 (these estimates include the $1.30 airport fee and $2 tunnel toll cabbies legitimately may add on to the metered fare).

Half a dozen **bus** companies ply long-distance routes between Logan and Cape Cod, central Massachusetts, and the rest of New England, stopping first in downtown Boston; $6 lands you a comfortable and quick ride to South Station aboard any of these.

*a passenger plane
from the 1930s*

AIRLINE TOLL-FREE PHONE NUMBERS

DOMESTIC

AirTran, tel. (800) 247-8726, www.airtran.com
America West, tel. (800) 235-9292, www.americawest.com
American Airlines/American Eagle, tel. (800) 433-7300, www.aa.com
Business Express/Delta Connection, tel. (800) 345-3400
Cape Air, tel. (800) 352-0714, www.capeair.com
Colgan Air/Continental Connection, tel. (800) 272-5488
Comair, tel. (800) 354-9822, www.fly-comair.com
Continental/Continental Express, tel. (800) 525-0280, www.flycontinental.com
Delta Air Lines/Delta Express/Delta Shuttle (to LaGuardia, NY), tel. (800) 221-1212,
    www.delta-air.com
Eastwind Airlines, tel. (800) 644-3592, www.eastwindairlines.com
Frontier Airlines, tel. (800) 432-1359, www.frontierairlines.com
Kiwi Air, tel. (800) 538-5494, www.jetkiwi.com
MetroJet, tel. (888) 638-7653, www.metrojet.com
Midway Airlines, tel. (800) 446-4392, www.midwayair.com
Midwest Express, tel. (800) 452-2022, www.midwestexpress.com
National Air, tel. (800) 248-9538
Northwest/NW Airlink, tel. (800) 225-2525, www.nwa.com
PanAm, tel. (800) 359-7262, www.carnivalair.com
Southwest Airlines, tel. (800) 435-9792, www.iflyswa.com
Spirit Airlines, tel. (800) 772-7117
TWA, tel. (800) 221-2000, www.twa.com
United/United Express, tel. (800) 241-6522, www.ual.com
US Airways/US Airways Express/US Airways Shuttle (to LaGuardia, NY), tel. (800) 428-4322,
    www.usairways.com

INTERNATIONAL

Aer Lingus, tel. (800) 223-6537, www.aerlingus.ie
Air Atlantic/Canadian Air, tel. (800) 426-7000, www.airatlantic.com
Air Canada/Air Alliance/Air Nova, tel. (800) 776-3000, www.aircanada.ca
Air France, tel. (800) 237-2747, www.airfrance.com
Alitalia, tel. (800) 223-5730, www.alitalia.com/english
American Trans Air, tel. (800) 225-2995
British Airways, tel. (800) 247-9297, www.british-airways.com
Icelandair, tel. (800) 223-5500, www.icelandair.is
KLM, tel. (800) 374-7747, www.klm.nl
Korean Air, tel. (800) 438-5000, www.koreanair.com
Lufthansa, tel. (800) 645-3880, www.lufthansa.com
Olympic, tel. (800) 223-1226, agn.hol.gr/info/olympic1.htm
Sabena, tel. (800) 955-2000, www.sabena.com
SwissAir, tel. (800) 221-4750, www.swissair.com
TAP Air Portugal, tel. (800) 221-7370, www.tap-airportugal.de
Virgin Atlantic Airways, tel. (800) 862-8621, www.fly.virgin.com`

Drivers can make change on bills up to a $20, though exact fare is always appreciated. Departures from the posted curbside bus stops at each terminal's baggage claim level are typically every 15-30 minutes until 11:15 p.m. **Logan Express** buses operate between the airport and outlying suburbs and cities including Quincy, Braintree, Natick, Framingham, and Woburn ($6-8; every 30-60 minutes).

Fixed-schedule services such as **Back Bay Coach,** tel. (617) 698-6188, and **City Transportation,** tel. (617) 561-9000, make frequent rounds between Logan and a dozen downtown and Back Bay hotels for $7.50 pp (slightly more for Allston or Brookline). Or make an appointment with **U.S. Shuttle,** tel. (617) 894-3100, from the airport or Boston/Cambridge, or, from outside the 617 area code, tel. (800) 714-1115 ($7 and up per person depending on destination), for door-to-door pickup or drop-off anywhere in the greater metro area. To check whether your hotel or inn has an airport courtesy van, look for the phone-equipped displays generally tucked away to the side of each baggage claim area.

Next to courtesy vans, the cheapest of all the airport-city transit options is the **Blue Line subway** inbound to downtown Government Center (85 cents!), with connections to the rest of the Massachusett Bay Transit Authority's subway and trolley lines; catch the designated free bus (the #22 or #33) to the subway from outside the lower level of your terminal.

Trains

North and South Stations are the two main passenger rail terminals connecting Boston with New England and the nation.

South Station, a magnificent building from the golden age of rail, provides interstate service via **Amtrak** to downtown Boston from western Massachusetts, Albany, and the Great Lakes, plus coastal Connecticut, New York City, and points south. Located on Atlantic Ave. and Summer St. down by the Waterfront. For Amtrak info and ticketing, call (800) 872-7245 or visit the Web site www.amtrak.com. South Station is also where you can catch MBTA **Commuter Rail,** tel. (800) 392-6099 from outside Boston, or (617) 222-3200, to Worcester, Providence, and intermediate destinations throughout southeastern Massachusetts.

North Station, on the ground level of the Fleet-Center, on Causeway St. near the I-93 bridge over the Charles, provides Commuter Rail service to Concord, Lowell, Salem, Cape Ann, and other points on the North Shore and in the Merrimack Valley. It's also slated to provide Amtrak service to coastal New Hampshire and Portland, Maine, beginning in 1999. The two stations have no *direct* public transportation link between them, but both are on the subway line. Most New England destinations are served by several daily departures. For anyone staying in the Back Bay or South End, most trains to and from South Station also make stops at Back Bay Station, on Dartmouth St.

Up until very recently, train travel in the Northeast, as in much of the country, was guaranteed to give migraines to the sort of traveler who asks, "Are we there yet?" minutes after sitting down. But the increasingly sclerotic condition of roads and airports has made railroad time competitive over certain routes—even without factoring in the convenience of not worrying about traffic or parking or whether the airport cabbie speaks a language you recognize. Of course, there's no getting around the fact that trains *feel* slow, so if you can't relax and enjoy a book, a nap, the scenery, or the savings, don't call Amtrak.

If you *do* choose the train and will be traveling the always-crowded New York-Boston route, consider springing for a seat in the club car—it's roomier and more relaxing than the regular coaches, and handier to a ready flow of libation. And try to avoid the infamous "Roach Coaches," the trains that make the coastal-route run at either end of prep school vacations (last weeks of August, January, and May, and mid-December), lest your quiet contemplation of the austere Connecticut seashore be shattered by hordes of rambunctious Manhattan adolescents heading to or from prestigious boarding schools.

Buses

All major intercity and interstate buses arrive and depart from the **South Station Transportation Center,** the boxy modern building on Atlantic Ave. propped up over the far end of the train station's rail platforms. If arriving from the distant south or west, New York City is likely to be part of your itinerary, whether you like it or not.

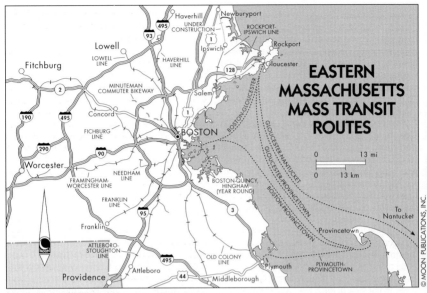

EASTERN
MASSACHUSETTS
MASS TRANSIT
ROUTES

© MOON PUBLICATIONS, INC.

Springfield-based **Peter Pan Bus Lines,** tel. (800) 237-8747, www.peterpan-bus.com, has the most expeditious express buses (4.5 hours) from New York's Port Authority bus terminal, with additional express connections from Philadelphia, Baltimore, and Washington. Reliable **Greyhound,** tel. (800) 231-2222, also has "express" service from New York (which makes a 15-minute stop in Hartford, Connecticut, plus runs from Albany and points west. It also serves Connecticut's Foxwoods Casino. If you don't really care (within reason) how long it takes to get here from New York and you want to enjoy the journey, book a space aboard the **East Coast Explorer,** tel. (800) 610-2680, a three-season, twice-weekly van service that spends an entire day meandering along a scenic route to and from Manhattan, stopping at half a dozen interesting sights along the way, all for only a few dollars more than the regular bus. It'll even drop you off at hotels and hostels around town.

Bus Service within New England and up-state New York: Peter Pan Bus Lines is again recommended for local service to such regional destinations as Worcester, the Pioneer Valley, and Williamstown; Albany, New York; and Hartford or New Haven, Connecticut. If bound for Providence, Rhode Island, or Bangor, Maine, go with Bonanza. For Hanover, New Hampshire, Vermont, Maine, and Montreal, **Vermont Transit,** tel. (800) 451-3292, is best. Central New Hampshire (including the AMC Pinkham Notch base camp on the Appalachian Trail, but excluding Hanover) and coastal Maine are served by **Concord Trailways,** tel. (800) 639-3317, while **C&J Trailways,** tel. (800) 258-7111, covers the New Hampshire seacoast with an intermediate stop on the North Shore at Newburyport.

Bus Transport within Eastern Massachusetts: The principal carriers are **Bonanza Bus Lines,** tel. (888) 751-8800, www.bonanzabus .com, serving Fall River, New Bedford, and upper Cape Cod; **Plymouth & Brockton Street Railway,** tel. (617) 773-9401, www.p-b.com, serving the South Shore and all Cape Cod (name notwithstanding, this *is* a bus company); and **American Eagle,** tel. (508) 993-5040, to New Bedford and Fairhaven.

Despite its recent construction, the bus terminal is not particularly comfortable for long waits; if you have a lot of time to kill before catching a bus out of town, you may find the grand concourse and food court at next-door South Station more interesting.

Car Rentals

All the major national car-rental companies are represented around the metro area, mostly at Logan Airport and near downtown hotels. **Alamo,** tel. (800) 327-9633, and **National Car Rental,** tel. (800) 227-7368, have airport offices, while **Avis,** tel. (800) 831-2847; **Budget,** tel. (800) 527-0700; **Dollar Rent A Car,** tel. (800) 800-4000; **Hertz,** tel. (800) 654-3131; and **Thrifty Car Rental,** tel. (800) 367-2277, all have downtown and Cambridge locations in addition to their airport lots. Among the most widespread and affordable is **Enterprise Rent-a-Car,** with offices in downtown, Copley Square, Cambridge, Brookline, and outside Logan, tel. (800) 736-8222. Average rental rates are generally much higher than the southern or western U.S., plus there's a $10 fee per rental to help defray the cost of constructing the city's new convention center, so be prepared for sticker shock.

GETTING AROUND TOWN

Boston's small size compensates somewhat for the absence of an easily navigable street grid over most of the city—even when lost, you probably aren't too far from where you really want to be. City blocks in the shapes of trapezoids and triangles and streets that seem to be parallel and perpendicular at the same time all take some getting used to. However, just remember *not* to assume that four right turns will always bring you back to where you began and you'll at least be in the right frame of mind.

When asking directions, be warned: first, several major avenues are abbreviated when spoken (Massachusetts as "Mass," Commonwealth as "Comm," and Dorchester as "Dot"); second, many residents have no clue as to the names of the streets they use every day. In truth, it wouldn't really matter much if they did—signs are options rather than standard equipment in many parts of town anyway.

Since nearly every hotel, restaurant, university, and tourist attraction mentioned in this chapter is accessible via Massachusetts Bay Transit Authority (MBTA) subways, buses, trolleys, boats, or commuter trains, public transit is your best option for getting around Boston and 77 adja-

For the latest Boston weather, call the Bell Atlantic Accu-Weather forecast, tel. (617) 936-1234.

cent communities. Over 700,000 daily commuters who use the **MBTA** know that despite occasional delays and crowds, it beats sitting in gridlocked traffic or trying to find affordable parking. If you do decide to sacrifice peace of mind for the right to boast of having driven in Boston, be prepared to pay dearly: with 150,000 cars competing daily for only 9,000 metered parking spaces, parking garages—though pricey—are your surest bet. Don't be tempted to park illegally in residents-only spots or other questionable curbsites—the city tickets and tows with frightening efficiency.

Taxis: Cabs are, of course, another option, and a less expensive one than in most other American cities. Service within 12 miles of downtown is charged by meter, but destinations outside the 12-mile radius are all assigned flat rates by the Boston Police Department. So, if you're taking a cab to Cape Ann, Plymouth, Maynard, or other distant places, ask the driver for the predetermined rate. Note that *all* of the communities and attractions mentioned in the Boston proper sections are within the meter limit. Remember during peak traffic times to take into account not only the length of your ride, but the duration. Aside from the method of hailing a cab from the streetside, going to a taxi stand at any of the larger hotels or calling for a pickup is the best way to catch a ride.

Selected taxicab companies in Boston:

Boston Cab, tel. (617) 262-CABS
Checker Cab, tel. (617) 536-7000
ITOA, tel. (617) 426-8700
Red & White Cab, tel. (617) 242-8000
Town Taxi, tel. (617) 536-5000

And in Cambridge:

Ambassador Brattle Cab, tel. (617) 492-1100
Checker Cab of Cambridge, tel. (617) 497-9000
Yellow Cab, tel. (617) 547-3000

For help locating property accidentally left behind in a Boston cab, call the Boston Police Hackney Hotline, tel. (617) 536-TAXI.

Public Transit

Unless you're chaperoning a large family entourage, the Massachusett Bay Transit Authority (MBTA)—**"the T"**—is your most affordable means of getting around the city. Except for crosstown travel—that is, a route circumventing downtown, such as from the Museum of Fine Arts to Harvard Square—it's reasonably rapid and convenient, too. (The only crosstown service is by bus—usually more than one, but transfers aren't free.) The four color-coded Boston subway and trolley lines are well explained by schematic maps throughout the system and aboard each vehicle. Pocket-sized copies are also available at Park St. and selected other stations. Since the system is a "hub and spoke" design, with all fixed rail lines running to and from downtown

Boston, there are two principal directions used on T signage and by anyone who may supply you with directions:

Inbound trains head toward the system's downtown hub.

Outbound trains head away from downtown.

MBTA **Passports,** for unlimited one-, three-, or seven-day travel ($5, $9, or $18) on all but the suburban components of the system may be purchased daily at the Airport, Government Center, Back Bay, and Hynes Convention Center subway stations; at both North and South Stations; at the newsstand in the Alewife terminal of the Red Line in Cambridge (except Sundays); or from the downtown visitor center on Boston Common. Many hotel concierge desks sell them, too. Otherwise, the standard fare is an 85-cent token for the subway, 60 cents exact change for buses. Certain idiosyncrasies should be noted: Green Line surface streetcars require a token or 85 cents exact change for inbound

THE BIG DIG

Short of visiting Boston inside a sealed coffin, it would be difficult to miss the sights, sounds, and traffic tie-ups of the Central Artery/Third Harbor Tunnel Project, better known as the Big Dig. The largest public works project in U.S. history, this multibillion-dollar feat of engineering and logistics is utterly transforming the face of the city. When completed sometime around 2005, it will have taken the present six-lane elevated portion of I-93 through downtown (the old Central Artery, less than two miles long), and replaced it with an eight- to 10-lane underground highway. Two massive new bridges over the mouth of the Charles, the MassPike (I-90) extension to Logan Airport via the Ted Williams Tunnel beneath Boston Harbor, and a new six-lane interchange between I-93 and I-90 are also part of the project. Meanwhile the T is taking advantage of having the downtown pried open like a sardine tin to reconfigure a couple subway stations and build from scratch an underground transitway to the newly christened Seaport District in South Boston. Needless to say, it's all raising quite a bit of dust—not to mention tempers, as commuters cope with fresh road closings, direction changes, pedestrian barriers, and other detours on an almost daily basis.

Critics are almost as numerous as the army of workers burrowing beneath the city. They cite huge cost overruns, broken promises, and bad design (the Charles River crossing is particularly reviled by those who anticipate having to live in its huge shadow). Worse, cuts to public transit improvements and anti-pollution technology may jeopardize the very cornerstone of the project: bringing Boston into long-overdue compliance with Federal Clean Air Act.

What isn't disputed is the Big Dig's record of engineering feats. Whether relocating 10,000 miles of utility cables and pipes, or constructing a concrete highway tunnel within mere feet of the subway, Amtrak rails, and the general mail distribution center for the entire city—without disrupting service to any of them—the project has made a permanent mark on the history of civil engineering. And though these often earn it comparison to other megasized construction projects such as the Channel Tunnel and the Panama Canal, the Big Dig is, in one respect, infinitely more difficult. It has to be built right in the backyard of tens of thousands of residents, not one of whom has been forced to move. Mitigating the impact of construction on neighbors and allowing the city to carry about its business as usual is easily its most amazing accomplishment of all.

rides (more on the "D" branch, whose fare runs $1-2 on the aboveground portion), but *all outbound rides westward are free if you board aboveground.* The fares are higher for express buses to or from communities outside Boston, and on the Braintree branch

For traffic conditions in the Boston area—including airport roadways and all numbered state and federal highways —call SMARTraveler, tel. (617) 374-1234.

PASSPORT

of the Red Line; observe the signs explaining the fare, or ask the driver or token collector for details. Tokens are sold at collector's booths in subway stations, or at token machines (examine the LED text display on the machine before feeding it your bills—when machines are unable to give change they say so). At Prudential and Symphony stations, the collector's booth is no longer staffed, so proceed through the open gate by the turnstiles and pay at the farebox at the front of the trolley with exact change or a token.

The T does *not* run 24 hours; trains and trolleys generally start rolling 5-6 a.m. and operate through midnight or shortly after; buses start at the same time and usually run until about 1 a.m. Service is reduced on Sundays and holidays, except on the Blue Line, to and from the airport.

Red, Orange, and Blue Line subways are wheelchair accessible via elevators at many, but not all, stations; consult the system map available from visitor information booths to identify those that are. Wheelchair access to Green Line streetcars is planned but not yet available. All bus routes have at least some lift-equipped

vehicles; to find out whether a lift bus is in service on a specific route—or to schedule one a day in advance—call (800) LIFT-BUS.

All MBTA subway, bus, and ferry schedules and fares are available by phone when there's a live operator available, generally until 8 p.m.; tel. (617) 222-3200 or, outside Boston, (800) 392-6100. Automated Commuter Rail departure and fare info, while rather tedious to extract, is available from the same number 24 hours a day. If you plan on being in the area for a while or you intend to rely on the T to get to many different parts of the city or region, you should invest in the handy book, *Car-Free in Boston: The Guide to Public Transit in Greater Boston & New England,* published by the nonprofit Association for Public Transportation, tel. (617) 482-0282. It's available in bookstores, newsstands, all CVS pharmacies, and information centers throughout the city.

Driving? You Crazy?

There's only one word of advice for anyone thinking of driving into Boston: DON'T. Most of the city was laid out centuries before the automobile existed, and it shows. Narrow, often one-way streets, adhering to long-buried footpaths and shorelines, routinely baffle drivers raised on the nice platted grids of most North American cities. Irregular intersections and infamous rotaries help terrorize novices, while an obstinate resistance to street signs and virtually no legal parking help to confuse and frustrate. To top it all off, Bostonians have a well-deserved reputation for driving as if it's a contact sport. All of which is why hundreds of thousands of residents daily use the best alternatives: their feet and the T. If you value your peace of mind, do likewise.

Since the ratio of cars downtown to on-street parking downtown is almost 20:1, competition for a metered spot is fierce. Paid parking lots

MBTA LOST AND FOUND PHONE NUMBERS

Blue Line, tel. (617) 722-5533
Green Line, tel. (617) 722-5221
Orange Line, tel. (617) 722-5403
Red Line, tel. (617) 722-5317

Mattapan High-Speed Line, tel. (617) 722-5213

Buses, tel. (617) 722-5607

Commuter Rail/North Station, tel. (617) 722-3600

HELL ON WHEELS: DRIVING IN BOSTON

So, you've chosen to ignore all the advice and drive Boston anyway. In the interests of full disclosure, here's a sneak peek at a few favorite local driving maneuvers (don't try these at home).

Team Turning. A single car needing to make a left turn across traffic turns slightly, waiting for a break in the on-coming stream; using it as a shield, three other cars pull up beside it in parallel. When the break comes—usually just before a fast-moving truck or bus—all four cars leap in unison to complete their turn, trying to merge into the single lane before being broadsided by that bus or semi. A great spectator event.

The Smerge. Whenever a handful of streets merge into one another at acute angles, the resulting expanse of pavement is traditionally left unmarked, so that drivers may define their own lanes—and refuse to merge until at least two carlengths after there is absolutely no other choice. In slow-moving rush-hour traffic, the result—a smerge—resembles an entire theater audience trying to exit through a single set of double doors. Once you've mastered the smerge, the next step is the high-speed rotary.

The Nose-First-Noodge. The solution to poor visibility around cars parked beside driveways or side streets, this fearless move simply involves boldly driving halfway into heavy cross traffic, forcing vehicles to swerve or screech to a halt—thus allowing a proper exit to be completed.

Eye Contact. Strictly *verboten*. An adversary who

JEFF PERK

sees the whites of a fellow driver's eyes will seize the initiative. Make eye contact and one of you will have to blink first; avoid it and you'll be telling the truth when you tell the officer filling out the accident report, "I never saw it coming."

---

will save you endless circling around the block, but be prepared to fork over a hefty chunk of change for the privilege: day rates of $6-10 plus $2 per hour are typical, and even after 6 p.m. parking near restaurant and theater hot spots often runs a flat $8-12. The city's most reasonable evening rate is in the underground Boston Common Garage: 4 p.m.-10 a.m., it's a flat $7. Even if others seem to be getting away with it, *don't* be tempted into parking in a tow zone, and *never* think you can get away with sneaking into a resident-permit parking zone; while some scofflaws get lucky, the city's treasury reaps millions of dollars each year from fools whose luck ran out.

If your car gets towed in Boston, call the Transportation Department Tow Line, tel. (617)

635-3900; in Cambridge, call (617)349-3300; and in Brookline, call (617) 730-2230. If your vehicle was towed rather than stolen, you'll be told who has it and given a number to call for directions and terms of payment. If you're lucky, you'll have been towed by the City of Boston: its fees begin below $30, it accepts credit cards, and its tow lot is within a couple dollars' cab ride of the T. Private tow companies charge $50-80 or more, typically won't take anything other than hard cash, and are often located in the most Godforsaken industrial limits of the metropolitan area. The towing fees are entirely separate from the bright hazard-orange ticket you'll find tucked under your windshield wiper. Lest you think of trying to collect a sheaf of them as souvenirs or to trade with friends, be warned that it takes only a few before your towed car will be wearing a Denver Boot—a giant yellow steel spur that renders driving impossible. Finally, if you accrue any Boston parking tickets during your stay, you may pay them by phone with a Visa card by calling (617) 635-3888; for Cambridge parking tickets, call (617) 491-7277.

Using Your Feet
In his rhapsodic *About Boston: Sight, Sound, Flavor, and Inflection,* poet David McCord wrote, "A pedestrian is a man in danger of his life; a walker is a man in possession of his soul." Where better to connect the sole of your shoes to the soul of your being than in "America's Walking City," where insouciant native Bosto-

nians walk the way Parisians drive—striding between all traffic, stopped or in motion. To a walker, all those light-running cabbies and commuters, double-parked delivery vans, and irksome one-way streets are merely local idiosyncrasies to be savored. Get in a car and the flavor of this bedlam instantly sours. Walkers find views of the city no drivers can ever see without endangering life and limb. Walkers who make wrong turns simply turn around and retrace their steps; drivers who do this end up circling the Public Garden six times. Walkers in Boston experience serendipity. Drivers in Boston experience frustration and despair. But don't take my word for it—try walking around a little bit and see for yourself.

INFORMATION AND SERVICES

Local bookstores are the best source of additional information about Boston, from historic neighborhood guides and street maps to glossy coffee table books. Otherwise, for a full supply of rack cards advertising commercial tours and attractions—or if you need directions to something around downtown—drop in on the Boston Common **Visitor Information Center,** tel. (617) 536-4100. Just don't expect this business-sponsored operation to help you stray far off the well-trod tourist path. Visitors who cross the river will find the **Cambridge Information Kiosk,** by the entrance to the Harvard Square T station, a much more informed resource, well equipped with excellent maps, event calendars, and a decent little brochure outlining a walking tour of Old Cambridge. (Don't be tempted by the free map offer at the usually adjacent sightseeing tour counter— the maps aren't even worth giving away.) Advance planners looking for the most comprehensive accommodations listings should call the **Massachusetts Office of Travel and Tourism,** tel. (800) 447-MASS, and request a copy of the state's *Getaway Guide.* Or point your Web browser to **www.boston.com,** a service of the *Boston Globe,* and follow the links for travel information.

It's impossible to recommend any all-encompassing Boston street map since none of the major brands commercially available—Rand McNally, Gousha, Arrow—has kept pace with the

city's evolution. (To be fair, neither has Boston's own planning agency.) "Don't drive today with yesterday's map," declares one, trumpeting its inclusion of newly constructed airport roadways even as significant citywide alterations—some well over a decade old—continue to be omitted. The worst offender of all is the American Automobile Association's "downtown and vicinity" map, offered free to AAA members, possibly the most erroneous and carelessly rendered piece of cartography you'll find for the Hub. Comprehensiveness—it shows every street in Boston and surrounding communities—is its only saving grace. For consolation, look for Hedberg Maps' "Professor Pathfinder's" series of university-and-vicinity maps. Although they only cover selected smaller portions of the metro area—the MIT map includes most of Back Bay, but not downtown, for example—they are unsurpassed in accuracy, legibility, and graphic detail. Though available at most area bookstores and newsstands, call (800) 933-6277 or e-mail HedbergMap@aol.com to find out where to obtain them in advance. Back Bay shoppers will want to keep an eye out for Hedberg's free "Newbury Street League" pocket map and business directory, available from many Newbury St. shops and at various information kiosks around Boston. Harvard Square visitors should drop two bits at the Cambridge Information Kiosk for Hedberg's map of that lively ivy quarter of town.

HEALTH AND SAFETY

In Boston, as in the rest of the U.S., emergency medical services are obtained by dialing 911. If you have a medical or dental emergency, but not one that requires an ambulance trip to an emergency room, try **Inn-House Doctor,** tel. (617) 859-1776. Its doctors and pediatricians make house calls 24 hours a day, seven days a week, and accept almost any form of payment you have, whether credit card, check, or cash.

Prescriptions
If you use any sort of prescription medication, be sure to bring the *medicine* (not the prescription) when you come to the state. Massachusetts pharmacists are prohibited from refilling any prescription from out of state.

Replacement Eyeglasses
Should you lose or break your prescription glasses and need new ones, like, *now,* make your way to **Cohen's Fashion Optical,** 380 Boylston St. between Arlington and Berkeley, near the corner of the Public Garden, tel. (617) 266-0561. These specialists in same-day service are competitively priced, friendly, and prompt. Open 10 a.m.-7 p.m. Mon.-Fri., 10 a.m.-6 p.m. Saturday.

Personal Safety
Most casual travelers to Boston need not be unduly anxious about coming to visit the big, bad city. Boston may be big, but it really isn't all that bad, and if residents never waste time worrying about making headlines as victims of gang wars, mafia crossfire, or serial killing sprees, neither should you. Although Seattle may be able to boast less violence, Boston does have a lower homicide rate than Kansas City, Missouri; Nashville, Tennessee; Charlotte, North Carolina; Jacksonville, Florida; Oklahoma City, Oklahoma; Denver, Colorado; and half a dozen other U.S. urban areas of comparable size. New Orleans, with nearly the same population, has about *six times* as many murders annually as Boston. *Laissez les bon temps roulez,* indeed. For what the statistics are worth, Boston is even safer than parts of Cape Cod. If you're really looking for something to worry about, consider that over 10,000 cars are stolen in an average year here.

a peony (Paeonia officinalis), *named after the Greek physician-god of healing, Paeon*

So guard your wheels. Nonetheless, Boston's relatively good record is no reason for complacency: take all common-sense precautions about not leaving your possessions unattended, not walking alone through unlit, unoccupied parks or back streets at night, and not carrying excessive cash or valuables.

Liquor Laws
Each state sets its own legal drinking age; in the state of Massachusetts one must be 21 years or older. Valid identification (passport or international driver's license along with your home country license) is required to purchase alcoholic beverages in stores or bars. Many clubs won't admit anyone under the legal drinking age. At these places, you'll be asked for photo I.D. at the door. Nightclubs that advertise "18-plus" shows provide fluorescent wristbands to patrons who can prove they're 21 or over, without which the club bartenders will refuse to serve you alcohol. Happy hours are illegal, and bars close at 2 a.m. or earlier. Taking your libation to go? Hard alcohol, beer, and wine are sold in package liquor ("packy") stores. Supermarkets can't sell liquor, and only a few sell beer and wine. Thanks to the persistence of age-old "blue laws," no packaged liquor, beer, or wine may be sold on Sundays, except at a bonded winery, or during the annual December holiday exemption traditionally granted by the state legislature.

Take note that many areas have open container laws, meaning you can't walk down the street with an open beer or bottle of whiskey in hand, though if you keep a low profile at your outdoor picnic, it shouldn't be an issue.

Smoking Laws

Smoking a cigarette in the U.S. can not always be done anytime, anyplace, at least not legally. Most indoor public places in the Greater Boston area prohibit smoking, from office buildings and markets to buses and subway stations. Even in other outdoor public areas, be alert for posted No Smoking signs. Boston, Brookline, and Cambridge have all banned smoking in restaurants—except where separately enclosed seating areas can be established—and Brookline has even banned smoking in bars. The bottom line is, if at all unsure, ask.

Tick-Borne Diseases

Massachusetts may not boast exotic dangers like tarantulas or green mambas, and even its once-widespread timber rattlers have all but vanished from the state's forests. But the state *is* home to both the bloodsucking wood or dog tick and the more notorious deer tick, *Ixodes dammini,* which, as its Latin name suggests, is a little damn thing—no bigger than the period at the end of this sentence. Though indigenous throughout the state, these ticks are most common in eastern Massachusetts. Should you choose to venture farther afield and check out any of the day hikes suggested outside of the city, or on the Harbor Islands, it is wise to to take precautions against being bitten.

Wear a hat and light-colored clothes with long sleeves and legs that may be tucked into socks. Commercial tick repellent is also advisable. Avoid favorite tick habitats such as tall grasses and the edges of woods and meadows (they drop out of trees when detecting movement). If you do find a tick on yourself, there's still no reason for panic, but early removal dramatically improves chances for avoiding illness (it usually takes a day or two for any infectious agents to be transmitted to the host). The deer tick's larval stage, which it reaches in July and August, is when it is believed to be *most* capable of passing on bacteria or parasites, but it is infectious throughout its life.

Above all, use the proper removal technique (described by Dirk Schroeder in Moon's *Staying Healthy in Asia, Africa, and Latin America*): if it isn't visibly walking and can't be lightly brushed away, use tweezers to grasp the tick's head parts as close to your skin as possible and apply slow steady traction. (Don't squeeze—you don't want its saliva in your skin.) Don't attempt to get ticks out of your skin by burning them or coating them with anything like nail polish or petroleum jelly. If you remove a tick before it has been attached for more than 24 hours, you greatly reduce your risk of infection. After you've removed the tick, wash the bite with soap and clean water, and watch for signs of infection over the following days.

Precautions against tick bites are advisable because of the diseases they can transmit to their hosts. Dog ticks carry Rocky Mountain spotted fever, while deer ticks have been identified as carriers of Lyme disease, human babesiosis, and human granulocytic ehrlichiosis (HGE). None of these maladies is serious if treated early and properly, since all are caused by either bacteria or microscopic parasites susceptible to antibiotics.

MONEY AND BANKING

Foreign Exchange

Don't take it personally, but if you're traveling from abroad, you'll find Americans tend to prefer U.S. dollars or traveler's checks in dollar denominations. Bring these with you and you'll save yourself the hassle of shopping for the best exchange rates—or even finding a place willing to perform exchanges in the first place. If you have to choose between cash and traveler's checks, the security-conscious tourist will opt for the checks. True to the vendors' claims, almost everyone but taxi drivers will treat them like cash.

When taking care of your exchange needs keep in mind that despite competition among the city's banks and brokers, there's enough range in rates and fees to make shopping around worth a few local phone calls.

Another option is automatic teller machines (ATMs). These are more commonplace and convenient than banks and permit you to make dol-

FOREIGN EXCHANGE BROKERS

Exchange rates are quite competitive from one company to the next, typically varying by no more than one percent. But, if you want to be sure you get the best deal, do a little comparison shopping by telephone.

AMERICAN EXPRESS TRAVEL SERVICES

Fee ($1) charged for exchanging currency; 10 major currencies accepted. American Express traveler's checks are cashed for free; no other brands are accepted.

Offices:
1 Court St., downtown Boston, tel. (617) 723-3077; open Mon.-Fri.
39 JFK St., Harvard Square, Cambridge, tel. (617) 349-1818; open Mon.-Sat.

THOMAS COOK CURRENCY SERVICES

Fee ($4 or 2%, whichever is greater) charged for either exchanging currency or cashing traveler's checks; 120 currencies accepted. Fee is waived on Thomas Cook checks.

Office:
399 Boylston St., Back Bay, tel. (800) 287-7362 or, in Canada, (800) 561-4212; open Mon.-Sat.

BANKBOSTON

Fee (the greater of $2.50 or 1%) charged on all foreign currencies or traveler's checks. All major brands of dollar-denominated checks are cashed for free.

Offices include:
1414 Mass Ave., Harvard Square, Cambridge, tel. (617) 556-6050; open Mon.-Sat.
175 Federal St., downtown Boston, tel. (617) 788-5000; open Mon.-Fri.
Logan Airport, Terminal C, tel. (617) 569-1172; open daily
Logan Airport, Terminal E, tel. (617) 567-2313; open daily

USTRUST

Flat fee ($2) charged on foreign currencies, principally those of Canada, Japan, and Western Europe.

Offices include:
30 Court St., Government Center, tel. (617) 726-7152; open Mon.-Fri. (over 20 foreign currencies accepted)
92 State St., near Faneuil Hall, tel. (617) 720-5724; open Mon.-Fri.
535 Boylston St., Copley Square, tel. (617) 726-7075; open Mon.-Sat.
671 Mass. Ave., Central Square, Cambridge, tel. (617) 497-6070; open Mon.-Sat.

Massachusetts Bay coins

Statewide sales tax on all goods, except food and clothing, is five percent, while lodging tax is 12.45% in Boston, Brookline, Cambridge, and Worcester; 4.7-9.7% elsewhere. B&Bs with three or fewer rooms are tax-free.

lar cash advances against your Visa or Master-Card—or to make withdrawals from your home bank account if you carry a Cirrus- or Plus-affiliated debit card.

Be aware that different brands of traveler's checks are *not* treated equal if they're in the denominations of your own national currency. BankBoston and the Thomas Cook Foreign Exchange office in Boston will accept all major brands, but American Express representatives will only cash their own. Foreign-denominated checks are cashed for free only by local affiliates of the issuer—and only AmEx has a large number of such offices outside of Greater Boston. By the way, Thomas Cook Travel and Thomas Cook Foreign Exchange are related but wholly distinct entities, although the distinction is blurred by the fact that in other parts of the country Cook Exchange facilities are inside Cook Travel storefronts. American banking regulations prohibit Cook Travel from taking your foreign currency or checks—although their many offices certainly can help expedite the paperwork if you need emergency assistance with replacing lost or stolen Thomas Cook traveler's checks.

ATMs

With the exception of the Boston Harbor Islands, every attraction and restaurant in this book is within a few blocks of an ATM. Most belong to the Cirrus, Plus, and NYCE banking networks. For the moment Boston is blissfully free of the odious practice of adding a surcharge for users who aren't account holders with a given ATM's proprietor, and if consumer advocates have their way, the Massachusetts legislature will possibly have banned such fees statewide by the time you read this. In any event, machines that *do* apply these charges are required to carry prominent notices to that effect, or to alert you before you consummate your transaction, so at least you needn't worry about being charged unknowingly.

Tipping

Who to tip? When to tip? How much to tip? These are questions even most Americans puzzle over, but no other act, or lack of action, can arouse quite the same level of friendliness, or contempt, in a waitperson.

Generally, 15% of your restaurant bill (to be precise, your bill including all drinks but before tax) is the minimum acceptable tip; 18-20% is otherwise standard. Larger tips are certainly okay for extraordinary service—did the staff go out of the way to make your visit pleasant?—and highly appreciated. Smaller tips (or no tip) are also acceptable in the case of very poor service.

Also keep an eye out for tip jars. Many cafes, coffeehouses, and ice cream shops that don't provide table service leave a jar or can on the counter for gratuities. In such cases, tipping is far more discretionary than at a sit-down restaurant. As for fast food outlets—McDonald's, Taco Bell, Au Bon Pain, etc.—tipping is entirely unnecessary.

Remember, tips are a way for you to express your level of satisfaction with the service, not a right.

Hotel desk clerks and restaurant hosts can be tipped when some special service is performed (special table, reservations on short/no notice), but otherwise not. Taxi drivers usually receive a 15% tip, though again, your tip can reflect the length of your ride, and the driver's attitude.

COMMUNICATIONS AND MEASUREMENTS

Mail

There are **post offices** throughout the city, most open weekdays 9 a.m.-5 p.m. and Saturdays until noon or 2 p.m. Selected high-volume branches stay open later (for example, the Harvard Square branch handles stamp sales weekdays until 7:30 p.m., Saturdays till 5 p.m.), but if the itch to write home strikes at a truly odd hour, head down to Boston's general mail facility, tel. (617) 451-9922, next to South Station: its full-service counter never closes. A first-class letter sent in the continental U.S. will require postage of 32 cents; a postcard is 20 cents.

post rider

For large parcels, the best one-stop shop for packing materials and delivery services is any of the dozen **Mailboxes Etc.** stores around town, which will arrange pickup by any of the major private couriers, from **UPS** to **Federal Express.** FedEx, tel. (800) 463-3339, and **Emery Worldwide,** tel. (800) 443-6379, also have their own network of drop-off centers, most conveniently downtown in the Financial District; call for directions to the nearest one.

Telephone

Public phones are widely available on street corners, outside convenience stores and gas stations. Until quite recently most still only required a dime, but consolidation in the regional phone industry—mergers among the so-called Baby Bells—have brought repeated price hikes. In a curious example of "competitive pressure" forcing prices *up,* the monopolistic local phone company, Bell Atlantic, requires 35 cents to complete local calls at any of its payphones. If you're lucky, you may stumble upon a payphone maintained by one of several third-party phone companies, most of which still charge but 25 cents. Dialing directions are provided on the face of the phone; if necessary press "0" for operator assistance. To place a local toll call (to communities in the 781 or 978 area codes, adjacent to Boston and Cambridge), or a long distance call, simply dial the number and an automated voice will tell you how much money to deposit. Since many of long distance service providers lurking behind otherwise identical-looking payphones

take great delight in absolutely fleecing unwary phone users, calling collect to anyone anywhere at any time is highly inadvisable without first dialing an access code that routes your call through a competitve, trustworthy service provider whose rates are familar to you. Alternatively, you can purchase prepaid **phone cards** in varying denominations at virtually every post office, convenience store, and copy shop in town, or even at specially marked ATMs.

In an emergency, when an ambulance, fire-fighters or police are required, you can dial 911 and be instantly connected with an emergency dispatcher; otherwise dial "0" for operator. The dispatcher's computer will track your number and address, enabling the authorities to locate you should the call be cut off, or if you hang up. (Standard procedure in Boston requires sending a police patrol car to confirm you weren't co-erced into ending the call, so even if you dial 911 in error, cops show up anyway.)

Since telephone directories are rarely available at public phone booths in Greater Boston—lobby payphones in upscale hotels are among the sole exceptions—if you need to find a phone number you must dial 411, for directory information.

Photocopying, Faxes, and E-mail

Photocopying and fax services are also nearly ubiquitous, from small mom 'n' pop markets to every copy shop in the city (these last are generally the least expensive and most reliable). Even e-mail isn't hard to find: several coffee-houses have **public Internet access** for a modest hourly charge, including downtown's Boston Globe Store at the corner of Washington and School St., across from the Borders Books superstore; the Cybersmith on Church St. in Harvard Square; and the Barefoot Café on Centre St. in Jamaica Plain. Most Kinko's copy shops around town do, too; look for their 24-hour storefronts next to the Copley Plaza Hotel in Back Bay, across from Government Center downtown, in Post Office Square in the Financial District, and next to the Harvard Square post office.

Newspapers

The mainstream daily *Boston Globe* is the largest-circulation paper in the region and worth picking up on Thursdays for the "Calendar" section, which offers a preview of the coming week's

*New England
Telephone operators,
circa 1915*

events and activities. A subsidiary of the *New York Times,* the *Globe* fits well within its parent organization's conservative respectability; newcomers to its pages will find only faint traces of the liberalism that Kennedy-bashers might imagine and expect. At least it has some very good investigative stories on occasion, which is vastly more than can be said of most of the competition. The large, highly educated young demographic in the city would seem ideally suited to support a thriving alternative press, but, judging from the content of the various weeklies, informative journalism takes a back seat to personal ads and movie reviews, executive career moves, and society gossip. Visitors accustomed to the tradition of provocative alternative free weeklies such as are found in cities coast to coast will be disappointed to find the most provocative content in the local variant, the *Phoenix,* is its massive quantity of adult escort and phone-sex ads—which apparently make an insufficient subsidy, since the cover price is $1.50. (Similar editions *are* available free in Worcester and Providence, RI.) Still, the *Phoenix,* which hits newsstands on Thursdays, offers the most comprehensive band listings for clubhoppers keen to catch a few gigs by local musicians.

Radio
When it comes to radio, Boston displays a bit

more evidence that it values diversity, vitality, and experimentation. The usual range of adult-oriented album rock, oldies, Top 40, and AM talk radio occupy much of the dial, but among the local FM stations are not one but two NPR affiliates (the classical-music-minded **WGBH 89.7** and the all-news **WBUR 90.9,** the home of "Car Talk") plus several college stations upholding their breed's national reputation for independence and nonconformity. Tune in to **WZBC 90.3** from Boston College for the best dose of truly alternative musical programming, or sample some of the runners-up: **WMFO 91.5,** from Tufts University, and **WMBR 88.1,** from MIT. (WMBR is also where devotees of Pacifica News will find their favorite alternative to the mainstream media, weekdays at 5 p.m.) Folk and acoustic listeners should turn the dial to the University of Massachusetts's station, **WUMB 91.9,** or, for a mix of acoustic, bluegrass, and classical, listen in on Harvard University's **WHRB 95.3.** None of these college stations have very strong signals, so your hotel's bedside radio or that Walkman you wear while jogging may be inadequate, but it's worth a try.

Measurements
Except for some beverage containers and nutritional information labels on packaged food, the metric system is just about nonexistent in Mass-

achusetts. For help converting from the modified English measuring system, consult the conversion table at the back of this book.

Electricity

Electric current is 110-120 volts, 60-cycle; appliances manufactured for use in most Asian and European countries will need an adaptor to operate safely outside their typical system of 220-240 volt, 50-cycle current, as well as a plug adaptor for the flat two-pin style of the U.S. plug.

Business Hours

Hours vary depending on the type of business. Generally speaking banks are open Mon.-Fri. 9 a.m.-5 p.m., although most of Boston major consumer banks also open their neighborhood branches—and select locations in downtown and Back Bay—for a half day Saturday. Other public and private businesses keep the general hours of 9 a.m.-5 p.m. daily, though hours will vary. Many retail stores are open extended hours, particularly around such popular shopping venues as Copley Square, Newbury Street, and Harvard Square. Many convenience stores (Store 24, Christy's, Seven-Eleven), some "super" supermarkets (Super Stop & Shop, Super Star Market), a few gas stations, and all Kinko's copy shops stay open around the clock. When in doubt, call ahead and confirm hours of operation.

Holidays

Certain public holidays in the U.S. you can bet will shut down the whole country (Christmas Day, New Year's Day, July 4th, and Thanksgiving, the fourth Thursday in November). Others only affect private businesses, banks, government offices, mail and package delivery services, and schools. Retail stores, on the other hand, typically stay open, often with special holiday sales and extended hours. These legal holidays, which whenever possible are observed on a Monday or Friday to create a three-day weekend, include the following: New Year's Day (January 1); Rev. Martin Luther King Jr.'s birthday (third Monday in January); Presidents' Day (third Monday in February); Memorial Day (last Monday in May); Labor Day (first Monday in September); Columbus Day (second Monday of October); and Veterans' Day (November 11).

Additionally, the City of Boston observes three other holidays, which only affect municipal workers (including parking meter enforcers, hurrah!) and the Boston Public Library: Patriots Day (April 19, observed the third Monday of April); Evacuation Day (March 17, coincidentally Saint Patrick's Day); and Bunker Hill Day (observed by the city on the Friday closest to June 17, but the National Park Service parades and reenactments occur on the closest weekend).

Time Zones

Boston functions on eastern standard time, five hours ahead of Greenwich mean time. The sprawling continental U.S. contains four time zones. For a specific breakdown of time zone borders in the rest of the country, consult the map in the local phone books, which contain combination area code/time zone maps in the front. All states, with the exception of Hawaii, convert to daylight saving time from midnight on the first Sunday in April to midnight on the last Sunday in October. Daylight saving time advances the clock one hour across U.S. time zones.

In an emergency, when an ambulance, firefighter, or police are required, dial 911.

APPENDIX

QUICK REFERENCE GUIDE: RESTAURANTS BY CUISINE

All addresses are in Boston unless otherwise noted. Restaurants are listed under more than one heading when appropriate.

AMERICAN, TRIED AND TRUE

Amrhein's, 80 W. Broadway St., South Boston, tel. (617) 268-6189
Buzzy's Fabulous Roast Beef, 327 Cambridge St., tel. (617) 242-7722
Charlie's Sandwich Shoppe, 429 Columbus Ave., tel. (617) 536-7669
Doyle's, 3484 Washington St., Jamaica Plain, tel. (617) 524-2345
Durgin-Park, 5 Faneuil Hall Marketplace, tel. (617) 227-2038
Fuddruckers', 137 Stuart St., tel. (617) 723-3833
Green Dragon Tavern, 11 Marshall St., tel. (800) 543-9002 or (617) 367-0055
IHOP, 500 Commonwealth Ave., tel. (617) 859-0458
Kelly's World Famous Roast Beef, 410 Revere Beach Blvd., Revere, tel. (781) 284-9129
Marshall's, 15 Union St., tel. (617) 523-9396
Mr. and Mrs. Bartley's Burger Cottage, 1246 Mass. Ave., Cambridge, tel. (617) 354-6559
The Paramount, 44 Charles St., tel. (617) 720-1152
Redbones, 55 Chester St., Somerville, tel. (617) 628-2200
The Rosebud Diner, 381 Summer St., Somerville, tel. (617) 666-6015
Sorella's, 388 Centre St., Jamaica Plain, tel. (617) 524-2016
Warren Tavern, 2 Pleasant St., Charlestown, tel. (617) 241-8142

AMERICAN, CONTEMPORARY OR ECLECTIC

Biba, 272 Boylston St., tel. (617) 426-7878
Black Crow Caffé, 2 Perkins St., Jamaica Plain, tel. (617) 983-2747
Centre Street Cafe, 669A Centre St., Jamaica Plain, tel. (617) 524-9217
Claremont Cafe, 535 Columbus Ave., tel. (617) 247-9001
East Coast Grill & Raw Bar, 1271 Cambridge St., Cambridge, tel. (617) 491-6568
Gargoyles, 215 Elm St., Somerville, tel. (617) 776-5300
Henrietta's Table, The Charles Hotel, 1 Bennett St., Cambridge, tel. (617) 864-1200
Johnny D's Up-Town Restaurant & Music Club, 17 Holland St., Somerville, tel. (617) 776-2004
Metropolis Cafe, 584 Tremont St., tel. (617) 247-2931
Mildred's, 552 Tremont St., tel. (617) 426-0008
North East Brewing Company, 1314 Comm. Ave., Allston, tel. (617) 566-6699
Parish Cafe, 361 Boylston St., tel. (617) 247-4777
Rialto, The Charles Hotel, 1 Bennett St., Cambridge, tel. (617) 661-5050
Santa Barbara Cafe, 1 Arrow St., Cambridge, tel. (617) 547-5508

AMERICAN, CONTEMPORARY OR ECLECTIC (cont.)

75 Chestnut, 75 Chestnut St., tel. (617) 227-2175
Sonsie, 327 Newbury St., tel. (617) 351-2500
Small Planet Bar and Grill, 565 Boylston St., tel. (617) 536-4477
Tallulah's Tap & Grille, 65 Holland St., Somerville, tel. (617) 628-0880
The Tam O'Shanter, 299 Harvard St., Brookline, tel. (617) 277-0982
Tremont 647, 647 Tremont St., tel. (617) 266-4600

BAKERIES

Biga Breads Cafe, 197 Eighth St., Charlestown Navy Yard, tel. (617) 242-1006
Biscotti Pasticceria, 95 Salem St., tel. (617) 227-8365
Bova's Bakery, 76 Prince St., tel. (800) 965-7217 or (617) 523-5601
Carberry's Bakery & Coffee House, 74 Prospect St., Cambridge, tel. (617) 576-3530
Hing Shing Bakery, 67 Beach St., tel. (617) 451-1162
Japonaise Bakery, 1020 Beacon St., Brookline, tel. (617) 566-7730
Kam Lung Bakery, 77 Harrison Ave., tel. (617) 542-2229
Mike's Pastry, 300 Hanover St., tel. (617) 742-3050
Modern Pastry Shop, 257 Hanover St., tel. (617) 523-3783
Rosie's Bakery, 2 South Station, tel. (617) 439-4684
Sorelle Bakery Cafe, 1 Monument Ave., Charlestown, tel. (617) 242-2125

BARBECUE

East Coast Grill & Raw Bar, 1271 Cambridge St., Cambridge, tel. (617) 491-6568
Redbones, 55 Chester St., Somerville, tel. (617) 628-2200

BRAZILIAN

Buteco, 130 Jersey St., tel. (617) 247-9508
Café Brazil, 421 Cambridge St., Allston, tel. (617) 789-5980

BREWPUBS, OR EXCEPTIONAL BEER MENUS

Brew Moon, 115 Stuart St., tel. (617) 523-6467
Doyle's, 3484 Washington St., Jamaica Plain, tel. (617) 524-2345
North East Brewing Company, 1314 Comm. Ave., Allston, tel. (617) 566-6699
Redbones, 55 Chester St., Somerville, tel. (617) 628-2200
Sunset Grill & Tap, 130 Brighton Ave., Allston, tel. (617) 254-1331

CAJUN/SOUTHERN

Bob the Chef, 604 Columbus Ave., tel. (617) 536-6204
Dixie Kitchen, 182 Mass. Ave., tel. (617) 536-3068
Redbones, 55 Chester St., Somerville, tel. (617) 628-2200

CAMBODIAN

Elephant Walk, 900 Beacon St., tel. (617) 247-1500

CARIBBEAN

Legal C Bar and Grille, 27 Columbus Ave., tel. (617) 426-5566
Rhythm & Spice, 315 Mass. Ave., Cambridge, tel. (617) 497-0977

CHINESE

Buddha's Delight, 5 Beach St., tel. (617) 351-2395
Buddha's Delight Too, 404 Harvard St., Brookline, tel. (617) 739-8830
Chef Chang's House, 1006 Beacon St., Brookline, tel. (617) 277-4226
Chef Chow's House, 230 Harvard St., Brookline, tel. (617) 739-2469
China Pearl, 9 Tyler St., tel. (617) 426-4338
Chinatown Cafe, 262 Harrison St., tel. (617) 695-9888
Chinatown Eatery, 44-46 Beach St., no phone
East Ocean City, 25-29 Beach St., tel. (617) 542-2504
Emperor Garden Restaurant (aka Empire Garden), 690 Washington St.,
   tel. (617) 482-8898
Golden Palace, 14 Tyler St., tel. (617) 423-4565
Grand Chau Chow Seafood, 41-45 Beach St., tel. (617) 292-5166
Hing Shing Bakery, 67 Beach St., tel. (617) 451-1162
Jumbo Seafood Restaurant, 7 Hudson St., tel. (617) 542-2823
Kam Lung Bakery, 77 Harrison Ave., tel. (617) 542-2229
Mary Chung Restaurant, 464 Mass. Ave., Cambridge, tel. (617) 864-1991
Shalom Hunan, Harvard St., Brookline, tel. (617) 731-9760

CHOCOLATE

Cafe Fleuri, Le Meridien Hotel, tel. (617) 451-1900
Teuscher of Switzerland, 230 Newbury St., tel. (617) 536-1922

COFFEEHOUSES AND HANGOUTS

Cafe Algiers, 40 Brattle St., Cambridge, tel. (617) 492-1557
Cafe Pamplona, 12 Bow St., Cambridge, no phone
Cafe Paradiso, 1 Eliot Square, Cambridge, tel. (617) 868-3240
Caffè dello Sport, 307 Hanover St., tel. (617) 523-5063
Cafe Graffiti, 307 Hanover St., tel. (617) 367-2494
Caffè Paradiso, 255 Hanover St., tel. (617) 742-1768
Carberry's Bakery & Coffee House, 74 Prospect St., Cambridge, tel. (617) 576-3530
Cybersmith, 36 Church St., Cambridge, tel. (617) 492-5857
Hazel's Cup & Saucer, 130 Dartmouth St., tel. (617) 262-4393
The Other Side Cosmic Cafe, 407 Newbury St., tel. (617) 536-9477
Phoenix Coffeehouse, 675 Mass. Ave., Cambridge, tel. (617) 547-2255
Someday Cafe, 51 Davis Square, Somerville, tel. (617) 623-3323
Starbucks, everywhere
Tar Bar, 4 Columbus Ave., tel. (617) 423-7283
Tealuxe, 0 Brattle St., Cambridge, tel. (617) 441-0077
1369 Cafe, 757 Mass. Ave., Cambridge, tel. (617) 576-4600
Trident Booksellers & Cafe, 338 Newbury St., tel. (617) 267-888

CUBAN

El Oriental de Cuba, 416 Centre St., Jamaica Plain, tel. (617) 524-6464
Mucho Gusto Cafe & Collectibles, 1124 Boylston St., tel. (617) 236-1020

DELI COUNTERS OR MARKET TAKE OUT

Bay State Lobster Company, 395 Commercial St., tel. (617) 523-7960
Darwin's Ltd., 148 Mt. Auburn St., Cambridge, tel. (617) 354-5233
DeLuca's Market, 11 Charles St., tel. (617) 523-4343
Savenor's Supermarket, 160 Charles St., tel. (617) 723-6328

ETHIOPIAN-ERITREAN

Asmara, 739 Mass. Ave., Cambridge, tel. (617) 864-7447
Mass Cafe, 605 Mass. Ave., tel. (617) 262-7704

FAST FOOD CHAINS

Au Bon Pain, Harvard Square, Cambridge, tel. (617) 497-9797, and over 30 other locations
Fuddruckers', 137 Stuart St., tel. (617) 723-3833
IHOP, 500 Commonwealth Ave., tel. (617) 859-0458
McDonald's, at Boston Common, Museum Wharf, South Station, Kenmore Square,
    Coolidge Corner, and a couple dozen other locations around town

FRENCH

Ben's Cafe, 45 School St., tel. (617) 227-3370
Elephant Walk, 900 Beacon St., tel. (617) 247-1500
Hamersley's Bistro, 553 Tremont St., tel. (617) 423-2700
Maison Robert, 45 School St., tel. (617) 227-3370

GREEK

Steve's Greek & American Cuisine, 316 Newbury St., tel. (617) 267-1817

ICE CREAM

Ben & Jerry's Ice Cream, 174 Newbury St., tel. (617) 536-5456, and 20 Park Plaza, tel.
    (617) 426-0890
Billings & Stover Apothecaries, 41A Brattle St., tel. (617) 547-0502
Emack & Bolio's Ice Cream, 290 Newbury St., tel. (617) 247-8772
Herrell's Ice Cream, 155 Brighton Ave, Allston, tel. (617) 782-9599, and 15 Dunster St.
    (Harvard Square), Cambridge, tel. (617) 497-2179
J P Licks Homemade, 659 Centre St., Jamaica Plain, tel. (617) 524-6740; 311A Harvard St.
    (Coolidge Corner), Brookline, tel. (617) 738-8252; and 352 Newbury St. (Back Bay), tel.
    (617) 236-1666
Steve's Ice Cream, Faneuil Hall Marketplace, tel. (617) 367-0569
Toscanini's Ice Cream, 899 Main St., Cambridge, tel. (617) 491-5877, and 1310 Mass.
    Ave., Cambridge, tel. (617) 354-9350

INDIAN

Bombay Club, 57 JFK St., Cambridge, tel. (617) 661-8100
Cafe of India, 52A Brattle St., Cambridge, tel. (617) 661-0683
Gandhi, 704 Mass. Ave., Cambridge, tel. (617) 491-1104
India House, 239 Harvard St., Brookline, tel. (617) 739-9300
Indian Globe, 474 Mass. Ave., Cambridge, tel. (617) 868-1866
India Quality Restaurant, 536 Comm. Ave., tel. (617) 267-4499
Rangoli, 129 Brighton Ave., tel. (617) 562-0200

Tandoor House, 569 Mass. Ave., Cambridge, tel. (617) 661-9001
Tanjore, 18 Eliot St., Cambridge, tel. (617) 868-1900

IRISH PUBS

The Black Rose, 160 State St., tel. (617) 742-2286
Brendan Behan Pub, 378 Centre St., Jamaica Plain, tel. (617) 522-5386
The Burren, 247 Elm St., in Davis Square, Somerville, tel. (617) 776-6896
Doyle's, 3484 Washington St., Jamaica Plain, tel. (617) 524-2345
The Druid, 1357 Cambridge St., Cambridge, tel. (617) 497-0965
Grand Canal, 57 Canal St., tel. (617) 523-1112
The Irish Embassy, 234 Friend St., tel. (617) 742-6618
McGann's, 197 Portland St., tel. (617) 227-4059
Mr. Dooley's Boston Tavern, 77 Broad St., tel. (800) 560-5655 or (617) 338-5656
Plough and Stars, 912 Mass. Ave., Cambridge, tel. (617) 441-3455
The Thirsty Scholar, 70 Beacon St., on the Cambridge/Somerville line, tel. (617) 497-2294

ITALIAN

Al Capone's, 102 Broad St., tel. (617) 227-2692
Anchovies, 433 Columbus Ave., tel. (617) 266-5088
Antico Forno, 93 Salem St., tel. (617) 723-6733
Armani Cafe, 214 Newbury St., tel. (617) 437-0909
Artú, 6 Prince St., tel. (617) 742-4336
Biscotti Pasticceria, 95 Salem St., tel. (617) 227-8365
Bova's Bakery, 76 Prince St., tel. (800) 965-7217 or (617) 523-5601
Carlo's Cucina Italiana, 131 Brighton Ave., Allston, tel. (617) 254-9759
The Daily Catch, 323 Hanover St., tel. (617) 523-8567
The Dogwood Café, 3172 Washington St., Jamaica Plain, tel. (617) 522-7997
Figs, 42 Charles St., tel. (617) 742-FIGS
Figs, 67 Main St., Charlestown, tel. (617) 242-2229
Galleria Italiana, 177 Tremont St., tel. (617) 423-2092
Gabriele's, 1 First Ave., Charlestown Navy Yard, tel. (617) 242-4040
Marcuccio's, 125 Salem St., tel. (617) 723-1807
Metropolis Cafe, 584 Tremont St., tel. (617) 247-2931
Mike's Pastry, 300 Hanover St., tel. (617) 742-3050
Modern Pastry Shop, 257 Hanover St., tel. (617) 523-3783
Nicole's, 54 Salem St., tel. (617) 742-6999
Panificio, 144 Charles St., tel. (617) 227-4340
Pizzeria Regina, 11 1/2 Thatcher St., tel. (617) 227-0765
Pomodoro, 319 Hanover St., tel. (617) 367-4348
Ristorante Saraceno, 286 Hanover, tel. (617) 227-5888
Terramia Ristorante, 98 Salem St., tel. (617) 523-3112

JAPANESE AND KOREAN

Arirang, 162 Mass. Ave., tel. (617) 536-1277
Cafe Mami, 1815 Mass. Ave., Porter Square Exchange, Cambridge, tel. (617) 547-9130
Ginza, 14 Hudson St., tel. (617) 338-2261
Ginza, 1002 Beacon St., Brookline, tel. (617) 566-9688

JAPANESE AND KOREAN (cont.)

JP Seafood Cafe, 730 Centre St., Jamaica Plain, tel. (617) 983-5177
Jae's Cafe & Grill, 520 Columbus Ave., tel. (617) 421-9405
Jae's Korean Grill, 212 Stuart St., tel. (617) 451-7788
Japonaise Bakery, 1020 Beacon St., Brookline, tel. (617) 566-7730
Koreana, 154 Prospect St., Cambridge, tel. (617) 576-8661
Kotobukiya, 1815 Mass. Ave., Porter Square Exchange, Cambridge,
    tel. (617) 492-4655
Nara Japanese Cuisine, 85 Wendell St., tel. (617) 338-5935
Sapporo Ramen, 1815 Mass. Ave., Porter Square Exchange, Cambridge,
    tel. (617) 876-4805
Suishaya, Beach St. and Tyler, tel. (617) 423-3848
Tanpopo, 1815 Mass. Ave. in the Porter Square Exchange, Cambridge, tel. (617) 868-5457

KOSHER

Jerusalem Café, 423 Harvard St., Brookline, tel. (617) 278-0200
Milk Street Cafe, 50 Milk St., tel. (617) 542-2433
Shalom Hunan, Harvard St., Brookline, tel. (617) 731-9760
Rami's, 324 Harvard St., Brookline, tel. (617) 738-3577

MALAYSIAN

Pandan Leaf, 250 Harvard St., Brookline, tel. (617) 566-9393
Penang, 685-691 Washington St., tel. (617) 451-6373

MEDITERRANEAN

Cena, 14 Westland Ave., tel. (617) 262-1485

MEXICAN/TEX-MEX

Anna's Taqueria, 1412 Beacon St., Brookline, tel. (617) 739-7300
Baja Mexican Cantina, 111 Dartmouth St., tel. (617) 262-7575
Tacos el Charro, 349 Centre St., Jamaica Plain, tel. (617) 522-2578

MIDDLE EASTERN

Anais, 333 Washington St., second floor, tel. (617) 367-8157
Barefoot Café, 697 Centre St., Jamaica Plain, tel. (617) 983-CAFE
Cafe Jaffa, 48 Gloucester St., tel. (617) 536-0230
Jerusalem Café, 423 Harvard St., Brookline, tel. (617) 278-0200
Rami's, 324 Harvard St., Brookline, tel. (617) 738-3577
Shawarma King, 1383 Beacon St., Brookline, tel. (617) 731-6035
Sultan's Kitchen, 72 Broad St., tel. (617) 728-2828
Zaatar's Oven, 242 Harvard St., Brookline, tel. (617) 731-6836

NEW ENGLAND

Durgin-Park, 5 Faneuil Hall Marketplace, tel. (617) 227-2038
Henrietta's Table, The Charles Hotel, 1 Bennett St., Cambridge, tel. (617) 864-1200

NORTH AFRICAN

Casablanca, 40 Brattle St., Cambridge, tel. (617) 876-0999

PERSIAN

Lala Rokh, 97 Mt. Vernon St., tel. (617) 720-5511

PIZZA

Al Capone's, 102 Broad St., tel. (617) 227-2692

Bella Luna, 405 Centre St., Jamaica Plain, tel. (617) 524-6060

Bertucci's Brick Oven Pizzeria, 21 Brattle St., Cambridge, tel. (617) 864-4748, and Faneuil Hall Marketplace, tel. (617) 227-7889

The Dogwood Café, 3172 Washington St., Jamaica Plain, tel. (617) 522-7997

Emilio's, 536 Tremont St., tel. (617) 423-4083

Figs, 42 Charles St., tel. (617) 742-FIGS

Figs, 67 Main St., Charlestown, tel. (617) 242-2229

Pizzeria Regina, 11^1/$_2$ Thacher St., tel. (617) 227-0765

Pizzeria Uno, Harvard Square, Cambridge, tel. (617) 497-1530; 280 Huntington Ave. (Symphony), tel. (617) 424-1697; and Kenmore Square, tel. (617) 262-4911

PUB GRUB AND WATERING HOLES

Audubon Circle Restaurant, 838 Beacon, tel. (617) 421-1910

The Bull & Finch Pub (a.k.a. Cheers), 84 Beacon St., tel. (617) 227-9605

Doyle's, 3484 Washington St., Jamaica Plain, tel. (617) 524-2345

Marshall's, 15 Union St., tel. (617) 523-9396

Sunset Grill & Tap, 130 Brighton Ave., Allston, tel. (617) 254-1331

Tar Bar, 4 Columbus Ave., tel. (617) 423-7283

PUERTO RICAN

Miami Cafe, 68 Aguadilla St., tel. (617) 859-8105

SANDWICH JOINTS

Anais, 333 Washington St., second floor, tel. (617) 367-8157

Au Bon Pain, Harvard Square, Cambridge, tel. (617) 497-9797, and over 30 other locations around town

Biga Breads Cafe, 197 Eighth St., Charlestown Navy Yard, tel. (617) 242-1006

Buzzy's Fabulous Roast Beef, 327 Cambridge St., tel. (617) 242-7722

Carberry's Bakery & Coffee House, 74 Prospect St., Cambridge, tel. (617) 576-3530

Charlie's Sandwich Shoppe, 429 Columbus Ave., tel. (617) 536-7669

Hazel's Cup & Saucer, 130 Dartmouth St., tel. (617) 262-4393

Kelly's World Famous Roast Beef, 410 Revere Beach Blvd., Revere, tel. (781) 284-9129

Milk Street Cafe, 50 Milk St., tel. (617) 542-2433

The Other Side Cosmic Cafe, 407 Newbury St., tel. (617) 536-9477

Panificio, 144 Charles St., tel. (617) 227-4340

Parish Cafe, 361 Boylston St., tel. (617) 247-4777

Santa Barbara Cafe, 1 Arrow St., Cambridge, tel. (617) 547-5508

Sorelle Bakery Cafe, 1 Monument Ave., Charlestown, tel. (617) 242-2125

Stuff-It, 8^1/$_2$ Eliot St., Cambridge, tel. (617) 497-2220

Sultan's Kitchen, 72 Broad St., tel. (617) 728-2828

The Wrap, 71 Mt. Auburn St., Cambridge, tel. (617) 354-5838

Zaatar's Oven, 242 Harvard St., Brookline, tel. (617) 731-6836

SEAFOOD

Bay State Lobster Company, 395 Commercial St., tel. (617) 523-7960
The Daily Catch, 323 Hanover St., tel. (617) 523-8567
Dolphin Seafood, 1105 Mass. Ave., Cambridge, tel. (617) 661-2937
East Coast Grill & Raw Bar, 1271 Cambridge St., Cambridge, tel. (617) 491-6568
East Ocean City 25-29 Beach St., tel. (617) 542-2504
Ginza, 14 Hudson St., tel. (617) 338-2261
Ginza, 1002 Beacon St., Brookline, tel. (617) 566-9688
Grand Chau Chow Seafood, 41-45 Beach St., tel. (617) 292-5166
JP Seafood Cafe, 730 Centre St., Jamaica Plain, tel. (617) 983-5177
Jumbo Seafood Restaurant, 7 Hudson St., tel. (617) 542-2823
Kelly's World Famous Roast Beef, 410 Revere Beach Blvd., Revere, tel. (781) 284-9129
Kotobukiya, 1815 Mass. Ave. in the Porter Square Exchange, Cambridge,
    tel. (617) 492-4655
Legal C Bar and Grille, 27 Columbus Ave., tel. (617) 426-5566
Legal Seafoods, Park Plaza, 35 Columbus Ave., tel. (5617) 426-4444
Marshall's, 15 Union St., tel. (617) 523-9396
Nara Japanese Cuisine, 85 Wendell St., tel. (617) 338-5935
Skipjack's Seafood Emporium, 500 Boylston St., tel. (617) 536-3500
Suishaya, Beach St. and Tyler, tel. (617) 423-3848

SPANISH

Iruña, 56 JFK St., Cambridge, tel. (617) 868-5633

THAI

Bangkok Cuisine, 177A Mass. Ave., tel. (617) 262-5377
Bangkok House Thai, 50 JFK St., Cambridge, tel. (617) 547-6666
Brown Sugar Cafe, 129 Jersey St., tel. (617) 266-2928
Rod Dee Thai Cuisine, 1430 Beacon St., Brookline, tel. (617) 738-4977

TURKISH

Sultan's Kitchen, 72 Broad St., tel. (617) 728-2828

VEGETARIAN

Buddha's Delight, 5 Beach St., tel. (617) 351-2395
Centre Street Cafe, 669A Centre St., Jamaica Plain, tel. (617) 524-9217
Masao's Kitchen, Porter Square Exchange, Cambridge, tel. (617) 497-7348
Milk Street Cafe, 50 Milk St., tel. (617) 542-2433
Five Seasons, 1634 Beacon St., Brookline, tel. (617) 731-2500
Johnny D's Up-Town Restaurant & Music Club, 17 Holland St., Somerville, tel. (617) 776-2004

VIETNAMESE

Pho Pasteur, 137 Brighton Ave., Allston, tel. (617) 783-2340, and 35 Dunster St., Cambridge, tel. (617) 864-4100
Sài Gòn, 431 Cambridge St., Allston, tel. (617) 254-3373
Viet Hông, 182 Brighton Ave., Allston, tel. (617) 254-3600
V. Majestic, 164 Brighton Ave., Allston, tel. (617) 782-6088

ACCOMMODATIONS BY PRICE (HIGH SEASON)

BUDGET: UNDER $35

BeanTown Hostel, 222-224 Friend St., tel. (617) 723-0800, e-mail BeanTown@aol.com
Hostelling International Boston, 16 Hemenway, tel. (617) 536-1027
Irish Embassy Hostel, 232 Friend St., tel. (617) 973-4841, e-mail EmbassyH@aol.com

INEXPENSIVE: $35-60

Boston YMCA, 316 Huntington Ave., tel. (617) 536-7800 (late June to September only)

MODERATE: $60-85

Anthony's Town House, 1085 Beacon St. in Brookline, tel. (617) 566-3972
Beacon Street Guest House, 1047 Beacon St. in Brookline, tel. (800) 872-7211 or (617) 232-0292
Constitution Inn at the Armed Forces YMCA, 150 Second Ave., in the Charlestown Navy Yard, tel. (800) 495-9622 or (617) 241-8400
Farrington Inn, 23 Farrington St. in Allston, tel. (800) 76-SLEEP or (617) 787-1860, or from the U.K., tel. (0800) 896-040
Four Seasons B&B, 15 Madoc St., Newton, tel. (617) 928-1128

EXPENSIVE: $85-110

A Friendly Inn at Harvard Square, 1673 Cambridge St., Cambridge, tel. (617) 547-7851
Hotel Buckminster, 645 Beacon St., tel. (800) 727-2825 or (617) 236-7050
Prospect Place, Central Square, Cambridge, tel. (800) 769-5303 or (617) 864-7500
Susse Chalet Inn—Cambridge, 211 Concord Turnpike (Rt. 2), tel. (800) 258-1980 or (617) 661-7800
Taylor House B&B, Jamaica Plain, tel. (888) 228-2956 or (617) 983-9334, e-mail taylorbb@ziplink.net

PREMIUM: $110-150

The Bertram Inn, 92 Sewall Ave., Brookline, tel. (800) 295-3822 or 566-2234, Web site www.bertraminn.com
Best Western Terrace Motor Lodge, 1650 Commonwealth Ave., Brighton, tel. (800) 528-1234 or (617) 566-6260
The College Club, 44 Commonwealth Ave., tel. (617) 536-9510
Copley House, 239 W. Newton St., tel. (800) 331-1318 or (617) 236-8300
The Copley Inn, 19 Garrison St., tel. (800) 232-0306 or (617) 236-0300
Days Inn, 1234 Soldiers Field Rd., Allston, tel. (800) 325-2525 or (617) 254-1234
The Eliot & Pickett Houses, 6 Mt. Vernon Pl., tel. (617) 248-8707, e-mail P&E@uua.org
Howard Johnson Inn—Boston/Fenway, 1271 Boylston St., tel. (800) I-GO-HOJO or (617) 267-8300
Irving House, 24 Irving St., Cambridge, tel. (800) 854-8249 out of state, or (617) 547-4600 locally
John Jeffries House, 14 Embankment Rd., tel. (617) 367-1866
Mary Prentiss Inn, 6 Prentiss St., Cambridge, tel. (617) 661-2929
Newbury Guest House, 261 Newbury St., tel. (800) 437-7668 or (617) 437-7666
Shawmut Inn, 280 Friend St., tel. (800) 350-7784 reservations, (617) 720-5544 information

LUXURY: $150+

Back Bay Hilton, 40 Dalton St., tel. (800) 874-0663 or (617) 236-1100

Best Western Homestead Inn, 220 Alewife Brook Parkway, tel. (800) 528-1234 or (617) 491-8000

Boston Harbor Hotel, 70 Rowes Wharf, tel. (800) 752-7077 or (617) 439-7000

Boston Park Plaza Hotel, 64 Arlington St., tel. (800) 225-2008 or (617) 426-2000

The Charles Hotel in Harvard Square, 1 Bennett St., Cambridge, tel. (800) 882-1818 or (617) 864-1200

Clarendon Square B&B, tel. (617) 536-2229, e-mail ClarSqrBnB@aol.com

The Colonnade Hotel, 120 Huntington Ave., tel. (800) 962-3030 or (617) 424-7000

Copley Square Hotel, 47 Huntington Ave., tel. (800) 225-7062 or (617) 536-9000

The Eliot Hotel, 370 Comm. Ave., tel. (800) 44-ELIOT or (617) 267-1607

The Fairmont Copley Plaza, 138 St. James St., tel. (800) 527-4727 or (617) 267-5300

Four Seasons Hotel, 200 Boylston St., tel. (800) 332-3442 or (617) 338-4400

Holiday Inn Boston—Logan Airport, 225 McClellan Hwy. (Rt. 1A), tel. (800) HOLIDAY or (617) 569-5250

Isaac Harding House, 288 Harvard St., Cambridge, tel. (617) 876-2888

Le Meridien Boston, 250 Franklin St., tel. (800) 543-4300 or (617) 451-1900

The Lenox Hotel, 710 Boylston St., tel. (800) 225-7676 or (617) 536-5300

Radisson Hotel Boston, 200 Stuart St., tel. (800) 333-3333 or (617) 482-1800

Ramada Inn Logan Airport, 75 Service Rd., Logan International Airport, tel. (800) 228-3344 or (617) 569-9300

The Ritz-Carlton, 15 Arlington St., tel. (800) 241-3333 or (617) 536-5700

Royal Sonesta Hotel, 5 Cambridge Parkway, Cambridge, tel. (800) SONESTA or (617) 491-3600

Seaport Hotel & Conference Center, Seaport Lane (off Northern Ave.), South Boston, tel. (800) WTC-HOTEL

Tremont House Boston, a Wyndham Grand Heritage Hotel, 275 Tremont St., tel. (800) 331-9998 or (617) 426-1400

University Park Hotel at MIT, 20 Sidney St., tel. (800) 222-8733 or (617) 577-0200

The Westin Hotel, Copley Place, 10 Huntington Ave., tel. (800) 228-3000 or (617) 262-9600

ACCOMMODATIONS BY LOCATION

AIRPORT VICINITY

Holiday Inn Boston—Logan Airport, 225 McClellan Hwy. (Rt. 1A), tel. (800) HOLIDAY or (617) 569-5250—luxury

Ramada Inn Logan Airport, 75 Service Rd., Logan International Airport, tel. (800) 228-3344 or (617) 569-9300—luxury

BEACON HILL AND THE WEST END

BeanTown Hostel, 222-224 Friend St., tel. (617) 723-0800, e-mail BeanTown@aol.com—budget

The Eliot & Pickett Houses, 6 Mt. Vernon Pl., tel. (617) 248-8707, e-mail P&E@uua.org—premium

Irish Embassy Hostel, 232 Friend St., tel. (617) 973-4841, e-mail EmbassyH@aol.com—budget

John Jeffries House, 14 Embankment Rd., tel. (617) 367-1866—premium

Shawmut Inn, 280 Friend St., tel. (800) 350-7784 reservations, (617) 720-5544 information—premium

DOWNTOWN AND WATERFRONT

Boston Harbor Hotel, 70 Rowes Wharf, tel. (800) 752-7077 or (617) 439-7000—luxury

Le Meridien Boston, 250 Franklin St., tel. (800) 543-4300 or (617) 451-1900—luxury

Radisson Hotel Boston, 200 Stuart St., tel. (800) 333-3333 or (617) 482-1800—luxury

Seaport Hotel & Conference Center, Seaport Lane (off Northern Ave.), South Boston, tel. (800) WTC-HOTEL—luxury

Tremont House Boston, a Wyndham Grand Heritage Hotel, 275 Tremont St., tel. (800) 331-9998 or (617) 426-1400—luxury

CHARLESTOWN

Constitution Inn at the Armed Forces YMCA, 150 Second Ave., in the Charlestown Navy Yard, tel. (800) 495-9622 or (617) 241-8400—moderate

PARK PLAZA

Boston Park Plaza Hotel, 64 Arlington St., tel. (800) 225-2008 or (617) 426-2000—luxury

Four Seasons Hotel, 200 Boylston St., tel. (800) 332-3442 or (617) 338-4400—luxury

BACK BAY

Back Bay Hilton, 40 Dalton St., tel. (800) 874-0663 or (617) 236-1100—luxury

The College Club, 44 Commonwealth Ave., tel. (617) 536-9510—premium

The Colonnade Hotel, 120 Huntington Ave., tel. (800) 962-3030 or (617) 424-7000—luxury

Copley House, 239 W. Newton St., tel. (800) 331-1318 or (617) 236-8300—premium

The Copley Inn, 19 Garrison St., tel. (800) 232-0306 or (617) 236-0300—premium

Copley Square Hotel, 47 Huntington Ave., tel. (800) 225-7062 or (617) 536-9000—luxury

The Eliot Hotel, 370 Comm. Ave., tel. (800) 44-ELIOT or (617) 267-1607—luxury

The Fairmont Copley Plaza, 138 St. James St., tel. (800) 527-4727 or (617) 267-5300—luxury

BACK BAY (cont.)

The Lenox Hotel, 710 Boylston St., tel. (800) 225-7676 or (617) 536-5300—luxury
Newbury Guest House, 261 Newbury St., tel. (800) 437-7668 or (617) 437-7666—premium
The Ritz-Carlton, 15 Arlington St., tel. (800) 241-3333 or (617) 536-5700—luxury
The Westin Hotel, Copley Place, 10 Huntington Ave., tel. (800) 228-3000 or (617) 262-9600—luxury

SOUTH END

Boston YMCA, 316 Huntington Ave., tel. (617) 536-7800 (late June to September only)—inexpensive
Clarendon Square B&B, tel. (617) 536-2229, e-mail ClarSqrBnB@aol.com—luxury

FENWAY

Hostelling International Boston, 16 Hemenway, tel. (617) 536-1027—budget
Hotel Buckminster, 645 Beacon St., tel. (800) 727-2825 or (617) 236-7050—expensive
Howard Johnson Inn—Boston/Fenway, 1271 Boylston St., tel. (800) I-GO-HOJO or (617) 267-8300—premium

JAMAICA PLAIN

Taylor House B&B, tel. (888) 228-2956 or (617) 983-9334, e-mail taylorbb@ziplink.net—expensive

ALLSTON-BRIGHTON

Best Western Terrace Motor Lodge, 1650 Commonwealth Ave., Brighton, tel. (800) 528-1234 or (617) 566-6260—premium
Days Inn, 1234 Soldiers Field Rd., Allston, tel. (800) 325-2525 or (617) 254-1234—premium
Farrington Inn, 23 Farrington St. in Allston, tel. (800) 76-SLEEP or (617) 787-1860, or, from the U.K., (0800) 896-040—moderate

BROOKLINE

Anthony's Town House, 1085 Beacon St., tel. (617) 566-3972—moderate
Beacon Street Guest House, 1047 Beacon St., tel. (800) 872-7211 or (617) 232-0292—moderate
The Bertram Inn, 92 Sewall Ave., tel. (800) 295-3822 or 566-2234, Web site www.bertraminn.com—premium

CAMBRIDGE

Best Western Homestead Inn, 220 Alewife Brook Parkway, tel. (800) 528-1234 or (617) 491-8000—luxury
The Charles Hotel in Harvard Square, 1 Bennett St., tel. (800) 882-1818 or (617) 864-1200—luxury
A Friendly Inn at Harvard Square, 1673 Cambridge St., tel. (617) 547-7851—expensive
Irving House, 24 Irving St., tel. (800) 854-8249 out of state, or (617) 547-4600—premium
Isaac Harding House, 288 Harvard St., tel. (617) 876-2888—luxury
Mary Prentiss Inn, 6 Prentiss St., tel. (617) 661-2929—premium
Prospect Place, Central Square, tel. (800) 769-5303 or (617) 864-7500—expensive

Royal Sonesta Hotel, 5 Cambridge Parkway, tel. (800) SONESTA or (617) 491-3600—
luxury
Susse Chalet Inn—Cambridge, 211 Concord Turnpike (Rt. 2), tel. (800) 258-1980 or (617)
661-7800—expensive
University Park Hotel at MIT, 20 Sidney St., tel. (800) 222-8733 or (617) 577-0200—luxury

GREATER BOSTON FESTIVALS AND EVENTS
All events are free unless otherwise noted.

January
Over a number of weeks at the beginning of
the year, the luxurious Boston Harbor Hotel
dispels crème de la crème doldrums with its annual **Boston
Wine Festival,** comprising a series of expert-
guided winetastings and glamorous, expensive dinners. Call (617) 439-7000 for details.

February
The first Friday evening of the month, Boston's
social crème de la crème continue to keep
old Jack Frost firmly at bay by attending the
annual **Anthony Spinazzola Gala Festival of
Food & Wine,** a largely black-tie affair at the
World Trade Center. Proceeds benefit a local
nonprofit organization that promotes culinary
education on the one hand and works to erad-
icate hunger and homelessness on the other.
Call the Anthony Spinazzola Foundation at
(617) 344-4413 for tickets or info.

March
On the Sunday closest to March 17, South
Boston hosts its annual **St. Patrick's Day Parade.** New York City's is larger—so is
Holyoke's, in Massachusett's own Pioneer
Valley—but if your family includes any young
aficionado of fire engines, this one will be a far
better treat, since it seems as if the Boston
Fire Department's entire truck and ladder inventory takes part. Thanks to a little cleverness on the part of James Michael Curley,
St. Patrick's Day itself, March 17, is also a
holiday for all state and city employees who

work within Suffolk County—i.e., Boston. To
make it palatable to the anti-Irish legislators
who had to approve of the measure back in
1938, the holiday *supposedly* celebrates
Evacuation Day—that is, the anniversary of
the British troop withdrawal from Boston during the Revolutionary War. So don't plan to
visit the Boston Public Library this day; it'll be
closed. On the other hand, Boston parking
restrictions take a holiday, too, meaning that
car owners have a 24-hour reprieve from feeding Boston parking meters (Brookline, Cambridge, and other adjacent communities do
not observe this holiday, so their parking regulations remain fully in force).

April
The third Monday of the month is **Patriots
Day,** celebrating colonial armed resistance
to the British at Lexington and Concord back
in 1775. It's also Marathon Day—the Boston
Marathon shares the holiday with the American Revolution. The Olympics-inspired foot-
race and reenactments of Paul Revere's and
William Dawes's rides both begin mid-morn-
ing. The MetroWest area also hosts battle
reenactments on April 19; call (617) 536-4100
for more information.

May
The month begins with the annual **Harvard
Square Book Festival,** tel. (617) 876-0786,
which rouses hibernating synapses with a
week of authors' readings and bookstore ap-

pearances. The festival's free outdoor book fair coincides with Harvard University's **Arts First,** tel. (617) 354-8047, a performance-filled Fri.-Sun. celebration of student and alumni arts, music, and theater. If that's not enough for you, the Harvard Square Business Association shuts down the square to all but foot traffic during its own food-, merchandise-, and fun-filled party, **May Fair,** on the first Sunday. Call (617) 491-3434 for details. Across the river, Boston waits until the third weekend before it finally believes that spring isn't just a hallucination induced by collective cabin fever. That's the Saturday that the **Boston Kite Festival,** tel. (617) 635-4505, brightens the skies over Franklin Park with thousands upon thousands of kites. The day after that, the Arnold Arboretum celebrates springtime with **Lilac Sunday,** tel. (617) 524-1718, showcasing over 400 varieties of these showy flowers.

June

On a Sunday early in June, the **Dragon Boat Festival** brings international competitors to the Charles River near Harvard Square for a day of racing in honor of Qu Yuan (343-277 B.C.), a faithful minister to the King of Chu and exalted Chinese poet (one of the illustrated scrolls of his revered masterpiece, *The Nine Songs,* is in the collection of the MFA). Call the Dragon Boat Line, tel. (617) 426-6500 ext. 778, at the Children's Museum for the specific date.

June 17, the anniversary of the Revolutionary Battle of Bunker Hill, is celebrated in Charlestown with a parade. **Bunker Hill Day** is also another Suffolk County holiday for municipal employees—which means street parking is free all day in Boston.

July

For a solid week leading up to July 4, Boston celebrates its waterfront with **Harborfest.** Brochures listing all the special tours, cruises, parades, concerts, Sunday **Chowderfest,** and the like are available from the various information booths around town, or call (617) 227-1528. On Independence Day itself, a sea of cheerful humanity lines the Charles River with

motor boats and the banks with picnic blankets to hear the Boston Pops Orchestra perform its free annual Esplanade concert, with its climactic bell-ringing, howitzer-thundering, fireworks-exploding rendition of Tchaikovsky's 1812 Overture. Roads along both banks are closed to traffic, but the T runs extra trains. Loudspeakers are strung in trees so even MIT students in Cambridge can sing along with full symphonic accompaniment to that other 1812 wartime composition and Pops standard, "The Star-Spangled Banner." The evening ends with several tons of colorful pyrotechnica being detonated over the assembled crowd, a good half hour of high explosive entertainment visible and audible from almost anywhere around the lower Charles River Basin.

July 14, **Bastille Day,** is celebrated with a block party on Back Bay's Marlborough St. in front of (and inside) the French Library, tel. (617) 266-4351, at 53 Marlborough St. (admission).

July also marks the start of the North End **Italian festivals,** tel. (617) 536-4100, a series of feasts and processions that run sporadically through September, each honoring a different saint or madonna.

August

The second Saturday of the month, the **Cambridge Carnival International,** tel. (617) 661-0457, spices up Central Square with a colorful parade, performance stages, and flavors of both the Caribbean and Latin America. Across the river, the giant **Caribbean Carnival** finishes out the month with an entire week of awards banquets, costume competitions, coronations, and parades through Dorchester (call Shirley Shillingford, tel. 617-534-5832 ext. 111, for details).

Chinatown celebrates the **August Moon Festival,** tel. (617) 542-2574, late in the month with a parade, music, and lucky moon cakes that help usher in an auspicious harvest.

September

The Saturday after Labor Day, tens of thousands of people head down to the banks of the Charles between Harvard's Weld Boathouse and Western Ave. for the **Cambridge River Festival,** tel. (617) 349-4380, comprising music stages, a gospel tent, wandering street performers, a petting zoo, and a block-long gauntlet of ethnic food vendors.

On a midmonth Sunday, the Cambridge **World Fair,** tel. (617) 8868-FAIR, prolongs summer with a hot program of music and food around Central Square, showcasing another typically Cantabrigian range of cultures and tastes.

Autumn in Boston ushers in "open studios" season: nearly every weekend until Thanksgiving finds one or another of the area's various artist associations throwing open their workspace doors to buyers and browsers. The season kicks into full swing in late September with the huge **South End Open Studios,** showcasing the talents of over 200 established and emerging artists throughout the South End (shuttle buses available). Contact the United South End Artists, Inc., P.O. Box 181114, Boston, MA 02118 for specifics, or tel. (617) 262-1803.

October
During the course of a midmonth weekend, the **Fort Point Arts Community Open Studios** draws droves of window-shoppers and would-be art collectors into the studios and galleries of the nearly 300 artists who live or work among the beautiful old warehouses and lofts across the Fort Point Channel from downtown. Call (617) 423-4299 for more info.

In celebration of Halloween, The Revolving Museum transmogrifies for the months of October and November into **Murdock's Haunted House,** tel. (617) 439-8617, a "huge kinetic domain of pleasure, madness, and sensuality." Who said Boston was prudish and predictable?

The second Sunday of the month, a few blocks around Harvard Square are closed off for the annual **Oktoberfest,** tel. (617) 491-3434, with music, food, and lots of streetside shopping. Don't look for fountains of free beer, though—an oompah band is about as close to Munich as it gets. Since it's on a Sunday in a state with stiff blue laws, liquor stores are all closed, too.

The fourth weekend brings the **Head of the Charles Regatta,** tel. (617) 864-8415.

November
For well over a century, an institution in Boston's North End has quietly shunned the aesthetic of the assembly line and devoted itself instead to producing master craftsmen: bookbinders, jewelers, locksmiths, joiners, and makers of fine musical instruments, among others. On Friday and Saturday of the first weekend of November, the widely anticipated **North Bennet Street School Open House,** 39 Bennet St., tel. (617) 227-0155, gives the public a chance to see (and buy) the exquisite, handcrafted results of the students' labors.

December
On December 31, **First Night,** tel. (617) 542-1399, rings in the New Year with a huge panoply of arts and entertainment, including an afternoon Children's Festival, a sunset parade through Back Bay, evening concerts and shop-window performance art, ice sculpting, fireworks over Boston Harbor, and the countdown to midnight at the Custom House Tower clock. Special buttons granting admission to paid events go on sale all over town at the beginning of the month; look for the special displays at local Starbucks, supermarkets, and other retailers. All MBTA trains and buses are free after about 8 p.m.

BOOKLIST

OTHER TRAVEL GUIDES

Association for Public Transportation. *Car-Free in Boston: The Guide to Public Transit in Greater Boston and New England.* Boston: A.P.T., 1995. This handy, regularly updated guide is a boon companion for anyone considering extended travels on bus or rail outside of Boston proper. Available at bookstores, newstands, and selected convenience stores all over Eastern Massachusetts, or by mail from the Association for Public Transportation directly (P.O. Box 1029, Boston, MA 02205, tel. 617-482-0282).

Chesler, Bernice. *In & Out of Boston with & without Children.* Chester, CT: Globe Pequot Press, 1992. If you've got kids, you may feel I've slighted your young ones. You won't feel that way with Chesler's volume (which covers eastern Massachusetts).

Harris, John. *Historic Walks in Old Boston.* Chester, CT: Globe Pequot Press, 1993. If my breezy dollops of history whet your appetite for a more, consider picking up this thoroughly erudite volume, which engagingly recounts what happened behind nearly every doorway of Boston proper—and to whom, and when, and with what consequence.

Sweetser, M. F. *King's Handbook of Boston Harbor.* Boston: Friends of Boston Harbor, Inc. Like the rest of the Moses King Corp.'s series of 19th-century guidebooks, this title is copiously illustrated; thoroughly descriptive; and rich in history, anecdote, and verse (including many sailors' shanties). The final 1888 edition has become a collector's item, but this modern paperback reissue by the Friends of Boston Harbor—a community advocacy group whose volunteers contribute mightily to visitor programs on the Boston Harbor Islands—is readily available in Boston bookstores or directly from the Friends themselves (P.O. Box 9025, Boston, MA 02114, tel. 617-740-4290; ISBN 1557091080).

Waldstein, Mark. *Mr. Cheap's Boston.* Cheshire, CT: Bob Adam's Inc., 1995. Good, extensive listings of everything that can be had for a fair price (or less) around the metro area. Every consumer category you could ask for, plus cheap eats. Not recommended so much for tourists (unless you want to know where to get cheap furniture or auto parts), but for anyone seeking to cut the costs of even temporary residency, this book will pay for itself.

Wilson, Susan. *Boston Sites and Insights.* Boston: Beacon Press, 1994. Thorough, informative, and well-written, this guide (by a *Boston Globe* reporter) lists about 100 Boston-area attractions, from familiar must-see sights to the lesser known, and provides the essential background to each. Recommended.

RECREATION GUIDES

Angiolillo, Paul. *Mountain Biking Southern New England.* Birmingham, AL: Menasha Ridge Press, 1993. A Falcon Guide, one of Dennis Coello's "America by Mountain Bike" series. Thorough, well-organized, informative. Describes 33 rides throughout Massachusetts.

Appalachian Mountain Club. *AMC Massachusetts and Rhode Island Trail Guide.* Boston: Appalachian Mountain Club Books, 1995. Long considered the definitive resource for serious hikers. The density of information is sometimes difficult to navigate, but there's no arguing with its thoroughness. Includes a pocket of topo maps to such popular hiking areas as Mt. Greylock and the Blue Hills.

Stone, Howard. *Short Bike Rides/Eastern Massachusetts.* Chester, CT: Globe Pequot Press, 1997. Though not as descriptive (or digressive) as some of the other suggestions above, this book is sufficiently informative and well-mapped to guide you around a number of scenic and not-too-tiring loop rides throughout the state.

Tougias, Michael. *Exploring the Hidden Charles: a Guide to Outdoor Activities on Boston's Celebrated River.* Boston: Appalachian Mountain Club Books, 1997.

FIELD GUIDES TO ALL THAT BREATHES~AND SOME THINGS THAT DON'T: PLANTS, BIRDS, ANIMALS, ROCKS, ART, AND ARCHITECTURE

Carlock, Marty. *A Guide to Public Art in Greater Boston, from Newburyport to Plymouth.* Boston: The Harvard Common Press, 1993. A detailed, well-organized, and well-written guide to exactly what the title says: public art around Boston and much of eastern Massachusetts. Artists' careers, numerous photos of the works themselves, and precise addresses so that you can find everything. Highly recommended.

Corbett, William. *Literary New England, A History and Guide.* Winchester, MA: Faber and Faber, 1993. Excellent companion for anyone who wants to find out more about the state's (and the region's) connection to the printed word, written by a poet who puts them together quite eloquently himself. Addresses and occasional directions for hard-to-find places are provided for historic sites, graves, and museums accessible to the public and pertinent to the subject. Highly recommended.

Skehan, James William. *Puddingstone, Drumlins, & Ancient Volcanos: a Geologic Field Guide along Historic Trails of Greater Boston.* WesStone Press, 1979.

Southworth, Susan, and Michael Southworth. *AIA Guide to Boston.* Chester, CT: Globe Pequot Press, 1992. Very detailed and authoritative. A worthy companion for architecture aficionados.

FOOD AND LODGING GUIDES

B & J Publications. *Campus Lodging Guide.* P.O. Box 5486, Fullerton, CA 92838-0486. To order this $14.95 publication, call (800) 525-6633 or (714) 525-6683, or visit the publisher's Web site, www.campus-lodging.com, to download a mail-in order form. You don't have to doctor the date on your old student ID to take advantage of these 600-plus U.S. and international college and university lodgings. Availability is highly seasonal (although about 90 offer year-round rooms), but with this guide at hand, you'll have all the information you need to plan a truly budget-friendly vacation. As a bonus, it also includes economy-class motel chains, plus information on home exchanges, inexpensive B&Bs, and other vital trip-planning data. While there are no listings for Boston beyond the YMCAs already covered in the preceding pages, regional travelers will find details for about half a dozen colleges around New England with dorm rooms to spare during the summer months.

Benson, John. *Transformative Adventures, Vacations & Retreats.* Portland, OR: New Millennium Publishing (tel. 503-297-7321), 1994. A national compendium of places that offer special opportunities to rejuvenate your mind, body, and spirit. Over a dozen Massachusetts centers are included, offering everything from macrobiotic clinics to mud baths, Ayurvedic healing to Zen meditation.

Hyman, Mildred. *Elderhostels: The Students' Choice.* Santa Fe, NM: John Muir Publications, 1991. (Publisher's address: P.O. Box 613, Santa Fe NM 87504, tel. 505-982-4078.) State-by-state list of Elderhostel programs, including about a half dozen in Massachusetts. The author surveyed program participants about everything from dorm conditions and food quality to teacher preparedness and overall atmosphere. Provides all essential names and numbers.

Williams, Jim. *The Hostel Handbook.* Self-published; for residents of the U.S. or Canada, send US$4 or C$5 by check or money order (payable to Jim Williams) to 722 Saint Nicholas Ave., New York, NY 10031. International orders are US$6 and must be paid with American Express money orders or traveler's checks drawn on a U.S. bank. E-mail infohostel@aol.com, or visit www.hostels.com/handbook/ for further info. Every hostel in the U.S. and Canada, regardless of affiliation, is listed in this handy pocket reference, which is updated by the author (gregarious owner of New York's Sugarhill Hostel) each winter. Good transportation and safety tips add icing to the cake.

HISTORY

Primary Documents

Apess, William. *On Our Own Ground: The Complete Writings of William Apess, a Pequot.* Edited by Barry O'Connell. Amherst, MA: University of Massachusetts Press, 1992. Apess's was the first Native American autobiography published, in 1829. His writings cover history, politics, and his own life as an Indian who had assimilated well among the English colonists.

Arber, Edward, ed. *Travels and Works of Captain John Smith.* Birmingham, England: English Scholar's Library, 1884. The writings of the man who named New England, and whose map, used by the Mayflower Pilgrims, already contained the name of their settlement—Plimoth—thanks to the arbitrary choice of 10-year-old heir-apparent Prince Charles, with whom Smith wished to gain favor.

Biggar, H.P., ed. *The Works of Samuel de Champlain.* Six-volume work includes the observant French captain's detailed log of his anchorages along the Massachusetts coast during his 1605-8 voyage, with descriptions and harbor chart for the Indian village at Patuxet (which, of course, became the site of the Pilgrims' Plimoth Plantation).

Bradford, William. *Of Plymouth Plantation, 1620-1647.* Edited by Samuel Eliot Morison. New York: Alfred A. Knopf, 1952. The leader and sometime governor of the Pilgrim settlement in Plymouth tells the story in his own inimitable style (helpfully edited, annotated, and indexed by one of the foremost scholars of colonial and maritime history). Unless you have a special interest in Bradford's orthography, no other edition can compare—which is why this one has never gone out of print.

Burrage, Henry S., ed. *Early English and French Voyages, Chiefly From Hakluyt, 1534-1608.* New York: Barnes & Noble, 1959, c. 1906. There were two 16th-century Richard Hakluyts—an uncle and his nephew. Each supported English colonial ventures in the New World. Burrage draws on the younger Hakluyt's 1589 *Principall navigations, voiages, and discoveries of the English nation,* compiled from interviews and first-person accounts. Precolonial Massachusetts and its inhabitants are described by several of the explorers featured.

Heath, Dwight B., ed. *Mourt's Relation.* Bedford, MA: Applewood Books, 1963. First published in 1622 as *A Relation or Journall of the beginning and proceedings of the English Plantation setled at Plimoth in New England, by certaine English Adventurers both Merchants and others* (shortened in 1736 to a title taken from "G. Mourt," unknown signer of the introduction), this volume is believed to have been taken in large part from the letters and journals of Edward Winslow, one of the Pilgrim leaders. Although clearly conceived as a bit of PR on behalf of the widely condemned "Separatists" (it omits, for example, any mention of the settlers' high mortality over their first winter), it is unique in its day-to-day detail, most of which can only have been written on the spot—unlike Bradford's history of the colony's early days, written several decades after the fact.

Higginson, Rev. Francis. "New England Plantation." In *Proceedings of the Massachusetts Historical Society,* 62, pp. 305-321. Boston: The Massachusetts Historical Society, 1929. A description penned in 1630.

Maverick, Samuel. "A Briefe Description of New England." Boston: The Massachusetts Historical Society, *Proceedings of the Massachusetts Historical Society,* 2nd Series, vol. I (1884-5), pp. 231-249. A rather detailed description, dated 1660, by a trader who settled in what's now East Boston several years before John Winthrop and his Puritan flock.

Morton, Thomas. *The New English Canaan.* Annotated by Charles Francis Adams. Boston: Massachusetts Historical Society, 1883. Although roundly excoriated by the Puritans for his moral laxity, Morton is illuminating in his description of the Massachusetts Bay Colony—

this is an account written by an unsympathetic eyewitness. Its accuracy in many details was endorsed by Samuel Maverick (above).

Winthrop, John. *The Journal of John Winthrop, 1630-1649*. Edited by Richard S. Dunn. Cambridge: Belknap Press of Harvard University Press, 1996. The first governor of the Massachusetts Bay Colony, whose painted portrait has become the archetype of Puritan severity, tells his version of the founding of the theocracy whose legacy, some say, endures well unto this day.

Wood, William. *New England's Prospect*. Edited by Alden T. Vaughan. Amherst, MA: University of Massachusetts Press, 1993. The 1634 description of what had only recently been christened "New England," by one of its early English settlers. This was one of the most persuasive accounts—widely consulted by prospective colonists.

Wroth, L.C., ed. *The Voyages of Giovanni de Verrazzano, 1524-1528*. New Haven, CT: Yale University Press, 1970. Includes the Florentine navigator's descriptions of the Massachusetts coast, particularly Martha's Vineyard and Cape Cod (before either island or the commonwealth had those names), written during his attempt to find a sea lane to the Far East.

Native Americans and Indian-Colonial Interaction

Bourne, Russell. *The Red King's Rebellion: Racial Politics in New England, 1675-1678*. New York: Oxford University Press, 1990. An exceptional work on King Philip's War, this book is less concerned with a definitive interpretation of motives (a controversial arena) than with describing the social fabric rent by that conflict—a topic frequently slighted.

Cronon, William. *Changes in the Land: Indians, Colonists and the Ecology of New England*. New York: Hill and Wang, 1983. Articulate and meticulously researched. The curious reader will easily amass a vast additional reading list on its interdisciplinary content—colonial history, Indian history, ecology, anthropology—from the exceptional bibliographic essay that ends this highly recommended, prize-winning book.

Foreman, Carolyn T. *Indians Abroad, 1493-1938*. 1943. Samoset and Squanto, two vital figures in colonial American history, are among the Indians whose experiences as slaves, curiosities, and ambassadors to the Old World are described in this volume.

Jennings, Francis. *The Invasion of America: Indians, Colonialism, and the Cant of Conquest*. New York: W.W. Norton, 1975. One of the major so-called revisionist histories, scrutinizing the motives of the Pilgrim/Puritan migration to these shores. Was war a deliberate strategy to abet land-grabbing (itself a policy stemming from a strict interpretation of Scripture)? Read the evidence in this impressive work.

Russell, Howard S. *Indian New England Before the Mayflower*. Hanover, NH: University Press of New England, 1980. Although it's been criticized for being uninformed about anthropological theory, little else can match this volume's detailed explication of the quotidian life among Native Americans, their farming practices, building styles, social organization, and the like. Contains a well-reasoned rebuff to those who cast doubt on Squanto's teaching the Pilgrims to use fish as fertilizer.

Salisbury, Neal. *Manitow and Providence: Indians, Europeans, and the Making of New England, 1500-1643*. New York: Oxford University Press, 1982. Argues against crediting manifest superiority of Europeans for their success in displacing New England's Native Americans, and gives credit instead to the spread of Western Europe's social and economic revolution to America. Well researched and full of fascinating details culled from primary sources, this book is highly recommended despite at least one minor but highly conjectural interpretation of the historical record.

Simmons, William. *Spirit of the New England Tribes: Indian History and Folklore, 1620-1984*. Hanover, NH: University Press of New England, 1986. Though academic in its rigor (presenting multiple versions of stories to illustrate comparative points), this is possibly the best source of the region's Native American myths and legends in print.

The Revolution

Bailyn, Bernard. *The Ideological Origins of the American Revolution.* Cambridge: Belknap Press of Harvard University Press, 1967. This Pulitzer Prize-winning work has become one of the standard texts on the American Revolution. A generation after publication, it still holds up admirably well, although readers who have grown up with the recent novelistic trends in literary social studies will find the style less lively than what they're accustomed to.

Bobrick, Benson. *Angel in the Whirlwind: the Triumph of the American Revolution.* New York: Penguin Books, 1998. Eminently readable, thorough, and detailed—even without the weight of academic footnotes. George Washington and Benedict Arnold are the contrapuntal figures central to the story, but a large cast of supporting characters puts in memorable appearances as well.

Commager, Henry Steele, and Richard B. Morris, eds. *The Spirit of 'Seventy-Six: The Story of the American Revolution as Told by Participants.* Indianapolis, IN: Bobbs-Merrill, 1958. The authors, distinguished historians, produced a benchmark document in this two-volume anthology, deftly weaving together diaries, letters, affidavits, military reports, and other written miscellany, with just enough introductory notes to give it all a narrative frame. Reprinted by New York's Da Capo Press in 1995.

Cook, Don. *The Long Fuse: How England Lost the American Colonies, 1760-1785.* New York: Atlantic Monthly Press, 1996. In contrast to the usual arguments in favor of wily patriots and their Yankee strategems on and off the battlefield, this volume makes a plausible case for what might be called the predecessor of the Vietnam syndrome. In other words, England's rotten political establishment and inconsistent military will may have been just as critical to American victory as anything done on this side of the Atlantic.

Fischer, David Hackett. *Paul Revere's Ride.* New York: Oxford University Press, 1994. A can't-put-it-down story of that famous silversmith and patriot, brimming with historical anecdotes

about the American Revolution. Some scholars take issue with Fischer's reliance on certain 20th-century sources—for the name of Revere's horse, for example—and question, in general, the degree of importance imputed to Revere, but critiques notwithstanding, this book will provocatively enlighten anyone raised with the standard glossy high-school review of American history.

Labaree, Benjamin Woods. *The Boston Tea Party.* NY: Oxford University Press, 1964. (Reprinted by Northeastern University, 1979.) A definitive examination of one of the most famous events on the road to Revolution.

Langguth, A. J. *Patriots: The Men Who Started the American Revolution.* New York: Simon and Schuster, 1988. This is not a book for readers who love the broad-brush or kid-glove approach to history. Packed with intimate detail, this work breathes life and dimension into events and people who otherwise are but names and phrases memorized in order to pass high school tests. The bitterness of a commander fatally let down by a timid fellow officer; the survival tactics of soldiers on a forced march in wintertime, turning flour sacks into footwear and making soup out of ducks' bones; the legendary strengths and utterly human failings of well-known American heroes; the circumstances behind individual deaths on the battlefield: out of a mountain of such omniscient little snapshots and soundbites comes a powerful sensation of being a true eyewitness to history.

Mackesy, Piers. *The War for America, 1775-1783.* Lincoln, NE: Bison Books, University of Nebraska, 1993. First published in 1964, this exhaustive work by a British military historian is arguably the ultimate reference volume for anyone interested in the battlefield history of the American Revolution, rather than its underlying politics.

Maier, Pauline. *From Resistance to Revolution: Colonial Radicals and the Development of American Opposition to Britain, 1765-1776.* New York: Knopf, 1973. Applying the same nearly x-ray vision more recently applied to the making of the Declaration of Independence, Ms. Maier, an MIT professor of history, here charts the evolution of the ideology that gave birth to a nation.

Middlekauff, Robert. *The Glorious Cause: The American Revolution, 1763-1789.* New York: Oxford University Press, 1986. The second volume in the Oxford History of the United States series, this is a good starting point for would-be students of the Revolution, rich in anecdote and narrative color. It also pays more than average attention to events in England that influenced the initiation of hostilities and the conduct of the war.

Tuchman, Barbara W. *The First Salute.* New York: Knopf, 1988. The Revolution as told by one of history's best narrators, with emphasis on the American patriots' European predecessors, the repercussions throughout the Old World after the Americans' success, and the critical military skills of particular generals and admirals—among them George Washington.

Tyler, John. *Smugglers and Patriots: Boston Merchants and the Advent of the American Revolution.* Boston: Northeastern University Press, 1986. Historians of the Revolution usually fall into two camps, explaining the motivations of America's early rebels in terms of either economic self-interest or pure ideology. Tyler's meticulous analysis reveals the merchant class to be a more politically divided lobby than some historians suggest (notably Arthur Schlesinger Sr., in his influential *The Colonial Merchants and the American Revolution, 1763-1776*), but he also confirms that threats to the livelihoods of many Boston traders are inextricably linked to their patriotism.

Zobel, Hiller B. *The Boston Massacre.* New York: W.W. Norton, 1970. Long before acquiring notoriety as the Boston judge who overturned the jury verdict in the closely watched 1997 trial of a young British nanny accused of murder, Zobel was known to students of American history for two primary achievements: editing John Adams' legal papers, and penning this book. For its clarity, thoroughness, evenhanded treatment of conflicting evidence, and avoidance of legal technicalities, this is the definitive study of one of the most mythic events of the Revolutionary era.

You won't find a better dissection of the massacre, its prelude, and its aftermath.

Other Historical Works

McManis, Douglas. *Colonial New England, a Historical Geography.* New York: Oxford University Press, 1975. An excellent introduction to all aspects of the region's colonial history, from exploration to demographics and commerce.

Morison, Samuel Eliot. *Builders of the Bay Colony.* Boston: Northeastern University Press, 1981. One of the most engaging historical writers in American literature, in my opinion. Written in anticipation of the state Tercentennary, these essays are the best distillation of the record on early Puritan and Pilgrim leaders (all men—alas, women are not considered).

Morison, Samuel Eliot. *The Maritime History of Massachusetts 1783-1860.* Boston: Northeastern University Press, 1979. Another classic, written with a clear love of the sea and sailing.

Porter, Katherine Anne. *The Never-Ending Wrong.* Boston: Little, Brown, 1977. A passionate dissection of the Sacco and Vanzetti case.

Russell, Francis. *A City in Terror: 1919, The Boston Police Strike.* New York: Viking Press, 1975. A detailed recapitulation of a restive era in the history of organized labor, focusing upon the strike that gave conservative Governor Calvin Coolidge the national recognition that took him to the White House. A good, sometimes quite colorful narrative.

Stilgoe, John R. *Common Landscape of America, 1580-1845.* New York: Oxford University Press, 1985. The Harvard professor famous for his undergraduate course on cultural geography (commonly known as "Gas Stations") has a number of sublimely entertaining and seriously informative books to his credit, most of which are recommended. This is one of several that use Massachusetts examples and experiences to illustrate Americans' changing attitudes toward "the traditional arrangement of space and structure," here focusing particularly on the conflict between rural and urban visions.

Willison, George S. *Saints and Strangers.* 1945. The *Mayflower* carried two very different groups of passengers on its 1620 voyage—those whom we now call Pilgrims (and who called themselves "Saints"), and the profit-minded colonists chosen by the "Merchant Adventurers" who financed the whole endeavor to accompany them. The motives, interests, and objectives of these factions are not as uniform as our high-school social studies texts would have had us believe, as this very thorough analysis reveals.

BIOGRAPHY
AND RECOLLECTION

This is an entirely arbitrary sampling of books whose characterizations of the state, in sum or in part, constitute tiny fragments in what could be considered the mosaic of contemporary Massachusetts.

Beatty, Jack. *The Rascal King: The Life and Times of James Michael Curley, 1874-1958.* Reading, MA: Addison-Wesley, 1992. Massachusetts' most colorful politician, James M. Curley was immortalized in Edwin O'Connor's bestselling 1956 novel, *The Last Hurrah,* and its equally successful movie version starring Spencer Tracy. Though virtually adopted as his official biography, both book and film are in fact romanticized views of a life that was in fact *not* his. For the real scoop on the populist mayor, congressman, and governor, check out this thorough biography.

Cohen, Cynthia, ed. *From Hearing My Mother Talk: Stories of Cambridge Women.* Cambridge: The Cambridge Arts Council, 1979. A small treasure, out of print for lack of funding, in which elderly Cantabrigians reminisce about everything from the profound to the profoundly ordinary. The Oral History Center, housed on the campus of Northeastern University, grew out of this work and has published several others, equally fascinating. Contact the OHC at 403 Richards Hall, Northeastern University, Boston, MA 02115 (or call 617-373-4814) to inquire about their availability, or to lobby for reprinting.

Hentoff, Nathaniel. *Boston Boy.* New York: Knopf, 1986. Notable in large part because of its rare glimpse into Boston's jazz scene.

Shand-Tucci, Douglass. *The Art of Scandal: the Life and Times of Isabella Stewart Gardner.* New York: HarperCollins, 1997. Fine, thoroughly researched bio of "Mrs. Jack" Gardner, wife of a Boston Brahmin; mentor and patron of writers, painters, and such other social untouchables as Jews and blacks; loyal Red Sox fan; and an underappreciated influence on the birth of American good taste. The home she designed herself, containing the art she amassed—considered the nation's first great art collection—is now one of Massachusetts's finest museums.

Shand-Tucci, Douglass. *Boston Bohemia, 1881-1900, Ralph Adams Cram: Life and Architecture.* Amherst, MA: University of Massachusetts Press, 1994. Mixing biography (of arguably the nation's finest church architect) with architectural history, this multilayered book also probes the Boston society of Cram's contemporaries, including John Singleton Copley, John Singer Sargent, and Isabella Stewart Gardner. Noteworthy in part for identifying the significant contributions of gays to Boston's cultural Belle Epoque (Cram, the author suggests, was probably a homosexual).

Von Mehren, Joan. *Minerva and the Muse.* Amherst, MA: University of Massachusetts Press, 1995. An acclaimed biography of Margaret Fuller, literary critic and first editor of *The Dial,* the Transcendentalist literary magazine published between 1840 and 1844.

Von Schmidt, Eric, and Jim Rooney. *Baby, Let Me Follow You Down: The Illustrated Story of the Cambridge Folk Years.* Amherst, MA: University of Massachusetts Press, 1994. A comprehensive oral history of one of the most celebrated music scenes in the country.

X, Malcolm, and Alex Haley. *The Autobiography of Malcolm X.* New York: Ballantine Books, 1973. Malcolm X may be remembered more for his ministry within the Nation of Islam, his so-called radical politics, and his assassination, but the foundation of his very public life is inextricably bound up with his often mispent years as Malcolm "Red" Little of Boston, years detailed in this justly famous book. The local jail in which Malcolm served time is long gone, by the way, but the movie used an equally atmospheric substitute: the now-abandoned Charles Street Jail, whose old gray stones still stand between the eponymous Red Line station and Mass. General Hospital.

MISCELLANEOUS

Amory, Cleveland. *The Proper Bostonians.* New York: E.P. Dutton, 1947. You won't find a more engaging portrait of the titular ruling elite of Boston's Brahmin past, told with mostly affectionate wit and humor. The anecdotal descriptions of the city's First Families and their milieu are recommended even now for their ability to illuminate the roots of contemporary Boston folkways, although some of the tales—regarding the colorful Isabella Stewart Gardner, for example—have been proven to be more fable than fact.

Davison, Peter. *The Fading Smile: Poetry in Boston, 1955-1960.* New York: Knopf, 1994. Davison, himself a poet and local editor, reminisces about the poets he knew in the local heyday of that art: Frost, Richard Willbur, L.E. Sissman, Sylvia Plath, Philip Booth, and others.

Hoerr, John P. *We Can't Eat Prestige: The Women Who Organized Harvard.* Philadelphia: Temple University Press, 1997. A timely tale of labor history in modern, anti-union America.

Kurlansky, Mark. *Cod: A Biography of the Fish that Changed the World.* New York: Penguin Books, 1998. A highly readable exploration of one of the economic mainstays of the Bay State.

Lukas, J. Anthony. *Common Ground: A Turbulent Decade in the Lives of Three American Families.* New York: Vintage Books, 1986. A Pulitzer Prize-winning account of three Boston families during the city's school busing crisis of the early 1970s, when the Federal District Court ordered an end to racial segregation in the city's public schools (served as the basis of a four-hour PBS

documentary in 1990). Dramatic events, dramatically told—highly recommended.

McCord, David T.W. *About Boston: Sight, Sound, Flavor and Inflection.* Boston: Little, Brown and Company, 1973. First published in 1948, but still one of the most lyrical introductions to Boston.

Saxenian, AnnaLee. *Regional Advantage: Culture and Competition in Silicon Valley and Route 128.* Cambridge: Harvard University Press, 1994. A careful dissection of the corporate failures of Rt. 128, "America's Technology Highway," and how it lost its hegemony of the high-tech industry to California's Silicon Valley.

Thoreau, Henry David. *Walden.* New York: Bantam Books, 1962 (first published 1854). What, you're visiting Concord and haven't read this? Shame! Get thee to a bookstore or library now!

Whitehill, Walter Muir. *Boston: A Topographical History.* Cambridge: Harvard University Press, 1959. One of the definitive texts on the evolution of Boston's cityscape. Well illustrated, dense with facts, and possibly a little disorientingly specific for the reader unfamiliar with Boston. Still, after a visit, this volume will surely help elucidate the methods to the city's apparent madness.

PUBLISHERS

The following publishers are all highly recommended for consistently offering good nonfiction books on Boston-related topics (a tiny sampling of which appear among the entries above). Contact the publishers directly for complete catalogues of their currently available titles and new releases.

Applewood Books, 128 The Great Road, Bedford, MA 01730, tel. (800) 277-5312 or (781) 271-0055, fax (781) 271-0056, Web site www.awb.com. Reprints works from the 17th and 18th centuries.

Arcadia, 1 Washington Center, Dover, NH 03820, tel. (603) 743-4266, fax 743-4267. Arcadia's "Images of America" series, of town- and neighborhood-specific collections of annotated historical photos, includes numerous entries on

Boston's various neighborhoods, not to mention *Trolleys Under the Hub,* published to coincide with the centennial of the Boston subway.

The University of Massachusetts Press, P.O. Box 429, Amherst, MA 01004, tel. (413) 545-2217, fax 545-1226, Web site www.vyne. com/umasspress/. Although UMass Press titles cover many disciplines of both academic and general interest, and are international in subject, a significant proportion have some connection with Massachusetts.

ACCOMMODATIONS INDEX

RESTAURANT INDEX

GENERAL INDEX

A

Abiel Smith School: 16
A.C. Cruise Line: whalewatching 65
accommodations: 79-90; see also Accommodations
Index
Accommodations Express: 80
acoustic music: 75
activities: film 78; nightclubs and coffeehouses 73-
77; outdoor activities 58-61; performing arts 67-73;
poetry 77-78; spectator sports 61-63; tours 63-67
Adams, John: 142
Adams, Samuel: 22, 24, 129
Adams National Historic Site: 142
African-Americana: Abiel Smith School 16; African
American people 15-16, 38; African Meeting
House 16; Black Heritage Trail 16; Boston African-
American National Historic Site 16; Huntington
Theatre Company 69; Museum of Afro American
History 16; Museum of the National Center for
Afro-American Artists 43; Muhammad's Mosque of
Islam #11 43; see also specific African-American
African Meeting House: 16
Agassiz, Louis: 55
air travel: 148-151

airline toll-free phone numbers: 150
airport transportation: 149-151
airports: Logan International Airport: 26, 148-149
A Joyful Noise: 68
Alan Rohan Crite House Museum: 38
Albee, Edward: 29
Alcott, Louisa May: 14, 131
Algonquian language: 3
Algonquin Club: 21
Alley Cat Lounge: 74
AMC (Appalachian Mountain Club): 17
American Express: 160
American Repertory Theatre: 69
American Revolution: 6; see also historical
attractions; history; specific place; specific person
American Textile History Museum: 126
Amory, Cleveland: 9
anarchists: 11
Anderson Bridge: 33
Appalachian Mountain Club: 17
Arabella: 4
archaeology: 3; King Aspeltas burial chamber 43;
Museum of Fine Arts 40-41; Peabody Museum of
Archaeology and Ethnology 52; Salem Village

ARCHITECTURE AND ARCHITECTS

general discussion: 8
Adams National Historic Site: 142
The Architects Collaborative: 133
Bauhaus school of architecture: 53, 133
Beacon Hill: 14-18
Blackall, Clarence: 29
Brattle Street: 53
Breuer, Marcel: 133
Bulfinch, Charles: 14, 15, 16, 23-24, 50
Charleston: 31
Codman House: 133-134
Commonwealth Avenue Mall: 34
Copley Square: 35-36
Cossutta, Araldo: 37
Emerson, William Ralph: 14
Faneuil Hall: 23-24
The First Church of Christ, Scientist: 37
Gardner-Pingree House: 117
Gehry, Frank: 35
Gibson House Museum: 34

Gropius House: 133
Gropius, Walter: 53, 133
Harvard Yard: 50
Hooper-Lee-Nichols House: 53-54
Le Corbusier: 52
McIntire, Samuel: 117, 118
Moneo, José Rafael: 137
Museum of the National Center for Afro-American
Artists: 43
Park Street Church: 21-22
Pei, I. M.: 37, 40, 44, 57
Richardson, Henry Hobson: 34, 36
Saarinen, Eero: 57
Science Center: 51
Sert, José Luis: 51
Sullivan, Louis: 133
three-deckers: 9
Weisner Building: 57
Wellesley College: 136-137
Wren, Sir Christopher: 30

AUTHORS

CEMETERIES AND BURYING GROUNDS

FESTIVALS AND EVENTS

Goose, Elizabeth Foster: 22
Gould, Robert: 17
Granary Burying Ground: 22
Grand Canal: 75
gratuities: 161
grave rubbings: 22
Great Brook Farm State Park: 126
Great Elm: 20
Great Fire: 8-9
Greater Merrimack Convention & Visitors Bureau: 122
Greenspan, Alan: 26
Green Street Studios: 70
Gropius House: 133
Gropius, Walter: 53, 133

H
hackers: 56-57
Hale, Edward Everett: 43
Hale Reservation: 138
Hancock-Clarke House: 130
Hancock, John: 22, 129

Hancock Tower: 36
Handel & Haydn Society: 71-72
harbor cruises: 65-66
Harbor Express: 121, 143
Harborfest: 178
Harper's Ferry: 76
Harpoon Brewery: 67
Harpoon Brewstock: 67
Harrison Gray Otis House: 15
Hart Nautical Galleries: 57
Harvard Bridge: 33
Harvard Film Archive: 52, 78
Harvard, John: 31, 50
Harvard Library: 50
Harvard Museum of Cultural and Natural History: 52
Harvard Semitic Museum: 52
Harvard Square: 46-55
Harvard Square Book Festival: 178
Harvard University: 5, 8, 47-55
Harvard University Art Museums: 52-53
Harvard University museums: 40

HISTORICAL ATTRACTIONS

Abiel Smith School: 16
Adams National Historic Site: 142
African Meeting House: 16
Armory of the Ancient and Honorable Artillery
    Company: 24
Battle Green: 61, 130
Beaver II: 27
Boston African-American National Historic Site: 16
Boston Common: 20
Boston Harbor Islands National Park Area: 58-59, 60
Boston National Historical Park: 18-19
Boston Stone: 24
Boston Tea Party Ship & Museum: 27
Buckman Tavern: 130
Bunker Hill Monument: 32-33
Codman House: 133-134
Ebenezer Hancock House: 24
Emerson House: 131
Freedom Trail: 18-19
Gropius House: 133
Hancock-Clarke House: 130
Holocaust Memorial: 25
The House of Seven Gables: 118
John Fitzgerald Kennedy Birthplace National
    Historic Site: 44-45
Longfellow National Historic Site: 53
Lowell National Historical Park: 123-124

Minute Man National Historical Park: 128
Munroe Tavern: 130
Museum of Afro American History: 16
New Old South Church: 36
North Bridge: 130-131
The Old Manse: 131
Old North Church: 30
Old Schwamb Mill museum: 61
Old South Meeting House: 8, 22
Old State House: 23
Orchard House: 131
Paul Revere House: 30
Pierce-Hichborne House: 30
Plymouth Rock: 145
Rebecca Nurse Homestead: 119
Robert Gould Shaw Memorial: 17
Salem Maritime National Historic Site: 117
Salem Village Parsonage Archaeological Site: 119
Trinity Church 36
USS *Cassin Young:* 32
USS *Constitution:* 32
Walden Pond State Reservation: 132
The Wayside: 131
The Witch House: 119
Women's Heritage Trail: 19

see also cemeteries and burying grounds; *specific place*

MUSEUMS

REENACTMENTS

Adams National Historic Site: 142
Boston Massacre (at the Old State House): 23
Boston Tea Party: 27
colonial town meetings (at the Faneuil Hall Marketplace): 24
famous people interred in the Granary Burying Ground 22
Mayflower II: 145
Plimoth Plantation: 144-145
Signing of the Declaration of Independence (at the Old State House): 23

Red Sox: 12
Regattabar: 76
Regattabar Jazz Festival: 76
religion: 4-6, 9, 16; *see also* houses of worship
Revere, Paul: 22, 30, 129, 130; Paul Revere House 30; Paul Revere Mall 30
Revolution: *see* American Revolution; New England Revolution (soccer team)
The Revolving Museum: 28
Richardson, Henry Hobson: 34, 36
Rickey, George: 133
Riverbend Park: 54
Robert Gould Shaw Memorial: 17
Rocky Narrows Reservation: 140
Rocky Woods Reservation: 140
Roosevelt, Franklin: 10
Ropes Mansion: 117
Rose Garden: 39-40
Rowes Wharf: 26
rowing: *see* boats/boating
Roxbury: 41-44
The Roxy: 73
royal charters: 5
running: 62; *see also* walking/jogging; hiking
Russell Bird Sanctuary: 126
Russell, Francis: 11
Ryles: 76, 77

S

Saarinen, Eero: 57
Sacco, Nicola: 11
Sackler Museum: 53
Sackler, Arthur: 53
Sacred Cod: 17
safety: 158
Saint-Gaudens, Augustus: 17, 36

"Saints:" 4
Salem: 116-121; food and drink 120
Salem Beer Works: 120
Salem Maritime National Historic Site: 117
Salem's Museum of Myths & Monsters: 118
Salem Village Parsonage Archaeological Site: 119
Salem Visitor Center: 117-118
Salem Wax Museum of Witches & Seafarers: 118
Salem Witch Museum: 118
Sam Adams Lager: 67
Sampas, Stella: 122
Samuel Adams brewery: 43
Sandy Pond: 133
Sanger, Margaret: 22-23
Sargent, John Singer: 36
The Scarlet Letter: 22
Schön, Nancy: 34
Science at Sea excursions: 26
Science Center: 51
Science Park: 17-18
Scottish Fiddle Rally: 68
Scullers Jazz Club: 76
sculptors: 17; Arneson, Robert 133; Bartholdi, Frédéric Auguste 34; French, Daniel Chester 43, 50, 130, 132; Kitson, H.H. 130; LeWitt, Sol 133; Matisse, Paul 57, 133; Milmore, Martin 43; Moore, Henry 52, 57; Pitynski, Andrzei 20; Rickey, George 133; Saint-Gaudens, Augustus 17, 36; Schön, Nancy 34; Wilson, John 43; *see also* artists, architects
seafood: 92-93; *see also* Restaurant Index
Second Church of Christ burying ground: 44
Sert, José Luis: 51

SELF-GUIDED TOURS

Black Heritage Trail: 16
Chinatown: 29
Freedom Trail: 18-19
Harvard Yard: 50
Hidden Garden Tour: 15
Longfellow National Historic Site: 53
Massachusetts Institute of Technology: 57
McIntire District: 118
Mount Auburn Cemetery: 54-55
Newbury Street art galleries: 35
Rocky Woods Reservation: 140
Waterfront: 25
Women's Heritage Trail: 19

see also tours; *specific place*

ABOUT THE AUTHOR

Author and photographer Jeff Perk has fished for trout in Lake Taupo, climbed Mt. Roraima, catalogued Cuzco's desserts, baked Sachertortes in Bora Bora, and as a result has never gotten around to owning a TV. After years of South American backpacking, South Pacific yacht-hitching, and squeezing through slot canyons in the American Southwest, Jeff finally sat still long enough to write the *Massachusetts Handbook.* He also has been a contributor to Moon's bestselling *Road Trip USA,* by the indefatigable Jamie Jensen. When not wearing out his tires or shoes, the author bounces to the salsa beat of Jamaica Plain, Massachusetts.

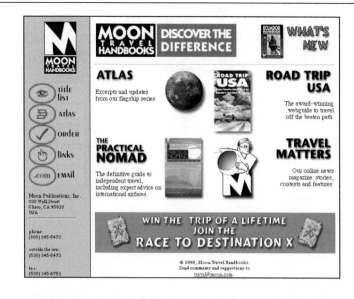

MOON
TRAVEL
HANDBOOKS

LOSE YOURSELF
IN THE EXPERIENCE,
NOT THE CROWD

For 25 years, Moon Travel Handbooks have been the guidebooks of choice for adventurous travelers. Our award-winning Handbook series provides focused, comprehensive coverage of distinct destinations all over the world. Each Handbook is like an entire bookcase of cultural insight and introductory information in one portable volume. Our goal at Moon is to give travelers all the background and practical information they'll need for an extraordinary travel experience.

The following pages include a complete list of Handbooks, covering North America and Hawaii, Mexico, Latin America and the Caribbean, and Asia and the Pacific. To purchase Moon Travel Handbooks, check your local bookstore or order by phone: (800) 345-5473 M-F 8 am.-5 p.m. PST or outside the U.S. phone: (530) 345-5473.

"An in-depth dunk into the land, the people and their history, arts, and politics."
—*Student Travels*

"I consider these books to be superior to Lonely Planet. When Moon produces a book it is more humorous, incisive, and off-beat."
—*Toronto Sun*

"Outdoor enthusiasts gravitate to the well-written Moon Travel Handbooks. In addition to politically correct historic and cultural features, the series focuses on flora, fauna and outdoor recreation. Maps and meticulous directions also are a trademark of Moon guides."
—*Houston Chronicle*

"Moon [Travel Handbooks] . . . bring a healthy respect to the places they investigate. Best of all, they provide a host of odd nuggets that give a place texture and prod the wary traveler from the beaten path. The finest are written with such care and insight they deserve listing as literature."
—*American Geographical Society*

"Moon Travel Handbooks offer in-depth historical essays and useful maps, enhanced by a sense of humor and a neat, compact format."
—*Swing*

"Perfect for the more adventurous, these are long on history, sightseeing and nitty-gritty information and very price-specific."
—*Columbus Dispatch*

"Moon guides manage to be comprehensive and countercultural at the same time . . . Handbooks are packed with maps, photographs, drawings, and sidebars that constitute a college-level introduction to each country's history, culture, people, and crafts."
—*National Geographic Traveler*

"Few travel guides do a better job helping travelers create their own itineraries than the Moon Travel Handbook series. The authors have a knack for homing in on the essentials."
—**Colorado Springs** *Gazette Telegraph*

MEXICO

"These books will delight the armchair traveler, aid the un-
decided person in selecting a destination, and guide
the seasoned road warrior looking for lesser-known
hideaways."

—*Mexican Meanderings* Newsletter

"From tourist traps to off-the-beaten track hideaways,
these guides offer consistent, accurate details without
pretension."

—*Foreign Service Journal*

Archaeological Mexico	**$19.95**
Andrew Coe	420 pages, 27 maps
Baja Handbook	**$16.95**
Joe Cummings	540 pages, 46 maps
Cabo Handbook	**$14.95**
Joe Cummings	270 pages, 17 maps
Cancún Handbook	**$14.95**
Chicki Mallan	240 pages, 25 maps
Colonial Mexico	**$18.95**
Chicki Mallan	400 pages, 38 maps
Mexico Handbook	**$21.95**
Joe Cummings and Chicki Mallan	1,200 pages, 201 maps
Northern Mexico Handbook	**$17.95**
Joe Cummings	610 pages, 69 maps
Pacific Mexico Handbook	**$17.95**
Bruce Whipperman	580 pages, 68 maps
Puerto Vallarta Handbook	**$14.95**
Bruce Whipperman	330 pages, 36 maps
Yucatán Handbook	**$16.95**
Chicki Mallan	400 pages, 52 maps

LATIN AMERICA AND THE CARIBBEAN

"Solidly packed with practical information and full of significant cultural asides that will enlighten you on the whys and wherefores of things you might easily see but not easily grasp."

—*Boston Globe*

Belize Handbook	**$15.95**
Chicki Mallan and Patti Lange	390 pages, 45 maps
Caribbean Vacations	**$18.95**
Karl Luntta	910 pages, 64 maps
Costa Rica Handbook	**$19.95**
Christopher P. Baker	780 pages, 73 maps
Cuba Handbook	**$19.95**
Christopher P. Baker	740 pages, 70 maps
Dominican Republic Handbook	**$15.95**
Gaylord Dold	420 pages, 24 maps
Ecuador Handbook	**$16.95**
Julian Smith	450 pages, 43 maps
Honduras Handbook	**$15.95**
Chris Humphrey	330 pages, 40 maps
Jamaica Handbook	**$15.95**
Karl Luntta	330 pages, 17 maps
Virgin Islands Handbook	**$13.95**
Karl Luntta	220 pages, 19 maps

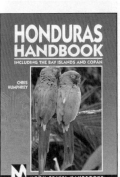

NORTH AMERICA AND HAWAII

"These domestic guides convey the same sense of exoticism that their foreign counterparts do, making home-country travel seem like far-flung adventure."

—*Sierra Magazine*

Alaska-Yukon Handbook	**$17.95**
Deke Castleman and Don Pitcher	530 pages, 92 maps
Alberta and the Northwest Territories Handbook	**$17.95**
Andrew Hempstead and Nadina Purdon	530 pages, 72 maps,
Arizona Traveler's Handbook	**$17.95**
Bill Weir and Robert Blake	512 pages, 54 maps
Atlantic Canada Handbook	**$17.95**
Nan Drosdick and Mark Morris	460 pages, 61 maps
Big Island of Hawaii Handbook	**$15.95**
J.D. Bisignani	390 pages, 23 maps

Boston Handbook	**$13.95**
Jeff Perk	200 pages, 20 maps
British Columbia Handbook	**$16.95**
Jane King and Andrew Hempstead	430 pages, 69 maps
Colorado Handbook	**$18.95**
Stephen Metzger	480 pages, 59 maps
Georgia Handbook	**$17.95**
Kap Stann	370 pages, 50 maps
Hawaii Handbook	**$19.95**
J.D. Bisignani	1,030 pages, 90 maps
Honolulu-Waikiki Handbook	**$14.95**
J.D. Bisignani	400 pages, 20 maps
Idaho Handbook	**$18.95**
Don Root	610 pages, 42 maps
Kauai Handbook	**$15.95**
J.D. Bisignani	320 pages, 23 maps
Maine Handbook	**$18.95**
Kathleen M. Brandes	660 pages, 27 maps
Massachusetts Handbook	**$18.95**
Jeff Perk	600 pages, 23 maps
Maui Handbook	**$15.95**
J.D. Bisignani	420 pages, 35 maps
Michigan Handbook	**$15.95**
Tina Lassen	300 pages, 30 maps
Montana Handbook	**$17.95**
Judy Jewell and W.C. McRae	480 pages, 52 maps
Nevada Handbook	**$18.95**
Deke Castleman	530 pages, 40 maps
New Hampshire Handbook	**$18.95**
Steve Lantos	500 pages, 18 maps
New Mexico Handbook	**$15.95**
Stephen Metzger	360 pages, 47 maps
New York Handbook	**$19.95**
Christiane Bird	780 pages, 95 maps
New York City Handbook	**$13.95**
Christiane Bird	300 pages, 20 maps
North Carolina Handbook	**$14.95**
Rob Hirtz and Jenny Daughtry Hirtz	275 pages, 25 maps
Northern California Handbook	**$19.95**
Kim Weir	800 pages, 50 maps
Oregon Handbook	**$17.95**
Stuart Warren and Ted Long Ishikawa	588 pages, 34 maps
Pennsylvania Handbook	**$18.95**
Joanne Miller	448 pages, 40 maps

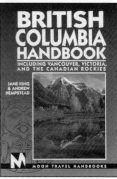

Road Trip USA	**$22.50**
Jamie Jensen	800 pages, 165 maps
Santa Fe-Taos Handbook	**$13.95**
Stephen Metzger	160 pages, 13 maps
Southern California Handbook	**$19.95**
Kim Weir	720 pages, 26 maps
Tennessee Handbook	**$17.95**
Jeff Bradley	530 pages, 44 maps
Texas Handbook	**$18.95**
Joe Cummings	690 pages, 70 maps
Utah Handbook	**$17.95**
Bill Weir and W.C. McRae	490 pages, 40 maps
Virginia Handbook	**$15.95**
Julian Smith	340 pages, 30 maps
Washington Handbook	**$19.95**
Don Pitcher	870 pages, 113 maps
Wisconsin Handbook	**$18.95**
Thomas Huhti	590 pages, 69 maps
Wyoming Handbook	**$17.95**
Don Pitcher	610 pages, 80 maps

ASIA AND THE PACIFIC

"Scores of maps, detailed practical info down to business hours of small-town libraries. You can't beat the Asian titles for sheer heft. (The) series is sort of an American Lonely Planet, with better writing but fewer titles. (The) individual voice of researchers comes through."

—Travel & Leisure

Australia Handbook	**$21.95**
Marael Johnson, Andrew Hempstead, and Nadina Purdon	940 pages, 141 maps
Bali Handbook	**$19.95**
Bill Dalton	750 pages, 54 maps
Bangkok Handbook	**$13.95**
Michael Buckley	244 pages, 30 maps
Fiji Islands Handbook	**$14.95**
David Stanley	300 pages, 38 maps
Hong Kong Handbook	**$16.95**
Kerry Moran	378 pages, 49 maps
Indonesia Handbook	**$25.00**
Bill Dalton	1,380 pages, 249 maps

Micronesia Handbook	$14.95
Neil M. Levy	340 pages, 70 maps
Nepal Handbook	**$18.95**
Kerry Moran	490 pages, 51 maps
New Zealand Handbook	**$19.95**
Jane King	620 pages, 81 maps
Outback Australia Handbook	**$18.95**
Marael Johnson	450 pages, 57 maps
Philippines Handbook	**$17.95**
Peter Harper and Laurie Fullerton	670 pages, 116 maps
Singapore Handbook	**$15.95**
Carl Parkes	350 pages, 29 maps
South Korea Handbook	**$19.95**
Robert Nilsen	820 pages, 141 maps
South Pacific Handbook	**$22.95**
David Stanley	920 pages, 147 maps
Southeast Asia Handbook	**$21.95**
Carl Parkes	1,080 pages, 204 maps
Tahiti-Polynesia Handbook	**$15.95**
David Stanley	380 pages, 35 maps
Thailand Handbook	**$19.95**
Carl Parkes	860 pages, 142 maps
Vietnam, Cambodia & Laos Handbook	**$18.95**
Michael Buckley	760 pages, 116 maps

OTHER GREAT TITLES FROM MOON

"For hardy wanderers, few guides come more highly
recommended than the Handbooks. They include
good maps, steer clear of fluff and flackery, and offer
plenty of money-saving tips. They also give you the
kind of information that visitors to strange lands—on
any budget—need to survive."

—US News & World Report

Moon Handbook	**$10.00**
Carl Koppeschaar	141 pages, 8 maps
The Practical Nomad: How to Travel Around the World	**$17.95**
Edward Hasbrouck	575 pages
Staying Healthy in Asia, Africa, and Latin America	**$11.95**
Dirk Schroeder	230 pages, 4 maps

MOONBELTS

Looking for comfort and a way to keep your most important articles safe while traveling? These were our own concerns and that is why we created the Moonbelt. Made of heavy-duty Cordura nylon, the Moonbelt offers maximum protection for your money and important papers. Designed for all-weather comfort, this pouch slips under your shirt or waistband, rendering it virtually undetectable and inaccessible to pickpockets. It features a one-inch high-test quick-release buckle so there's no fumbling for the strap or repeated adjustments. This handy buckle opens and closes with a touch, but won't come undone until you want it to. Moonbelts accommodate traveler's checks, passport, cash, photos, etc. Measures 5 x 9 inches and fits waists up to 48˝.

Available in black only. **US$8.95**
Sales tax (7.25%) for California residents
$1.50 for 1st Class shipping & handling.

To order, call (800) 345-5473
outside the US (530) 345-5473 or fax (530) 345-6751

Make checks or money orders payable to:
MOON TRAVEL HANDBOOKS
PO Box 3040, Chico, CA 95927-3040 U.S.A.
We accept Visa, MasterCard, or Discover.

MOON TRAVEL HANDBOOKS

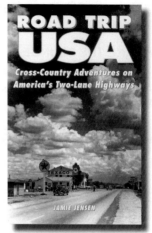

THE PRACTICAL NOMAD

✈ TAKE THE PLUNGE

"The greatest barriers to long-term travel by Americans are the disempowered feelings that leave them afraid to ask for the time off. Just do it."

✈ TAKE NOTHING FOR GRANTED

"Even 'What time is it?' is a highly politicized question in some areas, and the answer may depend on your informant's ethnicity and political allegiance as well as the proximity of the secret police."

✈ TAKE THIS BOOK

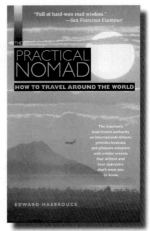

$17.95   576 pages

With experience helping thousands of his globetrotting clients plan their trips around the world, travel industry insider Edward Hasbrouck provides the secrets that can save readers money and valuable travel time.
An indispensable complement to destination-specific travel guides, *The Practical Nomad* includes:

airfare strategies

ticket discounts

long-term travel considerations

travel documents

border crossings

entry requirements

government offices

travel publications

Internet information resources

WHERE TO BUY MOON TRAVEL HANDBOOKS

BOOKSTORES AND LIBRARIES: Moon Travel Handbooks are distributed worldwide. Please contact our sales manager for a list of wholesalers and distributors in your area.

TRAVELERS: We would like to have Moon Travel Handbooks available throughout the world. Please ask your bookstore to write or call us for ordering information. If your bookstore will not order our guides for you, please contact us for a free catalog.

Moon Travel Handbooks
P.O. Box 3040
Chico, CA 95927-3040 U.S.A.
tel.: (800) 345-5473, outside the U.S. (530) 345-5473
fax: (530) 345-6751
e-mail: travel@moon.com

IMPORTANT ORDERING INFORMATION

PRICES: All prices are subject to change. We always ship the most current edition. We will let you know if there is a price increase on the book you order.

SHIPPING AND HANDLING OPTIONS: Domestic UPS or USPS first class (allow 10 working days for delivery): $4.50 for the first item, $1.00 for each additional item.

Moonbelt shipping is $1.50 for one, 50 cents for each additional belt.

UPS 2nd Day Air or Printed Airmail requires a special quote.

International Surface Bookrate 8-12 weeks delivery: $4.00 for the first item, $1.00 for each additional item. Note: We cannot guarantee international surface bookrate shipping. We recommend sending international orders via air mail, which requires a special quote.

FOREIGN ORDERS: Orders that originate outside the U.S.A. must be paid for with an international money order, a check in U.S. currency drawn on a major U.S. bank based in the U.S.A., or Visa, MasterCard, or Discover.

TELEPHONE ORDERS: We accept Visa, MasterCard, or Discover payments. Call in your order: (800) 345-5473, 8 a.m.-5 p.m. Pacific standard time. Outside the U.S. the number is (530) 345-5473.

INTERNET ORDERS: Visit our site at: www.moon.com

NOTES

ORDER FORM

Prices are subject to change without notice. Be sure to call (800) 345-5473,
or (530) 345-5473 from outside the U.S. 8 a.m.–5 p.m. PST for current prices and editions.
(See important ordering information on preceding page.)

ame: _____Date: _____

treet: _____

ity: _____Daytime Phone: _____

tate or Country: _____Zip Code: _____

QUANTITY	TITLE	PRICE

Taxable Total_____

Sales Tax (7.25%) for California Residents_____

Shipping & Handling_____

TOTAL_____

Ship: ☐ UPS (no P.O. Boxes) ☐ 1st class ☐ International surface mail

Ship to: ☐ address above ☐ other _____

_____

ake checks payable to: **MOON TRAVEL HANDBOOKS**, P.O. Box 3040, Chico, CA 95927-3040
.S.A. We accept Visa, MasterCard, or Discover. **To Order**: Call in your Visa, MasterCard, or Discover number,
send a written order with your Visa, MasterCard, or Discover number and expiration date clearly written.

rd Number: ☐ **Visa** ☐ **MasterCard** ☐ **Discover**

☐ ☐ ☐ ☐ ☐ ☐ ☐ ☐ ☐ ☐ ☐ ☐ ☐ ☐ ☐ ☐

act Name on Card: _____

piration date:_____

gnature: _____

U.S.~METRIC CONVERSION

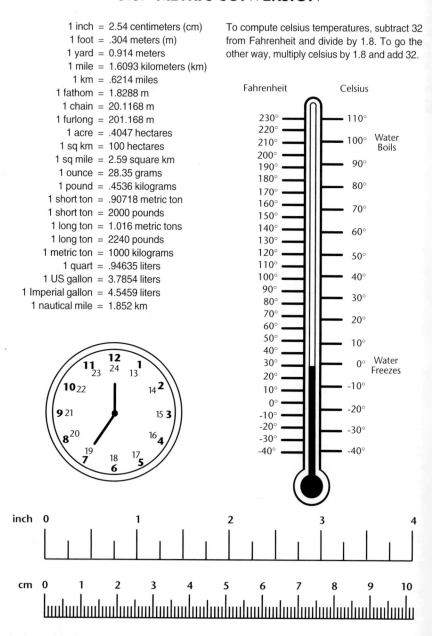

1 inch	=	2.54 centimeters (cm)
1 foot	=	.304 meters (m)
1 yard	=	0.914 meters
1 mile	=	1.6093 kilometers (km)
1 km	=	.6214 miles
1 fathom	=	1.8288 m
1 chain	=	20.1168 m
1 furlong	=	201.168 m
1 acre	=	.4047 hectares
1 sq km	=	100 hectares
1 sq mile	=	2.59 square km
1 ounce	=	28.35 grams
1 pound	=	.4536 kilograms
1 short ton	=	.90718 metric ton
1 short ton	=	2000 pounds
1 long ton	=	1.016 metric tons
1 long ton	=	2240 pounds
1 metric ton	=	1000 kilograms
1 quart	=	.94635 liters
1 US gallon	=	3.7854 liters
1 Imperial gallon	=	4.5459 liters
1 nautical mile	=	1.852 km

To compute celsius temperatures, subtract 32 from Fahrenheit and divide by 1.8. To go the other way, multiply celsius by 1.8 and add 32.

Fahrenheit   Celsius

230°   110°
220°
210°   100°   Water Boils
200°
190°   90°
180°
170°   80°
160°
150°   70°
140°   60°
130°
120°   50°
110°
100°   40°
90°
80°   30°
70°
60°   20°
50°
40°   10°
30°
20°   0°   Water Freezes
10°
0°   -10°
-10°   -20°
-20°   -30°
-30°
-40°   -40°

inch 0   1   2   3   4

cm 0 1 2 3 4 5 6 7 8 9 10